Iranian Romance in the Digital Age

Sex, Family and Culture in the Middle East Series

This innovative series explores the connections and influences impacting ideas about marriage, sexuality, and family throughout history in the MENA region and until the present day. Individual volumes consider the ancient, early Islamic, medieval, early modern, and contemporary periods to investigate how traditions and practices have evolved and interacted across time and countries.

Series Editors:

Janet Afary, Professor and Mellichamp Chair in Global Religion and Modernity, UC Santa Barbara

Claudia Yaghoobi, Roshan Institute Assistant Professor in Persian Studies, The University of North Carolina at Chapel Hill

Iranian Romance in the Digital Age

From Arranged Marriage to White Marriage

Edited by
Janet Afary and Jesilyn Faust

I.B. TAURIS
LONDON • NEW YORK • OXFORD • NEW DELHI • SYDNEY

I.B. TAURIS
Bloomsbury Publishing Plc
50 Bedford Square, London, WC1B 3DP, UK
1385 Broadway, New York, NY 10018, USA
29 Earlsfort Terrace, Dublin 2, Ireland

BLOOMSBURY, I.B. TAURIS and the I.B. Tauris logo are trademarks of Bloomsbury Publishing Plc

First published in Great Britain 2021
This paperback edition published in 2022

Copyright © Janet Afary and Jesilyn Faust, 2021

Janet Afary, Jesilyn Faust and contributors have asserted their right under the Copyright, Designs and Patents Act, 1988, to be identified as Author of this work.

Copyright Individual Chapters © 2021 Janet Afary, Jesilyn Faust, Masserat Amir-Ebrahimi, Ashraf Zahedi, Amir Mirfakhraie, Gholam Reza Vatandoust, Maryam Sheipari, Vahideh Golzard, Cristina Miguel, Azal Ahmadi, Soraya Tremayne, Erika Friedl, Mary Elaine Hegland, Behrouz Alikhani, Roger Friedland

For legal purposes, the Acknowledgments on p. vii constitute an extension of this copyright page.

Series design: Adriana Brioso
Cover image © TIBO D'HERMY/Gamma-Rapho/Getty Images

All rights reserved. No part of this publication may be reproduced or transmitted in any form or by any means, electronic or mechanical, including photocopying, recording, or any information storage or retrieval system, without prior permission in writing from the publishers.

Bloomsbury Publishing Plc does not have any control over, or responsibility for, any third-party websites referred to or in this book. All internet addresses given in this book were correct at the time of going to press. The author and publisher regret any inconvenience caused if addresses have changed or sites have ceased to exist, but can accept no responsibility for any such changes.

A catalogue record for this book is available from the British Library.

A catalog record for this book is available from the Library of Congress.

ISBN: HB: 978-0-7556-1827-9
PB: 978-0-7556-3957-1
ePDF: 978-0-7556-1829-3
eBook: 978-0-7556-1828-6

Series: Sex, Family and Culture in the Middle East

Typeset by Deanta Global Publishing Services, Chennai, India

To find out more about our authors and books visit www.bloomsbury.com and sign up for our newsletters.

Contents

Acknowledgments	vii
Glossary	viii
Introduction *Janet Afary and Jesilyn Faust*	1

Part One Norms, Romance, and the Breakdown of Arranged Urban Marriage

1. The Emergence of Independent Women in Iran: A Generational Perspective *Masserat Amir-Ebrahimi* — 11
2. Romancing Filipinas: Challenges and Promises of Transnational Families in Iran *Ashraf Zahedi* — 32
3. Beyond the *Sharia*: "White Marriage" in the Islamic Republic of Iran *Gholam Reza Vatandoust and Maryam Sheipari* — 55
4. School Textbooks, Ideological Codes, and the Construction of the Standard Iranian Family *Amir Mirfakhraie* — 79

Part Two Online Dating, Hymenoplasty, and Assisted Reproductive Technologies

5. Negotiating Intimacy through Social Media: Challenges and Opportunities for Muslim Women in Iran *Vahideh Golzard and Cristina Miguel* — 111
6. Recreating Virginity in Iran: Hymenoplasty as a Form of Resistance *Azal Ahmadi* — 125
7. Whither Kinship?: Assisted Reproductive Technologies and Relatedness in the Islamic Republic of Iran *Soraya Tremayne* — 141

Part Three Reconstructing Hierarchies: Rural and Tribal Marriages

8. How Marriage Changed in Boir Ahmad, 1900–2015 *Erika Friedl* — 155
9. Changing Perceptions and Practices of Marriage among People of Aliabad from 1978 to 2018: New Problems and Challenges *Mary Elaine Hegland* — 174

10 Changing Established-Outsider Relations?: A Case Study of Bakhtiaris
    in Iran *Behrouz Alikhani*   197

Epilogue: The Rise in Non-standard Marriages in the Region
    Janet Afary and Roger Friedland   214

Bibliography   219
Notes on the Contributors   239
Index   243

Acknowledgments

This volume emerged out of a conference on the *Changing Nature of Family and Marriage in Iran* held at the University of California, Santa Barbara, in November 2017 and a subsequent international call for papers. We are grateful to Dr. Haleh Emrani and the late Ahmad Gramian of the Gramian-Emrani Foundation, who generously supported the conference and helped with the publication of this volume. Additional funding was provided by the Duncan and Suzanne Mellichamp Funds, the American Institute of Iranian Studies (AIIA), the Baha'i Institute of Higher Education (BIHE), the Center for Middle East Studies (UCSB), the Cross-Cultural Research and Education Institute (CREI), and the Department of Religious Studies (UCSB). We offer special thanks to Sophie Rudland, our Commissioning Editor at I. B. Tauris/Bloomsbury, for her enthusiastic support throughout this project and to Nicholas Murray and Lui Cordero for their careful editorial assistance.

We dedicate this volume to the memory of Dr. Farokhru Parsay, medical doctor, educator, and dedicated supporter of Iranian women's rights. Dr. Parsay served as the Principal of Nourbakhsh High School, a highly respected public school for girls in Tehran that produced numerous accomplished graduates during and after her tenure. She went on to become the first woman member of parliament and the first woman cabinet minister, serving as Iran's Minister of Education. Dr. Parsay was instrumental in winning women's suffrage in 1963 and helped push through the Family Protection Law in 1968. Soon after the 1979 Revolution, she was arrested for these activities and executed by a firing squad in May 1980.

Glossary

ʻashāyir(pl.) ʻashireh (sing)	Tribe
ahle kitab	people of the book (Jews and Christians)
andaruni	inner compartment, occupied by wives, children, and female servants; women's quarters
aqd nāmeh	marriage contract
fadākāri	sacrifice
faqih	religious scholar
fatwā	religious ruling
fiqh	jurisprudence
gheyrat	honor
govāhiye bekārat	virginity certificate
ĥījāb	literally meaning "cover" in Arabic; a scarf or veil designed to cover the head and neck of a woman; religious covering; a modest attire and a headscarf
hodud	part of sharia Islamic law that pertains to actions that transgress the limits/laws set by God
ʻidda	waiting period for a woman after divorce
Ijtihād	certificate received by a cleric granting him the right to interpret the laws of Shi'i Islam
jahiziyeh.(or jahiz)	trousseau, assets or goods a woman brings to her husband in marriage; dowry
kadkhodā	village elder
khāstegāri	marriage proposal
mahriyeh (also mahr/mehriyeh/mehr)	marriage portion payable to the wife by husband at any time after the marriage, but usually paid after divorce or death of the husband, with some similarities to alimony
marja' (sing.) (marāje' (pl.)	religious source of emulation in Shi'i tradition

muburāt	divorce by mutual agreement
mutʻa	Arabic term for temporary marriage
neʻmat	blessings
nafaqeh	maintenance paid by husband to wife for daily necessities of life
nejāsat	ritual impurity, uncleanliness, from a religious point of view
nekāh daʼem (or simply nekāh)	formal marriage; permanent marriage; contracted through civil law
sharia	Islamic law; rules and regulations that are derived in principle from the Qurʼan and traditions relating to the words and deeds of the Prophet; these rules govern the lives of Muslims
pardeh-ye bekārat	hymen
pishraft	progress
sigheh (verb)	to utter the formula for any contract; to engage in temporary marriage in colloquial Persian
sigheh (noun)	Persian term for temporary marriage; a renewable contract of marriage for a defined duration, from a few hours to ninety-nine years; also a wife in such a marriage
talāq	divorce initiated by a husband; repudiation
zinā	fornication; one of the actions that transgresses the hodud ordinances

Introduction

Janet Afary and Jesilyn Faust

Soon after the 1979 Iranian Revolution, the new government of the Islamic Republic instituted a dramatic reversal in women's rights. The state revived many premodern social conventions, such as mandatory veiling, easy divorce for men, child marriage, and polygamy but enforced them through modern means and institutions. Women accused of improper veiling were flogged, and those accused of premarital or extramarital sex were imprisoned, or in some cases stoned to death, while openly gay men were severely punished and even executed.

These harshly misogynistic laws existed alongside populist social and economic programs that benefited the poor urban and rural sectors of society, including women. After initially encouraging pronatalist policies in the early 1980s, the state reversed course and established a popular and comprehensive family-planning program in the late 1980s. The results of this program, coupled with a literacy campaign that targeted rural women, were quite dramatic. In less than one generation, a unique demographic transition took place. Population growth dropped from 4.06 percent (in 1984) to 1.15 percent (in 1993), while total fertility rate dropped from 6.4 births per woman (in 1984) to 1.9 in 2010 (Aloosh & Saghai 2016). The United Nations Population Division described this transition as the largest percentage change in the world during 1975–80 and 2005–10 (Aghajanian et al. 2018). As a result of this decline, there was a substantial increase in the age at first marriage for both women and men. The number of formal marriages declined markedly while rates of temporary marriage and, gradually, cohabitation increased.

Studies of birth control and family planning in the United States suggest that what happened in the West is very similar to what has happened in Iran. In the last two centuries in Europe and the United States, as a result of industrialization, urbanization, vaccination, better hygiene, and the adoption of contraceptive technologies, the institution of marriage went through a profound change. People began to live longer, and as fertility rates dropped, marriage became more than an institution for procreation. Women's demands for emotional and sexual intimacy increased. The emphasis on romantic, (hetero)sexual love led to new forms of normative heterosexuality. Good sex in marriage became important, and romantic love seemed necessary to a good marriage. Attitudes toward premarital sex also changed, with sex outside marriage becoming more acceptable. Widespread use of contraceptives helped make marriage a more companionate union. Birth control also opened the door to other nonreproductive forms of relations "from childless marriages to casual encounters to non-heterosexual relationships" (Ball 2005, 23). As women became more sexually assertive, they also became less tolerant of men's extramarital affairs, both heterosexual and homosexual. Gradually, as old social hierarchies broke down, racial and ethnic divisions lessened, leading to more intermarriages.

In Iran too, as the birth rate dropped and mass vaccination and better hygiene took root, life expectancy increased. Changing gender norms saturated society through the international media, and women's expectations of marriage shifted. Iranians had practiced arranged marriages for centuries, with less normative weight given to romantic love. During the Pahlavi era, companionate marriages gradually gained ground among the elite and the new urban middle classes. Nonetheless, parents still played a key role in introducing prospective couples, approving marriages, and negotiating dowry and *mahriyeh*. In the 1950s and 1960s, strictly arranged unions, and also polygamy, gradually gave way to more companionate monogamous marriages in urban communities. The emergence of the nuclear family among the new middle classes reduced the authority of the extended family. However, in rural communities, arranged marriages remained the norm, and the powers of the extended family were not diminished.

As elsewhere in the world, urban professional men, who became economically independent from their fathers, were the first to claim their right to marry for love. Young men took a more assertive part in choosing their spouses, and young urban women gradually gained more rights in choosing their partners from a range of potential suitors who were approved by their parents.

Soon a rising generation of educated women, among them university professors, lawyers, members of parliament, and leaders of the state-sponsored Women's Organization of Iran (WOI), began to cautiously campaign for new laws granting women substantially greater marital rights. In the 1960s and 1970s, abortion was legalized, and birth control became available. Laws were ratified that granted women greater rights to divorce and prevented a man from taking a second wife, without authorization from the first wife. The courts began to grant divorced women custody of their children until they reached eighteen, so long as the women did not remarry. These changes were more dramatic than similar ones in Europe, mainly because they took place over a relatively short period of about forty years and, as a result, became the source of great social anxiety within the more traditional middle classes.

By the 1970s, the new middle classes had changed so much that they hardly understood their more religious and conservative compatriots. The more modern urbanites simply assumed it was a matter of time before others would join them in embracing these changes. In reality, women and their families from the old middle classes continued to observe the veil. Few women from the bazaar or clerical middle classes went to the university. Most entered arranged marriages while still in high school. Some endured polygamy, but they seldom petitioned for divorce. In their extended families, marriage was still an institution for procreation rather than for emotional intimacy and female sexual fulfillment. By the 1970s, Iranian society was in the midst of a backlash against these gender reforms, a reaction that would become a major contributing factor to the 1979 Islamic Revolution.[1]

---

[1] For details, see Janet Afary, *Sexual Politics in Modern Iran* (Cambridge: Cambridge University Press, 2009), chapter 7.

But the institution of marriage continued to change despite all attempts by the new Islamist state to reverse the clock. The young rural men and women who were recruited into the regime's militia received many economic and social benefits, as well as a salary. Young Islamists met at their workplaces and soon began to enter more often into companionate marriages that were blessed by the regime. By the second decade of the twenty-first century, even in tribal and rural communities, strictly arranged marriages and endogamous marriages (within kinship groups) were no longer the norm. Marriage was seen less and less as merely an institution for procreation, and women came to expect intimacy and spontaneity along with a greater degree of emotional and sexual closeness. Moreover, the mean age of marriage for girls went up, and dating became a more acceptable part of life. The present study examines some of these dramatic changes in the institution of marriage from an interdisciplinary perspective, considering the research of ethnographers, medical anthropologists, sociologists, historians, feminist scholars, and educators, all with deep understanding of Iranian society, culture, and politics.

Part One looks at changes in urban marriages, including transnational marriages, new forms of cohabitation, known as "white marriages," and the visible emergence of a new group of professional women who live independent lives and have chosen not to marry or remarry. Masserat Amir-Ebrahimi, looks at the emergence of independent, urban middle-class women in Tehran and their challenges. They gained this independence sometimes through higher education and work and sometimes by living alone or outside the conventional norms of the traditional family. Two generations of women have played a particularly important role in breaking down the gender norms of Iranian society: (1) Those who went to school in the 1960s and 1970s and, hence, were adults at the time of the 1979 revolution and (2) those who were born after the Islamic Revolution and have no personal recollection of the prerevolutionary era. During the era of Muhammad Reza Shah Pahlavi, secular middle-class women had experienced unprecedented changes in their public and private lives. Some went to college, entered the job market, and became the first women in their families to become economically independent. As a rebellious generation, these women were active participants in the early stages of the 1979 revolution when they fought for the overthrow of the monarchy with the hope of establishing a more democratic government. After the foundation of the Islamic Republic, women from this generation faced many new restrictions on their rights and in their daily lives, restrictions that were based on the sharia. However, through time, they learned how to resist and overcome some of these limitations. The "Second Generation," those who were children and teenagers during the early years of the revolution, experienced enormous hardship and are commonly referred to as the "burned generation." Today, forty years after the revolution, members of the "Third Generation," have become new social actors. Members of this generation were born after the revolution and grew up under the precepts of the Islamic Republic as well as the influence of new technologies. They are more educated than their mothers and grandmothers and more active. They also have a greater awareness of their rights. As a result, they are altering society and the structure of family—sometimes by postponing marriage, by living alone, or by living outside the conventional norms of the traditional family.

Ashraf Zahedi looks at transnational marriages between Christian Filipina women and Muslim Iranian men and the social experiences of their bicultural children. The Cultural Revolution of 1980, and the subsequent closure of Iranian universities from 1980–3, compelled many young Iranians to pursue higher education overseas in Asia, Europe, and the United States. Although most students preferred Western (particularly American) universities, obtaining a student visa from the United States proved to be very difficult as Iran and the United States had no diplomatic relations, and there was no consulate inside Iran to issue visas. The quality of education, geographical proximity, and the lower cost of education made the Philippines a popular alternative and a country of choice for many Iranian students, the majority of whom were men. Some of these men were more secular; others were more religious. Some opposed the postrevolutionary regime; others supported it and benefited from its scholarship. Interactions of Iranian men with Filipinas led to intimate relationships and, in a number of cases, marriages. Eventually, many Filipina wives followed their husbands and settled in Iran. These transnational marriages have been challenged by two negative perceptions—that of Iranian men as "Muslim terrorists" in the Philippines and that of Filipinas as "foreign maids" in Iranian society. The main burden, however, has been placed on Filipina brides. They have had to go through a mandatory process of conversion to Islam, migrate to Iran, learn the Persian language, and adjust to the Iranian culture, which is vastly different from their own. Zahedi examines the complexities of Filipinas' migration and highlights their varied experiences in transnational marriages. She argues that, despite personal and social challenges, these transnational couples have managed to transcend their cultural and religious differences and build a life together based on affection and shared views of family life. Additionally, she examines the lived experience of their bicultural and bilingual children and shows that race, culture, and nationality are not fixed categories. As social constructs, they are thus imprecise, unstable, and subject to change.

Gholam Reza Vatandoust and Maryam Sheipari explore a new phenomenon called "white marriage" that is gaining popularity in urban communities. Despite severe government prohibitions on mingling of unrelated men and women, a growing number of urban couples have chosen to cohabit, without entering into either a formal or a temporary marriage, thereby ignoring social and religious stigma as well as possible state persecution. While the government is aware of such so-called illegal cohabitations, it has been unable to prevent the practice and has had to suffice to harsh verbal condemnations and threats. As such, white marriages pose severe challenges to the theocratic regime. Vatandoust and Sheipari examine the social and political implications of "white marriage" and why it has become popular in urban communities. They interview a group of highly educated professional women, as well as a group of carpet weavers, and ask what they think about the arrangement. They also report on the results of a survey they conducted on the subject with both Iranians and Iranian-Canadians to see if there were differences in opinion on this matter between people residing inside Iran and those living in the diaspora. Finally, they review the state's positions on the subject of "white marriage," from initial denials to strong reactions and, ultimately, hostile indifference.

Amir Mirfakhraie looks at what Iranian students and adult learners read about the family in their textbooks. How are gender relations and diversity represented in constructions of the family? What are the ideological characteristics of the ideal family?

And do curricular images of the family and family relations reflect the lived-experiences of the students? He deconstructs representations of the family in language, social studies, geography, history, and provincial studies textbooks, as well as select teachers' guide booklets and literacy program books. Mirfakhraie looks at the categories and discourses that frame the construction of the family and highlights how "race" (whiteness), theories about Aryan migration, ethnicity, gender, sexuality, ability, development, love for nation (Īrān-dūstī), martyrdom, and velāyat-e-faqih (leadership by clerical ruler) are incorporated in both texts and images. He suggests that the images of the ideal family or the *Standard Iranian Family* are based on several interlocking and conflicting biases. He concludes that these are often racist, monolithic, sexist, heterosexist, modernist, conservative, Persian-centric, and Islamic-centric constructs. Although Iranian textbooks have been revised since 2000 based on the pedagogical assumptions which claim to be influenced by human rights precepts and global educational theories, the *ideological codes* that inform representations of the family and nation offer oppressive, essentialist, racialized, ableist, pro-state/leadership, and heteronormative constructions that exclude diversity. To develop effective anti-oppressive and anti-hegemonic subaltern forms of knowledge, Iranian curricula writers need to account for how they exclude and silence the historical memories of diverse forms of families in the constructions of difference and subaltern marginalized peoples in Iran.

Part Two of this volume explores the way technology and social media has impacted and altered the institution of family, including marriage. Vahideh Golzard and Cristina Miguel look at how Iranian women negotiate intimacy in the age of social media. The internet has opened up new opportunities for users to communicate in very personal ways. Social media platforms allow users to disclose themselves to contribute to social interaction. Self-disclosure in social media amplifies the various levels of intimacy, depending on users' desires, which help to set a new form of visibility that alters the traditional notions of privacy. Online intimacy is usually achieved through reciprocal visual and textual self-disclosures, which in turn may lead to face-to-face encounters. In Iran, social media platforms have become powerful tools for political and interpersonal communication. They open new ways for their users, particularly women, to negotiate their intimate relationships with their family, (potential) partners, or friends. For Iranian women, social media allows room for self-expression, a way to combat loneliness and create meaningful relationships with like-minded people. At the same time, women are confronted by a number of risks associated with social media interactions in Iran, such as censorship, online (sexual) harassment, or cybercrime. Based on in-depth interviews and participant observation with women in Tehran, Golzard and Miguel explore the extent to which social media platforms (blogs, Facebook, and dating sites) have created both challenges and opportunities for women by transforming the ways in which young women create and maintain intimate relationships online.

Azal Ahmadi writes about the practice of hymenoplasty in Iran. Hymenoplasty is a controversial surgery, where a woman who has had sexual intercourse secretly undergoes a surgery that repairs her hymen shortly before marriage so her husband would think he is marrying a virgin. There is evidence of the practice going back to the mid-nineteenth century, if not before.[2] In Iran and other Middle Eastern countries, and

[2] See Ibid., 27–30.

even in diaspora communities, where a woman's failure to present herself as virginal for marriage may result in severe social repercussions, this covert practice remains popular. Critical literature surrounding this clandestine surgery is sparse. During ethnographic fieldwork in Tehran, Ahmadi interviewed women who had undergone hymenoplasty or knew of the practice, as well as physicians who performed it. The resulting narratives and discourses suggest that hymenoplasty is a covert form of resistance against socioculturally prescribed sexual inegalitarianism, one that restricts women to the social sphere of premarital chastity. By manipulating the medicalization of virginity, women covertly resist the dichotomous gendered classifications that constrain them. These classifications regard women who do remain virgin until marriage as normal and others who engage in premarital sex as deviant.

Soraya Tremayne looks at how assisted reproductive technologies (ARTs) have contributed to the evolving nature of marriage and family formation in Iran. Family and kinship remain foundational and sacrosanct institutions in Iranian culture, acting as guiding principles of social organization. Their significance has not diminished in the face of major changes that have taken place in all aspects of reproductive life in Iran during the past few decades. Islamic laws and practices, which are intensely focused on the protection of family and its perpetuity, and which determine the parameters of relatedness, predominantly through biological lineage, further frame and strengthen cultural values and norms in relation to family kinship. To ensure the continuity of the family and lineage, the pressure on individuals to reproduce is intense, and infertile couples are often marginalized and have to carry the burden of their barrenness. However, even for fertile couples, reproducing per se is not unconditional or sufficient to make them welcome or full members of their kin group. The unity of the family being the ultimate priority, those individuals, including children, who do not have a biological link with the family or their kin group are rarely welcome members of the kin group. As infertility is such a major stigma, it is understandable that when ARTs were first introduced to Iran, they were received with open arms and legitimized in a relatively short time, with the full endorsement of leading Shia scholars. Tremayne focuses on how ARTs have become instrumental in the hands of infertile couples, who tend to use them to perpetuate their lineage and forge new bonds with their kin group, who are the donors or recipients of gamete. ARTs' contribution to procreation, thus, goes even further than offering a cure for infertility. It has become instrumental in allowing infertile couples to interpret the rules and to use ARTs in such a way that these technologies would meet their understanding of kinship and maintain the integrity of their lineage as they perceive it.

Part Three examines marital changes in the rural and tribal sectors of society. As rates of urbanization have dramatically increased in the last three decades, many formerly rural areas have turned into suburbs of large cities, while other rural and tribal areas have undergone significant changes due to access to amenities, as well as better means of transportation and communication. Erika Friedl looks at the historical evolution of the institution of marriage in the village of Deh Koh in southwest Iran, where she has conducted ethnographic research in the span of several years from 1965 and 2015. She looks at three major politico/economic time frames: (1) the patrilineal, authoritarian, and violent era of the *khan*s, which lasted through the mid-twentieth century; (2) the modernist era of the authoritarian Pahlavi shahs, especially the era of Muhammad Reza Shah (1941–79); and the androcentric and authoritarian clerical leadership, which since 1979 has spearheaded an economically struggling and rapidly globalizing population. These three periods share a patrilineal bias with male dominance in most aspects of life. Historically, intertribal fighting encouraged a strict male-female labor division with a matching gendered philosophy. These factors impacted the politics of marriage and family relations. However, over time, arranging a marriage, negotiating the contract, and celebrating the union became increasingly expensive though the practice itself remained highly popular. Today, this cultural lag has created problems especially in the cash-strapped new tribal middle classes, where people's criteria for spousal selection and couples' expectations of a good life are exceeding their financial resources. As birth rates fall, the age of marriage rises, divorce increases, and the care of children and old people have become problematic. As a result, residents of Deh Koh increasingly criticize customary relations and their own assumptions of marital life.

Anthropologist Mary Elaine Hegland conducted participant observation in the village of Aliabad near Shiraz for about three years between 1978 and 2018. She writes that in 1978, marriage was perceived as automatic and an early point in the life cycle; not too complicated or difficult for parents to attain for their children; and of absolute necessity for both men and women, alongside becoming parents, to be accepted as a complete human being. Forty years later, some but not all attitudes about marriage have changed. These changes have been encouraged by economic and living-style improvements, changes in the means of subsistence, better transportation, travel, communication, and social media, access to global culture, increased education, and wider and more varied social networks especially for young people. By 2018, young people of Aliabad had become more active in choosing their spouses, and young women especially held higher expectations from marriage. Yet, for many Aliabadi people, marriage was now more economically difficult to attain and fraught with potential pitfalls. In spite of the perceived possible dangers, and the terrible expenses for parents, for the great majority of Aliabadis, marriage has remained a highly desired achievement. Parents still consider the marriage of their children to be a supreme duty of theirs, and this encourages them to make every effort to make it possible. However, for present-day Aliabadis, marriage is no longer a taken-for-granted step in the life cycle followed by a more-or-less functional partnership. Marriage has diversified into additional possible images, practices, choices, and pressures. It has become a realm replete with complications, conflicts, and paradoxes—as well as with potentially greater possibilities for companionship and intimacy. Young people want to receive full economic support from their families but also live independent lives.

Anthropologist Behrouz Alikhani looks at the evolution of marriage among Bakhtiari tribes of Iran who reside in the north and east Khuzestan, south Lorestan, Chaharmahal and Bakhtiari, and west Isfahan provinces of Iran. Alikhani looks at the manner in which education and employment are breaking down entrenched social classes within tribes and allowing for intermarriages between established and marginal tribes, which had been hitherto taboo. As a result of the revolution, clans that were considered marginal and inferior to the established and more respectable tribes have gained access to greater education, jobs, land, and power—including greater authority within the institutions of the Islamic Republic. These changes have increased the self-esteem of marginal tribes while also elevating their social class in the eyes of the more established tribes. As a result, the community is beginning to see a greater number of marriages between the established and marginal tribes, particularly when a young man and woman of a marginal tribe has accumulated both economic and social capital by virtue of becoming a highly respected professional in Iranian society.

In the epilogue, Janet Afary and Roger Friedland show that the institution of marriage is going through dramatic changes throughout the Middle East, North Africa, and South Asia. Throughout the region, marriage is delayed and the age at first marriage for both men and women has gone up. There is also a significant increase in the rates of nonstandard marriages. A Facebook survey by the authors shows that an overwhelming number of women in such nonstandard unions are employed, with some supporting their male partner financially.

This volume maps the dramatic changes in romance and family structure in Iran in the last four decades. While in some ways the decline of marriage in Iran mirrors a decline in marriage happening worldwide, the impact under a religious authoritarian regime is far greater. With demographic and economic challenges, the younger generation is turning to technology to help fulfill their desires for romance and family. Yet Iran remains a land of deep contradictions, not just in politics, but also in love, sex, and marriage. Many women now earn a living and financially support their families. A significant number of urban women have also chosen to stay single or, if divorced and widowed, never to remarry. Yet textbooks remain deeply conservative, portraying women as primarily wives and mothers. Young people date online, and many urban women engage in premarital sex with their boyfriends. But, when the relationship does not end in marriage, the women undergo hymenoplasty before getting married to an available male partner. Anachronistic laws declare intimacy between unrelated men and women unlawful, and, from time to time, severely punish people for breaching the law. At the same time, couples brazenly elect to cohabit in "white marriages" rather than enter into a formal or temporary marriage. Families continue to place a high value on formal marriage and having children. They go to ART clinics to receive the latest Western technology to conceive. Yet the desire to have a child to whom one is related by blood is so strong that occasionally husbands and doctors secretly collude to impregnate a wife with the semen of a close relative. In many ways, the political and economic ties that used to uphold the old social hierarchies of tribes have broken down. Yet members of high-status tribes, even if relegated to a modest income and standard of living, continue to look down upon marginal tribes of their own community who have moved up the economic hierarchy and often refuse to consider their members as suitable marriage partners. In rural and tribal communities, families have become much smaller, with both men and women marrying much later. Yet couples tend to demand all the old economic perks of traditional marriages, which today are simply beyond the reach of most families. They opt for extravagant weddings, a fully furnished home, and all the accompanying luxuries. They also expect their parents to pay for everything, and the parents themselves willingly take on these ruinous expenses that leave them impoverished in their old age. At the same time, the newlyweds want to live independent lives away from the extended family, and expects to have little obligation for the care of their parents in their old age. It is unclear how these dramatic contradictions can be resolved. Iranian society seems to be reaching a breaking point not just politically, with periodic street protests and demonstrations, but also socially and culturally in terms of attitudes toward love, sex, and marriage.

Part One

Norms, Romance, and the Breakdown of Arranged Urban Marriage

1

The Emergence of Independent Women in Iran

A Generational Perspective

Masserat Amir-Ebrahimi

In the Islamic Republic of Iran, the family is considered a fundamental social institution, and marriage is seen as an obligation for anyone who is physically and financially qualified. During the Iran–Iraq War (1980–8), married couples and extended families received many more privileges than single people from the government. Even after the war ended, married couples received preferential treatment in the job market, with regard to acquiring loans, rental accommodations, travel, among other things. Single people, especially single women, were last in line for all government privileges.

Despite these privileges, the structure of family appears to be fracturing. In the last decade, the rate of marriage has declined significantly, and divorce rates have increased in cities such as Tehran (one divorce for three marriages in 2018). In addition, the age of women at first marriage has risen considerably. In 2016,[1] nearly 37 percent of women living in Tehran between the ages of twenty and thirty-five had never been married. This delay in the age of marriage has been accompanied by a drop in fertility rates (from 6.4 percent in 1986 to 1.8 percent in 2014 and then a small increase to 2.0 percent in 2018 nationwide). These changes are accompanied by a general rise in the number of households composed of elderly, single people. They were also influenced by the rise of individualism among younger generations and a dramatic increase in the number of women who are heads of their household. In ten years from 2006 to 2016, the number of women who were heads of their households doubled, growing from 1.6 million (9.4 percent) in 2006 to 3.06 million in 2016 (12.7 percent). Of this group, around 1.36 million women (44.4 percent) were living alone. Besides single households, the number of young, unmarried people who were cohabiting with a roommate or a partner has been rising. This new phenomenon, which would have been unimaginable until a few years ago, is called "white marriage" or "married singles" by the media, as a way of giving it a certain religious legitimacy. As Azad-Armaki et al. have argued, this new type

---

[1] Most of the statistics come from different national censuses.

of household and cohabitation is mostly the result of globalization along with important economic, cultural, and social changes that have taken place in Iran.²

Living alone is a dramatically new phenomenon for Iranian women. Until recently, living alone was considered a sad "fate," a life reserved to widows, the elderly, migrants, prostitutes, and—in general—destitute poor people. In Muhammad Reza Shah Pahlavi's time, living alone was not common. In 1976, single households constituted 7.2 percent of all households in Tehran. Of this number, 49.7 percent was people who were less than thirty-five years old—most probably rural migrants who came to Tehran in search of better jobs. These individuals would eventually get married after their economic situation stabilized. About 22 percent of single households were elderly, which shows the prevalence of the extended family, and women represented only 31.2 percent of single households. Thus, living alone was mostly a masculine phenomenon and reserved for young people.

Forty years later, in 2016, the official rate of single households in Tehran has increased to 10.1 percent. This may not seem like a significant increase; however, the distribution is now very different. In 2016, youth under thirty-five constituted 19.7 percent of single households, whereas the elderly (more than sixty years old) composed 47.4 percent of single households. More surprisingly, living alone has become mostly feminized; indeed, 61.3 percent of all single households in Tehran were composed of women in 2016, so the rate had doubled since 1976. Among them, 62.2 percent were more than sixty years old. Such changes in the composition of single households in the last forty years show that the structure of the Iranian family has altered significantly.

These statistics point to two changes: (1) the transformation of the structure of the family from an extended family to a nuclear one based on growing individualism and (2) greater independence of women, who are living alone, sometimes by choice and sometimes because they have no other option.

Today there are two types of single households: one is the traditional single household, which is based on quasi-obligation, because there is no other choice. These single people either have no family or are abandoned by them; they are old, migrants, or poor. On the other hand, the modern single household is based on individualism and independence. In these cases, living alone is a choice rather than a fate imposed on the person.

In his book on single people and singlehood, J. C. Bologne explains this new lifestyle as it emerged in the West. The rise of single households was linked to the emergence of the "modern woman" or "*la femme moderne*" in the twentieth century. It was related to the fact that divorce was no longer a stigma, as well as to the fact that a significant number of women had attended college, had jobs, and, therefore, could afford to live independently. The rise of single households was also related to harsh economic times. Dramatic shifts in social and, especially, technological factors in everyday life, from the introduction of refrigerators and microwaves to the arrival of television and the

---

² T. Azad-Armaki, M. H. Sharifi-Saee, M. Isaari, and S. Talebi, "Cohabitation, the Emergence of New Forms of Family in Tehran," in *Jame'e Pajouhi-Farhangi Quarterly*. Institute of Human Science and Cultural Studies, 3rd year, Number 1 (Tehran 2012), 65.

internet, all made this lifestyle possible.³ For many women who choose to live alone, acquiring some independence and freedom have been the most important reasons. However, living alone and staying single often remains a big challenge for most women, especially in traditional and more family-oriented societies. Tuula Gordon rightly points out that "constructing an independent life, reaching the status of 'the individual' and obtaining full social citizenship are still areas of struggle. . . . Single women are still marginalized in familyist societies and many of them experience multiple marginalizations."⁴ In Iran, despite persistent negative views of singlehood, which make life harder for single women living alone, the new trend of globalization and greater exposure to modern lifestyles have facilitated this new type of household. In fact, with the massive entrance of women into higher education, the emergence of a larger job market (formal and informal), the construction of smaller rental apartments, the advent of satellite TV and social media into everyday life, as well as the emergence of new public spaces, living alone has become more bearable and plausible. In no small measure, women's greater self-esteem and self-awareness have contributed to this trend.

However, traditional familial expectations lead many women to hide their way of life from their families or neighbors; they do not declare that they are living alone so as not to attract other people's attention. In my research, I encountered young women, especially those who had migrated from the provinces to Tehran and left their families behind, who said they were occasionally sharing their apartment with a partner, a friend, or a family member but were actually living alone for most of the time. For a variety of cultural and economic reasons, they did not declare that they lived in a single household. Thus, the number of single households among youth may be much higher than what is declared officially. Although there is no indication as to who is living alone by choice and who is doing so out of necessity or social obligation, we can assume that this new type of single household is popular among those with economic advantages, especially in big cities and among middle-aged and middle- and upper-class women. In the 2016 census, 42.9 percent of female single households in Tehran were headed by women between the ages of fifty-five and seventy-four. These are women who at the advent of the revolution were aged between eighteen and thirty-seven years. Some of these women had acquired a certain degree of independence from their families during the shah's time, because they worked and had a salary. Some had also been deeply involved in the early stages of the revolution, when hundreds of thousands of youth joined the movement. These women had a very different life experience compared to their mothers or even their daughters who grew up after the institution of the Islamic Republic, with its limitations and some mandatory segregated spaces.⁵ They are the only generation who lived their youth in the free public spaces of the prerevolutionary era but also experienced the enclosed and segregated spaces

---

3   Jean Claude Bologne, *Histoire du célibat et des célibataires* (Paris: Fayard, 2004), 297–300.
4   Tuula Gordon, *Single Women: On the Margins?* (Hampshire: Macmillan Press LTD, 1994), 197.
5   Gender segregation does not apply to every situation and every public space. Only some spaces are segregated, such as schools and stadiums, as well as urban buses. At workplaces, universities, concerts, and other such public gatherings, unrelated men and women can sit together and work in the same space. In the metro, there are two special wagons for women, but women can also board the other wagons.

that were mandated after the revolution.⁶ This generation, which was born between 1942 and 1961 (roughly corresponding to the baby boomer generation), like their counterparts in Western countries, was a rebellious generation. Their children and grandchildren, those who were born around the time of the revolution (1976–91),⁷ were between the ages of twenty-five and forty when the last census was taken in 2016. Known as the Third Generation, this latter group has introduced major social changes to Iranian society. These two generations, the ones who were principal actors of the revolution (the First Generation) and the ones who have introduced important social changes after the revolution (the Third Generation), are my focus in this article.⁸ Women from the First Generation (never married, divorced, or widowed) account for a significant share of single households in Tehran (42.9 percent). Members of the Third Generation, however, often lack the economic opportunities and resources to rent or own an apartment on their own, especially with the high inflation in recent decades. Officially, women of the Third Generation compose only 12.9 percent of the women who are living alone in Tehran; as mentioned, however, they may be far more numerous. Both generations of women have tried to gain their independence within a society that has little respect for women who choose to live alone. To understand their trajectory, a glance at some important, historical, and social events and challenges that women have faced from the shah's time until now is necessary. To trace their trajectory, I need to explain briefly my approach to a theory of generations, especially since the label the "Third Generation" was self-imposed by the "Children of the Revolution," for whom life in Iran has been divided into a "Pre- and Postrevolutionary Period."

The Concept of Generational Theory Applied to the Iranian Case

The term "generation" has multiple meanings, depending on different schools of thought. The oldest and the most common approach is the genealogical one, where the average age of a generation from the birth of a parent to the birth of a child is between twenty and twenty-five years, even if this could change case by case and according to the dominant cultural practices. After the First World War, Karl Mannheim (1893–1947) proposed a new approach to generations. He defined a *generation* as a cohort or a group of people who were born during a certain historical period and were bonded

---

⁶ Masserat Amir-Ebrahimi, "Conquering Enclosed Public Spaces," in *Cities: The International Journal of Urban Policy and Planning* (Elsevier, volume 23:6, 2006), 455–61.
⁷ These dates correspond to the Iranian dates of 1355–70.
⁸ This chapter is part of a larger study based on twenty-five in depth interviews and four focus groups (peer groups of three to six persons) with women aged between twenty-five and sixty-nine years old, which I conducted during 2015–16. All these women were residents of Tehran, had university degrees, and were working and living alone or outside the conventional norms of the traditional family context of family. In this total sample of forty women, there were fifteen divorced and twenty-five single women. Twelve of them had migrated from different provinces to Tehran. Of these, nine younger ones came to Tehran as students, and three older women had moved to Tehran when they were younger and with their families. Sixteen of the total sample were between fifty and seventy years old, five were in their forties, and eighteen were between twenty-five and forty years old.

by shared experience, one that could eventually result in a distinct self-consciousness, a worldview or an approach to political action.⁹

According to this theory, what distinguished one generation from another is their experience in young adulthood with regard to the major social and political events they faced, experiences that differentiated them in addition to their age from the older (parents) and the newer generation (younger siblings/children). Important historical events and social changes can influence the value systems and beliefs of individuals in a society and foster a collective consciousness that permits that generation to react to or intervene significantly in social changes. In Iran, this generational approach becomes very important after the Islamic Revolution when important social changes occurred.

The Emergence of the New Concept of Generation in Iran

Until a few years ago, the concept of generation in Iran was based on the classical gap between parents and children. However, around 2002, a new concept of generation was spread in the Iranian blogosphere by some young bloggers who called themselves the bloggers of the "Third Generation" *Nasl-e Sevvom* or "the sixties" *dahe-ye shasti*, the decade of the 1360s corresponding to the decade of the 1980s. This generation, which was born around the time of the revolution and is known as the "Children of the Revolution," considers the Islamic Revolution of 1979 a departure point for their generational classification. They consider their parents the First Generation, the ones who were often actors in the revolution. This Third Generation makes a clear distinction also between itself, a generation that struggled hard, and those who were born later in the 1990s (in 1370 or *dahe-ye haftaadi*). Thus, based on their classification, the four generations are as follows:

(1) **The First Generation.** Members of this generation were usually parents of "Children of the Revolution." They were predominantly born between 1941 and 1961 (from 1320 to 1340 in the Iranian calendar) during the reign of Mohammad Reza Shah Pahlavi (1941–79). They were at least eighteen years old at the time of the revolution. This generation lived and passed their teens and young adulthood and, in some cases, their adult years during the shah's time. The older ones had the full experience of living their youth in two different worlds—the secular Pahlavi monarchy and the Islamic Republic. Women of this generation were the only ones who experienced a "free public space" in their young adulthood— they were legally free to choose to wear or not wear the Islamic *ḥijāb*, and they could, for the first time, enjoy some freedom in the new modern public spaces. Under Mohammad Reza Shah's regime, there were greater social and individual freedoms, but political repression was also significant. The upheaval and

---

⁹ Karl Mannheim, cited by Semi Purhonen, "Zeitgeist, Identity and Politics in the Modern Meaning of the Concept of Generation," in *The Routledge International Handbook on Narrative and Life History*, General Editor: Ivor Goodson (and Part editors) (London and New York: Routledge, 2017), 167–78.

social movements of the 1960s and 1970s in Western countries, along with the discourses of Leftist social movements, had an important impact on this First Generation and encouraged them in their struggle against the dictatorship of the shah. As Edmunds and Turner point out, in the 1960s, the concept of generation changed, and this generation—those who lived in the West and others who lived in developing societies that adopted a more modern/Western life—became the first truly global generation, in the sense that they had a common experience of global consumerism, global music, and communication systems.[10]

This generation, both those who were secular and those who were devout, constituted the grassroots of the 1979 Revolution. After the revolution, men and some women of this generation participated massively in the Iran–Iraq War as soldiers and aid workers. As veterans of war, the survivors then moved up the political hierarchy and formed the new generation of Iran's political class. Although some women served as nurses' aides and volunteer supporters, most women had to manage to live without men during the war and deal with wartime issues. They also had to adapt themselves to the new social order, which was vastly different from the previous one.

Some members of the First Generation, both men and women, were Leftist activists who were jailed and/or persecuted in the 1980s. The more modern, middle-class women had the hardest time adjusting and surviving under the Islamic Republic, learning step-by-step how to become Islamic citizens to survive. Some of these women formed the core of the first resistance to the Islamist state and initiated acts of civil disobedience aimed at preventing the complete Islamization of the Iranian society.

(2) **The Second Generation** was born between the mid-1960s and the mid-1970s, and, at the time of the revolution, they were less than eighteen years old. Most were too young to participate in the revolution, but many participated in the Iran–Iraq war. They were the first young generation to experience the Islamization of public spaces in the schools and on the street. They barely experienced any type of leisure activity during the Iran–Iraq War and their teenage years. Many of them, like younger members of the First Generation, encountered the 1980–3 Cultural Revolution. This was a period when the state closed down all universities, expelled or forcibly retired many professors, and implemented the policy of Islamization of students and faculty members at Iranian universities. Some other members of the Second Generation, especially those living in urban and more modern areas, experienced the unprecedented brutality of the morality police in public, and even in private spaces, and during family gatherings. Many felt their youth was lost due to the revolution and the war, and they called themselves the Burned Generation (*Nasl-e Soukhteh*).

(3) **The Third Generation** is composed of those who were born around or after the Islamic Revolution in the late 1970s and in the 1980s. They did not experience the early years of the revolution and were very young during the war. As the

---

[10] June Edmunds and B. S. Turner, *Generations, Culture and Society* (Philadelphia: Open University Press, 2002), 5.

first bloggers in the Iranian blogosphere, some called themselves members of the Third Generation *Nasl-e Sevvom* or "*daheh-ye shasti*" (sixties generation; according to the Iranian calendar, they were born in 1360s, corresponding to 1980s).

This generation is the baby boomer generation of Iran, a time when fertility rates were at their peak. In 2016, those who were born between 1976 and 1991 (twenty-five to thirty-nine years) constituted 29.8 percent of the Iranian population. This generation has been the source of many social changes in Iran. They were the first young generation to connect to the world through satellite TV, and later the internet and the mobile phone. The famous Iranian blogosphere (*Weblogestan*) is mostly their creation.[11] Deeply influenced by the time of the reform, when Mohammad Khatami was president of the republic (1997–2005), they became a political generation that later constituted the grassroots of the Green Movement in 2009, a peaceful protest of millions of Iranians against the reelection of Mahmoud Ahmadinejad (2005–13), when their votes in the 2009 presidential election were ignored. They are also those who started the sexual revolution in Iran, and some of them are now changing the family structure in today's Iran by staying single or living as unmarried couples. Since 1998, women of this generation have conquered and feminized universities and public spaces with their important presence. They have also changed the drab and dark appearance of Iranian public spaces by bringing colors and fashion to them, and have challenged the morality police with their semi-*ḥijāb* using fashion as a feminist tool.

(4) **The Fourth Generation**, or *dahe-ye haftaadi*, are those who were born between 1991 and 2001 (from 1370 to 1380 in the Iranian calendar) after the Iran–Iraq war. In 2016, they were less than twenty-five years old. Most of them grew up with the newest technology—the internet, mobile phones, and satellite TV. Their formative political years were during the presidency of Mahmoud Ahmadinejad and the repression that followed the Green Movement. Thus, members of this generation are more or less disillusioned by politics.

Unlike the Third Generation, most members of the Fourth Generation are often the only children of their family. In the 1990s, the state pursued a progressive family-control policy and encouraged low fertility rates. As only children, members of the Fourth Generation often have all the attention of their parents as well as their grandparents and have experienced a somewhat easier and different life than earlier generations. In some ways, they inherited everything that the Third Generation had fought for—technology, sexual revolution, and even strategies of resistance. Members of the 1990s generation are marrying earlier but also divorcing earlier than previous generations. During Ahmadinejad's presidency and when Mohammad Qalibaf was mayor of Tehran (2005–17), consumerism became a widely accepted part of life in urban milieus.

---

[11] Masserat Amir-Ebrahimi, "Weblogs and the Emergence of a New Public Sphere in Iran," in *Publics, Politics and Participation: Locating the Public Sphere in the Middle East and North Africa*, ed. Seteny Shami (New York: SSRC Books, 2009), 326–56.

New public spaces, such as shopping malls, cafes, and restaurants, which emerged in large numbers, provided more freedom in the new public spaces and helped this generation to ignore their political and sociocultural differences with the state, at least for a while. This generation is more hedonistic, individualistic, and more consumerist. It is attached to its daily life and its pleasures. Today, it has also become the most transgressive, uncontrollable, and challenging generation for the Islamic Republic. Members of this generation were behind the grassroots demonstrations of January 2018 and in November 2019 in different cities, calling for economic changes. Some members of this group were also behind calls for the return of the royal dynasty.

Broadly speaking, it seems that members of the First and Third generations, who are the main age groups for this study, have played a formative role in bringing about deep social and political changes in Iran: The First Generation made the revolution, and the Third Generation brought significant social changes during the Islamic Republic. Members of the Second Generation were too young to participate to the revolution or to resist its new social changes. Members of the Fourth Generation and beyond are still too young to have an independent life and so, for the purposes of this study, have been omitted. Many members of the Third and Fourth Generations, who seem to be the most transgressive agents of change, had rebellious mothers who struggled hard for their freedom and resisted the complete Islamization of public spaces. These women continued to attend the universities and go to work despite the limitations and frequent humiliations they faced. They maintained their individuality in the face of repression and punishment. They remained present in different public spheres and prepared the ground for the transition to the new generations.

Lives of Urban, Middle-Class Women before the Revolution

Mohammad Reza Shah Pahlavi's reign (1941–79) was an important era for Iranian middle-class women because this was a unique time in Iranian history. Women entered colleges and the job market in much larger numbers than before. They had the choice of wearing a veil in public. When the Family Protection Law and the Family Protection Courts were implemented in 1967 and later in 1975, women also gained some rights in the private sphere and in marriage, such as the right to divorce and to child custody after divorce, among others.[12] A significant characteristic of this period was the existence of an important duality between women from the more traditional and observant rural majority and the traditional urban middle classes (the *bazaari* and clerical families) and those from the more modern and Westernized urban middle classes, who were still a minority. In Tehran, the northern neighborhoods were more modern, with new public spaces, cinemas, theaters, restaurants, and parks, while the

---

[12] See Janet Afary, *Sexual Politics in Modern Iran*, (Cambridge: Cambridge University Press, 2009) and Nikki Keddie, *Modern Iran, Roots and Results of Revolution* (New Haven and London: Yale University Press, 2003).

old center and south of Tehran were more traditional and religious. Neighborhoods in southern Tehran were quite impoverished. This area was more like a poor dormitory for low-income workers and lacked many basic public services and public spaces.[13]

This duality was perceptible also in the appearance of women. In traditional neighborhoods, women were mostly veiled and usually confined to the enclosed spaces of their neighborhoods. Few of them were active in the labor market or permitted by their families to go to college. While in the more modern neighborhoods, women enjoyed more freedom. They could go to the university, work, and wear what they liked. They also enjoyed some amenities in the new public spaces, which became part of their everyday lives. Some of these women tried to gain their independence vis-à-vis their families by postponing their marriage. Sometimes, they married the person they wanted; if the marriage did not work out, they opted for a divorce and lived independently.[14] Some of these women became political actors at the end of the 1970s and near the revolution.

Gaining Independence within the Family

Pamela Karimi explains in detail the impact of Truman's Point Four Program, which was introduced in Iran in 1950 during the premiership of Ali Razmara (1950–1). The program helped reorient the Iranian economy toward mass-market consumption and, in the process, created a new image of the modern woman. Such new images were also promulgated through TV, movies, and women's magazines, which had an important influence on women. In the process, women also began to rethink their place within the home.[15] This eventually led to new conflicts between parents and daughters and gave young women the desire to be more independent and live a freer life. Until this time, most young women got married after finishing high school. Now, some resisted early marriage and, instead, entered the university, or the job market, or both and gained more independence. Later, they married based on their personal choice rather than their parent's choice.

In 1976, female students comprised 35.1 percent of all students at colleges and universities in Tehran, and 11.6 percent of workers. Sixty-nine percent of these women were working as specialists, clerks, and managers. For some young, middle-class women, having a job and a salary were very important and helped them become more independent from their families. Some of my middle-aged interviewees began working as early as seventeen or eighteen, even before finishing high school. According to them, having their own salary released them from the harsh pressure of family and gave them some autonomy and independence. They could avoid obligatory marriage and other family pressures. At that time, living alone for a woman was not common in Iran. By working and earning their own salary, these young women managed to change their

---

[13] Amir-Ebrahimi, "Conquering Enclosed Public Spaces," 456.
[14] Afary, *Sexual Politics in Modern Iran*, 218.
[15] Pamela Karimi, *Domesticity and Consumer Culture in Iran, Interior Revolutions of the Modern Era* (London and New York: Routledge, 2013), 90–4.

relationships with their parents and acquire some independence and freedom, which were very valuable. Zari (born in 1954), a divorced English teacher, said,

> I was 20 years old and I liked to go out with my friends, but my father was reluctant and did not want me to go out. One day he told me that he won't pay me my pocket money if I went out anymore. So I tried to find a job and I became an English teacher and in this way earned my freedom from my dad. When I could make enough, and no longer needed to ask him for money, the power relation between us changed. He could not control me as before nor ask me where I was or tell me what to do.

Despite the Pahlavi state's image of highly emancipated and educated young Iranian women, many middle-class families were still reluctant to send their daughters to the university because they did not value higher education for young women. This attitude was more common in religious and traditional families, but it also existed in many modern families where higher education was seen as unattractive for young women. However, young women themselves were highly influenced by the image of the "modern educated woman" and her better economic situation, and some tried to overcome family limitations by working, earning their own income, and even paying their own college tuition without the help of their parents. Narges (born in 1950), a divorced journalist, recalls,

> I was living in Tabriz until my father died. He was a very religious man and believed women should not even go to high school. When he died, I was 15 years old and we moved to Tehran where my uncles were living. My family still did not want me to finish high school, but I insisted so much that finally my mom agreed to let me attend night school on the condition that I wear a chador in school. In the night class I was the only *chadori* girl and I was ashamed of this. So I would take off my chador before entering class. Later when my brother was arrested for his political activities, in late 1960s, I began to work for a newspaper at the age of 17 to help my family and to earn a living. My mother cried for a week but then she accepted. I was the first woman in my family to unveil, to work for a living, and later to go to the university with my own means and to become independent.

In the late 1960s and 1970s, the image of the "liberated woman" was very fashionable and advertised by the regime of the Shah as a role model for Iranian women. Women's magazines such as *Zan-e Rouz* (Today's woman) or *Ettela'at-e Banovan* (Women's information) along with cinema, radio, and television were all promoting this image of a liberated, Westernized, fashionable, and active woman. The media presented mostly Western values, standards, and cultural practices in their programs and shows. The new magazines were full of stories about the lives of Iranian or Western actresses, successful women, love stories, and Western fashion. The lives of the more traditional women, who lived completely outside this context, were completely ignored. Most of these women had very limited education or were illiterate. They often remained confined to the enclosed spaces of their homes and neighborhoods.

Private Life: Love and Politics in the 1970s

The new lifestyle led to new laws that directly affected the private lives of families and couples. In 1966, Muhammad Reza Shah approved the formation of the Women's Organization of Iran. This new institution, with numerous branches throughout the country, proposed a series of reforms in family and marriage laws. The laws were to be carried out by special courts known as the "Family Protection Courts." Even if these laws were not universally applied, or ignored, and even disapproved of by more traditional women under the influence of the clergy, they remained an important step toward changing the unequal treatment of the sexes, especially in urban areas.[16] On the other hand, under the influence of Western culture, feminist magazines, cinema, and literature, including the hippie culture of "free love" in the late 1960s and 1970s, romantic love gradually became an important ingredient of life for the youth and a "must" for many in modern, urban, middle-class families. As Janet Afary points out in detail, in the 1970s, in modern urban areas, arranged marriages were losing ground as marriages became more companionate, based on love rather than parents' decisions. Young men and women would date for several months before marriage in the new middle classes.[17] Cinemas and clubs in northern Tehran were prime dating locations, where prospective couples could meet and experience some moments of privacy and intimacy.[18] Despite this acceptance of courtship by more modern families, maintaining virginity until marriage was still essential for young women. Having a sexual relationship before marriage was extremely worrisome for them. However, by the late 1970s, the situation had slightly changed, and younger women in the new middle classes, those born in the 1950s, became more rebellious and liberated in their private lives.

If the Western hippie counterculture, with its slogans of love and peace, attracted many youths from the urban, modern middle classes, others were more fascinated by the new Western political ideologies, from existentialism to Leftist and Maoist social movements. Leftist guerrilla organizations (Marxist and Islamist) emerged in the late 1960s and became popular within the youth culture a few years before the revolution. Another important influence was the revolutionary discourse of Ali Shari'ati on militant Islam, which inflamed more religious youths. In the second half of the 1970s, youths were getting more politically active. Some leftists were also involved in partisan underground movements. Marriage in these groups was influenced by their ideology—political fascination replaced romantic love, and rebellion took the place of

---

[16] See Afary, *Sexual Politics in Modern Iran*; 212 N. Keddie, *Modern Iran, Roots and Results of Revolution* (New Haven and London: Yale University Press, 2003), 167 and Azadeh Kian-Thiébaut, "From Motherhood to Equal Rights Advocates: The Weakening of Patriarchal Order," *Iranian Studies* 38, no. 1 (2005): 467.
[17] Afary, *Sexual Politics in Modern Iran*, 215.
[18] Idem. 159.

bourgeois values.¹⁹ Many political young people married on the basis of their shared political values and adherence to an organization rather than love or family obligation. Goli (born in 1952), a divorced employee, recalls,

> I was working since I finished high school and was very interested in politics. So I married a man who was an active leftist intellectual. I was not in love with him but I thought marrying him will be the best way to be able to work for my people, because he knew politics and philosophy well and I was mostly attracted by his way of thinking.

Soheila (born in 1950), another divorced artist, remembers those days:

> In those years we were very rebellious, even in marriage. For leftist youth, marriage was not so important, especially in its traditional form. To avoid customary marriage traditions, young people often just went to a notary public's office to register their marriage, far from all these splendors of today's ceremonies. The only fact that counted was mutual attraction. In the beginning of the 1970's it was the time of Love and Peace. But later, near the Revolution, things changed. Leftist youths, influenced by secular or Islamist revolutionary ideas, began to suppress their sexual instincts, and soon considered sex a luxury concern. We were politicized and adopted an anti-imperialist point of view but at the same time we belonged to the middle classes and so we had our own leisure and night gatherings. But because we considered ourselves leftist and responsible, we observed some sexual "redlines" and did not cross them and stayed faithful to our modest beliefs and values.

Larger numbers of young men and women encountered each other in universities or on the job market in the 1970s. In addition, during the social upheavals that led to the revolution, interaction between young men and women became more common, especially among the urban middle classes. This generation was becoming more rebellious not only in the political arena but also in their private lives.

Women, Freedom, Revolution, and Public Spaces

The revolution was the beginning of a new era and a new life in many ways. In prerevolutionary Iran, the authority of the monarchic state—the old over the young, men over women, parents over children, and the rich over the poor—was indisputable; after the revolution, the old authority would fracture on many levels. The 1979 Revolution marked the beginning of the end of the old authority and the birth of a new one, which, despite its freshness, was still based on tradition and

---

¹⁹ See Mehrangiz Kar. She gives an interesting personal and political account on the lives of women before and during the revolution in her book, *"Shuresh, ravâyati zananeh az enghelâb"* (Rebellion, a Feminine Narration of the Iranian Revolution) (Baran, Sweden, 2006).

religion.[20] In that moment between the death of the old authority and the birth of the new one, public spaces became free spaces and truly "spaces for the public" for the first time. The freedom of political expression, the excitement, the joy of victory, and camaraderie gave youth a new boost and energy. For many Iranian youth, it was an unforgettable moment. Briefly, public spaces became huge scenes where all types of political and cultural tendencies could be demonstrated. Human rights attorney Mehrangiz Kar provides an interesting account of that time when pop music and American movie posters coexisted side by side with religious songs, while books that had been politically banned were sold by young peddlers on the streets. During this period, youth and women had some valuable experiences of "freedom," which were unique and particular to the time. As Soheila (born in 1950) points out,

> During the revolution, women were gaining some freedoms and men were losing some advantages of the traditional society. Everything was under the influence of the revolution and politics. We no longer had a "normal" life.

Some parents in the more secular social classes remained faithful to the Shah's regime or at least cautious about political change. But their children were often transported by the revolutionary zeal. They stood up to their parents and the old authority and some even gained new authority at home due to their sympathy with the revolutionary state. The gap between parents and children became deeper. Young revolutionary women became more independent; some left home to join their comrades in team houses, where they lived together for months, sometimes without sending any news about their whereabouts to their families. Even within traditional and religious families, religious young women became freer and participated in politico-religious seminars and various demonstrations.

Revolutionary youths were spending days and nights with their comrades and their peers, discussing politics. Sometimes they traveled together to join other revolutionary groups. In this new life, politics and comrades replaced family for some and gave young people a new identity. It also changed interactions between men and women. This generation was idealist, hoping for a better future and a new and still unknown world. The revolution gave this generation a strong collective identity that they had never experienced before. Fariba (born in 1950), a journalist, recalls,

> There were such an excitement and energy in the air that I think it was the best period of my whole life. It was important that we were involved in the movement, the movement itself was not so important, the "moment" was important, not the future! Revolution gave us an identity that we never had before. We were unique! But a few years later, we lost this identity and our uniqueness and again we became nobody. During the revolution everything was different, we had the greatest freedom; nobody was asking us where you were going and what you were doing.

---

[20] Amir-Ebrahimi, "Conquering Enclosed Public Spaces," 456.

The End of the Dream and the Building of the Islamic Republic

Soon after the victory of the revolution, the political atmosphere changed, and a new authority based on Islamic precepts was established as the only law of the land. Despite their undeniable role in the revolution, urban, middle-class women, much sooner than other classes and segments of society, lost many of their rights in both the private and public spaces. The Family Protection Law, which was an important milestone for women, was abrogated just a few days after the February Revolution and the *ḥijāb* and modest clothing soon became compulsory for all. In the following months and years, innumerable restrictions and limitations based on the sharia were imposed on women. In contrast, men regained many "religious" rights over women, including the right to polygamy and the right to control the conduct of their wives. To travel, study, and work, wives needed a husband's permission. Men also gained the unilateral right to divorce and to have both guardianship and even custody of small children after divorce. More secular and "Westernized" female employees were the first targets of the persecution and "purification" in the public and private sectors. Women who were able to escape this cleansing trend had to comply fully with the new Islamic laws by becoming almost invisible. They did so by observing their black *ḥijāb* and performing the required Islamist attitudes. Nevertheless, these women formed the first core of female resistance to the total masculinization of public spaces and administration, despite the harsh pressure and humiliation they endured for decades.

The 1980s were the hardest years in the recent history of Iranian society. On the one hand, during the eight years of the Iran–Iraq War, several hundred thousand young men were killed; on the other hand, a vast purge happened within the Leftist and oppositional groups. Thousands were imprisoned, executed, or forced to flee from Iran. This decade was the period of transition from a secular monarchic era to a new kind of religious republic. During these years, many gatherings or public events were prohibited. Most public spaces became huge stages for acting out "revolutionary roles." New patterns of behavior and predetermined social roles based on Islamic and "traditional" values were imposed on appearance, body language, and speech.[21] Adaptation to these new roles became crucial in every social negotiation of the postrevolutionary period. The Iranian middle classes, which had enjoyed some cultural freedom during the Shah's period, learned how to organize their lives in the enclosed spaces of their homes. As noted earlier, during the early 1980s, known as the period of the Cultural Revolution, universities were closed, and young people had very few occasions for outdoor leisure that would be safe from the persecution of the Revolutionary Guards (Pasdaran). Thus, for many, the only solution was marrying soon. The rate of employment of women plummeted, while the birth rate rose dramatically.

But the 1980s also had a surprising new effect on the relationship between parents and children, especially among the urban middle classes. During the shah's period, the most difficult struggle of youths was inside their homes and within the private spaces,

---

[21] Amir-Ebrahimi, "Weblogs and the Emergence of a New Public Sphere in Iran," 328.

but they enjoyed some freedom in public spaces. After the revolution, the situation was reversed. Women and youth were the first targets of the Revolutionary Guards, the supposed guardians of public morality in public spaces. They could be arrested at any time for "un-Islamic" appearance or behavior or for their social interaction with members of the opposite sex. Faced with the harsh control of the Revolutionary Guards, parents in modern, middle-class families gradually became accomplices of their children. Parents also had guilty feelings about what had taken place after the revolution and how the social freedoms they had taken for granted became social sins, punishable by an ever-vigilant state. As a result parents became more understanding of their children and gradually assumed the role of mediators between them and the state.[22] In other words, once the state took over what had customarily been parental authority in private spaces and began to enforce its ideological position in both public and private spaces (parties held in private homes could be raided by the Pasdaran, who could arrest the participating youth), a new relationship between parents and children emerged. This new relationship was "no longer founded on authority but on dialogue and persuasion."[23]

This period was crucial and contributed to the new forms of civil resistance that gradually began to take shape. Paradoxically, by adapting and conforming their appearances and behavior to predetermined Islamic sociocultural models, Iranian youth and women gradually introduced major and irreversible social changes. By making small and seemingly unimportant, yet continuous and cumulative changes in their appearance, demeanor, and social position, they ultimately changed the dominant models of self-presentation and created new and spontaneous forms.[24]

Post-Khomeinism and the Era of Transition

After the war and the death of Ayatollah Khomeini in 1989, a new era of transition began that resulted, as Azadeh Kian has argued, in "the weakening of the patriarchal order and male domination in both public and private spheres." Women's presence increased in the public sphere, and they began to challenge the patriarchal system and the prevalent gender inequality of traditional Iranian society. At the same time, and within the private sphere, they questioned the very institution of the patriarchal family, which is founded on highly regimented gendered roles and male domination.[25] These social and political changes, including the ones listed below, have transformed Iranian society and have had an important impact on the everyday lives of women and youth, empowering them and giving them more independence.

- **Opening of New Public Spaces/Public Spheres.** After the war, the new mayor of Tehran, GH Karbaschi (1989–96) implemented an active sociocultural policy

[22] Pardis Mahdavi, *Passionate Uprisings: Iran Sexual Revolution* (Palo Alto, CA: Stanford University Press, 2009), 273.
[23] Kian-Thiébaut, "From Motherhood to Equal Rights Advocates," 46.
[24] Amir-Ebrahimi, "Conquering Enclosed Public Spaces," 460.
[25] Kian-Thiébaut, "From Motherhood to Equal Rights Advocates," 46.

with the aim of creating new public spaces such as cultural centers, sport centers, parks, malls, and theaters in different neighborhoods of Tehran, including in poor areas of the city. These new public spaces had an important impact on the lives of women and youth who until then had very limited access to social and physical activities, especially in the more traditional neighborhoods. These cultural centers, which offered a variety of classes in the arts, computers, languages, and sports enhanced the self-awareness of women and youth and opened up new horizons for them. During the presidency of M. Khatami (1997–2005), state control of public spaces somewhat diminished, and public life gained some stability. In the last two decades, increasing outdoor recreational spaces, together with the emergence of a new consumerist culture, have created new lifestyles and forms of leisure. Though these new developments were periodically threatened by the resurgence of more conservative policies, especially during the presidency of M. Ahmadinejad (2005–12), they have continued and even expanded.

- **New Technology.** In the 1980s, with the government ban on the Video Cassette Recorder (VCR) and the Video Home System (VHS), smuggled videos conquered private spaces. Although satellite TV was banned in the 1990s (and remains so to this day), a great majority of Iranians ignored the ban and used satellite TV, even though they could be subject to periodic fines for doing so. In 2001, when it became possible to type in Persian on the internet, the new medium became an important public sphere. The Iranian blogosphere and, later, social networks, such as Facebook, Twitter, Instagram, Telegram, and WhatsApp have significantly affected the lives of Iranians. As with other new technologies in Iran, many of these social networks have been blocked by the government, but today most people access them easily via the Virtual Private Network (VPN). In this new virtual space, women and youth can interact, dialogue, and write about their concerns, desires, and frustrations, revealing their private lives and unspoken thoughts.[26]
- **Sexual Revolution.** Pardis Mahdavi (2009) conducted an interesting research on the sexual behavior of youth and found that many members of the Third Generation have evaded various bans and limitations in their relationships. In 2014, the Research Center of the Islamic Legislative Assembly affiliated with the Iranian Parliament, published a controversial report on sexual relationships of youth in Iran, which was soon removed from their website.[27] The report concluded that in 2008, nationwide and out of 141,552 high school students (girls and boys mostly from the Third Generation), 74.3 percent were engaged in some kind of relationship with a member of the opposite sex.[28]

---

[26] Amir-Ebrahimi, "Weblogs and the Emergence of a New Public Sphere in Iran."
[27] Report of the Iranian Parliament's Legal Research Group: "*Provisory Marriage and Its Impact on the Adjustment of Illegitimate Sexual Relation,*" May 2014 (The Research Center of Majlis has published: The shocking statistics about sexual relationship in Iran (August 9, 2014 accessed on February 7, 2019), https://www.eghtesadnews.com/بخش-اخبار-2/102836-آمار-های-تکان-دهنده-از-روابط-جنسی.
[28] This report did not clarify what was the nature of these relationships. According to limitations imposed by the Islamic morality on the relationships between unrelated men and women, one can assume that this number includes any kind of relation, from platonic to sexual ones.

- **Higher Education.** In 1998, for the first time, 52 percent of the entrants to Iranian universities were women. This percentage increased every year, so that in some campuses more than 70 percent of first-year students were women. When Ahmadinejad became president, he tried to reverse this trend by imposing new quotas and limiting women's entry into some fields in higher education and even in the job market, demanding that they stay home. Despite his efforts, however, women have held their ground and continue to constitute a majority of the students at Iranian universities.
- **Employment.** Despite their success in higher education, Iranian women have not made much progress in the job market. Today, a significant number of women with college degrees are unemployed or underemployed. In the last forty years, formal rates for women's employment in the paid sector have never gone above 16 percent nationwide (in 2018), but this number does not adequately reflect the situation on the ground. Faced with both state-sponsored and traditional gender discrimination in a male-dominated job market, high inflation, and massive unemployment, and encouraged by the growth of individualism and greater independence, many women are now quietly self-employed and constitute an important segment of the informal job market. Some run their own private business; others are working as after-school tutors, or private teachers in the arts and languages, or as yoga and fitness instructors, as well as academics. Some provide necessary home services, such as catering, tailoring, or cleaning. The less-educated women work as peddlers inside the metro. Some of these young women from the Third Generation hold multiple jobs, none of which are declared. Maliheh is a good example; she is a young divorcee (born in 1984) who holds several different jobs:

> I began working as assistant yoga teacher when I was 20 years old. After my divorce, not only did I continue teaching my yoga classes, but I am now also providing medical massage for clients. From time to time, I work at a coffee shop. In addition, and with the help of my friends, we organize tours around the country, adding to my income. So I currently have four jobs and I earn very well! Many of my friends are doing the same, they work hard, and make a good income, and live independently.

This informal job market has allowed many young women to live alone or to share an apartment with a friend, and thus live more independent lives.

Living as a Single Woman in Tehran in the Twenty-First Century

For a long time, living alone had a highly negative connotation in Iran and was considered a suspicious lifestyle, bordering on immorality. Landlords did not want to rent their apartments to single people, and the term "*khaneh-ye mojaradi*" (bachelor apartment/home) suggested a place where illegal or suspicious activities might be taking place. In recent years, landlords have become more willing to rent to young people who live alone, especially in some gentrified central neighborhoods of Tehran.

In the first decade of the revolution, living alone was culturally, socially, and especially economically hard. But that has also gradually changed. Several factors have helped: many women have graduated from universities; informal markets have expanded, new possibilities opened up for earning money; smaller and more affordable apartments became available; and a significant number of young men and women have migrated to Tehran and other big cities to attend college or find employment. In 2012, according to the Ministry of Youth and Sport, between 25 and 30 percent of youth were living alone, especially in Tehran, Shiraz, Mashhad, Esfahan, Tabriz, and Ahvaz, where important universities are located.[29]

The new trend of single or small households led to the construction of new apartment buildings with smaller floor plans. In 2016, 76.8 percent of all dwellings in Tehran were less than 100 square meters and, therefore, more affordable for singles or young couples. In addition, when a family's financial situation allowed, single-family dwellings were transformed into apartments that allowed elderly parents and their grown children to live independently but close to one another in the same building. Today, many Tehrani single women within the middle and upper classes are living independent lives and have their privacy, but they are also next to their families and benefit from their support and security. Their situation is quite different from that of young women from small cities who have moved to Tehran to study and find jobs but then decided to stay in Tehran, partly to stay far from their more traditional families, who would not grant them similar privacy in their hometowns. These young women from other cities or small towns are an important percentage of young, single, or unconventional households in the major cities. Often they live with roommates or a partner.

Migrant Women versus Tehrani Women

Nine of my younger interlocutors were women who had migrated from different provinces to study in Tehran. Some of them came from families where girls were highly controlled. For these young women, going to college in another city was the only way to experience some freedom and independence. Most of them, after experiencing this life of greater "independence," no longer wanted to go back home. So when they finished college, they found jobs, rented apartments, and stayed in Tehran. Research on the lives of female college students shows that one of the most important motivations of young women for going to the university, especially in other cities, was experiencing an independent life, free from family restrictions.[30]

Migrant students usually live in a university dormitory at first. But the dorms are often overcrowded, and, in addition, the university staff adopts the position of

---

[29] "The Boom of Single Household Rental," in *Donyay-e Eqtesad*, http://www.donya-e-eqtesad.com/news/518816/, October 2012, accessed in August 28, 2018.
[30] Somayeh Fereidooni, *Girls' Narrative of University Experience* (Tehran: Jamee-shenasan, 2015), 114–21.

in loco parentis. As in dorms in the United States or Europe in the 1950s, staff members establish rigid curfews for when students must be back in their rooms and who can visit them, and they even report students' comings and goings to their parents.

Students often choose, therefore, to move to a "pension," another name for a shared communal apartment. In this new living arrangement, women are less restricted, but living in a communal apartment is not easy either. Residents are usually mixed—students, employees, divorced women, and sometimes runaway girls all share bathrooms, a kitchen, and even bedrooms. Thus, as soon as a young woman can afford it, she will try to rent an apartment alone or share one with friends to have a more independent life and experience greater freedom of mobility.

Such independence and freedom are not always accompanied by a sense of security. Many young women, especially those from small towns, do not feel secure in Tehran. Some of my young interviewees had to move several times because of different types of harassments. This is another reason why young woman who live alone do not always declare that fact; instead, they give the impression to their neighbors and family members that they are living with friends or family.

Yassi (born in 1985) is an accountant from Mazandaran in the Caspian Sea region who came to Tehran when she was eighteen. One difference between her life and those of other migrant women is that she belongs to a well-to-do family in Sari (the provincial capital of Mazandaran) and also has an aunt in Tehran. Thus, she could live with her aunt until she finished her studies. She then found a job and, with the help of her parents, rented an apartment in the northern, more upscale part of Tehran. As she recalled in the interview, her path to independence had three phases—coming to Tehran, taking a job, and renting her own apartment—a path that is more or less identical to that of other young girls who come from the provinces. Yet even Yassi, whose parents are wealthy, modern, and understanding, does not want to return to her city:

> In a small town you can never have any independence. You have nothing to do. Your friends are very limited. You cannot meet interesting people. You cannot find a job you like. So, I told my parents I really cannot go back, I would be miserable back home! At the same time, I have now been living alone in Tehran for ten years. I can no longer go back to my parent's house and live again under their authority.

Maryam (born in 1982) is another young woman from Mazandaran who works as a social worker at an NGO. She came to Tehran when she was eighteen to attend the university. She lived for a couple of years in a dormitory and then rented an apartment. She comes from a small, religious town in Mazandaran, where the community and her family exert severe control over young women. In her town she used to wear the chador, but when she came to Tehran, she changed to more modern outfits. Her most important experience of living in Tehran was the "freedom" she experienced due to her anonymity in public spaces:

> Living in Tehran has been great. When I arrived in Tehran, I loved walking alone for hours, nobody paid any attention to me and I was not afraid of anyone. I felt I was in control of my life here. I did not want to lose this opportunity. I experienced

a bad economic situation and my family could not help me. So I found a job in a newspaper bureau and then my life became much easier. After a few years, when I returned to my town I saw that all my female cousins were married, had children, and lived "normal" lives as housewives, but for me everything had changed. I did not want to live this "normal" life. Today my work, my friends, and my freedom are my most important belongings.

However, even in Tehran, living alone for a woman is not an easy task, not just economically but also culturally. Young women who live alone, far from the family, need to adopt several survival strategies to remain safe, and they are especially careful in selecting their companions to avoid meddling by parents and neighbors. Sara (born in 1976) is a Tehrani writer. She was divorced twelve years ago, after a short marriage, and has been living alone:

> For a young woman to live alone in Iran requires some particular intelligence and strategies in order not to attract problems or too much attention from her neighbors. For instance, I try not to make much noise. Nor do I enter my apartment with my boyfriend. We never enter together. First, I enter and then a few minutes later he arrives.

This is a common strategy for young women who live alone. They fear what people in the neighborhood might think and how they might react, and they also fear alerting the morality police. Young women are, therefore, very circumspect about their relationships with men and do not fully trust their neighbors. This sense of insecurity is in direct relationship to the neighborhood in which they live: Is the community more modern or traditional? What type of building is it (a big and more anonymous complex or a small and more intimate apartment building)? How old is the woman? What is her social position? What is her status in the building (owner or renter)? Tenants are more careful than those who own their units. For most of these young women, having some family and relatives in the same town provides a measure of safety.

Thus, migrants and Tehrani women usually have different experiences with regard to living alone. Tehrani women have their families in the same city, the same neighborhood, or perhaps even the same building. Migrant women usually live far from their families and beyond their control. Yet, both share some common factors that have to do not with their origin but with their gender.

The Trajectory of Independent Women in Iran

For most women, regardless of their generation, choosing to be independent and living alone is not easy; it requires a great deal of effort, intelligence, tolerance, and endurance. Until recently, just renting an apartment was difficult for a single woman, because people were very judgmental and suspicious. However, in the last few years these attitudes have changed somewhat, in part, because more female migrants are coming to the cities, either as students or as employees. Another important factor is that women and men in all sectors of society are delaying marriage; thus, singlehood and single households have become a more common social reality. A large number of more "traditional" single households (i.e., people who live alone out of necessity) still exist. However, there is also an undeniable new trend of "modern" single households that is due to desire among the more educated and capable women for greater independence. These women are more aware of their rights, and they prefer to live alone. They are willing to confront the accompanying challenges to enjoy their independence. They prefer this life to that of a woman who lives in a miserable marriage, especially in a country where patriarchal laws strongly favor men in divorce proceedings. Most young women with whom I have talked were planning to marry some day and to have children. In reality after a couple of years of independent living, their expectations of life and marriage change, which makes marriage more difficult for them.

As Jean Claude Bologne notes, the modern style of singlehood depends very much on the ability to extend sociability, using all the technological tools that are available to overcome "loneliness" in old age.[31] In fact, "loneliness" is still the biggest fear of most people who live alone, but nowadays it seems easier to tolerate this loneliness, especially among the younger, more educated urban populations. The opening of new public spaces—cafes, malls, restaurants, cinemas, sport centers, parks—and the spread of smartphones and the new social media have all added sociability to the lives of people. These aspects of social life were nonexistent until a short while ago. These new social spaces (physical and virtual) play an important role in the lives of young and middle-aged single women and compensate for their occasional loneliness.

Women's search for greater independence started during the Pahlavi regime. At first, they could only find it by taking a job, securing an income, and becoming economically independent. Later, during the chaos of the revolutionary time, women and youth experienced a new type of freedom and independence that was both more volatile and more intense. Under the Islamic Republic, people—especially women and youth—gradually learned how to live under a seemingly permanent paradox, where tradition and stillness coexisted with modernity and movement. This paradox provoked new types of resistance, one form of which involved changes in the structure of the family. In the last half century, Iranian women have become the most important agents of change in their society, despite the many types of segregation, persecution, restriction, and marginalization that they have endured. Living independently has become itself a form of resistance for women who want to take their lives into their own hands.

---

[31] Bologne, *Histoire du célibat et des célibataires*, 374.

2

Romancing Filipinas

Challenges and Promises of Transnational Families in Iran

Ashraf Zahedi

The Iranian Revolution of 1979 and the Cultural Revolution and subsequent closure of Iranian universities in 1980–3 compelled many young Iranians to pursue higher education overseas in Asia, Europe, and the United States. Although most students preferred Western (particularly American) universities, obtaining a student visa from the United States proved to be very difficult in the 1980s, as Iran and the United States had no diplomatic relations, and there was no consulate inside Iran to issue visas. The quality of education, geographical proximity, and the lower cost of education made the Philippines a popular alternative and the country of choice for many Iranian students, the majority of whom were men. While some of these men were secular, others were religious. Some opposed the postrevolutionary regime, but others supported it and benefited from its scholarships. Interactions of Iranian men with Filipinas led to intimate relationships and marriages in many cases.

These transnational marriages have been challenged by the negative perception of Iranian men as "Muslim terrorists" by Filipinos, and of Filipinas as "foreign maids" by Iranians. The main burden, however, has been placed on Filipina brides, who have had to go through a process of mandatory conversion to Islam, migrate to Iran, learn the Persian language, and adjust to Iranian culture, which is vastly different from their own. This chapter examines the complexities of migration for Filipinas and highlights their varied experiences in transnational marriages. I argue that, despite personal and social challenges, these transnational couples have managed to transcend their cultural and religious differences and build lives together based on affection and shared views of family life. Additionally, I examine the lived experience of their biracial, bicultural, and bilingual children. In so doing, I aim to demonstrate that race, culture, and nationality are not fixed categories—as social constructs, they are imprecise, unstable, and subject to change.

Filipinas in Transnational Spaces

Much has been written about Filipinas working overseas.[1] "Filipinas bodies," in Tolentino's[2] words, have served in many sectors, including health care, hospitality, and domestic work, contributing to keeping the Philippine economy afloat and sustaining family members back home. The presence of Filipinas in transnational space needs to be examined in the context of socioeconomic and political developments in the Philippines and the global labor market. These developments have had a significant impact on the interactions of Filipinas with foreign men and on their transnational marriages.

Employment opportunities in the Philippines have been diminishing since the 1970s, and the state has actively encouraged the most important single export of the Philippines—its people. While Filipino labor migration dates back to the 1940s, former President Ferdinand Marcos (1917–89) expedited and facilitated the migration of Filipinos overseas in the 1970s to alleviate unemployment in the Philippines.[3] Labor export has resulted in substantial remittances from overseas, which have supported families in the Philippines and significantly[4] helped the state by providing much-needed foreign exchange to pay its foreign debts and balance its trade deficit.[5]

While the range of opportunities has continued to narrow in the Philippines, overseas employment opportunities have expanded. These parallel developments have had a clear gender implication. As Western women leave their domestic work in favor of professional work outside the home, Filipinas and women from developing countries fill the domestic needs and provide care,[6] making care the Philippines' "primary export."[7] About "two-thirds of Filipino migrant workers are women."[8] Like all Philippine citizens, Filipinas are driven to seek employment abroad due to limited opportunities in the Philippines and their desire to help their families and fulfill family obligations.[9] Family obligations reinforced by a culture of expectation and reciprocation

---

[1] Nicole Constable, *Romance on a Global Stage* (Berkeley: University of California Press, 2003); Nicole Constable, "A Transnational Perspective on Divorce and Marriage: Filipina Wives and Workers," *Identities: Global Studies in Culture and Power*, 10 (2003): 163–80; Nicole Constable, "A Tale of Two Marriages: International Matchmaking and Gendered Mobility," in *Cross-Border Marriages: Gender and Mobility in Transnational Asia*, ed. Nicole Constable (Philadelphia: University of Pennsylvania Press, 2005), 167–86; Yen Le Espiritu, *Home Bound: Filipino American Lives Across Cultures, Communities, and Countries* (Berkeley: University of California Press, 2003); Rachel Paddock, "The Care Crisis in the Philippines: Children and Transnational Families in the New Global Economy," in *Global Women: Nannies, Maids, and Sex Workers in the New Economy*, eds. Barbara Ehrenreich and Arlie Hochschild (New York: Metropolitan Books, 2002), 39–54; and Roland Tolentino, "Bodies, Letters, Catalogs: Filipinas in Transnational Space," *Social Text*, 48 (1996): 49–76.
[2] Tolentino, "Bodies, Letters, Catalogs: Filipinas in Transnational Space," 53.
[3] Constable, *Romance on a Global Stage*, 121.
[4] Constable, "A Tale of Two Marriages," 124.
[5] Le Espiritu, *Home Bound*, 90.
[6] Tolentino, "Bodies, Letters, Catalogs: Filipinas in Transnational Space," 66.
[7] Rachel Parrenas, "The Care Crisis in the Philippines: Children and Transnational Families in the New Global Economy," in *Global Women: Nannies, Maids, and Sex Workers in the New Economy*, eds. Barbara Ehrenreich and Arlie Hochschild (New York: Metropolitan Books, 2002), 41.
[8] Ibid., 39.
[9] Elisabeth Zontini, "Immigrant Women in Barcelona: Coping with the Consequences of Transnational Lives," *Journal of Ethnic and Migration Studies*, 30 (2004): 119–20.

play a significant role in compelling overseas workers to remit their savings to their families back home.[10] While most Filipinas are labor migrants, some are "marriage migrants." As Nicole Constable points out, marriage to a "foreigner constitutes another important pattern of migration."[11]

Migration and Transnational Marriages

The formation of transnational communities facilitated by sociopolitical events (such as war and revolution), the flow of capital, and the movement of labor in the late twentieth century, has resulted in a substantial increase in the rate of marriage migration around the globe. The majority of marriage migrants are women, but in recent years, male marriage migrants have joined transnational communities as well, adding to the diversity of marriage migration.[12] Transnational communities, like other communities, usually seek to preserve their identity and heritage and to prefer marriage within the group. The literature on transnational marriages points to the importance of shared race, ethnicity, religion, and national origin for couples in transnational communities.[13] Research, however, suggests an emerging trend of cross-ethnic and cross-nationality marriages among second-generation Muslim migrants in Europe, (e.g., German Turks have married Muslims of European transnational communities).[14] Nevertheless, the preference for ethnically endogamous marriages—the desirability of co-ethnic status and shared culture—continues to prevail.[15]

Although interethnic marriages are increasing, the number of transnational interfaith marriages is still relatively small. Many of these marriages have been between Christian and Jews.[16] Research on interfaith marriages highlights the merits and challenges of such marriages. In general, as Marranci points out, religious groups "tend to have rules"[17] with different levels of rigidity with regard to rejecting interfaith

---

[10] Constable, *Romance on a Global Stage*; Espiritu, *Home Bound*; and Zontini, "Immigrant Women in Barcelona," 1113–44.
[11] Constable, *Romance on a Global Stage*, 121.
[12] Kathrine Charsley, "Unhappy Husbands: Masculinity and Migration in Transnational Pakistani Marriages," *Journal of Royal Anthropological Institute*, 11 (2005): 85–115.
[13] Elisabeth Beck-Gernsheim, "Transnational Lives, Transnational Marriages: A Review of Evidence from Migrant Communities in Europe," *Global Networks*, 7 (2007): 271; Katharine Charsley and Alison Shaw, "South Asian Transnational Marriages in Comparative Perspective," *Global Networks*, 6 (2006): 331; and Nicola Mooney, "Aspiration, Reunification and Gender Transformation in Jat Sikh Marriages from India to Canada," *Global Networks*, 6 (2006): 389.
[14] Gaby Strassburger, "Transnational or Interethnic Marriages of Turkish Migrants: The (In)Significance of Religious or Ethnic Affiliations," in *Muslim Networks and Transnational Communities in and Across Europe*, eds. Stefano Allievi and Jorgen Nielson (Boston: Brill, 2003), 217.
[15] Charsley, "Unhappy Husbands," 88; Gabriele Marranci, "Muslim Marriages in Northern Ireland," in *Migration and Marriage: Heterogamy and Homogamy in a Changing World*, eds. Barbara Waldis and Reginald Byron (Berlin: LIT Verlag Berlin-Hamburg Munster, 2006), 48.
[16] Gabrielle Glaser, *Stranger to the Tribe: Portraits of Interfaith Marriage* (Boston: Houghton Mifflin, 1997); Evelyn Kaye, *Crosscurrents: Children, Families, and Religion* (New York: C.N. Potter, 1980); Egon Mayer, *Love and Tradition: Marriages Between Jews and Christians* (New York: Plenum Press, 1985); and Susan Schneider, *Intermarriages: The Challenge of Living with Differences Between Christians and Jews* (New York: Free Press, 1989).
[17] Marranci, "Muslim Marriages in Northern Ireland," 41.

marriages. More importantly, civil laws governing marriage that are based on religious laws, as is the case in Iran, not only discourage interfaith marriages but also require non-Muslims who do enter into them to convert to Islam, so that such couples effectively end up with the same religion, at least on paper. Regardless of the endogamous or exogamous patterns of transnational marriages, these marriages often lead to chain migration, paving the way for migration of other family members.[18]

Transnational marriages of Filipinas demonstrate that they have crossed not only ethnic and racial barriers but religious ones as well. Filipinas have married people of diverse backgrounds throughout the world. Marriage agencies have played a significant role in encouraging and facilitating these marriages. The inclination of Filipinas to become marriage migrants has occasionally raised concerns about their motives. Scholars who have examined and analyzed the motives and intentions of these migrant brides, pen pals, mail-order brides, and worker wives[19] highlight that their motives range from wanting romantic love to needing better economic opportunities. Having the option of divorce could play a part in their motives as well. Legal sanctions against divorce in the primarily Catholic Philippines have worked against women who are trapped in difficult marriages. Thus, transnational marriages give women the option of divorce and the opportunity for self-fulfillment in marriage.[20] What is more, employment opportunities, or the lack thereof, have made Filipino men less sought after by Filipina women. Research indicates that Filipinas who choose to be marriage migrants are not helpless victims; they are informed managers of their own lives and use their agency to improve their life chances.[21] As Nakamatsu points out, "Their agency is expressed in their making decisions that change their life course to their own advantage."[22] The dichotomous characterization of Filipinas as victims or gold diggers is not an accurate portrayal. Like other people, they make decisions based on the opportunities and resources available to them. Thus, the marriages of Filipina migrants, as Constable notes, "are intertwined in a complex and paradoxical way with global, local, and personal factors."[23]

---

[18] Beck-Gernsheim, "Transnational Lives, Transnational Marriages," 271; Mooney, "Aspiration, Reunification and Gender Transformation in Jat Sikh Marriages from India to Canada," 395; Charsley and Shaw, "South Asian Transnational Marriages in Comparative Perspective," 335.

[19] Constable, *Romance on a Global Stage*; Teresita Del Rosario, "Bridal Diaspora: Migration and Marriage Among Filipino Women," *Indian Journal of Gender Studies*, 12 (2005): 253–73; Nicola Piper and Mina Roces, eds. *Wife or Workers* (Oxford: Rowman & Littlefield Publishers, Inc., 2003); Nobue Suzuki, "Tripartite Desires: Filipina-Japanese Marriages and Fantasies of Transnational Traversal," in *Cross-Border Marriages: Gender and Mobility in Transnational Asia*, eds. Nicola Piper and Mina Roces (Philadelphia: University of Pennsylvania Press, 2005), 124–44.

[20] Constable, "A Transnational Perspective on Divorce and Marriage," 164.

[21] Constable, *Romance on a Global Stage*, 93; Mina Roces, "Sisterhood Is Local: Filipino Women in Mount Isa," in *Wife or Worker*, eds. Nicola Piper and Mina Roces (Oxford: Rowman & Littlefield Publishers, Inc., 2003), 75; and Zontini, "Immigrant Women in Barcelona," 1130.

[22] Tomoko Nakamatsu, "Complex Power and Diverse Responses: Transnational Marriage Migration and Women's Agency," in *The Agency of Women in Asia*, ed. Lyn Parker (Singapore: Cavendish, Marshall International, 2005), 163.

[23] Constable, "A Transnational Perspective on Divorce and Marriage," 163.

Though marriage migration is a relatively new phenomenon, interracial marriages in the Philippines have a long history.[24] Historically, Filipinas have married foreign men, ranging from Spanish colonizers to Japanese invaders and American soldiers. In particular, aside from the opportunities in the West, the perceived characteristics of Caucasian men have made marriage to Western men very desirable for Filipinas, many of whom find the physical features and fair complexions of Caucasian men very attractive.[25] Their attraction to Western men is also shaped by the common perception of Western men as open-minded, liberal, and egalitarian.[26] However, opportunities to marry Western men are limited, and thousands of Filipinas marry non-Western men of different races and nationalities every year.

In marriages involving men from the United States or Asia (particularly Japan, Korea, or China), the husbands usually share some commonalities with their Filipina wives—for example, in terms of religion (such as Christianity) or at least an Asian background. The marriages of Filipinas and Iranian men are unique in that they usually do not share race, ethnicity, language, or religion, nor do they conform to the Filipina's desired ideal. The physical features of Iranian men do not match Caucasian features and complexion. Iranian men, in general, are not considered to be open-minded or liberal as Western men. Moreover, while marrying Western men would allow Filipinas to facilitate migration of family members to the West, Iran was and still is a place where few foreigners would like to settle, which means these women would not encourage their family members to migrate to Iran. What is more, employment opportunities in Iran are limited, and even Iranians have been facing severe unemployment and underemployment. Not only is Iran economically undesirable, but the political environment, dominant Islamic rules, and female dress codes make Iran an unlikely choice for Filipina migration.

In the absence of favorable socioeconomic factors, what compelled these Filipinas to marry Iranian men and migrate to Iran? Though love is cited as the main reason for these marriages, love is often intertwined with the "political economy and cultural logics of desire."[27] There are practical considerations that come into play as well, such as financial well-being, commitment to marriage, opportunity for employment, family obligation, and characteristics of future husbands. These considerations are important in marital choices all over the world. Love and attraction are important, but weighing perceived risks and gains is part of a rational choice.[28] The women were graduating from college in the late 1980s, after the Philippine Revolution of 1986 when economic uncertainties compelled many educated Filipinos to seek employment abroad. Marrying educated Iranian men, though they were not the ideal Western husbands,

---

[24] Chester Hunt and Richard Coller, "Intermarriage and Cultural Change: A Study of Philippine-American Marriages," *Social Forces*, 35 (1957): 224; and Victoria Reyes, *Filipina Military Brides: Negotiating Assimilation and Cultural Maintenance with a Bi-Cultural Setting*, A Senior Thesis, The Ohio State University, 2006, 3.

[25] Constable, *Romance on a Global Stage*, 122.

[26] Constable, "A Tale of Two Marriages," 168.

[27] Constable, *Romance on a Global Stage*, 116.

[28] Jutta Lauth Bacas, "Cross-Border Marriages and the Formation of Transnational Families: A Case Study of Greek-German Couples in Athens," 2002: 4. http://www.transcomm.ox.ac.uk/working%20papers/WPTC-02-10%Bacas.pdf. Accessed on December 15, 2018.

provided Filipinas economic security and respected status as married women devoted to raising their children (a culturally valued status in the Philippines), and it put an end to the possibility of having to perform undesired work abroad.

In addition, the literature on migration and transnational marriages has covered economic, social, and cultural factors influencing migration and transnational marriages, including marriage motives and the promises and challenges of these marriages. Yet religious conversion for the sake of marriage is an area of research that has not received the attention it deserves from scholars. In examining the case of Filipina brides in Iran, this chapter aims to fill this gap. While addressing socioeconomic and cultural factors, it also highlights mandatory conversion, thereby adding a new dimension to the analysis of transnational marriages in an Islamic context.

Research Methods

In conducting this research, I have drawn upon my academic training as a sociologist, my cultural background as a Persian-speaking native of Iran, and my personal ties to Filipinas in Iran. According to the Embassy of the Philippines in Iran, more than four hundred Filipina women who are married to Iranian nationals reside permanently in Iran.[29] I interviewed eleven of these women in Tehran in October 2005. Interviews were semistructured and conducted in English. I used the snowball model to identify interviewees. Some interviewees recruited other Filipinas and facilitated my interview with them and thus helped me with my snowball sampling research method. I intended to have a larger number of interviewees, but the Iranian regime's intimidation of scholars made my return to Iran risky. Thus, I had to base this chapter on the existing interviews.

All the interviewed brides had interesting life stories and were generous in sharing them with me. Their personal profiles would have enriched this chapter; given the political environment, however, I have changed their names and omitted any information that could help the Iranian authorities identify and intimidate these Filipinas. In addition to the brides, I also interviewed a number of mothers-in-law. These short interviews, conducted in the Persian language, explored their attitudes and feelings toward their Filipina daughters-in-law.

Two of the Filipinas had come to Iran before the revolution in the mid-1970s. They worked as nurses and later married Iranian men. The other interviewees had come to Iran between the mid-1980s and the mid-1990s. All of them had college degrees and were members of the middle and lower middle class in the Philippines. They were all Catholic. Seven of them had met their Iranian husbands in the Philippines, two in Iran, one in Japan, and one in Canada. All but one of the husbands had college education, and all belonged to the traditional or modern Iranian middle classes.

All but two interviewees were still married at the point of interview. One was divorced but still living in Iran; the other had become a widow only a year before but

---

[29] Personal interview with Henelito Sevilla, Jr, Staff at Embassy of Philippines in Tehran, October 15, 2005.

still lived in Iran. Both women indicated that they had well-paid professional jobs in Iran and, thus, could live comfortably. The other women were either working outside the house or were stay-at-home mothers. All of them had children. Some lived in houses at some distance from their Iranian in-laws; others lived in large apartments close to their in-laws.

I interviewed the brides at their homes while their young children played in an adjacent room. At that time, I wondered about the social experience of these biracial children and hoped to have an opportunity to interview them as adults. Thirteen years later, in 2018, I managed to get in touch with several Filipino-Iranian children and interviewed eight of them over the phone. Two of them were children of Filipina mothers whom I had interviewed in 2005.

The interviews with adult children were semistructured and conducted in Persian. Their ages ranged from nineteen to forty-one. They all had college degrees from Iran or from European, Asian, American, and Canadian universities. Some of them lived overseas. I changed the names of the interviewees to protect their identities.

Romancing and Marrying Iranian Men

University settings provide great opportunities for people of different nationalities to forge friendships that sometimes become romantic, and the relations of Iranian and Filipina students are no exception. Before the 1979 Iranian Revolution, young, urban, middle-class Iranian men could socialize with Iranian girls and experience romance. The postrevolutionary sex segregation in Iran, along with the mandatory ĥijāb, placed physical and emotional barriers between urban Iranian men and women that restricted their public interactions.

In the Philippines, young Iranian men were free to socialize with female students. In their eyes, Filipina girls were educated and modern, yet "untainted by feminism."[30] They were kind and warm like the Iranian girls. Unlike Western girls, who were viewed as unfaithful, selfish, and uncommitted to the family, Filipinas were perceived as loyal, selfless, and family-oriented. What is more, like Iranian girls, they were assumed to be virgins and sexually inexperienced before marriage.

In turn, Filipinas saw these young men as loving partners and good providers who would take care of them and their children. They did not view marrying Iranians as very different from other transnational marriages. However, unlike other family members who had married Christian or Buddhist husbands and moved overseas, marriage between Christian Filipinas and Muslim Iranians presented a problem. Islam has been an integral part of the history of the Philippines, but the majority of Christian Filipinos have a negative view of Islam and of Muslims. Although marriages between Muslims and Christians have taken place in the Philippines,[31] there has been continuous tension between the Christian majority and the Muslim minority.

---

[30] Constable, *Romance on a Global Stage*, 94.
[31] Luis Lacar, "Balik-Islam: Christian Converts to Islam in the Philippines, 1970-1998," in *Muslim-Christian Marriages in the Philippines* (Quezon City, Philippines: New Day Publishers., 1980), 2001.

Given the existing negative perceptions about Muslim men, the parents of interviewed Filipinas were, to say the least, uncomfortable and worried. Many Filipino parents expressed dismay at the possibility that their daughters might marry Muslim men and some did their best to discourage them. Angelita's father, for example, did not approve of her marriage. Hoping that physical distance would discourage her Iranian suitor, he sent her to Germany. But that did not work. As Angelita joyously remarked, "He followed me to Germany and appealed to my parents to agree to our marriage. He was in tears, and my parents could no longer disagree."[32]

Indeed, many parents who initially opposed the marriage of their daughters gave their blessings once the Muslim Iranian men were introduced to them and expressed their love for their daughters. Mandatory conversion to Islam, however, was an unforeseen issue for the future brides. According to Iranian civil law, non-Muslims who marry Muslims are required to convert to Islam; otherwise, the marriage could not be registered. There is no civil marriage in Iran. Furthermore, although non-Muslims are expected to convert to Islam, the conversion of Muslims to other religions is regarded as a serious sin and apostasy, potentially punishable by death. Iranian grooms, therefore, regardless of their views on Christianity, could not consider conversion to Christianity.

There is no Islamic consensus on whether a Jewish or a Christian woman should convert to Islam for the sake of marrying a Muslim man. In the Qur'an, Christians and Jews are classified as *ahl-e ketab*, "People of the Book." They believe in a monolithic God and follow the Abrahamic tradition, as do the Muslims. As stated in the Qur'an, Al Baqarah Verse 2:221, Muslim men can marry "believing" Jewish and Christian women.[33] No conversion is required for these women, though it is hoped for. Yet some countries, including Iran, have made conversion a requirement for non-Muslim women marrying Muslim men. Conversion to Islam for the sake of marriage, in small numbers, has taken place elsewhere. Some Filipinas working in Hong Kong have married Muslim Pakistanis, but several had converted to Islam long before their marriage or after they started working in Hong Kong.[34] Thus, their cases do not represent conversion for the sake of marriage.

All the Filipinas that I interviewed indicated that they had always been religious and devoted Catholics but converted to Islam to fulfill the marriage requirement. Their conversion naturally did not sit well with their parents and officials of their church. A church wedding has been an important part of the image of marriage, and a few Filipinas never experienced that. Others, however, married in the church first before converting to Islam. Later, they had an Islamic ceremony. Only a very small number of Filipinas eventually became true converts.

But was love enough to prepare them for the challenges of moving to Iran, living with in-laws, learning a new language, adjusting to a different culture, and facing an unfamiliar sociopolitical environment? Apparently, it was—or had to be—once the Filipina brides landed in Tehran and faced life in the Islamic Republic of Iran. They

---

[32] Personal interview, October 20, 2005, Tehran.
[33] *Qur'an*. Translated by Muhammad Habib Shakir (New York: Tahrike Tarsile Qur'an, Inc., 1987).
[34] Sithi Hawwa, "From Cross to Crescent: Religious Conversion of Filipina Domestic Helpers in Hong Kong," *Islam and Christian and Muslim Relations*, 11 (2000): 347–67.

did not know much about Iran but had confidence in their ability to adjust and make the best of any situation as their fellow Filipinos have done all over the world. Filipinas have married foreign men and lived in small and remote places, from mining towns in Australia to farmlands in Japan and many other places in between.

The Persistent Image of Muslim Men and Filipina Women

People are often categorized into homogenized national, racial, ethnic, or religious categories. Each person is tied to a history that either fairly or unfairly projects certain images onto him or her. Muslim Iranian grooms and Filipina brides are no exceptions; both have been subject to a process of Othering within specific contexts. The Philippines is regarded as the only Christian country in Asia, yet Islam has long been part of Philippine history, having arrived in the Philippines in the fourteenth century.[35] At that time, Muslims lived on the southern island of Mindanao and had peaceful and harmonious relations with natives.[36] By the sixteenth century, when Spanish colonizers brought Christianity to the Philippines, Islam as a religion had already been well established.[37] Along with bringing Christianity to the Philippines, Spanish rulers brought an "attitude of enmity toward Islam"[38] and made major efforts to "eradicate" it.[39]

Muslim men have been not only characterized as polygamous and abusive of women but with the radicalization of some Muslim Filipinos and their anti-government violence some Christians also view Muslims as terrorists. For both religious groups, continued animosity has turned into mutual suspicion and hostility.[40] Such negative views of Muslims reflected on Muslim Iranian grooms. Rosie's mother expressed her fear and anxiety to her:

> How can you marry a Muslim man? He can divorce you any time he wants. He can marry other women and ask you to serve them. Muslim men are violent. Aren't you worried about that? I am very concerned about your safety. The thought of you living among all those Muslims worries me to death.[41]

Other Filipina brides have encountered their parents' belief that Muslim men would be involved in terrorist acts. Amanda's father conveyed his disappointment with her marital choice by declaring, "There is something about Islam that feeds into the use of

---

[35] Ibid., 348; Jeffrey Ayala Milligan, "Religious Identity, Political Autonomy and National Integrity: Implications for Educational Policy from Muslim-Christian Conflict in Southern Philippines," *Islam and Christian Muslim Relations*, 12 (2001): 437.
[36] Hawwa, "From Cross to Crescent," 348; Lacar, "Balik-Islam: Christian Converts to Islam in the Philippines, 1970-1998," 39.
[37] Milligan, "Religious Identity, Political Autonomy and National Integrity," 436.
[38] Hawwa, "From Cross to Crescent," 349.
[39] Lacar, "Balik-Islam: Christian Converts to Islam in the Philippines, 1970-1998," 41.
[40] Ibid., 63.
[41] Personal interview, October 5, 2005, Tehran.

terror. Look at the world, all terrorist groups are Muslim. You are so blinded by love that you cannot see that."[42]

Filipina brides also had to face Iranians' perception of them as Other. In Iran, though they were welcomed by their Iranian in-laws, there were occasional questions about their character and marriage motives. They have been viewed as poor girls with no education who could be after the assets of in-laws. Most Iranians, however, have no knowledge of the underlying structural causes of Filipinos' transnational mobility.

Since the oil boom of the 1970s in the Middle East and the subsequent increase in employment opportunities, thousands of Filipino labor migrants, both male and female, have found their way to Middle Eastern countries. Older Iranians remember the presence of Filipinas in Iran in the mid-1970s, when many of them worked as domestic workers, nannies, and nurses. It is the image of "maids" that has been sealed in many Iranians' minds. Some Iranians remark sarcastically that a Filipina bride is "yesterday's maid [who] has today become the lady of the house." Contrary to this perception, none of the Filipina brides I interviewed had worked as domestic servants. What is more, a significant number of Filipinas who have done domestic work throughout the world are high school or college graduates.

Dynamics of Family Relations

Away from their own families once they arrive in Iran, Filipina brides had little emotional and psychological security.[43] In a new country with a totally different culture, they often experienced a range of feelings common to other migrant brides: "disappointment, loneliness, and adjustment to a social reality that often bears little resemblance to earlier imaginings."[44] Lynda's words depicted this sense of disappointment: "I was just shocked and did not know how to relate to the new environment."[45] Loneliness was overwhelming for some. Rosie recalled those days, saying, "I longed for my family, my country, and the sound and smell of the Philippines. I missed my life there. In Iran, everything was foreign to me except my husband."[46]

In the beginning, unfortunately, they did not know of other brides and lacked any support network. In difficult times, people often take solace in religion and places of worship, but these Filipinas could not seek the comfort of the church. As new converts, they pretended to adhere to Islam in public, but privately they remained Catholic and sought comfort in their own religion in the privacy of their bedrooms: "My church is in my house. I live in my church," Rosie remarked.[47]

As foreign brides, they were eager to establish relations with their in-laws and secure their affection and acceptance. Not knowing the language made them very insecure in

[42] Personal interview, October 10, 2005 Tehran.
[43] Suzuki, "Tripartite Desires," 126.
[44] Constable, "A Tale of Two Marriages," 168.
[45] Personal interview, October 15, 2005, Tehran.
[46] Personal interview, October 5, 2005, Tehran.
[47] Personal interview, October 5, 2005, Tehran.

understanding what was going on around them and comprehending the views and feelings of their in-laws. Amanda recalled those days:

> I had to wait all day for my husband to return from work, but as soon as he got home, parents, siblings, friends, and relatives stopped by unannounced. None of them spoke English and [they] kept talking in Farsi [Persian]. It was very frustrating for me.[48]

Diwata took refuge in reading: "I used to read English books just to keep busy and not lose my mind. At that time [in the 1980s] there was no English TV channel in Iran."[49] Interestingly, all interviewees indicated that during these difficult times, they enjoyed the support and affection of their fathers-in-law, brothers-in-law, and other male relatives. Their disappointment was often with female in-laws.

A few Filipinas enjoyed the affection and respect of their mothers-in-law from the very beginning; some, however, had to prove themselves. Dalisay had taken care of her mother-in-law for years, but her mother-in-law still continued to see her as an outsider and Other:

> My mother-in-law is very religious and thinks of me as *najes*, impure. She says only Muslims go to heaven. This is very hard for me to take. You know, she is bedridden and needs me. I would be happy to help her, but she has a sharp tongue. Even her daughters do not help her. Thank God that my husband understands me and supports me.[50]

In facing all these challenges, the women hoped to depend on their husbands' support, but a few husbands used their wives' love to their own advantage. A few Filipinas complained that when they were dating their future husbands in the Philippines, the men had tried hard to please them and accommodate their needs and expectations. They also downplayed the cultural differences and were more agreeable to the wishes of their future Filipina brides. That changed after the marriage. An "unequal power distribution"[51] favoring the husbands shaped the lives of these couples in Iran, where the husbands were in their own territory and had cultural advantages.[52] Thus, they felt more comfortable in asserting their own needs and expectations.

Some husbands also used love as a means of control. Drawing on their wives' affection, these husbands framed their personal needs and desires as culturally valid expectations. Filipinas did not know whether their husbands' demands were based on their personality or cultural characteristics. They did not know how to decode these expectations and ended up complying with them. For example, a few husbands had

---

[48] Personal interview, October 10, 2005, Tehran.
[49] Personal interview, October 18, 2005, Tehran.
[50] Personal interview, October 20, 2005, Tehran.
[51] Reyes, *Filipina Military Brides*, 2.
[52] Michelle Lee and Nicola Piper, "Reflection on Transnational Life-Course and Migratory Patterns of Middle-Class Women—Preliminary Observation from Malaysia," in *Wife or Workers*, eds. Piper and Roces (Oxford: Rowman & Littlefield Publishers, Inc., 2003), 133.

higher expectations of their Filipina wives than they would have had of an Iranian wife. They wanted to prove to their families that their Filipina brides were better than the Iranian girls whom their parents wished they had married. Some husbands even encouraged their Filipina wives to be more accommodating to their in-laws. In so doing, a husband hoped to turn his foreign bride into "one of us,"[53] thus validating their own choice. Diwata questioned this expectation: "I do a lot for my mother-in-law. She is old and not in good health. She is physically and emotionally dependent on me. How come her other daughter-in-law never offers any help? No wonder I am my mother-in-law's favorite."[54]

In addition to adjusting to family expectations, Filipina brides were totally dependent on their husbands emotionally, socially, linguistically, and financially. For some of them, not having their own income was a problem. Not knowing the language limited their chances of employment. Thus, they could not fulfill the familial obligation of sending money home. Though their husbands provided a middle-class lifestyle for them, they did not have extra money to send to their families. What sustained them through this ordeal were the love of their husbands and the friendship of fellow Filipinas.

Adjustment and Social Integration

Filipina brides, like other Filipinos the world over, have shown great ability to adapt to the "demands and changing circumstances of the migrant setting," earning the label "expert migrants" from Zontini.[55] It has been argued that they are capable of mobilizing their "inner resources" to fit in and even to "reinvent themselves in an all but strange and sometimes hostile environment."[56] While they did not face any form of hostility from the Iranian society, they had to make emotional and cultural adjustments and face social challenges.

Emotional and Cultural Adjustment

The first challenge was to leave their family and migrate to another country. The emotional strain of the separation was intense, particularly for those whose parents could not visit them. Talking with their parents and siblings on the telephone was the only avenue in the 1980s. Since the 1990s, however, affordable phone cards, fax, and the internet have enabled them to establish more regular contact with their families. Traveling to the Philippines was the best way for these Filipinas to get an emotional and a psychological break and ease their loneliness. Some traveled every year, others less frequently. Loneliness was a prevailing feeling for Filipinas, and some in-laws did

---

[53] Lauth Bacas, "Cross-Border Marriages and the Formation of Transnational Families."
[54] Personal interview, October 18, 2005, Tehran.
[55] Zontini, "Immigrant Women in Barcelona," 1130.
[56] Rosario, "Bridal Diaspora: Migration and Marriage Among Filipino Women," 256.

not fully recognize that. Parvin, a mother-in-law, stated that her Filipina daughter-in-law

> Keeps calling her family in the Philippines and speaks for a long time. Long-distance calls are expensive; that is too much expense for my son. True that she did not demand an expensive wedding like Iranian girls do, but that would have been a one-time expense. If you add up all these phone calls, it would be equal to wedding expenses.[57]

While this was certainly an exaggeration, it was ironic that later on she mentioned that she takes pride in the affection of her two daughters, who lived in France and called her on a weekly basis. Parvin recognized the emotional needs of her daughters away from home, yet she failed to acknowledge the emotional needs of her Filipina daughter-in-law.

Motherhood eased the loneliness of these Filipinas and brought them much-needed power in the family. It provided them with physical and emotional spaces to reclaim themselves and establish their roots. Motherhood is a highly praised status in Iranian culture, leading to improved social standing of women in their families and, in turn, in society. As mothers, Filipinas gained more respect, and they capitalized on this respect to claim more authority and negotiate their relationships with their in-laws more effectively. Having children brought their in-laws closer to them. With increased understanding and intimate connections, they developed stronger emotional ties with their in-laws. Toran, a mother-in-law, expressed her affection by stating, "I wish my other son had married a Filipina. Rosie is kind and caring. She does not have too many demands and expectations like the Iranian girls do. I love her more than my own daughter."[58]

Not knowing the Persian language was a major barrier to their adjustment and interaction with Iranians. Over time, some mastered speaking the language; others also learned to read and write. They needed this command of the Persian language to survive in Iran. Not understanding the culture and its nuances was also difficult for the Filipinas. All interviewees found the cultural differences a challenge. Cultural differences were the cause of divorce for Gloria, but she was quick to point out that "it was the culture of my husband and his family, not the national culture that created tension between us."[59] Many stated that they could not relate to the Iranian culture in the beginning but gradually learned to appreciate it. Gloria stated that she really likes the Iranian culture and "would like to continue to live in Iran."[60] Mayumi seemed content about living in Iran, "I learned to love this country. The people are accommodating, especially my in-laws."[61] Filipinas had a positive view of Iran and believed that Iranians treated them well and were kind and accommodating. All but one had adjusted to family life and felt that their in-laws treated them well and respected them.

[57] Personal interview, October 12, 2005, Tehran.
[58] Personal interview, October 22, 2005, Tehran.
[59] Personal interview, October 25, 2005, Tehran.
[60] Ibid.
[61] Personal interview, October 28, 2005, Tehran.

Religion is another aspect of life in Iran that these Filipinas had difficulties adjusting to. They found the ever-present sounds and images of Shiite rituals overwhelming.[62] The fact that they did not have emotional and spiritual connections with these rituals made it more difficult for them. Nevertheless, a few Filipinas married to high-ranking officials of the regime had to participate in the rituals to secure social acceptance from their husbands, in-laws, and society at large. Some Filipinas even took lessons in Islam. It was reassuring for them that Jesus was a revered prophet for Muslims. In fact, Jesus is mentioned in the Qur'an ninety-three times.[63] But Mayumi believed, "There are different understandings of Christ [Jesus] in Islam. For Muslims, Christ is a prophet and a man. For us Catholics, Christ is the son of God."[64]

Many Filipinas pointed out that love for their religion sustained them and made their adjustment smoother. Likewise, they emphasized that their husbands' understandings of their religious needs were very important for their adjustment, and, in some cases, brought them closer. One husband had unofficially converted to Catholicism but did not publicize it, since his conversion would be considered apostasy and, therefore, punishable by death. Another husband demonstrated his inclination toward Catholicism by consenting to their children's baptism. A few months after the interviews, these two families migrated to the West.

Social Integration

Learning the Persian language was crucial for Filipinas' social integration. It was also crucial for getting a job, and jobs, in turn, increased their financial independence. Many of them had been or were employed in fields compatible with their education at the time of the interview. They faced no legal impediment to their employment. According to Iranian civil laws, a foreign woman who marries an Iranian man is automatically entitled to Iranian citizenship and authorized to work in Iran. In seeking employment, Filipinas had the support of their husbands as well as in-laws, whether secular or religious. While in the past only urban secular families supported women's employment outside the home, since the revolution, more and more urban religious families approve of women's employment. The clerical regime claims to have "purified the social atmosphere of old corrupt practices" in the workplace.[65] In this new setting, women can be employed without compromising their Islamic values.[66]

Employment provided the Filipinas the opportunity to engage with Iranians other than their in-laws and extended families and facilitated their integration into wider society. Those employed did not feel discriminated against or disadvantaged. Actually,

---

[62] For Filipinas' views on Shiite rituals, please refer to Ashraf Zahedi, "Negotiating between Shi'a and Catholic Rituals in Iran: A Case Study of Filipina Converts and Their Adult Children," *Anthropology of the Middle East*, 13 (2018): 82–96.
[63] Hawwa, "From Cross to Crescent," 357.
[64] Personal interview, October 28, 2005, Tehran.
[65] Afsaneh Najmabadi, "Hazards of Modernity and Morality: Women, State, and Ideology in Contemporary Iran," in *Women, Islam and the State*, ed. Denize Kandiyoti (Philadelphia: Temple University Press, 1991), 50.
[66] Ashraf Zahedi, "State Ideology and the Status of Iranian War Widows," *International Feminist Journal of Politics*, 8 (2006): 267–86, 280.

some Filipinas felt privileged because of their command of English. Employed Filipinas expressed a higher degree of social integration than those who were unemployed. Amanda prided herself on working and being a career woman:

> I have been working for many years now. I have a good position and deal with foreign relations and correspondence. I am appreciated at work and paid well. This job gives me the opportunity to see the other side of Iran, its work environment and its professional relationships. At work, I am just myself—not related to my husband and his relatives. I use my maiden name and enjoy having a professional identity.[67]

It is not customary for women in Iran to change their last names after marriage; thus, Filipinas could keep their maiden names and preserve their family and national identity.

Employment also enabled Filipinas to send money home and fulfill familial obligations and, in turn, feel good about themselves and their lives in Iran. A few complained that while their husbands spent too much money on their families, they were not as generous in sending money to the Filipinas' parents. Diwata, a stay-at-home mother, was frustrated, "I hate it that he secretly gives our money to his parents, you know. My parents could use some help too. They are living on a small pension."[68] She added, "I am planning to start a business and make my own money."[69] The frustration of Filipinas and the limited generosity of their husbands have cultural explanations based on differences in gendered obligation. While both Filipino sons and daughters are expected to send remittances to their families, only Iranian sons are expected to support their natal family financially. Since most Iranian women did not work outside home in the past and did not have their own income, they were not expected to help their natal families financially. What is more, it was not considered proper to receive money from an unemployed, married daughter since the money effectively belonged to the son-in-law; thus, it was culturally frowned upon. Though much has changed and Iranian women have been earning their own income, the old attitudes about remittances persist. Regardless of gender, not being able to send remittances and meet cultural obligations cause a lot of frustration.

Wearing the mandatory ḫijāb has been a serious impediment to the social adjustment of Filipinas. As people of tropical islands who are used to wearing light clothing, they found the ḫijāb confining, hot, and suffocating. "I used to get headaches when I covered my head,"[70] Lynda remarked. While most of them wore a scarf and long jacket, as is the norm in Tehran and other major cities, a few Filipinas married to high-ranking officials and living in small towns had to display their piety and wear a chador, the black veil, in public during the more repressive times of the Iran–Iraq War in the 1980s. All women in Iran have to wear the ḫijāb (modest clothing) in the public sphere,

---

[67] Personal interview, October 10, 2005, Tehran.
[68] Personal interview, 18 October 18, 2005, Tehran.
[69] Ibid.
[70] Personal interview, October 15, 2005, Tehran.

but some have to observe the ḥijāb even in the private sphere and when interacting with the males of the extended family. Though the more secular husbands opposed the compulsory ḥijāb and sympathized with their Filipina wives, the more religious husbands demanded that their Filipina wives wear the ḥijāb even inside the home in the presence of male relatives. Carmita remarked with frustration:

> For a while my brother-in-law was living with us, so I had to wear a scarf all the time. My hair started to fall out; I got rashes on my scalp. I was going crazy. Doesn't my husband remember how I dressed in the Philippines? Doesn't he remember that I had to convert for his sake, for his love, for the sake of a legal marriage, and not for any belief in Islam? He knows all these. I never believed in covering my head. Even most Iranians do not believe in the ḥijāb. Look at all those Iranian women who challenge the ḥijāb. You know what, I do not think even my husband believes in the ḥijāb, but he does not have the courage to challenge his friends and relatives who expect me to cover my head.[71]

As for the political system, interviewed Filipinas were not happy with the lack of democracy in Iran. Nevertheless, they were not inclined to criticize the regime directly. Often, they framed political issues as cultural ones. Perhaps criticizing the culture was safer than criticizing the regime. Their disengagement from politics, however, was not based on disinterest. These Filipinas had been politicized during the Philippine Revolution of 1986 and had a good grasp of politics at the international level. When it came to women's issues, they seemed to be more engaged. Many criticized gendered laws in Iran that privilege men, including the need for wives to obtain their husbands' permission to work or travel abroad, as these were the laws that directly affected them. These women found the political environment repressive, yet they appreciated the safety of living in Iran. As Mayumi remarked, "I like living here. It is safe for our children. Iran has European standards of living and Asian morality and family values."[72] Her view was shared by most of the Filipina interviewees.

They found the love of their husbands empowering and crucial for their adjustment and social integration. It was this love that sustained them through the ups and downs of life in Iran. Even Gloria, who had divorced her husband, believed in his love: "We loved each other, and I have no regrets marrying him."[73] For Narella, who lost her husband to a heart attack, love was the core of their relationship, "We loved each other. He loved me and understood me well. I would marry him again,"[74] she proclaimed with teary eyes. They all seemed assured of the love of their husbands, but this did not influence their judgment of Iranian men in general. Many stated that Iranian men were restrictive and possessive. Yet when asked if, given the choice, they would prefer their daughters to marry an Iranian man or a Filipino man, all, except one, preferred Iranian

---

[71] Personal interview, October 18, 2005, Tehran.
[72] Personal interview, October 28, 2005, Tehran.
[73] Personal interview, October 25, 2005, Tehran.
[74] Personal interview, October 24, 2005, Tehran.

men. They believed Iranian men were better providers, more responsible, and more committed to the family than Filipino men.

Now, after decades of living in Iran, most Filipinas felt at home. They had made a great deal of effort to adjust and socially integrate and so had their in-laws. As Romano has pointed out, "Learning to live with someone from a different culture, even when it involves conflict" can provide opportunities for growth.[75] They were on good terms with their in-laws and felt that their interactions with them had led to deeper understanding on both sides. My interviewees had mastered the language, learned the social and legal systems, and found ways to negotiate between their own culture and the Iranian culture and navigate between different religious terrains. They felt socially integrated, and all indicators of social integration such as residential integration, intermarriage, language use, legal integration, acquisition of citizenship, participation in the labor market, and access to social services applied to them.[76]

Though socially integrated, all the Filipinas except one noted that, if given the choice, they would like to leave Iran, not for the Philippines but for a Western country. A few had already been planning to migrate with their husbands and children. The desire to leave Iran for Western countries was often shared by their husbands and, in general, has been strong among many Iranians. Iranians and these Filipinas are both looking for better opportunities in Western countries.

Cultural Reproduction and Maintenance

Transnational marriages pose challenges to Filipinas living overseas. The rupture of natal family ties, emotional and social isolation, and the loss of identity can be very stressful. Yet, Filipinas have been more resourceful in establishing social networks and making a home away from home than many other migrants. They have constituted a home "by establishing social relations that validate them as individuals."[77] They have made the best of the situation by drawing on their religion, culture, and one another, and have established social networks and communities throughout the world. By so doing, they have eased their process of adjustment and, in turn, increased their chances of social integration. They have maintained their culture through forming Filipino cultural centers or associations.[78]

The church has played an important role in the lives of Filipinas who marry Christian men overseas and has often helped with their adjustment. Participation in church activities has helped them find fellow Filipinos and make friends with non-Filipinos. These emotional and religious ties, in turn, have facilitated their integration

---

[75] Dugan Romano, *Intercultural Marriage: Promises and Pitfalls* (Yarmouth: Nicholas Brealey Publishing Intercultural Press, 2001), ix.
[76] European Commission, *Migration and Social Integration of Migrants* (2003):11. http://ec.europa.edu/research/social-science/pdf/other_pubs/migrations_report-en.pdf (Accessed December 15, 2018).
[77] Janine Wiles, "Sense of Home in Transnational Space: New Zealanders in London," *Global Networks*, 7 (2008): 123.
[78] Rosario, "Bridal Diaspora: Migration and Marriage Among Filipino Women," 256.

in the host country. This was not the case for the Filipina brides interviewed in Iran. Nevertheless, they gradually organized religious gatherings in their houses, studied the Bible, and drew on their religion to ease their social adjustment. Attending Sunday religious gatherings was part of their lives. Through religious gatherings, they formed friendships with other Filipinas and their friendships served to sustain them emotionally, culturally, and psychologically.

In addition to religious gatherings, the Filipinas met for various social and cultural events, where they shared their life stories and drew on each other's advice. They found comfort in and gained strength from each other. Their sisterhood was similar to the sisterhoods formed in other parts of the world,[79] and the Filipina brides in Iran have been similarly empowered by this sisterhood. Though they have been divided by social class, region, and worldview, their commonalities in terms of nationality, language, religion, culture, and transnational marriage have nurtured their relationships.

What makes these gatherings unique is that they are mainly composed of women. There is only one similar case in an isolated mining town of Mount Isa in Australia where Filipina women created similar gatherings.[80] In the earlier years, the Embassy of the Philippines in Tehran served as a connecting center for Filipinos. With the help of the embassy, the Filipinas formed two all-female organizations—the Filipino-Irano Community Association, founded in 1987, and the Pinay-Irano Family Community founded in 2003.[81] These two organizations have created social spaces in which Filipinas can reclaim themselves.

These organizations serve to maintain Filipino culture, facilitate interaction among Filipinos and Filipino-Iranians, organize annual celebrations, and make connections with other Filipino transnational communities. The Filipinas interviewed were involved in a variety of organizational activities, from sponsoring cultural and religious events, including celebrations of Filipina national holidays, Christmas, and New Year parties, to raising funds and providing humanitarian assistance. These events provided opportunities to display cultural artifacts, use ethnic decorations, wear traditional Filipino customs, eat Filipino dishes, sing Filipino songs, and perform folk dances. My interviewees felt that these cultural events were crucial for preserving their national, religious, and cultural identities. In some cases, their husbands and children also participated in these activities, and the women used them to introduce their Filipino heritage to their children, instilling in them a sense of pride and identification with the Philippines.

The participation and involvement of Iranian husbands in these cultural events had a significant impact on the ethnic development of their bicultural and biracial children. Husbands' appreciation for Filipino culture has encouraged their children to learn their mother tongue, Tagalog. The knowledge of Tagalog, in turn, helped these children in their communication with their maternal grandparents back in the Philippines. These

---

[79] Roces, "Sisterhood Is Local," 73–100; Ibid., 253–73.
[80] Roces, "Sisterhood Is Local."
[81] Embassy of the Philippines, "Filipinos in Iran," http://tehranpe.dfa.gov.ph/index.php/site-administrator/press-release/87-filipinos-in-iran (Accessed December 15, 2018).

Filipino-Iranian children, who lived both in Iran and the Philippines, had affinity for both countries.

The Social Experiences of Filipino-Iranian Children

As stated before, Filipinos have historically married non-Filipinos of various nationalities, races, and religions. Thus the notion of identity, whether national, racial, or religious, is fluid for them. Unlike Filipinos, traditional Iranians' marriages were endogamous; thus, their notion of identity is less flexible. Accordingly, traditional Iranians have had less exposure to a wider definition of identity, in contrast to the experiences of Filipino-Iranian children.

The social experiences of these biracial, bilingual, and bicultural children add another dimension to transnational marriages inside Iran. Some Filipino-Iranian children were treated as Other in their early school years. Their experience seems to have been shaped by when they were born, their features, and their first names. Some of these children were born before the revolution. By the time they started school, Iran was going through Islamization, and the 1980–88 Iran–Iraq War was in progress. Most foreigners, who had been part of the public scene in Tehran and other major cities, had already left the country. People no longer heard non-Persian names. Lillian experienced some degree of Otherization. Her Filipino features and her non-Persian name did not help. She recalled, "My classmates found my name hard to pronounce. Even the teacher did not know how to pronounce my name. They made fun of my name. They saw me as a foreigner, and my Filipino features assured them that I was a foreigner."[82] But the fact that her last name was Persian (the name of her father) and she was fluent in Persian worked to her advantage, and gradually she was accepted as an Iranian.

By the time Parisa went to school, the Iran–Iraq War was over, and foreigners were returning to Iran. Parisa benefited from having Iranian features. "My name was a Persian name, I spoke Persian, and I looked Persian, so I was an Iranian. But when my classmates saw my mother, they started doubting whether I was really an Iranian,"[83] she remarked. Dariush's experience in school was not pleasant. "My features were not familiar to the fellow students, not even to my teachers. They wondered if I was an Arab or an Indian. I was ambiguous to them. They asked if I was a Muslim."[84] The fact that he was a Muslim helped his acceptance by his classmates, but it took some time.

Neema could not believe he was viewed as a foreigner. "My experiences in kindergarten and primary school were not good. Just because my features were different, my teachers and fellow students thought I was Chinese. Some thought I was from Afghanistan. I resented that they saw me as a foreigner, because inside me I was an Iranian,"[85] he stated. For Roya having Persian features did not help much. "My

---

[82] Phone interview, July 30, 2018.
[83] Phone interview, July 25, 2018.
[84] Phone interview, July 18, 2018.
[85] Phone interview, July 12, 2018.

school years were not that good. Children did not play with me. I looked Iranian, but others saw me as biracial and thus a foreigner. Perhaps this was because my mother was not an Iranian,"[86] she noted.

Roksana, who attended a government-run international school in Tehran, and was surrounded by non-Iranians, experienced another form of Otherization. "My features are Iranian, I speak Persian, and I had no problem passing as an Iranian. But sometimes I felt because I attended an international school and my Persian was not so good, some Iranians did not see me as fully Iranian. But I do consider myself fully Iranian,"[87] she remarked. Yasmin's experience in the international school was good but not so pleasant outside school. She recalled, "Because of my features, people thought I was Chinese. They kept staring at me, and I did not like it. They did not consider me a real Iranian. That was hard for me; I was just a human being. Shouldn't that be enough? Because of my experience, I prefer to socialize mostly with biracial children. We have similar experiences."[88]

While some Filipino-Iranians encountered negative reactions in school, over time their classmates accepted them as Iranians and established closer relationships with them. Many Filipino-Iranian children believed this turnaround was ostensibly because of their own efforts to forge friendships with school children and gradually gain their trust. Over time, their schoolmates learned to accept them as Filipino-Iranian children.

The interviewed children clearly viewed themselves as biracial and took pride in having two national identities. Some had frequently traveled to the Philippines and visited their maternal grandparents and their extended families. Some were born in the Philippines. Most of them speak Tagalog, the main language of the Philippines, as well as English. It was not uncommon for these children to attend university in the Philippines, where the language of instruction is English.

Yet a few Filipino-Iranian children had no Filipino experience. Roya said, "I have never been to the Philippines. My mother went there every year but did not take me with her. I have not seen my Filipino side of family. My grandparents were too old and passed away."[89] Roya's parents got a divorce when she was eight years old, but her mother, who has a well-paid job, still lives in Iran.

When asked how they identified themselves in terms of national identity, some Filipino-Iranian children were clear in privileging their Iranian nationality. Roya felt, "Perhaps because I was raised in Iran and have command of the Persian language and do not speak Tagalog, I do not feel I belong to the Philippines, I belong to Iran."[90] Others, however, allowed for a wider sense of national identities. Yasmin, who currently lives in Canada, stated, "Where do I belong, Iran or the Philippines? Actually, neither. I belong to Canada. It is a more open society. I am selective when I want to be Iranian, Filipino, or Canadian, [it] all depends on how I feel."[91]

---

[86] Phone interview, July 5, 2018.
[87] Phone interview, July 9, 2018.
[88] Phone interview, July 15, 2018.
[89] Phone interview, July 5, 2018.
[90] Ibid.
[91] Phone interview, July 15, 2018.

Neema had no preference, "I feel I am at home in Iran. I am at home in the Philippines as well. Honestly, I cannot choose. I belong to both places. We are all interconnected, we are just human beings."[92] Lillian had similar feelings, "I lived in Iran and the Philippines. I feel I am both Iranian and Filipina. I am proud to be biracial, it is really a privilege. I have benefited from this privilege in my career and my social relations."[93] Bardia, while expressing his pride in being an Iranian, said, "I am troubled by the notion of having a fixed national identity. My features are ambiguous, and I like that. The fact that so many people, Latin Americans, Middle Easterners and Asians, see me as one of their own makes me happy. Why should I be limited by where I was born? I belong to many places, at least socially."[94]

It seems these children were flexible with the national identity of their spouses as well. "When I came of age, I was in the Philippines, and I thought I would marry a Filipino man. But when I returned to Iran, I preferred an Iranian man. May be, unconsciously, it was because of language. My deeper understanding of Iranian literature, jokes, and satire drew me to an Iranian man, my husband," Lillian remarked.[95]

Parisa, who has married a non-Iranian man, expressed a similar thought, "It did not matter. I could be happy with an Iranian man or a Filipino. It was just fate, I guess."[96] Dariush, who has married a Filipina, remarked, "I wanted to have a compatible partner; she just happened to be a Filipino."[97] Neema expressed a similar view, "I do not want to limit myself to any particular country or race. It is all about how I feel about my future wife." [98]

Roksana had a clear idea of who she wanted to marry: "I think I have more in common with biracial and bicultural people. They have different world views. I can relate to them. We have shared experiences."[99] Yasmin was more emphatic about her marital choice: "I do not want to marry an Iranian man. I feel more attracted to Asian men in general."[100] Roya's preference, however, was an Iranian partner, "I prefer to marry an Iranian man. My preference is based on common culture and language."[101] According to my interviews, Filipino-Iranians who live abroad tend to marry other Asians such as Chinese, Japanese, or Filipino.

These children had clear memories of how their mothers were treated by their paternal family members. Roksana felt that her father's family did their best to embrace her mother. "Actually, my grandfather and my uncle very much helped my mother to adjust to Iran and feel at home. Transnational marriages can be negative experiences. But lucky for us, my parents' marriage has worked,"[102] she stated with joy. "My mother's experience was very good. Though people saw her as a foreigner, they respected

---

[92] Phone interview, July 12, 2018.
[93] Phone interview, July 20, 2018.
[94] Phone interview, June 30, 2018.
[95] Phone interview, July 30, 2018.
[96] Phone interview, July 25, 2018.
[97] Phone interview, July 18, 2018.
[98] Phone interview, July 12, 2018.
[99] Phone interview, July 9, 2018.
[100] Phone interview, July 15, 2018.
[101] Phone interview, July 5, 2018.
[102] Phone interview, July 9, 2108.

her for her professionalism,"¹⁰³ Parisa stated. Likewise, Lillian said, "My mother was well-respected, and I would say she was even privileged for being educated and working professionally."¹⁰⁴ Neema, however, had a different experience, "My paternal grandparents did not treat my mother well. They criticized my father for marrying a non-Iranian. Sometimes they treated my mother like a maid, even though my mother had a college degree and was working professionally."¹⁰⁵

Many children pointed to cultural and religious differences in transnational marriages, but they were emphatic about the need to be flexible and accommodating. Dariush, who has married a non-Iranian, stated, "My parents' marriage was a solid example for me to follow. Certainly, there are challenges. But one needs to be flexible and adjust to new cultural experiences, respect each other's needs, and love each other."¹⁰⁶ Roya, whose parents had divorced, believed respect and understanding are crucial for the stability of a marriage. She commented, "My father recognized my mother's religious needs, but my mother did not understand my father's religious needs. She even ridiculed him for praying. They did not understand each other. They had different values."¹⁰⁷

Conclusion

This case study, though limited in its scope and number of interviewees, sheds light on the migration of Filipinas and deepens our understanding of their varied experiences in transnational marriages. My study demonstrates the resilience of these women and their determination to overcome sociocultural challenges by adjusting to a new environment, raising biracial, bicultural children, and helping to establish a transnational community. An examination of their lives supports the existing scholarly literature on Filipina agency and also shows the importance of social networks and transnational associations in cultural maintenance and social adjustment in a new country.

Another focus of this chapter has been the role of the state in sanctioning religiously endogamous marriage for transnational couples. Interestingly, most Filipino-Iranian couples viewed the conversion of the non-Muslim spouse as a legal formality and effectively lived their lives as interfaith transnational couples. Religious and cultural challenges notwithstanding, the majority of these Filipinas, given a choice, would prefer their daughters to do as they have done and marry Iranian men.

This study of Filipinas in Iran also directs our attention to the high value placed on motherhood in Iran and how motherhood can ease social adjustment for interethnic, interracial, and interfaith transnational couples. Filipina women have crossed national, cultural, and racial barriers, as well as religious ones, by marrying Muslim men and

---

[103] Ibid.
[104] Phone interview, July 30, 2018.
[105] Phone interview, July 12, 2018.
[106] Phone interview, July 18, 2018.
[107] Phone interview, July 5, 2018.

living under an Islamic theocracy. In doing so, they have managed to maintain a balance between their own religion and the religion of their husbands and their country. They have transcended all these barriers by drawing on the love of their husbands and the shared value they place on family life. I hope that this case study sets the stage for future research and establishes the basis for a more comprehensive examination of transnational marriages in both Iran and other Muslim-majority countries.

This case study also illustrates the varied experiences of biracial, bilingual, and bicultural children and compares the experiences of the mothers and their adult children. While Filipina mothers have no claim on Iranian national identity and culturally belong to the Philippines, their children have come to embrace more than one national identity. These children have effectively contested the singular meaning and singular image of being an Iranian. By their mere existence, they have compelled people surrounding them, from school to the community and the workplace, to examine the one-dimensional social meaning of race, nationality, and national identity.

This case study of Filipina mothers and their children is intended to shed light on the diversity of Iranian families and to demonstrate the growing changes in the institution of the Iranian family.

Acknowledgments

I would like to thank the Filipinas in Iran who trusted me with their life stories. Likewise, I would like to thank Filipino-Iranian children for sharing their social experiences in interviews with me. I am grateful to Mary Hegland for her insightful comments on an earlier version of this article. My thanks go to the Women's Studies International Forum as well for granting me permission to use an earlier version of this article, "Transnational Marriages of Filipinas and Iranian Men: Adjustment and Social Integration."

3

Beyond the *Sharia*

"White Marriage" in the Islamic Republic of Iran

Gholam Reza Vatandoust and Maryam Sheipari[1]

Introduction

Over the past four decades in Iran, legal and social mores in marriage and family have faced significant challenges. After the Islamic Revolution of 1979, the Family Protection Law of 1967[2] was abrogated and replaced by new legislation. These new laws claimed to "strengthen the institution of the family," and to "protect women and motherhood" in the Islamic Republic, but—in reality—they weakened the bonds of monogamous, heterosexual marriages.[3] Serious economic problems, unemployment, increasing poverty, and political and social unrest, together with rising expectations due to the introduction of the internet and social media, have further aggravated the situation, leading to a gradual decline in the number of marriages and a rise in divorce.[4] In the meantime, a new practice known as "white marriage" has emerged: men and women choose to live together in partnership, with little fear of social and religious stigma or legal prosecution. Since there are no registries for "white marriage" in government-sponsored notary public offices, the space for recording marital status remains "white" and clean on the identity cards that all Iranians must have, which is why the practice is called a "white marriage." While the government is aware of what it calls "illegal cohabitations," it has been unable to turn the rising tide or oppose the practice beyond harsh verbal

---

[1] Authors' note: The authors would like to express their gratitude to Dr. Bita Alaei for providing assistance with the statistical analysis of the data; to Dr. Zahra Afshar, who graciously helped by taking charge of the surveys in Tehran and to our PhD candidate Azadeh Vatandoust, who oversaw the surveys in Toronto on very short notice. While we are grateful to all, we take full responsibility for the content and analysis of the study.
[2] The Family Protection Law of 1967 is discussed at length in Gholam Reza Vatandoust, "The Status of Iranian Women during the Pahlavi Regime," in *Women and the Family in Iran*, ed. Asghar Fathi (Leiden: E.J. Brill, 1985), 114–21.
[3] See Marianne Boe, *Family Law in Contemporary Iran. Women's Rights Activism and Shari'a* (London: I.B. Tauris, 2015). See particularly chapter 3, 58–79.
[4] On the issue of the crisis of marriage and divorce, see Parvin Paidar, *Women and the Political Process in Twentieth Century Iran* (Cambridge: Cambridge University Press, 1995), 285–6 and 290–4.

condemnations and threats. Iran's marriage (*nekāh*) laws are part of the corpus of family laws that are rooted in the Twelver (*Ithna 'Ashari*) *Shi'a* doctrine of Islam. In legal terms, there are only two forms of marriage, formal (*nekāh da'em*) and temporary (*sigheh* or *mut'a*).⁵ White marriage is, thus, a new form of union and a severe challenge to the theocratic *Shi'a* regime.

Clerics and government officials have frequently advised young men and women to enter into a temporary marriage if they cannot for some reason choose a more durable, formal marriage. However, *sigheh* is despised by most Iranians, particularly among the more educated men and women, who find temporary marriage "offensive"⁶ and view it as nothing less than an official endorsement of prostitution. This has given way to the new alternative of white marriages, living together without fanfare but with mutual consent, which are on the rise.

The official Iranian narrative of legal marriage, both formal and temporary, is carefully and narrowly defined within the framework of *sharia* law. The idea of white marriage does not fall under either of the legal definitions of marriage (*sigheh* or *mut'a*). However, beyond the official legal definition of marriage, new lifestyles and living arrangements that have long been common in the West are now making inroads into Iranian society, as they are in some other Muslim-majority countries, such as Tunisia. White marriage is best defined as a consensual cohabitation of a man and a woman who have not formalized the relationship or engaged in the rituals that officially legitimize a marriage.⁷ Among the reasons for the rise of white marriage is the exorbitant cost of marriage. Separation and divorce are also long and exhaustive processes, especially for the woman. A wife has limited options and must prove her husband is either physically abusive, is psychologically impaired, or has failed to fulfill his (sexual or financial) obligations as a husband.⁸

A formal marriage must be registered in an officially designated marriage bureau. Failure to do so could result in a prison sentence of one year. Furthermore, in accordance with article 21 of the 2002 Family Protection Law of the Islamic Republic, the registration of a temporary marriage is required if/when the temporary (*sigheh*) wife becomes pregnant. Any other form of marital relationship outside the framework of a formal or a temporary marriage is considered forbidden (*haram*) according to *sharia* and illegal according to article 637 of the Islamic Code. Thus, individuals who engage in white marriages can be prosecuted and legally punished.⁹ This chapter is an inquiry into the social and political implications of white marriage, and how it has radically evolved. It begins with an interview with a young woman

---

5 For a historic account of temporary marriage in Iran, see Janet Afary, *Sexual Politic in Modern Iran* (Cambridge: Cambridge University Press, 2009), 60–6.
6 Ibid.
7 "Ezdevaj Sefeid," *Majaleyeh Khanevadeh, Mahnameyeh Behdasht va Ravan-e Jam'e*, no. 79, Winter (1396/2017): 6–7.
8 Ramin Mostaghim and Sarah Parvini, "White Marriage' a Growing Trend for Young Couples in Iran" Los Angeles Times, May 29, 2015.
9 Meysam Musavizadeh, Muhsen Bagheri Tavani, and Adeh Nahvi, "Deidghah-e huquqi nesbat be ezdevaj sefeid dar Iran," *Avalin Hamayesh Aseb va Aseb Zudaei Shekaf bein Nasli (Azmun-ha, Chalesh-ha, va rahkar-ha)*, Moasses-yeh Farhangi va Honari-yeh Bam. Pajuhesh-e Parvaz Junub (Bushehr, 1396/2017).

we have called Mariam, who is currently in a white marriage. Next, we turn to a roundtable discussion with eight professional women on the subject of white marriages followed by an interview with a group of five women, carpet weavers of meager means, who present their own take on the subject. In the next section, we turn to a quantitative analysis of the subject. We surveyed 172 Iranian men and women (122 Iranians living inside Iran and 50 Iranian–Canadians living in Toronto) and asked their opinion about white marriages. Both groups were asked to respond to four key questions to determine their degrees of approval of white marriages. We assumed that the Iranian–Canadians would respond differently than Iranians living inside Iran to the idea of cohabitation. Another initial assumption was that women would have a different perspective than men on white marriages. We also wanted to know if a woman's degree of education affected her views on cohabitation, and we were curious about other hidden factors that might determine a man's or woman's "conditional" acceptance of such unions. Finally, we sought to review the government's position on the subject of white marriages—from initial denial to strong reaction and finally hostile indifference.

Mariam's White Marriage

Mariam was born in the southern city of Shiraz and lived there until she was twenty-four. She then moved to Tehran to continue her studies and work. At the time of the study, she was twenty-eight and had a master's degree in literature. She was born into a relatively affluent, educated, upper-middle-class family. Her father was a dentist, and her mother was a housewife. She had two elder brothers and was the youngest in the family. She regarded her parents as open-minded, except when it came to choosing a husband, whereupon they became traditional and conservative and preferred a rich and an educated match for their only daughter.

Mariam and Ali were colleagues who worked in different departments of a government bureau. They had first met at a seminar three years earlier. Their friendship developed gradually, but they soon realized they liked each other and wanted to move on to a more serious relationship. A year and eight months later, they began dating. Ali was eight years older than Mariam. At the time, Mariam was living with a girlfriend in a small apartment, so Ali could visit her on the weekends. Later, she decided to move into an apartment of her own. After a while, Ali moved in with her; since then, they have been living together. Ali and his family are from Tehran.

Mariam openly admits that she has had several boyfriends before Ali. When asked how her present relationship developed, she described it as a simple friendship.

> However, after a while when I was able to know and trust Ali, we began thinking of marriage. As the relationship unfolded, we decided to find out if we could live together in the future, and we considered experiencing mutual partnership prior to marriage, since the downturn in the economic situation in Iran, compounded with our own poor financial health, left us with no option.

When Mariam was asked what memories come to mind when she reflected on her relationship, she admitted that she had always been financially and emotionally dependent on her family. Now Ali was her financial and emotional rock. Since she was certain that their goal was marriage, she felt secure living with Ali.

Mariam admitted that a critical factor in her decision was financial, but she also feared divorce. "If we were both employed and financially secure, we would have informed our parents and would have married without hesitation. But I also fear divorce. I like to have a secure marriage, and living together makes it possible to test our relationship." Mariam continued, "Though I have a relatively open-minded family, I am afraid to tell them about my relationship. But I think that my mother has already guessed. She constantly reminds me to be careful, so no man takes advantage of me." The couple lived on their meager income though Mariam was also partially dependent on her parents for financial support. This was perhaps another reason why they could not afford to get married.

Mariam described the cultural and financial differences between herself and Ali as points of contention in their relationship. She is from a relatively well-to-do family, but Ali comes from a family of civil servants with limited resources. "Ali has repeatedly warned me that I need to let go of my financial dependence on my family and try to become independent. He believes that we need to stand on our own feet in the future, without reliance on our parents."

When asked if she had other friends who were experiencing white marriage, Mariam's response was positive. "I was inspired by one of my close friends from Esfahan who moved in with her boyfriend in Tehran. They are now happily married." At the time of our interview, Mariam and Ali had been living together for ten months, and when asked how she would describe the benefits of cohabitation, she said, "getting to know one another intimately and learning about each other's inhibitions, behavior and psyche." Mariam also described some of the problems they had. She had to keep the relationship secret from her parents and extended family since neither family had been told of their cohabitation.

Mariam had no doubts about her plans for the future. She looked forward to eventually entering into a formal marriage with Ali and perhaps emigrating abroad together. She also added that, so far, they had no plans to have any children.

Mariam believed that, while her friends in Tehran supported her partnership, her friends in Shiraz constantly cautioned her to formalize her relationship with Ali. Her intuition told her that some of their mutual friends did not regard their relationship as a serious commitment. She was also uncomfortable with having to hide the truth from her parents. Another concern of Mariam was the government and its agencies. To avoid conflict, she was prepared to present herself as a single woman to avoid confrontation with government agents or the morality police. She had never encountered such a situation, but she was always fearful and had no ready answers if she were approached by the state about her living situation.

When Mariam was asked what cultural and political strategies might be useful in bringing about social change in modern Iran, particularly across genders, she said moderation and compromise with the world that surrounds us and a realization that the younger generations do not wish to abide by the policies and values of the past.

In her view, many traditions of the earlier generations were simply unacceptable to the youth. In any case, "We need to move on. The government should recognize that our values need to adjust and harmonize itself with the world around us. For now, values such as moderation, respect, and tolerance for the world have been initiated and endorsed only by the younger generations."

When Mariam was asked to compare her present union with the formal marriages of friends and family and to discuss its advantages and disadvantages, she said that the difficulties were numerous: "Having to live a double life, the fact that society is unwilling to recognize your relationship, fear that after losing your virginity, your parents will disapprove of your radical lifestyle." Mariam continued, "There is also a positive side to this relationship. I am away from my town, and Ali is my emotional support. We have sufficient time to know each other and we do not have to fear a lack of compatibility or divorce. We have the opportunity to prepare ourselves for a long life in the future. This form of relationship is necessary prior to marriage." Whether cohabitation prior to marriage can in fact become more acceptable in Iran's traditional society is an important question that involves further investigation.

The Professional Women

We arranged a roundtable discussion with eight educated professional women. Our circle included seven university professors and an established engineer. Four of these eight women were single, three were divorced, and one was married. They ranged in age from forty to forty-eight and are referred to under their pseudonyms here.[10]

Roya is a 43-year-old from Shiraz who was raised in a large, traditional family and was single at the time of the interview.

> My mother still questions where I go and with whom I speak over the phone. Though I am a university professor, my family sees me as a child in need of protection. Under present circumstances I won't consider a traditional marriage, much less a white marriage. A traditional marriage is simply an Islamic contract between a man and a woman that I cannot accept. I have given up on marriage altogether.

Nada is a 42-year-old who holds a PhD in physics and is also a university professor. She says, "I am a single woman. I live in a house all by myself. My mother, unlike Roya's mother, does not monitor my life. However, white marriage in its present form is a mistake. The only men who engage in white marriage are those who expect their female partners to pay for their expenses."

Sahar is in her mid-forties with a PhD in statistics. She is married with two sons. She believed that Nada and Roya had not taken account of why white marriage might be a suitable solution for the time.

---

[10] This discussion was conducted by Dr. Maryam Sheipari in Shiraz on December 28, 2018.

> You have never been married to know that if your husband turns ugly, there is no law that will protect you. You will then have to run around trying to liberate yourself from a failed marriage. You will have to spend years making your rounds from one legal court to the next and from one lawyer to another to get your problems solved, facing insults and humiliation throughout the ordeal. However, in a white marriage the absence of formality provides you with the opportunity to exit when you choose.

She also added,

> We are educated, in our mid-forties, and have a source of income, and if there is a man involved in our lives, it is because we cherish a healthy and loving relationship. Think about young men and women in their twenties who have no income, do not have strong religious beliefs, and do not have supportive mothers. In reality, women of our age need to serve as their mothers who no longer uphold traditional values and beliefs. It is natural that mothers like us may be more accepting of white marriage.

Shirin, forty-three, holds a PhD and is a professor in the humanities. She is divorced. She said, "You have yet to experience having to make the rounds in legal courts and law firms. You may be beaten or threatened frequently [by your husband], but when you have limited financial resources, you have no option but to accept and continue living in an unhappy marriage." She continued,

> Free women are better partners, and men who stay of their own free will are equally better. Men who go out and cheat on their wives will continue to do so, and marriage will not stop them. People will have to be free to choose. However, in Iran things are often different. Social pressure, fear of government intrusion, loss of face and personal shame are only some of the reasons that prevent people from getting to know each other. But the younger generation that speaks freely about personal relationships will lead the way in the future.

Negar is a 47-year-old with a PhD in political science, and Behnaz, forty-two, holds an MA degree; both are single. Both women are from Shiraz and grew up in large families with many brothers. Negar has had the experience of being in a deep romantic relationship with a man who has since left her. She believed,

> If when we had just been acquainted, and loved each other, we had had the opportunity to have an open relationship and had been able to know each other up close, and without fear of being known, perhaps our relationship would have evolved into a marriage. But when you see each other secretly, perhaps once a week, and fear those wanton eyes spotting you as you quietly sneak into cinemas together, life becomes unbearable. Gradually such relationships tend to cool off and dissipate.

Behnaz continued from where Negar had left. "I prefer a traditional marriage to any form of relationship, since I no longer have the strength to travel a journey halfway. At present, I have a boyfriend. We go to cafes, movies, and the marketplace together. I am waiting for the day he proposes marriage."

Both Soheila and Zahra, who were in their early forties, held MA degrees and were divorced. Soheila is a petroleum engineer. She earns a good salary and has no children. Zahra, on the other hand, has two children and is unemployed. She lives off her *mahriyeh*, which is deposited into her savings account. These two women had entirely different views. Soheila, who has a comfortable income, no child, and lives by herself, confidently said that she no longer wants to get married. But if she found a man she liked, and he was willing to accept her as she was, she would consider giving up her family and friends to live with him outside a formal marriage.

Zahra argued that, in essence, formal marriage is a mistake, so is having children, unless the husband is a type of person who is willing to accept responsibility. Human beings have the right to enjoy life even if the only way they can do so is by maintaining a secret relationship. In a society where men are privileged, having children is a mistake. And if the essence of cohabitation is to have children, there does not seem to be a positive alternative. But she pointed out that a white marriage was possible in larger cities such as Tehran, Shiraz, or Esfahan, where people were busy with their own lives and minded their own business. In smaller cities or towns, the situation was different. In a small town, cohabitation was not an option, and many women entered into totally inappropriate marriages to support themselves and their children. In one case she knew, in a small town near Shiraz, a thirty-year-old divorced woman had married an eighty-year-old man for the sake of supporting her children.

All eight discussants believed that they had been robbed of their youth, as they had not been given the opportunity to know themselves better nor to know a man intimately. In their lives, men were portrayed as untrustworthy, immoral, and selfish. If opportunities had been provided for men and women to spend time together, they might have been able to develop better relationships, regardless of whether one called it a traditional or a white marriage.

The Carpet Weavers of Shiraz[11]

In contrast to the professional women, who were willing to discuss the subject of white marriages openly, the five female carpet weavers we interviewed had no clear understanding of white marriages. Of the five, one had a high school diploma, and the other four had never finished high school. Ghohar, a 42-year-old, was a single woman who believed it was a man's responsibility to be the provider. However, in her case, she was single, living at home with her parents, and was expected to pay her share of the living expenses. "Once you are married, your husband is your family and he will pay for your expenses."

Mariam, who was forty-four and also single, had certain moral qualms about cohabitation. She said, "My problem is not my expenses. I consider it a sin to live with

---

[11] The discussion with the carpet weavers of Shiraz was conducted by Dr. Maryam Sheipari on January 16, 2019.

a man outside marriage. A woman must be married to be respected by society and to bid God's will. My brother says those who live with men outside marriage should be stoned to death. Perhaps that is too extreme, especially when there is love involved."

Zainab, a 48-year-old, was divorced and financially supported her only daughter. "My husband was an addict and I was able to get my divorce with great difficulty. Formal marriage is no good. Everyone should be able to make a choice. What is wrong with white marriage? God will accept it so long as the woman is not vile and is not with several men at the same time." Zainab, a good-natured person who constantly laughed, continued, "So long as she does not have a brother like ours. It is even better if you live in a place where you are less likely to be recognized. It is better that way."

Leyla, forty-two, had a high school degree and was expected to marry soon. She and her fiancée were not allowed to stay home alone. Her future husband was already married to another woman, but his first wife was unable to conceive a child. Leyla was asked how she felt about becoming a second wife. Her response was that "it is better than living at my father's home." Her father was old, and the living expenses of her old father, mother, and sisters were all her responsibility. "I would like to go somewhere else. Even if it means having to work for a living while married, I would like to have my own home. I have heard about white marriages from my fiancé. He said he could have had a similar relationship, but in order to please God, he has chosen otherwise."

Fariba, thirty-three years old, was the quietest. She kept silent until she was asked to speak. She then said,

> If I had the courage, I would have run away, but I am afraid I would end up somewhere worse than my parent's home. I wish there was a good man; I could work alongside him, then after living together we would get married. I think if a man knows that you belong to him, and you are supporting him at all times, he will accept you.

Fariba seemed to conclude that there was nothing wrong with a woman living with a man so long as it culminated in a marriage. However, she did not foresee this for herself and for her community of carpet weavers, who had a difficult life. "No man would come their way." This final sentence by Fariba was telling, as it pointed to the low social self-esteem of the carpet weavers of Shiraz, or perhaps the reality of their more traditional community. Her companions also seemed to agree. Somehow, they associated white marriages with women of higher social means and status.

Our Survey of White Marriages

Two sets of similar surveys were conducted in Iran and in Canada (Toronto) over a period of six months (122 surveys in Iran and 50 in Canada for a total of 172)[12] The

---

[12] In Iran, surveys were conducted over several months, mostly in June and July 2018. In Toronto they were administered in late July to mid-August 2018.

surveys in Iran (Table 3.1) included seventy women, of which forty-five were from Tehran and twenty-five were from other cities. Thirty-four of the fifty-two men in the Iranian survey were from Tehran, and eighteen were from other cities, such as Shiraz, Kerman, Zahedan, and Bandar Abbas.

The Iranian study group ranged in age from eighteen to fifty-five and was divided into three age groups of 18–30, 31–40, and 41–55. The educational level of those interviewed was an important factor in our selection. For example, in Table 3.1 (interviews conducted in Iran), 59.42 percent of the women and 42.30 percent of all the men held bachelor's degrees, and 28.99 percent of women and 36.53 percent of the men held university degrees equivalent to an MA or a PhD.

The interviews in Canada (Table 3.2) were somewhat different. Our total sample included twenty-five men and twenty-five women. All were residents of Toronto, and most were single (seventeen women and eighteen men), between the ages of eighteen and thirty (eighteen women and nineteen men). Forty-six percent held PhD degrees (eleven women and twelve men). Both groups were first asked if they were familiar with the concept of white marriages. If they answered in the affirmative, they were then required to respond to four key questions: (1) if they approved of white marriages, (2) if they conditionally approved of white marriages, (3) if they disapproved of white marriages, and (4) if they had no opinion about the union. They also had the opportunity to elaborate their views on the subject if they so desired.

Table 3.1 Total Surveys in Iran

Total Surveys In Iran			
Women	70	57.02%	
Men	52	42.97%	
Marital Status			
Marital Status	Single	Married	Divorced
Women	44 (63.76%)	21 (30.43%)	4 (5.79%)
Men	42 (80.76%)	9 (17.30%)	1 (1.92%)
Age Group			
	18–30	31–40	41–55
Women	32 (46.37%)	15 (21.73%)	22 (31.88%)
Men	40 (76.92%)	9 (17.30%)	3 (5.76%)
Education			
	Diploma and Below	BA or Equivalent	MA, PhD, or Equivalent
Women	8 (11.59%)	41 (59.42%)	20 (28.99%)
Men	11 (21.15%)	22 (42.30 %)	19 (36.53%)
Agree, Disagree, Conditionally Agree with White Marriage			
	Agree	Disagree	Conditionally Agree*
Women	24 (34.78%)	33 (47.82%)	12 (17.39%)
Men	20 (38.46%)	25 (48.07%)	7 (13.46%)

*Conditional acceptance implies that under proper social and cutural conditions or for a short period with the intent to marry.

Table 3.2 Total Surveys in Canada

Total Surveys in Canada				
Women	25	50%		
Men	25	50%		
Marital Status				
Marital Status	Single	Married	Divorced	
Women	17 (34%)	7 (14%)	1 (2%)	
Men	18 (36%)	6 (12%)	0	
Age Group				
	18–30	31–40	41–55	
Women	18 (72%)	6 (24%)	1 (4%)	
Men	19 (76%)	5 (20%)	1 (4%)	
Education				
	BA or Equivalent	MA or Equivalent	PhD	
Women	5 (20%)	9 (36%)	11 (44%)	
Men	3 (12%)	10 (40%)	12 (48%)	
Agree, Disagree, Conditionally Agree with White Marriage				
	Agree	Disagree	Conditionally Agree*	No Opinion
Women	9 (34%)	6 (26%)	5 (20%)	5 (20%)
Men	4 (16%)	10 (40%)	6 (24%)	5 (20%)

*Conditional acceptance implies that under proper social and cultural conditions or for a short period with the intent to marry.

The findings are presented in three graphs. In Graph 3.1, we see that, paradoxically, the total number of Iranians living inside Iran who agreed with white marriages (34.4 percent) exceeded the number of Iranian–Canadians who did so (24 percent) by more than 10 percent. The number that disagreed with white marriages in Iran (49.2 percent) also exceeded that in Canada (24 percent) by a much larger margin. In fact, by a margin of around 20 percent, more Iranians agreed to a conditional white marriage than Iranians of Canada. Overall, the Canadian survey is more homogeneous, with an equal number of Iranian–Canadians who agree (24 percent) or disagree (24 percent) with white marriages.[13]

Graph 3.2 demonstrates the educational levels of surveyed individuals in both Iran and Canada. In Iran, those who strongly disagreed with "white marriage" had a university degree equivalent to a BA, followed closely by those who agreed. The pattern repeated itself for groups with higher education (an MA or equivalent). However, there was a significant difference of opinion among Iranians in Canada. Ranking highest were those who conditionally agreed with "white marriages," followed closely by those who disagreed, and they all held MA and PhD degrees. Perhaps this could be explained by the fact that the survey was skewed from the start since most Iranian–Canadians interviewed represented a highly educated sample. Thirty-eight percent held MA degrees while 46 percent held a PhD.[14]

[13] See Graph 3.1.
[14] See Table 3.2.

Beyond the sharia

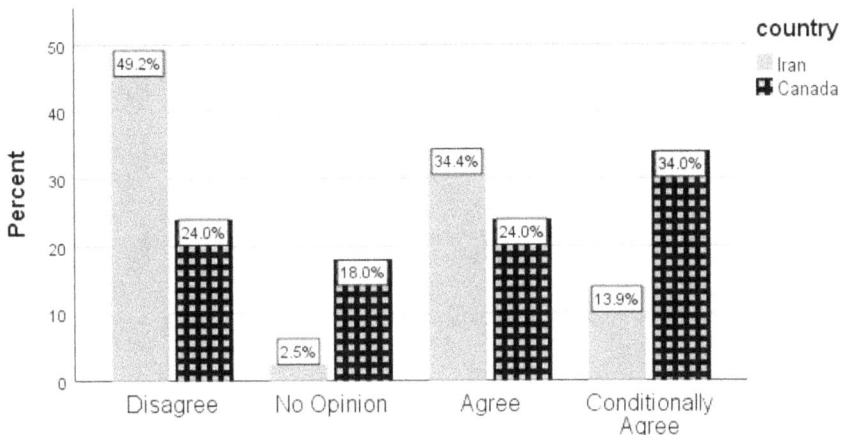

Graph 3.1 On "white marriage."

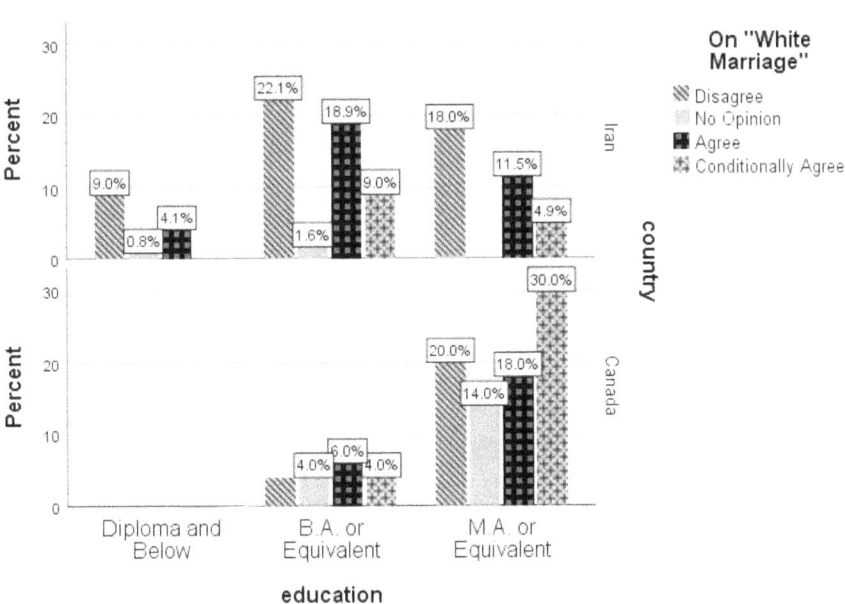

Graph 3.2 Education

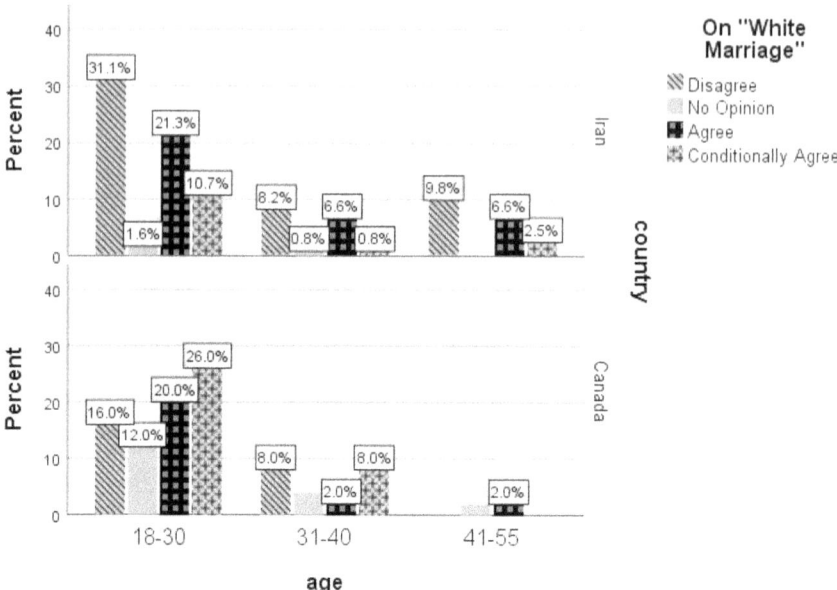

Graph 3.3 Age

Graph 3.3 compares the two samples of Iranians and Iranian–Canadians in terms of age distribution and their views on "white marriage"; that is, whether they (1) disagree, (2) have no opinion, (3) agree, or (4) conditionally agree. A major difference in this section was that in Iran a majority of those who agreed (23 percent) or disagreed (15 percent) fell into the lower-age category (18–30) and the percentage was high. In Canada, while the age group (18–30) remained the same as in Iran, the majority of those who conditionally agreed with "white marriages" was followed closely by those who agreed.[15] In both samples, the numbers that conditionally accepted "white marriages" are high.

In general, the following observations can be drawn from the surveys and the interviews conducted with the 122 Iranians in Iran and the 50 Iranians in Canada. Among those who were cohabiting or were themselves engaged in a "white marriage," most agreed that there was a general satisfaction in their relationship and that their long-term goal was marriage. While the number of those that actually engaged in white marriages in our sample was less than a handful, around a third of the positive respondents to the idea of cohabitation believed that a healthier relationship could emerge, leading to a long-term relationship and marriage. However, they were also aware that cultural issues made that very difficult in Iran and agreed that there was no real difference between a "white marriage" and a traditional one with regard to

---

[15] See Graph 3.3.

the emotional commitment of both parties. They also recognized that in a patriarchal society, the legal constraints and social pressures are much greater on women than on men. The major difference was that a "white marriage" was not registered. Couples in these relationships seemed to support each other financially and emotionally, and many of their immediate family members were aware of the relationship and did not directly interfere.

Based on the 122 interviews conducted inside Iran, one can divide the general views of men and women inside Iran into three categories. One group was opposed to "white marriages," a second group conditionally accepted it, while a third group supported it. The first group opposed white marriage because it offered no stability. For example, Mohammad, a thirty-year-old from Tehran,[16] believed that this form of relationship lacked responsibility and only fulfilled one's physical needs. Husain, a 38-year-old from Shiraz,[17] indicated that he did not trust women who entered such unions because, in his view, this suggested a lack of moral responsibility on their part. Shaqayeq, a thirty-year-old Tehrani woman,[18] claimed that these relationships undermined women's legal rights. Mehrnoush, twenty-eight and also from Tehran,[19] expressed her disapproval by stating that "our country is not at all ready to accept such a relationship." Mahsheed, a 39-year-old woman from Tehran,[20] added that in such cases it was the women who ultimately suffered. Zahra, Gohar, and Zeinat, all illiterate women from Shiraz,[21] believed that a white marriage was no different than having a boyfriend. "Men take advantage of you and then discard you." Among those interviewed, some men also pointed to the desire to live by choice. Saied, a man who was previously married, concluded that in a "white marriage" there was more loyalty and honesty involved "since you live together by choice and not by contract. Going through divorce in a formal marriage is a difficult and expensive venture and you often continue the marriage to avoid trouble. However, in the meantime you cheat and lie to sustain the relationship, even though you no longer love your partner."[22] On the contrary, Husain from Kerman said, "I am against 'white marriage' because of religious reasons and I prefer to escort my wife to our home after a formal wedding."[23] All of the individuals who opposed "white marriages" had a university education, except the last three men, who had very little education. They rejected white marriage on the grounds that it was an unstable union and that the existing laws provided no protection for the couple; they seldom mentioned religious reasons.

---

[16] Interview no. 77, Tehran, July 14, 2018.
[17] Interview no. 166, Shiraz, July 6, 2018.
[18] Interview no. 145, Tehran, July 19, 2018.
[19] Interview no. 138, Tehran, July 14, 2018.
[20] Interview no. 124, Tehran, July 14, 2018.
[21] Interview no. 160/161/162, Shiraz, June 21, 2018.
[22] Taqi Azad Armaki, "Khanevade-yeh sefeid, chaleshi buniyadi barayeh khanevadeh-yeh Irani," *Zanan Emruz*, I, no. 5, Mehr (1393/2014), 8.
[23] Interview no. 165, Kerman, July 29, 2018.

The second group conditionally accepted the idea of a "white marriage." Most believed that under current political conditions, the relationship would be paradoxical and of an uncertain future. Ibrahim, a 36-year-old man from Tehran,[24] claimed that Iranian society was full of serious contradictions. Another man, fifty-year-old Jafar, also from Tehran,[25] agreed with white marriages if in his view "the moral conditions" of society were appropriate. Two women—Elham, thirty-nine, and Mehrnoush,[26] both from Tehran—believed that if the nation adopted a more accepting attitude toward "white marriage," then there should be no problem. However, as the situation stood today, Iranian society remained intolerant of such relationships.

There was yet another group that conditionally accepted "white marriage" provided it was of a temporary nature—one that allowed partners to know each other, to resolve their financial issues, and to pave the way for their eventual formal marriage. This was an important consideration for individuals who viewed "white marriages" as a pathway toward formal marriage. They regarded a "white" relationship as a temporary one since Iranian society has not yet accepted the principle. In the surveys, two women Zahra and Haleh from Tehran[27] believed that if the partners were serious about marriage and wished to know each other, then it was acceptable. Even 36-year-old Hamid Reza from Tehran,[28] said, "I agree, since one will get to know one's partner and can make sure if one would like to live with that person in the future." Mariam, a 28-year-old from Tehran, who is now in a "white" relationship, was also in this category.[29]

The third group accepted "white marriages" unconditionally. Nahid from Shiraz, now in her mid-forties, pointed out, "I'm the only one who will decide the terms of my relationship. No one can harm me unless I decide otherwise."[30] Maryam, also from Shiraz, believed that in any form of marriage, be it "white" or registered, the [potential for] damage is real, and people will suffer once they are separated.[31] Thus, it makes no difference. Twenty-year-old Ali from Tehran also concurred, particularly when "one does not have economic issues and can live with the person one loves."[32]

The responses thus suggested that, for a majority, there were no major objections to the practice of "white marriage." Rather, because of the existing social mores, religious beliefs, and government restrictions, people accepted it conditionally.

---

[24] Interview no. 80, Tehran, July 15, 2018.
[25] Interview no. 86, Tehran, July 17, 2018.
[26] Interview no. 134, Tehran, July 15, 2018 and Interview no. 138, Tehran, July 18, 2018.
[27] Interview no. 149/150, Tehran, July 11, 2018.
[28] Interview no. 78, Tehran, July 15, 2018.
[29] Mariam granted us a full interview, which is provided in the text as Mariam's 'White Marriage.'
[30] Interview no. 152, Shiraz, July 25, 2018.
[31] Interview no. 159, Shiraz, June 25, 2018.
[32] Interview no. 81, Tehran, July 16, 2018.

Attitude of the Government of the Islamic Republic

The available research in Persian on contemporary practices of marriage and cohabitation are significantly limited, and what is available is often politicized. One set of official studies views relationships outside the legal definition of marriage as a form of deviance imported from the West. In one such study, "white marriage" was listed along with homosexuality, transsexuality, and even bestiality.[33]

The first periodical to publish significant investigative journalism on the subject of "white marriages" was the monthly magazine *Zanan* (Women), which was followed by the monthly magazine *Zanan-e Emruz* (Today's Women). Both journals were edited and published by the feminist Zahra Sherkat.[34]

In September 2014, the magazine published a groundbreaking study that shocked the nation despite the fact that the sample was random and limited to just thirteen individuals, eleven women and two men (mostly aged between 20 and 40)[35]. The writers noted that they had encountered a number of other couples in similar unions who were afraid or unwilling to discuss the matter openly.[36] This issue of the journal angered the Ministry of Guidance (*Ershad*), and on April 27, 2015, the government shut down *Zanan-e Emruz*, the only popular and reliable women's magazine in Iran, for having dedicated an entire issue to the concept of white marriages.[37] That same year, Siavash Shahriar, who led the Social and Cultural Affairs Department at the Office of the Governor of Tehran, promised that his office was trying to find solutions for the problem though nothing has since been proposed or presented. [38]

According to the study presented in *Zanan-e Emruz*, all those engaged in a "white marriage" had a university education, regardless of their social and family status. For those who had not previously married, such a relationship was an initial step toward a formal marriage, a period of getting to know one's future partner. However, those who had been married and divorced were not necessarily contemplating marriage and were content to remain in a white marriage.[39] Couples who engaged in such unions had to rely primarily on themselves for financial support and could not expect assistance from their parents. Often, both partners were employed and shared the cost of living; whoever earned more paid a bigger share. In such an arrangement traditional rules and mores no longer applied, and both partners were equal partners in the process.[40]

---

[33] Elahe Jafari, "Taghir-e mafhum-e khanevadeh as ezdevaj-e sefeid ta hamjesgaraei; neghahi be sabak zendeghi, Asib-ha va chalesh-ha," *Faslname-yeh Mutalle'at-e Siyanat as Huguqeh Zanan*, no. 8 (Summer 1396): 155.
[34] *Zanan* was published for sixteen years. Its license was revoked by the Press Supervisory Board of Iran on January 28, 2008, for "endangering the spiritual, mental and intellectual health of its readers, and threatening psychological security by deliberately offering a dark picture of the Islamic Republic."
[35] The magazine reemerged with a new license and under the new name of *Zanan-e Emruz* (Today's Women) on May 29, 2014.
[36] Azad Armaki, "Khanevade-yeh Sefeid, Chaleshi Buniyadi Barayeh Khanevadeh-yeh Irani," 10.
[37] http://www.bbc.com/persian/iran/2015/04/150427_l26_zanan_e_emrouz_suspended_iran_press
[38] "Can Iran Control Its Cohabiting Couples?" *BBC News*, December 5, 10, *Middle East* (2014). Available at http://www.bbc.com/news/world-middle-east-30391593.
[39] Ibid.
[40] Azad Armaki, "Khanevade-yeh sefeid, chaleshi buniyadi barayeh khanevadeh-yeh Irani," 10.

The Islamic Republic has remained in a state of perpetual denial, as evidenced by the paucity of official information on the issue of "white marriages." To date, there have been no government-sponsored studies on the subject. The only materials available are no more than hearsay journalistic writings and questionable secondary newspaper sources, often dismissed by government as of no serious consequence.

The official media, particularly the government-controlled television programs, have also remained mostly silent.[41] If they do present commentary on white marriage, they refer to it as sinful and shameful.[42] Other, more popular journals, particularly the ones related to youth and youth culture, followed suit shortly thereafter. White marriages continue to be viewed as a form of social deviance by the authorities and many publications affiliated with them. It is branded as a form of Western-inspired conspiracy, propagated by social media and satellite television, which has limited impact on the Iranian people and thus does not require serious government action. The daily paper *Kayhan*, notorious as the mouthpiece of the regime, has labeled white marriage an international conspiracy sponsored by the British Broadcasting Company (BBC) and other news outlets determined to undermine the institution of family in Iran[43]. There were legal and religious attempts to condemn the practice. In 2014, chief of staff of the Supreme Leader Mohammad Mohammadi Golpayegani referred to the phenomenon of a growing number of unmarried couples and called upon the Justice Department to crack down on those involved.[44] Ayatollah Golpayegani claimed that living together outside the bonds of marriage would affect the entire society, that "their legitimate (*halal*) existence will be extinguished," and that "future generations will turn out to be bastards."[45] Elsewhere, he is noted to have said that "It is the responsibility of Islamic Jurisprudence (*hokm-e Islami*) to resist these false relationships and to protect the faith."[46] The office of the Supreme Leader called for a show of "no mercy" for those living in such relationships.[47] In June 2016, the deputy of the office for Population Health announced that the Ministry of the Interior was soon going to engage in issues pertaining to the phenomenon—an announcement that was never pursued by the state. Other officials, recognizing that

---

[41] However, the earliest known officially acknowledged interview, in 2012, was granted by Sardar Talaei, a one-time commanding officer of the city of Tehran and the head of the Cultural and Social Commission of the Tehran City Council, in which he confirmed that "cohabitation does exist in northern areas of Tehran." Musavizadeh, Tavania and Nahvi, "Deidghah-e huquqi nesbat be ezdevaj-e sefeid dar Iran."

[42] The director of the office of the Supreme Leader, Ayatollah Golpayegani, who acknowledged the existence of cohabitation by referring to it as an absolutely shameful act. Masoud Golchin and Saed Safari, "Kalan shahr Tehran va zuhur neshaneha-yeh ulgu-yeh tazeh as ravabet zan va mard. Muttalleh zamineh, farayand va payamadha-yeh ham-khanegi," *Faslnameh Tahgigat-e Farhangi-e Iran* 10, no. 1, Spring (1396): 30.

[43] "Vaqti resanehayeh khareji saz-e ezdevaj-e sefeid ra kuk mikonand, naqsheyeh jadid shabakeha-yeh mahvareh-i barayeh takhrib-e khanevadeh dar Iran," *Keyhan*, 6 Bahman (1393/2014): 8.

[44] Mostaghim and Parvini, 'White Marriage' a Growing Trend for Young Couples in Iran."

[45] Golnaz Esfandiari, "Rise in Cohabitation Has Iran Officials Railing Against 'White Marriage,'" Radio Free Europe, Radio Liberty, December 6, 2014. http://www.rferl.org/articleprintview/26 728820.html. 1.

[46] "Ayatollah Muhammadi Golpayeghani ezdevaj sefeid sharm avar ast," *Ruznameyeh Sharq*, 10 Azar (1393/2014): 14.

[47] "'White Marriages,' Iran's Cohabiting Couples," *The Week*, 1–2.

the large number of such unions makes it impossible for the state to crack down, have tended to tone down the rhetoric. Muhammad Golzar, deputy for the Youth Affairs Organization, announced that "the available statistics on white marriage are relatively low and we need not raise concern about it."[48] Ashraf Borujerdi, another state-affiliated official, called white marriages a "passing fever" that should not be transformed into a serious social issue and suggested that the government should cease its interference in people's private lives, which could only "further aggravate the situation."[49]

White Marriage: A Social Enigma

Our survey, coupled with the existing literature in Persian on the subject, suggests that men are happier than women in a white marriage. One thirty-year-old man said, "I have sufficient problems of my own. I no longer wish to have to worry about mortgage payments and other issues that come along with a married life. Under present circumstances both my partner and I worry about our own problems."[50]

Life in the megacities of Iran imposes harsh conditions on most Iranian families, particularly the younger generations.[51] One of the interviewees mentioned that he and his partner were students who worked part-time to make ends meet, and under these circumstances they could not marry. Living together had reduced their cost of living and made it possible to afford their university expenses.[52]

Other important reasons included financial shortcomings, parental disagreements, differences in age and educational achievements, and duration of the partnership. For example, one of the interviewees indicated that "I really loved him very much to the point that I was willing to die for him and would not do anything to displease him."[53] However, such attachments often lead women to insist on a formal marriage, which can generate fear in the prospective male partner and cause him to withdraw from the relationship.[54] A woman's insistence on transforming a "white" relationship into a more

---

[48] "Amar-e ezdevaj sefeid bala neist," *Ruznameyeh Sharq*, 6 Urdibehest (1394/2015): 16.
[49] Yek Khabar, "Seh chehreh dar movred-e ezdevajeh sefeid," *Ruznameyeh Shargh*, 13 Azar (1393/2014).
[50] Ibid., 190.
[51] A 28-year-old man from a conservative background said he preferred to have his girlfriend live with her parents until they could afford a wedding. "If the husband cannot be a provider, he will have no authority to run his family." This comment obviously supported the traditional view of marriage, where the husband was expected to be the sole provider and to have the greatest authority in the family. See Raziyeh Makvand, "Negaresh zanan va mardan-e mojarad shahr-e Tehran be hambashi va barresi-ye 'avamel-e moasser bar an," Payan-nameh Karshenasi Arshad, Tehran: Al-Zahra University, 1396/2017. Ahmad, thirty-five and living in Tehran, disavowed a "white" relationship and regarded it as frivolous and void of responsibility, particularly for men. Nora, forty-three and also from Tehran, held a similar view to Ahmad's. Interview no. 165. Kerman, June 29, 2018.
[52] Nader Karimian and Samaneh Salari, "Rabet-e hamkhanegi dar Iran, barresi keifi va 'elal-e angezehayeh gerayesh be on," *Mutalle'at Ravanshenasi Baleini*, no. 21, Winter (1394/2015): 199.
[53] Abolfazl Zulfaghari and Akram Ramazani, "Aseib shenasi ravabet kharrej as urf dukhtaran," *Pajuhesh-nameyeh Madadkari-yeh Ejtema'i*, no. 4, Summer (1394/2015): 215.
[54] "Ezdevaj Sefeid," 6–7.

formal one could be due to her deep attachment to the institution of marriage or social pressures and/or the fear of uncertainty that comes with cohabitation.[55]

On the other hand, at least some women sought equality in partnership and viewed a formal marriage as nothing less than the undermining of their hard-earned independence. For these women, living with parents was living under constant surveillance. Mahnaz Kousha described this as the "invisible contract" that tended to restrict women's lives and granted priority to the institution of the family. "For some women, limited social rights pose a problem. The family reigns supreme so that all individual rights and needs must be curtailed in order to safeguard this primordial institution. Family is viewed as the primary focus for women. Anything that takes women's attention away from this primary responsibility must be minimal." [56]

However, not all women yielded to the demands and expectations of their families. For example, Nahid, from Shiraz, was very supportive of a white marriage because it gave her the opportunity to construct the relationship on her own terms.[57] Another woman claimed that while "*mahriyeh* and a living allowance are presumed to be a plus for a woman, it takes away her independence and she becomes dependent on her husband."[58]

Marriage and divorce laws have always privileged the husband. In the late twentieth century, many educated women with work experience decided that it was better to voluntarily forgo the *mahriyeh* in their marriage contract at the time of their marriage and, instead, stipulate in their contract that they had the right to divorce and to retain custody of any children conceived in the union in case of divorce or the death of their husband. In such instances, a marriage that fell apart was referred to as a consensual divorce or "*talāq-e tavafoghi*." Once divorce and custody laws became even more patriarchal after the revolution, this form of divorce became more common in the Islamic Republic whereby women gave up some financial rights in exchange for the right to divorce and custody of any children born out of the union.[59] One result of this change was that, as the economic advantages of marriage eroded, some urban women came to see less of a reason to marry; therefore, cohabitation became a viable alternative.

Life in the larger cities of Iran is more conducive to cohabitation although interviews with a number of young people from Kermanshah[60] and Zahedan[61] indicated that youth, in general, had few objections to cohabitation. Even in more conservative southern and south eastern cities, such as Bandar Abbas and Kerman, cases of cohabitation existed, although there were no precise statistics to substantiate the numbers. However,

---

[55] Mahnaz Kousha, *Voices from Iran: The Changing Lives of Iranian Women* (Syracuse: Syracuse University Press, 2002), 198–9.
[56] Ibid.
[57] Interview no. 152, Shiraz, July 5, 2018.
[58] Golchin and Safari, "Kalan shahr Tehran," 29–57.
[59] Consensual divorce is possible even if it is not stipulated in the marriage contract, providing both sides agree on the terms of divorce.
[60] For further information, see Mohsen Niazi and Leyla Parniyan, "Classification of Friendships Between Two Opposite Sexes Among Young Girls in the City of Kerman," *Zan dar Towse-ye va Siyasat*, no. 47, Winter (1393/2014): 559–76.
[61] Interview no. 141, Zahedan, 2017.

Tehran, both because of its size (more than ten million residents) and its level of social awareness, is an exception. One interviewee said, "I like Tehran. It will embrace you no matter who you are,"[62] which means that, whatever your lifestyle, you are always welcome in Tehran.

According to many young couples, freedom from parental intervention was perhaps one of the greater assets of a white marriage,[63] because either side could end the relationship at short notice and without much ado. There were no expectations on either side, and the economic liabilities were minimal.[64] Despite all odds, this new lifestyle has flourished alongside traditional weddings and festivities.[65] What makes white marriage different is that the "commitment" is neither "contractual" nor "permanent." Either partner can end it at will.[66] In this relationship, the couple's extended family exists on the fringes and bears no responsibility.[67] In an interview, some women claimed they had greater independence in this new lifestyle; they did not need "to bear the responsibilities or commitments of a married life."[68]

However, the negative consequences of cohabitation are far greater for women than for men. Women have no legal recourse in cases of abuse by their partner for fear of alerting the authorities to the nature of their relationship. They are more apt to hide themselves and their lifestyles from their family and friends for fear of being humiliated, and they face far more to risk than their male counterparts. For women, it is a lonely path to travel, and its consequences can be costly.

Still, white marriages are on the rise. When asked what they dreaded most about a white marriage, many of the respondents expressed social and legal concerns. A young man who seemed relatively content with his new lifestyle expressed fear as to how the couple's family might react to what they considered a form of moral degradation. Their condemnation would cast a shadow not just on the man or woman in such a union but on the entire family.

One individual who was in a white marriage said, "I'm a family man and I would like to continue to remain within the [extended] family circle. However, whenever I go to Yazd to visit my family, my partner and I will have to part and go our different ways. This is difficult to do."[69] Another said that he would like to engage in this new lifestyle but found it impossible.[70] Yet a third mentioned that "so far, my family is unaware of my relationship and if they do find out, they will be shocked and dismayed."[71]

A more serious outcome of a white marriage, particularly for a woman of child-bearing age, is pregnancy. The stigma involves not only the couple but also the child

---

62 Golchin and Safari, "Kalan shahr-e Tehran," 51.
63 Roya Karimi Majd, "Ezdevaj safeid, utaqi ba dar-e baz," *Radio Farda* (1395/2016): 2. Accessed June 13. http://www.radiofarda.com/articleprintview/27776567/html.
64 Esfandiari, "Rise in Cohabitation Has Iran Officials Railing Against 'White Marriage,'" 2.
65 Azad Armaki, "Khanevade-yeh sefeid, chaleshi buniyadi barayeh khanevadeh-yeh Irani," 6.
66 Majd, "Ezdevaj safeid, utaqi ba dar-e baz," 2
67 Ibid.
68 Ibid.
69 Golchin and Safari, "Kalan shahr Tehran," 51.
70 Interview no. 143, Bam, December 26, 2017.
71 Somayeh Qasemi and Hassan Muhadesi Gilavani, "Mutalleh jam'eh shenakhti durughgui dar Ravabet beyna jensi zuvjhayeh Tehran," *Pajuheshnam-e yeh Zanan Pajuheshga Ulum Ensani va Mutalle'at-e Farhangi* 8, no. 3, Fall (1393/2014): 110.

who is born out of wedlock. The authorities will not issue a birth certificate for a child without proof that the parents are married, and the child will, therefore, lack legal support, making it difficult for her or him to register in school. Currently, many children of illegal immigrants living and working in Iran, including Afghans, are faced with this dilemma. Illegal abortions are common and sometimes result in medical complications due to the malpractice of unlicensed and quack physicians. One respondent said that "a major development in our relationship involved an unwanted pregnancy that complicated our relationship and was only resolved after an abortion."[72]

When financial matters are involved, it is predominantly the woman who bears the brunt since neither side can litigate financial and security matters in a court of law. It is often the woman who must compromise, for she cannot litigate against a partner who does not legally exist.[73]

One of the more serious outcomes of a white marriage is that it can contribute to the practice of polygamy. An official registration of marriage in Iran involves inscribing the name of each party on the birth certificate of the other party. According to existing laws, a man is required to have the consent of his first wife to marry a second wife. However, when a woman agrees to live with a man without a formal marriage, knowing full well the repercussions, this opens the door for illegal polygamy. One woman who was interviewed described how she became the partner of a married man. "After my divorce, my family abandoned me, and my boss, who is a married man, rented a place for me and visits me daily."[74]

The question is, how long can young men and women in Iran can live such "a double life"?[75] Farangis, a female interviewee, listed the advantages of such a relationship, despite fears and concerns. She claimed that women felt more independent. Such a relationship did not have the complications of married life.[76] For Farangis, the biggest advantage of a white marriage was that it resembled a room with an open door. Whenever you choose, you can exit, and no one can stop you. However, if the room was comfortable, well lit, and well heated, why would you want to leave it? What was important was the recognition that the door was not shut. Marriage often gave you the feeling of living behind closed doors. When you decide to open the door and leave, you need to know if you have a key. "What if you are not granted the key? What will you do then?"[77]

Numerous fears prevail in white marriages. One fear is that the relationship might be discovered or reported to the moral police, who might come knocking at the door and even arrest the couple. The reactions of neighbors and families are other serious concerns. Marjan, who lives with her boyfriend in the city of Arak, said she had to change homes four times after landlords discovered that she and her partner were not married. To mask their relationship, many unmarried couples wear fake wedding rings

---

[72] Masoud Golchin and Saed Safari, "Kalan shahr Tehran," 151.
[73] Ibid., 32.
[74] Nader karimian Samaneh Salary, "Rabeteyeh hamkhanegi dar Iran," 191.
[75] Ibid., 3.
[76] Majd, "Ezdevaj safeid, utaqi ba dar-e baz," 1.
[77] Ibid. 2/2.

and memorize each other's family genealogies to make their phony marriages seem real in case they are questioned by the moral police.[78]

Some women entered a white marriage for a short period but ultimately decided to leave. Mina, thirty-two, was in such a relationship. She now has doubts regarding the sincerity of men who engage in a "white" relationship. "While women engage one hundred percent, men do not. It is women who end up losing. Men could be with you today and with someone else tomorrow."[79] Parisa, thirty-five, lived with a man for six years and now regrets the relationship. She feels she lost financially and emotionally and believes her partner took advantage of her in every conceivable way. Even now, he does not leave her alone. She stated that she would no longer engage in such a relationship and preferred a formal marriage.[80] Men, on the other hand, have much less to lose. In a white marriage, men do not have to pay for expensive weddings, or for *mahriyeh*, as stipulated in a formal marriage contract. Ali, a man from Tehran who was interviewed, pointed out that "it's expensive to get married and even more expensive to get a divorce. Why commit to something you're not sure of?"[81]

For those engaged in a white marriage, another consequence is its unpredictability. In such instances, once again, women encounter greater harm. One woman whose cohabitation with a male partner had ended abruptly said, "The wounds of the relationship are still with me, because my attachment to him—the lack of assurance that I have vis-à-vis others and in the next relationship . . . after a while I said I am not ready to form a new relationship, I'm not prepared to love another one."[82] A male interviewee who had experienced a white marriage confessed that "whenever I feel I can no longer continue, I can leave the relationship, without having to worry about legal litigations and demands for repayment of *jahiziyeh* or payment of *mahriyeh*."[83]

Men were generally more receptive of white marriage than women, for obvious reasons. Women tended to insist on changing a "white" relationship to a formal one. Mehrangiz Kar, a prominent lawyer and women's rights activist, has stated that women who are physically abused in such unions cannot seek help from the law for fear that they may be charged with adultery.[84] Consequently, women suffer more in Iran and other Islamic societies where the social and religious bonds are strong, and individuals can be ostracized and severely punished for relations outside the traditional codes of conduct.

Conclusion

After collecting, coding, and analyzing the data obtained from the 172 surveys conducted in Iran and Toronto, we tested two hypotheses. One was that both men

---

[78] Nader karimian Samaneh Salary, "Rabeteyeh hamkhanegi dar Iran," 2.
[79] Azad Armaki, "Khanevade-yeh sefeid, chaleshi buniyadi barayeh khanevadeh-yeh Irani," 13.
[80] Ibid., 14–15.
[81] Ibid.
[82] Golchin and Safari, "Kalan shahr Tehran," 151.
[83] Qasemi and Gilavani, "Mutalleh jam'eh shenakhti durughgu-ei dar ravabet bein-e jensi zuvjha-yeh Tehran," 51.
[84] "Can Iran Control Its Cohabiting Couples?" *BBC News*, BBC.com, December 10, 2014.

and women in Iran would have different views about white marriages, whereas men and women in Toronto would have similar views. The second was that women in Iran would have a different opinion than women in Canada, or that men in Iran would have a different opinion than men in Canada. In fact, our survey result showed that the results were practically the same in Iran and Toronto. We can thus conclude that, based on our samples, men and women living in Iran, in comparison with Iranians living in Canada, have similar perceptions about white marriages. This finding is significant, for it demonstrates that those surveyed in Toronto have the same concerns as those living in Iran. From opinions expressed, very few of the respondents looked upon white marriages from a purely religious perspective. On the contrary, most were primarily concerned with its social and cultural repercussions within Iran today.

The Islamic regime has often alluded to white marriages as "black marriages"[85] and presented the issue within the broader context of what it refers to as a conspiracy (*fetneh*) fomented by the Green Movement of 2009. This is a reference to a mass urban uprisings that was unleashed in Iran in spring 2009 as a result of a rigged presidential election. This discourse was coupled with the government's persistent narrative that the "enemy" (i.e., the United States) is set upon a change of regime and will do anything in its power to implement its plans. After President Trump abruptly left the 2015 Nuclear Agreement that had been negotiated during President Obama's administration, and reimposed severe sanctions on the nation, Iran's economy suffered greatly. In April 2018, Iran's currency went through a sharp devaluation, further adding legitimacy to the government's claim that foreign conspiracies were involved in Iran's social and domestic woes.

In a broader context, white marriages can also be seen as a reaction to the partial failure of the women's movement for legal reform, particularly the Campaign for One Million Signatures, where women vowed to change the laws pertaining to women's rights, such as those in marriage, polygamy, and divorce, and made a long list of other demands that have since been pushed to the background.[86] However, despite all the difficulties encountered by women and women's rights groups in Iran since the 1979 revolution, there has been an "incredible flourishing of women's intellectual and cultural production."[87] This ironically had its roots in attempts by the government of the Islamic Revolution. The government encouraged women from the more religious and socially conservative sectors to become more socially and politically active in pursuit of goals set by the Islamist state.

Antonio Gramsci's concept of state-administered hegemony provides a fresh perspective on understanding the major trends under the Islamic Republic.[88] Gramsci views the state as a hegemonic system that perpetuates itself by imposing its ideology and power through its organs and institutions. Thus, no matter what the state advocates,

---

[85] Nobles, "A Potential Dark Side to Iran's White Marriages," 2.
[86] See the Campaign for One Million Votes.
[87] See Afsaneh Najmabadi, "(Un)veiling Feminism," in *Women and Islam: Critical Concepts in Sociology*. Vol. III, ed. Haideh Moghissi (London: Taylor and Francis Ltd, 2005): 217–20.
[88] See Antonio Gramsci, *Selections from the Prison Notebooks* (London: Lawrence & Wishart, 1971) and *Selections from Political Writing, 1910-1920* (London: Lawrence & Wishart, 1977) for a full discourse on the subject.

it serves as a formidable system that controls many aspects of social and political life by enforcing its ideology and the state apparatus on its citizens. This concept was further developed by Louis Althusser, who presented Gramsci's theory of state hegemony from a structural perspective, showing how the ideological state apparatus transmits and dispenses ideology to the public at large.[89]

Both concepts of ideological and cultural hegemony could be applied to the Islamist regime, where state ideology reigns supreme and where patriarchy determines what is best for citizens and disseminates this ideology through different institutions of the state. Ideological hegemony serves as a system of thought control This can be accomplished through propaganda or through state-controlled media.

However, most educated urbanites in Iran do not view white marriage from the perspective of the state but in practical terms.[90] There seems to be a general consensus that a white marriage is no different in its emotional commitments than a real marriage. In several cases, divorced women, who were in a white marriage and were interviewed, preferred this relationship and had no intention of changing it to a formal marriage. One employed woman claimed to have informed her parents of the relationship and, since she was independent and divorced, her parents expressed no objection. Sara, who was twenty-nine at the time of the interview, mentioned that during her four years of formal marriage, she had been very lonely. According to her, divorce after a formal marriage is far more difficult than a separation after a white marriage. "In a divorce one has to bear the legal, social, and emotional costs of a separation, whereas in a white marriage it is only the emotions that take a toll."[91]

The women interviewed who preferred to stay in a white marriage and not turn it into a formal marriage, whether single or divorced, all had their reasons. They feared that there was no social compatibility between their families and their partners, or that their partners were in no position to make the serious financial and social commitments that were a prerequisite of marriage.[92] Cohabitation resulted in a more equitable relationship for both partners in comparison to a formal marriage. One woman pointed out that she had no obligation to take her partner's shirts to the dry cleaners or to cook for him, and that when she did, he was always grateful.

Support for traditional marriage remains strong, both among Iranians inside Iran and abroad. Women who contemplate turning a white marriage into a formal marriage are primarily those who want to have children at some point in the relationship.[93] However, many urban, educated women are skeptical about formal marriage. They tend to remember the relationships of their parents and are critical of the patriarchal attitude of their fathers.

Like most Middle Eastern societies, the Islamic Republic of Iran is founded on gender inequality, with discriminatory laws that assume women are in need of caretakers, be they fathers, husbands, or brothers. Recently the government coined a new phrase, "women who support themselves," or "women who are their own caretakers" (*zanan*

---

[89] See Louis Althusser, *On the Reproduction of Capitalism* (London: Verso, 2014).
[90] Esfandiari, "Rise in Cohabitation Has Iran Officials Railing Against 'White Marriage,'" 1.
[91] Azad Armaki, "Khanevade-yeh sefeid, chaleshi buniyadi barayeh khanevadeh Irani," 8.
[92] Ibid.
[93] Ibid.

khod sarparast), to define single women who support themselves. Iranian women have come a long way in realizing that they need to be agents of change and that the state should recognize them as such. After the failure of the One Million Signature Campaigns,[94] women realized that gender equality and democracy were inseparable and that they needed to promote democracy and civil rights to further their cause. As Azadeh Kian has eloquently stated, "Iranian women are increasingly well-educated. [They] marry later, have fewer children and more and more aspire to the equal sharing of responsibilities for home and children with men."[95] Indeed, Iranian women have proven themselves to be symbols of resilience and have gained international acclaim for their struggles for equal rights inside Iran, in the Middle East, and in diaspora communities.

---

[94] For the history of the movement, see Noushin Ahmadi Khorasani, *Iranian Women's One Million Signatures Campaign for Equality: The Inside Story* (Women's Learning Partnership for Rights Development and Peace, 2010). See also, *One Million Signatures Demanding Changes to Discriminatory Laws*. BBC Persian, Wednesday January 24, 2007.

[95] See Azadeh Kian's, "Gendered Citizenship and the Women's Movement in Iran," in *Iran: A Revolutionary Republic in Transition*, ed. Rouzbeh Parsi (European Union Institute for Security Studies, Chaillot Papers, 2012), 61–79.

4

School Textbooks, Ideological Codes, and the Construction of the Standard Iranian Family

Amir Mirfakhraie

Introduction

This chapter deconstructs the ideological codes that inform Iranian official knowledge about the family, men, women, children, rights, obligations, the nation, and the state by exploring the answers to several interrelated questions from an intersectional, post-structuralist, and anti-racist approach.[1] What do Iranian students read about the family in their grades one through nine and literacy program textbooks? How are gendered relations (e.g., in terms of the division of labor and citizens' rights and obligations toward other citizens, the nation, the state, and themselves) represented in constructions of the family? How are local forms of diversity and oppression reflected in images of the family? How have government policies influenced representations of the family? What are the ideological characteristics of the ideal family? Whose political and pedagogical frameworks inform the narration of nation and the family? What are the discourses that frame the depictions of the ideal family? Do curricular images of the family/family relations reflect the lived-experiences of Iranian citizens?

    I argue that the curricula narrate and frame the ideal family through several contradictory patriarchal, heterosexual, racialized, and religious-nationalist ideological codes, which "order and organize texts across discursive" political/educational/policy sites and practices, reflecting and framing "divergent topics and [factors]" that deal with contradictory audience and issues. As sets of complex master narratives, they offer orderly, homogenized, and essentialized schemes "that reproduce their organizations and logic" "in multiple and various sites" and offer a selective, official, and objective knowledge in the form of "syntax, categories, and vocabulary in the writing of texts and the production of talk and for interpreting sentences, written or

---

[1] For a detailed exploration of the theoretical and methodological frameworks drawn upon in this chapter see Amir Mirfakhraie, "*Curriculum Reform and Identity Politics in Iranian School Textbooks: National and Global Representations of "Race," Ethnicity, Social Class, and Gender*" (Doctoral dissertation, the University of British Columbia, 1998), https://open.library.ubc.ca/cIRcle/collections/ubctheses/24/items/1.0055443 1998; Idem, "Discursive Formations of Indigenous Peoples in Iranian School Textbooks: Racist Constructions of the Other," *Journal of Curriculum Studies* (2018). Accessed October 4, 2018. https://doi.org/10.1080/00220272.2018.1528302.

spoken, ordered by [them]."[2] Drawing upon Dorothy Smith's conceptualization of the Standard North American Family,[3] I also maintain that the Standard Iranian Family (SIF), or the ideal family, is an ideological, political, and economic construction that reaffirms the importance of order and hierarchy that must consciously be embraced and internalized by all citizens, as they accept Shi'a authority and actively promote the goals of the revolutionary Islamic leadership and the state. As an ideological code, the SIF legitimizes the nuclear family as the union of a legally married monogamous heteronormative Muslim couple who live in the same household with their children.[4] The ideal family is normalized as a white, heterosexual, able-bodied, Shi'a, middle-class, Persian, Islamist, and highly educated institution that must play an important role in the reproduction of the healthy, moral, and ethical Iranian-Islamic society. The SIF is romanticized as an institution that supports and cares for the state, its ruling elite, and the nation/country. It functions as a discourse of surveillance, situating those who are patriotic and support the ideology of the state as desirable citizens in opposition to those who are constructed as anti-Islamic/Iranian.

The curricula frame the SIF through a number of contradictory hegemonic discourses/ideological codes of *Ummat-e Islamī* (Islamic Nation/Community), Aryan thesis, *ḥijāb*, marriage, whiteness, *'ashayir* (nomadic tribes), ethnic clothing, color of skin, martyrdom, development, independence, freedom, caring, support for the *Velāyat-e Faqih*, hegemonic motherhood, and the cult of domesticity. These ideological codes intersect yet other discourses such as self-sacrifice, unselfishness, and monolithic, microstructural, conservative, racist, classist, ableist, and heterosexist biases in representing an ideal image of the family. As an ideological code, the SIF normalizes a patriarchal discourse as the main framework to imagine the ideal family. Several binary oppositions are invoked to situate the ideal citizen/family as a collective unit of sameness and central to an orderly reproduction of a moral society such as *bā-ḥejāb*/veiled and *bī-ḥijāb*/unveiled, *bā-īmān*/believer and *bī-īmān*/nonbeliever, *ḥalāl*/permitted and *ḥarām*/forbidden; and *maḥrām*/"a family member with whom modesty rules need not be observed" *and nāmāḥrām*/"a person with whom modesty rules must be observed." These discourses and their corresponding binary oppositions are reflections of the government's Islamic and civic principles, as an *ideological state apparatus*, which offer politicized narrations of imagining the nation/country/state and demarcating the roles and obligations of the ideal citizen. The narration of the SIF normalizes the discourses of Islamic Revolution, Imam's line (path), and Islamic leadership as important pedagogical messages of the education system, from Persian-, Shi'a-, and male-centric perspectives that rationalize and universalize a narrow and hegemonic yet transnational understanding of the nation/family.

---

[2] Dorothy E. Smith, "The Standard North American Family: SNAF as an Ideological Code," *Journal of Family Issues* 14, no. 1 (1993): 51–2. Accessed March 4, 2016. https://doi.org/10.1177%2F0192 513X93014001005.
[3] Ibid., 51–2.
[4] Ibid. 52.

Education, Pedagogy, Textbooks, and the State: Curricula and (Trans)National Ideological Codes

Since the Iranian Revolution of 1979, school textbooks have been revised based on the conflicting principles of Islamization, student-centered pedagogy, and global and supposedly "human rights" education. These revisions not only reflect the roles of transnational expert systems in the production of official knowledge about the self and the other[5] but also highlight how the pedagogical assumptions of curricula writers are framed from within the state's revolutionary Islamic-Iranian ideological educational policies that aim at promoting economic, scientific, and technological developments and establishing Iran as a formidable anti-imperialist (but not anti-capitalist) leader in the Islamic world.[6] For example, although the Ministry of Education has implemented a comprehensive national plan to incorporate citizenship education, including children's rights based on the principles of the Convention on the Rights of the Child,[7] the main function of the education system remains socializing students who not only obey religious laws of life but are also actively involved in establishing a global "social justice" community of believers, reflecting Islamic-Iranian norms/ethics/political values and Imam Khomeini's line (his socio-religious-political teachings) and his point of view on what constitutes justice.[8] The reproduction of a moral/ethical Islamic society, and its policies, is dependent on reinforcing the status and developmental role of the family and its effective partnership in the country's general formal educational system. It is also dependent on strengthening the family's foundation and enhancing the family's capabilities and skills to play this educational and nurturing role in conformity with the needs of an Islamic-Iranian society.[9] Although the authors of school textbooks consider the family an important partner in devising/teaching educational and pedagogical activities,[10] educational policy officials frame the role of the family through a pathological framework. That is, they assume it is the role of the educational system to provide "effective training sessions and rendering counseling services to the vulnerable and deleterious families for coordination of the objectives and pedagogical methods at school and family environments."[11]

---

[5] See Mirfakhraie, *Curriculum Reform and Identity Politics*; See also Ali Reza Kiamanesh, *UNICEF: Global Education in Iranian Guidance Schools: Achievements and Prospects* (Tehran: UNICEF Iran, 2004); Idem, *UNICEF: Global Education in Iranian Primary Schools: Achievements and Prospects* (Tehran: UNICEF Iran, 2004).

[6] In this chapter, the following abbreviations are used in referencing school textbooks and other government policy papers: Ministry of Education (MoE), Islamic Republic of Iran (IRI), The Iranian Textbook Publishing and Writing Company (ITPWC), and *Fundamental Reform Document of Education in the IRI* (FRDE). MoE, IRI. *FRDE* (N.p.; n.p., 2011). Accessed June 4, 2017. http://www.dres.ir/safeschool/Downloads/FRDE.pdf.

[7] Ministry of Foreign Affairs, IRI, *The Country Report of the IRI on the Ten Year Evaluation of Implementing the Commitments Undertaken in the World Summit for Children (WSC)* (N.p.: n.p., 2000), 2.

[8] MoE, *FRDE*, 16–17.

[9] Ibid., 18, 35.

[10] MoE, IRI, "A Word with Dear Teachers," in *Social Studies 4* (Tehran, Iran: ITPWC, 2015); Idem, *Social Studies 3* (Tehran, Iran: ITPWC, 2017).

[11] MoE, *FRDE*, 35.

Despite the essentialist and supposedly harmonious goals of the educational system and its (trans)national approach to curricula reconstruction, teachers are also encouraged to revise educational materials to account for local/regional needs and students' varied life experiences, allowing them to better situate their *selves*/lives in the context of micro and macrostructures of the family/school/village/city/country/region/globe.[12] This student-centered approach, nevertheless, is framed in light of the main goals of the educational system to legitimize the centrality of the Islamic-Iranian identity in ensuring "national solidarity" among diverse populations of Iran. It is the task of the ideal Iranian to "[honor] the noble and everlasting Islamic-Iranian values and mak[e] efforts to establish a society" that celebrates/affirms the belief in "Imam Mahdi and the establishment of the Mahdavi society."[13] A person's knowledge of Iran and the world is to be compatible with the Islamic norm system, and they must understand socioenvironmental/political/cultural/economic relations and structures as "the signs and symptoms demonstrating God's power in creation." The foremost pedagogical goal is to instill a pure Islamic ideology, as interpreted by Imam Khomeini, the Supreme Leader of the Islamic Revolution, "with special consideration for the privileged status of Iran within the Islamic world."[14] The discourses of Islamic Revolution, *Velāyat-e faqih, and* Islamic *Ummah* encode the state's curricula, its pedagogical policies, and its practices. The goal is to familiarize students with the basic roles of the family, to teach respect for family members, to promote the state's notion of an Iranian identity, to develop moral and ethical conceptions of their *selves* in light of strong affection for God's creations, and to instill morally sanctioned Islamic anti-discriminatory behaviors.[15]

As Patricia Higgins and Pirouz Shoar-Ghaffari have argued, the 1980s postrevolutionary textbooks placed less emphasis on the Persian identity of Iranians that characterized the prerevolutionary period. For example, the 1986–87 edition of Persian elementary textbooks did not contain as many poems by the poet, Firdawsī, whose *Shāhnāmah* focused on narrations about "pre-Islamic Kings."[16] In this chapter, I argue that Shiʿa/Islamic identities are interwoven with Persian/Aryan and white identities as important characteristics of the ideal family and citizen. In terms of representations of various class positions, the majority of pictures and the content of prerevolutionary curricula portrayed a middle-class lifestyle as the ideal form, without any real references to the working or lower middle-class social settings, a trend that has continued to the present time.[17] This is despite the fact that soon after the

---

[12] MoE, "Dear Student," in *Social Studies 3*, 2017; See also Idem, *Teacher's Guide Social Studies 3* (Tehran, Iran: ITPWC, 2013), 19.

[13] MoE, *FRDE*, 18.

[14] MoE, IRI, "Preface," Ali Reza Arafi, in *The Theoretical Foundations for Fundamental Transformation of the Education System in the IRI* (N.p.: n.p., n.d), 18.

[15] MoE, IRI, *Teacher's Guide Farsi 1* (Tehran, Iran: ITPWC, 2012), 34–7; Idem, *Teacher's Guide Social Studies 3*, 51, 62–5.

[16] Patricia J. Higgins and Pirouz Shoar-Ghaffari, "Changing Perception of Iranian Identity in Elementary School Textbooks," in *Childhood in the Muslim Middle East*, ed. Elizabeth Warnock Fernen (Austin: University of Texas Press, 1995), 335.

[17] Patricia J. Higgins and Pirouz Shoar-Ghaffari, "Women's Education in the IRI," in *The Eyes of the Storm: Women in Post-revolutionary Iran*, eds. Mahnaz Afkhami and Erika Friedl (Syracuse: Syracuse University Press, 1994), 19–43.

revolution textbooks began to offer more representations of the traditional lifestyles of working classes and the peasantry.[18] Furthermore, in her analysis of representations of masculinity and femininity in early postrevolutionary school textbooks, Adele Ferdows argues that women were mainly represented as mothers, caregivers, and unselfish individuals and that the textbooks portrayed men in leadership positions, inside and outside the structure of the family.[19] Patricia Higgins and Pirouz Shoar-Ghaffari have also maintained that there was a decrease in the visibility of women in postrevolutionary textbooks. Nevertheless, in the textbooks of both eras, women were portrayed as homemakers or else working as teachers and in agricultural occupations. In fact, "there was no difference in the occupations portrayed for men and women in the two sets of Persian language textbooks. Among males, intellectuals were the focus in 36-40 percent of the lessons" during both periods.[20] The dominant form of the family in both post- and prerevolutionary textbooks has been the nuclear family, composed of a father, a mother, and two children (a boy and a girl).[21]

In addition, as Golnar Mehran has argued, in reference to Iranian female adult education programs and textbooks, Iranian school textbooks were not written from the perspective of "empowerment theories" and, as such, lacked the potential to provide older students with critical thinking, literacy, and knowledge to assist them in overcoming their "subordinate position[s]."[22] Despite the stated goals of the government to "strengthen the social and political insight of girls and increase their self-confidence," contemporary postrevolutionary textbooks reinforce existing patriarchal "social and family responsibilities" of women.[23] Much like the pre-2003 curricula, most current textbooks also ensure the sanctity and stability of the family by socializing girls and boys according to their different gender roles[24] that portray religiously sanctioned images "of women's roles in the family, society, and education" and "the mutual rights of women, men, and the family at all levels."[25] Although postrevolutionary textbooks continue to offer Islamic-centric patriarchal constructions of the ideal family, the inclusion of the universal rights of the child has been a significant critical addition to Iranian curricula.

---

[18] Higgins and Shoar-Ghaffari, "Women's Education in the IRI."
[19] Adele K Ferdows, "Gender Roles in Iranian Public School Textbooks," in *Childhood in the Muslim Middle East*, ed. Elizabeth Warnock Fernen (Austin: University of Texas Press, 1995), 328, 332, 333.
[20] Higgins and Shoar-Ghaffari, "Changing Perception of Iranian Identity in Elementary School Textbooks," 358.
[21] Ibid.
[22] Golnar Mehran, "The Paradox of Tradition and Modernity in Female Education in the IRI," *Comparative Education Review* 47, no. 3 (2003): 271. See also Golnar Mehran, "The Socialization of School Children in the IRI," *Iranian Studies* 22 (1989): 35–50; Idem, "Ideology and Education in the IRI," *Compare* 20 (1990): 53–65; Idem, "The Creation of the New Muslim Woman: Female Education in the IRI," *Convergenc*, XXIV, no. 4 (1991): 42–51; Idem, "Social Implications of Literacy in Iran," *Comparative Education Review* 36, no. 2 (1992): 194–211; Idem, "The Creation of the New Muslim Women: Female Education in the IRI," *Convergence* XXIV, no. 4 (1993): 42–51; Idem, "A Study of Girls' Lack of Access to Primary Education in the IRI," *Compare: A Journal of Comparative Education* 27, no. 3 (1997): 263–77; Idem, "Lifelong Learning: New Opportunities for Women in a Muslim Country (Iran)," *Comparative Education* 35, no. 2 (1999): 201–15.
[23] Mehran, "The Paradox of Tradition and Modernity in Female Education in the IRI," 276.
[24] Ibid.
[25] Ibid., 284.

Discourses of Nuclear Family and Marriage: Exclusionary Heteronormative, Islamic-Centric, and Patriarchal Constructions of the Ideal Family

The discourses of nuclear family and marriage are the most prevalent and central frameworks through which the curricula construct/narrate the ideal family from heteronormative, patriarchal, ageist, sexist, and ableist perspectives as a legal union between a man and a woman.[26] Knowledge about why and how the nuclear family has become normalized as the main family structure is a silent aspect of the curricula. Although elementary social studies and Persian textbooks are inclusive of content that represent pastoral nomads (representing ethnic diversity through the discourse of 'ashayir), they do not include any knowledge about the family and the transformation of family structures in various Persianate and non-Persianate parts of Iran. Knowledge about various changes in the structure of the family is not included as part of the universal national curriculum. It is only in the context of provincial studies textbooks, each specific to a province, many of which are populated by non-Persianate ethnic groups, that this knowledge is discussed. For example, only students who live in the province of Kurdistan read about traditional dominant forms of kinship. They do so in the text's exploration of human geography in that province and through the introduction of the term "patrilineal" (*pedar tabāri*). They also learn how such traditional forms have now given way to the nuclear family, as a result of industrialization and urbanization.[27] Provincial textbooks do not explore the positive and/or negative implications of structural changes in the formation of the family in terms of power relations between men and women and/or parents and children. As Ahmad Mohammadpur,[28] in quoting one of his male research participants, points out, the role of Kurdish men in terms of enforcing traditional patriarchal values and ideals on women has been questioned by Kurdish women due to the rise of critical consciousness among younger Kurdish women who are better educated and have clearer understandings of their rights. The media's construction of modern family relations has also brought changes in the perceptions of women in terms of their ideals of the "perfect" family and the desired gendered family relations. Although the process of enculturation, due to external value systems and knowledge, has had positive and negative consequences for Kurdish tribal groups, how these value systems compete with traditional and time-honored norms and mores are not explicated for students who live in this province.[29] This and similar issues that explore the history of nondominant groups need to be included as part of the national curriculum. This knowledge also needs to be inclusive of ethnic women's

---

[26] MoE. *Social Studies 4*, 1999, 134; Idem, *Social Studies 4*, 2004, 108–9; Idem, *Farsi 1*, 2015, 2, 5; Idem, *Farsi 2* (Tehran, Iran: ITPWC, 2015), 6; Idem, *Farsi 3* (Tehran, Iran: ITPWC, 2013), 20; Idem, *Social Studies 3*, 2017, 12.

[27] MoE, IRI, *Provincial Studies: Kurdistan* (Tehran, Iran: ITPWC, 2016), 81.

[28] Ahmad Mohammadpur, "Disembedding the Traditional Family: Grounded Theory and the Study of Family Change Among Mangor and Gaverk Tribes of Iranian Kurdistan," *Journal of Comparative Family Studies* 44, Iss. 1 (2013): 117–XI32. Accessed June 8, 2018. https://ezproxy.kpu.ca:2443/login?url=https://search.proquest.com/docview/1431071305?accountid=35875.

[29] Ibid

historical memories and their multiple and intersecting experiences and issues, a process which requires a reassessment of the discourse of an "Aryan identity" as the basis for the narration of the nation.

School knowledge that is available to all Iranians, irrespective of provincial residence, does not explore how various Persian and non-Persian (Iranian) women have reconstructed their identities and rethought their relations within traditional (and modern) family structures.[30] For example, the authors of *Provincial Studies: Kurdistan*, conclude that in this region, parents in nuclear families continue to provide their children with care and protection, and grandparents are respected by younger generations. Referencing Western historians, the authors also maintain that, despite the prevalence of patrilineal relations in Kurdistan, Kurdish women have historically enjoyed equality, special status, privileges, and values that are well entrenched in this region's popular/traditional culture and mores. However, there are no explanations or examples provided to critically explore these important points and their implications for gendered relations of power. Instead, the text ends with a generalized statement about the importance of unique and unparalleled Kurdish marriage ceremonies, conceptualized as rites-of-passage into adulthood.[31] Lack of knowledge about how modern gendered relations are imagined and reflected upon places limits on the role of the curricula as textual spaces for developing critical self-reflections and reimagining how men and women of different ethnic and racial backgrounds relate to one another in light of structural changes. The curricula do not offer critical reflections on conflicting and contradictory factors that have led to rising critical consciousness and women's empowerment. Knowledge produced by women and men that highlight their reflexivity on the transformation of marriage practices and family relations is a necessary component of a progressive curriculum that is lacking in Iran. The images of the family and marriage normalize Islamic conception(s) of heterosexual marriage as timeless and central in the reproduction of the exalted community of sameness. In writing about the family, authors discount the history of change and transformation. As Ahmad Mohammadpur argues, the structure of the family has been affected by several historical factors such as infertility rates, a decrease in the rates of marriage and remarriage, a rise in divorce rates and single family composition, participation of women in paid employment, and the encroachment of state institutions into family affairs that are now compounded by the effects of the globalization of economy, culture, and information.[32] Existing research on the transformation of Iranian family structures highlight that power structures within families have been reformulated due to the changing attitudes of men and women with respect to the perceived rights of women.[33] The political economy of this shift has not been explored in any detail.

The discourse of the nuclear family intersects with the discourse of marriage in offering heteronormative constructions of the ideal family. The curricula present marriage (1) as a quintessential rite-of-passage with rich historical roots that is central

---

[30] As quoted in Ibid.
[31] MoE, *Provincial Studies: Kurdistan*, 2016, 81.
[32] Mohammadpur, "Disembedding the Traditional Family."
[33] Ibid.

to one's identity/self-conception and is sanctioned by the Prophet Muhammad and (2) as the most important obligation that God has placed on humans. Marriage, either in the form of *dāyemi* (formal) or *sigheh* (temporary) unions, is normalized as an omnipresent, constant, and timeless Islamic legal contract[34] and as the symbol of a complete ideal Muslim who follows the commands of God.[35] Elementary school knowledge about marriage contract is decontextualized and excludes any controversial information—for example, issues that involve female sexuality.[36] School knowledge does not reflect on the contradictory aspects of temporary marriage, as a solution to satisfying sexual needs and desires of the youth, widows, and/or single-parent families. The textbooks, including adult literacy textbooks (see further), also do not distinguish between sexual needs and promiscuity, which were the topics of heated public discursive formations in the media, following the comments made by the late president Rafsanjani in November 1990 during his Friday Prayer sermon in Tehran that acknowledged female sexuality.[37] The public involvement in taking sides between those who welcomed such an interpretation of temporary marriage, *mut'a* (*sigheh*, in Persian colloquialism), and those who considered it as a form of corruption leading to the dissolution of long-held values central to the reproduction of a healthy society[38] points to the diversity of views and ways of knowing that are not incorporated as part of the official knowledge about the family.

Iranian school textbooks exclude critical discussions of sexuality in framing the family as an important institution of Islamic Iran. The lack of historicizing of how men's and women's understandings of marriage, sexuality, family relations, and civil, social, and political rights have been affected by the nation-building process, Westernization, and the Iranian Revolution sanitizes the complex political economy of the family.[39] Instead, the curricula identify the first step in forming a healthy family as carefully choosing a *bā-īmān*/pious partner with good qualities, which results in the tranquility of the soul.[40] It is through marriage, as the indicator of a healthy emotional *self*, that well-adjusted individuals achieve spiritual completion.[41] An unmarried person is assumed to be an incomplete *self*, who has not fulfilled his/her religious requirement. In religious discourses, it is recommended that with marriage half of one's religion is preserved.[42]

---

[34] Literacy Movement Organization, MoE, IRI, *Women's Commandments* (Tehran, Iran: Literacy Movement Organization, 2012), 16–19.
[35] MoE, IRI, *Social Studies 3* (Tehran, Iran: ITPWC, 2015), 6; Idem, *Social Studies 3*, 2017, 16–17; Literacy Movement Organization, MoE, IRI, *Teaching Literacy 1* (Tehran, Iran: Literacy Movement Organization, 2014), 63.
[36] See Shahla Haeri, "No End in Sight: Politics, Paradox, and Gender Policies in Iran," *Boston University Law Review* 93 (1992): 1049–62.
[37] See Ibid.
[38] See Ibid., 1050–1.
[39] See Ibid.
[40] Literacy Movement Organization, MoE, IRI, *Social Studies* (Tehran, Iran: Literacy Movement Organization, 2014), 2; Idem, *Teaching Literacy 1*, 63; Idem, *Women's Commandments*, 16.
[41] MoE, *Women's Commandments*, 16.
[42] Ibid.

By institutionalizing and normalizing Islamic forms of marriage as the only viable and acceptable form of cohabitation that all men and women must undergo,[43] the curricula not only silence and exclude non-Muslim marriage practices but also depict those people who may not want to get married and/or have children as outsiders/abnormal selves. Moreover, despite the fact that the curricula frame marriage as an obligation and the right of all Iranians (read Muslims), the official knowledge disregards the social, economic, and psychological dilemmas that gay/lesbian/transgendered families/individuals face in contemporary Iran.[44] Furthermore, the institution of polygamy (both in its formal form and in its temporary marriage form), which the state has vehemently defended, violates the sanctity of the nuclear family and, in fact, makes the nuclear family a highly fragile institution.[45]

The patriarchal/heteronormative construction of marriage is framed with a sexist bias and in light of the intersections of the discourses of compulsory heterosexuality, hegemonic motherhood, the cult of domesticity, and *Velāyat-e Faqih*. It is also framed based on the binary oppositions of *bā-īmānī/bī-īmānī* and *nāmāḥrām/māḥrām* that demonize homosexual love, idealize the ability of women to have children as the basis for defining their femininity, and celebrate their reproductive/household managerial functions as central to perpetuating the leadership positions of men within the family.[46] The curricula fetishize the ideal woman as a mother whose domestic responsibilities are to ensure the reproduction of a peaceful cooperative household, much like Ḥaẓarat-e Zahra (the prophet's daughter and wife of Imam Ali) who, as a pious woman, created a serene household for her husband, Ḥaẓrat-e Ali.[47] It is through the discourses of unity and cooperation that marriage is framed as a practice that provides safety, strengthens kinship relations, and enables people to share their difficulties.[48] Marriage, moreover, symbolizes the strength of the community of believers and the level of collaboration within it through a heteronormative approach to the discourse of virginity, as a patriarchal invisible pedagogy that associates female purity to a woman's adherence to the dominant sexual mores: a virgin girl, that is a girl who has not yet married, needs the permission of her father or male guardian to get married.[49]

The curricula narrate the ideal Muslim, heterosexual, knowledgeable, and *bā-īmān* mother/sister/wife as someone who (1) supports/perpetuates the Imam's line and (2) controls and is aware of the temptations of looking/gazing,[50] because this is

---

[43] MoE, IRI, *Farsi 1* (Tehran, Iran: ITPWC, 2008), 75; Idem, *Social Studies 3*, 2017, 6.
[44] MoE, *Social Studies 7*, 2017, 2.
[45] Editorial comments by Janet Afary.
[46] Katerina Deliovsky, *White Femininity: Race, Gender, & Power* (Halifax, Nova Scotia: Fernwood Publishing, 2010), 55.
[47] Literacy Movement Organization, MoE, IRI, *Teaching Literacy 2* (Tehran, Iran: Literacy Movement Organization, 2014), 62.
[48] MoE, IRI, *Provincial Studies: Baluchistan* (Tehran, Iran: ITPWC, 2016), 61; Idem, *Provincial Studies: Bushehr* (Tehran, Iran: ITPWC, (2016), 65; Idem, *Provincial Studies: Hormozgan* (Tehran, Iran: ITPWC, 2016), 63; Idem, *Provincial Studies: Khuzestan* (Tehran, Iran: ITPWC, 2016), 63; Idem, *Provincial Studies: Semnan* (Tehran, Iran: ITPWC, 2016), 70; Idem, *Provincial Studies: Tehran* (Tehran, Iran: ITPWC, 2016), 43.
[49] MoE, *Women's Commandments*, 17.
[50] MoE, *Teaching Literacy 1*, 21; Idem, *The Role and Rights of Women in Islam* (Tehran, Iran: Literacy Movement Organization, 2014).

how the devil enters the core of one's soul.⁵¹ A woman must not look at the body of a *nāmāḥrām* man or another woman with lust or for pleasure. A man must do the same, unless he is looking at a woman's face and hands up to her wrists.⁵² Lesbian/homosexual/heterosexual love/feelings are viewed in light of binary oppositions of *bī-īmānī* and *nāmāḥrām* that are assumed to disrupt God's natural order on earth. These heteronormative depictions of the ideal forms of interpersonal relationships between men and women function as scripts and inform the dominant habitus. Transgressions of essentialized/idealized identities delineated by the dominant habitus place unruly women into the category of un-Islamic Other: their demonization is framed in light of actions that undermine the patriarchal/heteronormative structures of power. The curricula normalize a heteronormative and essentialist notion of femininity, through which women are required to fit their varied selves into and adjust who they are within the parameters of the state's religiously sanctioned habitus: *Bā-īmān* women control their (homo)sexuality, deny the devil a place in their "souls," and thus affirm the sanctity of the idealized patriarchal community of sameness.

The heterosexual bias of the curricula is also framed in light of two other biases of ableism and ageism. Although people with disabilities are presented in pictures and drawings of families, schools, and city life, the SIF is celebrated as an able-bodied unit that excludes people with visible forms of disabilities as parents or in leadership positions within the family.⁵³ The SIF only consists of able-bodied parents who may have children with disabilities: a healthy nation is not produced through the bodies of women with disabilities, and men with disabilities are not imagined as the leaders of the ideal family. The disability bias not only ignores/silences the historical memories of those families/individuals who deal with inequalities resulting from their disabilities but also intersects the ageist bias that offers limited depictions of the varied life experiences of elderly Iranians. The ageist bias, for example, constructs (widowed) grandparents as individuals who often live with their children or as individuals who lament the loss of their youth and the decline of their physical and mental abilities.⁵⁴ The curricula intertextually consider young able-bodied heterosexual individuals who are actively involved in the reproduction of a healthy nation as the most valued members of the ideal family and the nation.

Eurocentrism, Male-centrism and Constructions of Family Diversity: Patriarchy, Motherhood, Martyrdom, and the SIF

A male-centric bias frames the narration of the nation and constructions of all types of families: the ideal family (as an urbanized/middle-class/white nuclear family), extended family (composed of a father/mother/children/grandparents), and single-

---

⁵¹ MoE, *Women's Commandments*, 12.
⁵² Ibid.
⁵³ MoE, IRI, *Social Studies 3*, 2015, 15; Idem, *Social Studies 3*, 2017, 57, 61; Idem, *Social Studies 7*, 2017, 4.
⁵⁴ MoE, *Social Studies 3*, 2015, 19–20.

parent family. Through a male-centric framework, the curricula celebrate the formal marital union as the ideal form of marriage, omitting any references to multiple wives or *sigheh* families: the ideal household is one in which the ideal man has only one ideal wife and whose children are the biological outcome of such a union. Stepfamilies are excluded in representations of family diversity. A pervasive patriarchal discourse frames/informs constructions of the dominant habitus regarding marriage and all family types: the father is normalized as the rightful fair-minded owner/leader of the household, the family, the nation, and the state.[55] A hegemonic construction of masculinity is normalized as an axiom/maxim: male leadership is essential to the family's survival.[56] The patriarchal discourse, for example, informs the depictions of the Hashemi family's relations—"Ali is the child of Mr. Mahmood Hashemi"; "In the home of Mr. Hashemi";[57] "Ali and Maryam are the children of Mr. Mahmood Hashemi"; and "Tahereh *khānūm*, the mother of Ali and Maryam, is a housewife."[58] The father is epitomized as the subject to whom the children/the household belong. The curricula identify the mother as the *khānūm* (lady) of the private sphere of the household, a dependent female, and its manager. Moreover, the patriarchal discourse frames how various types of families/family relations are presented in light of the binary opposition of when the father is alive versus when he is deceased. For example, in representing a single-parent family, the authors state, "This is a picture of Reza's family. He lives with his mother and sister. Reza's father passed away."[59] Reza is positioned as the subject and the leader of this family whose father is deceased. The patriarchal discourse, furthermore, frames representations of historical exalted religious women (e.g., Ḥaẓarat-e Khadijeh, Ḥaẓarat-e Zahra, Ḥaẓarat-e Masomeh, all Muslims who are referred to as noble and virtuous women) as wives, mothers, and sisters of important exalted religious prophets/Imams.[60]

The patriarchal curricula formalize the presence of the father as central to the functioning of an orderly family and, in his absence, the son. The inclusion of single-parent families is due to the pedagogical goal of being inclusive of such family structures, by portraying them as normal and ensuring that students in these families are accepted and not alienated.[61] Still the curricula do not offer holistic images of the diversities of such family types. Representations of single-parent families (which are always represented as single-mother households) and extended families (where widowed grandmothers/women live with their paternal relatives) are only contextualized in light of the death of the male patriarch of the nuclear family, due to natural disasters

---

[55] MoE, *Social Studies 5*, 1993, 162, 168–9; Idem, *Social Studies 5*, 2001, 126; Idem, *Social Studies 5*, 2004, 118–19, 121, 132; Idem, *Social Studies 6*, 2004, 34, 47; Idem, *Social Studies 6* (Tehran, Iran: ITPWC, 2015), 49; Idem, *Social Studies 8*, 23–9; Idem, *History 8*, 1999, 36–9, 43, 86; Idem, *History 8*, 2002, 23–9, 36–9, 45–6, 72, 90; Idem, *History 8*, 2004, 3, 40–1, 51, 72, 90; Idem, *History 12* (Tehran, Iran: ITPWC, 2005), 26–7; Idem, *Farsi 3* (Tehran, Iran: ITPWC, 2001), 78–9; Idem *Farsi 3*, 2004, 103; Idem, *Farsi 3*, 2015, 73, 80; Idem, *Farsi 5* (Tehran, Iran: ITPWC, 2012), 131; Idem, *Farsi 5* (Tehran, Iran: ITPWC, 2015), 56–7; Idem, *Farsi 6* (Tehran, Iran: ITPWC, 2004), 158.
[56] MoE, *Farsi 2*, 2004, 53.
[57] MoE, IRI, *Social Studies 3* (Tehran, Iran: ITPWC, 2000), 1–3.
[58] MoE, *Social Studies 3*, 2004, 1–2.
[59] MoE, *Social Studies 3*, 2017, 12.
[60] Literacy Movement Organization, *The Role and Rights of Women in Islam*, 2–4.
[61] MoE, *Teacher's Guide Social Studies 3*, 70.

or war. When the father is deceased, the role of an ideal Muslim mother is (1) to help his children cope with such a loss that has left them devoid of his blessings (na'mat) and (2) to ensure they follow in his footsteps.[62] Widowed mothers are obligated to sacrifice themselves and reaffirm the centrality of the fathers' values and morality in their children. Not only are the varied agencies of widowed wives excluded and their independence deemphasized but the status of a woman, as the wife/mother in perpetuity, is also assumed to be natural.

The discourse of *martyrdom* is the most pervasive framework for depicting the lives of widowed women who always cohabit with their significant paternal male relatives after the death of their husbands in the Iran–Iraq War. In one depiction of a fatherless family, the widowed mother's status is secondary to the leadership position of her brother with whom she and her two sons now live. The real leader within such an extended family is the adult male of the ideal nuclear family, who also protects his sister and her children after the death of his brother-in-law.[63] In contrast, the curricula exclude any information about how families that have lost their mothers/sisters/daughters, due to sickness, natural disasters, or as martyrs of the Iran–Iraq War, have dealt with such tragedies. Although the curricula offer examples of several female martyrs (as mothers/single-women/never-married women) of the Iranian Revolution and the Iran–Iraq War, the authors do not explore how the husbands of martyred married women have socialized their children in light of the martyred mothers' virtues. The inclusion of female martyrs is narrated in light of the ideological codes of loving Iran, defending Iran, sacrifice, and the Islamic Revolution. They celebrate the role of men as the true leaders, heroes, and protectors of Iran.[64] Although female martyrs of the war are constructed as brave lionesses, the narration of female contributions to the war efforts locate them not at the front lines but as either cooks or nurses.[65] These are feminine occupations that do not highlight the role of women in various armed forces where they sometimes have held leadership roles. The inclusion of women martyrs and their roles during the revolution and the Iran–Iraq War in post-2010 editions of textbooks is an add-on approach to knowledge construction that continues to idealize the political and anti-hegemonic roles of male leadership as the main component of the category *mārdom* (people), which is also a Persianized and apolitical construct.[66] For example, non-Persian women's resistance in the cities of Khoramshar and Abadan is framed in light of the discourse of the borderland people of Iran (the reference is to non-Persian ethnic minorities of various ethnic provinces) who sacrificed their lives and "fought until their last blood" to protect their cities against Saddam's forces. The discourse of *mārdom*, which is presented as a unified and undifferentiated force, includes references to women who not only resisted the invading enemy and protected

---

[62] MoE, *Social Studies 6*, 2004, 17, 47.
[63] MoE, *Farsi 5*, 2004, 182–4.
[64] MoE, *Farsi 1*, 2015, 44–7, 88–100; Idem, *Farsi 3*, 2004, 104; Idem, *Farsi 3*, 2016, 51; Idem, *Provincial Studies: Bushehr*, 77; Idem, *Social Studies 9*, 2016, 104; Literacy Movement Organization, *Teaching Literacy 1*, 104; Idem, *Teaching Literacy 2*, 29, 105.
[65] MoE, *Social Studies 9*, 2016, 110; Idem, *History 8*, 2012, 112–14.
[66] MoE, *History 8*, 2009, 66–85.

Iran but also participated in the reconstruction of Iran after the war.[67] However, it is through an Islamic paternalistic framework that celebrates the political influences of Imam Khomeini, as the true leader of Iran and the protector of the nation, that Muslim women's participation in achieving freedom and independence is framed.[68] Women are identified as *fadākār* people (*mārdum*) who sacrificed their "meager wealth" for the revolution and the war effort.[69] Still, the role of women in the preservation and development of Iran is limited to that of the manager of the family, a family whose members are well aware of their status, roles, and obligation to society and the state. The discourses of *fadākāri* and martyrdom define and set limits to the main roles and functions of Iranians[70] through a patriarchal lens that undermines the economic, political, and cultural roles of women in the transformation and development of Iran. It is through a patriarchal discursive framing of hegemonic motherhood that women's ultimate divine roles are dictated: to encourage their husband/sons to sacrifice their lives and to become martyrs.[71] The curricula credit the success of the great men of Islam/Iran to the self-sacrifice/chastity/bravery of their mothers.[72] An ideal mother is someone who socializes future brave male martyrs within the context of a nuclear family; she does not undermine the leadership positions of men.

The curricula do not offer any representations of divorced women as the heads of single-parent homes. Although curricula authors recognize the existence of divorced families and the difficulties that these families face,[73] divorce, despite being viewed as a *ḥalāl* cancellation of the *aqd* (marriage) contract, is constructed as a reprehensible act by God.[74] Divorce is not a natural right of women; however, there are instances when a woman can divorce her husband (excluding *sigheh* marriages that have a specified expiration date).[75] Referencing Imam Khomeini's interpretation of Islamic laws, the right to divorce as a condition already formulated in the *aqd* (marriage contract) is acknowledged, especially in those cases when a man is morally corrupt, treats his wife unfairly, lives unethically, and is extremely violent towards her.[76] Although divorce is presented as an aberration of God's will, it is, nevertheless, condoned only when a woman is married to a *bī-īmān* (an irreligious) man. A patriarchal discourse envelopes discussions of divorced families that ultimately construct them in light of a medical model, as social pathologies with negative effects on both children and society: they are "broken," "disjointed," and "abnormal" units that undermine the sanctity of the SIF and male leadership.[77] It is only through the wives' and mothers' well-managed middle-class nuclear never-divorced Muslim family households that their husbands/sons can function as ideal sacrificing and faithful individuals.

[67] Literacy Movement Organization, *Teaching Literacy* 1, 85.
[68] Literacy Movement Organization, *Teaching Literacy* 1, 104; Idem, *Teaching Literacy* 2, 29.
[69] Literacy Movement Organization, *The Role and Rights of Women in Islam*, 20–1.
[70] MoE, *Farsi* 1, 2015, 44–7, 88–100.
[71] Literacy Movement Organization, *The Role and Rights of Women in Islam*, 12, 16.
[72] Ibid., 12; MoE, *Farsi* 6, 2004, 158.
[73] MoE, *Teacher's Guide Social Studies* 3, 70.
[74] Literacy Movement Organization, *Women's Commandments*, 19.
[75] Literacy Movement Organization, *The Role and Rights of Women in Islam*, 27.
[76] Ibid.
[77] MoE, *Teacher's Guide Social Studies* 3, 70.

Rights, Roles, and Obligations: Sexist Bias and Individual Pathologies

The curricula offer a pathologizing conception of childless families. They are constructed as disorderly units that have not been blessed with the love of "the creator of all creatures whom humans must obey."[78] The textbooks do not represent families that are or have chosen to remain childless. The family is defined as "the first and smallest society in which we live. A family begins with the marriage between a man and a woman. With the birth of children, the number of family member increases and its base becomes stronger. The existence of children in the family brings joy and happiness."[79] An ideal family is formed with the creation of children (conceptualized as the most important investment) that legitimates it as a joyous group and authenticates its reproductive function in the propagation of a just and moral Islamic society.[80] The tranquility of a happy household is framed as (1) the main responsibility of the wife/mother, where children learn to be "thankful to God for all his blessings and gifts" and follow the teachings and ideologies of the Supreme Leader(s) of Iran[81] and (2) the main venues for men to be able to perform their leadership roles.[82] The curricula idealize fertile women as child bearers and managers of households and fecund males as its leaders, who teach their children about Islamic values and socialize them as supporters of the Supreme Leader.[83] The main responsibility of morally veiled Muslim mothers who sacrifice themselves for the good of their husbands, children, and country is the reproduction of a well-organized cooperative family unit that consumes, saves, and conserves for the good of the nation. They must demonstrate to their children how to serve the interests of the group and cooperate with one another, follow rules, accept authority, and secure their revolution and independence by conserving resources and avoiding conspicuous consumption of luxury items.[84] Women's main economic contributions are considered to be due to their influences over their children, to purchase Iranian-made products, and to become frugal and environmentally conscious individuals.[85] Ideal mothers socialize rational children who do not spend more than they earn and save their money. The discourses of *isrāf* (avoiding waste) and *ṣarfe-jūī* (frugality) are central in imaging the obligations of the ideal mother.[86] It is the mothers' role to teach their children the Islamic ethic, but this can only be achieved in the context of a family that is led by a fair husband/father, one who is considerate of

---

[78] MoE, *Social Studies 5*, 2004, 135; Idem, *Social Studies 3*, 2015, 3.
[79] MoE, *Social Studies 3*, 2015, 12; Idem, *Social Studies 4* (Tehran, Iran: ITPWC, 1994), 134.
[80] MoE, *Social Studies 3*, 2017, 2–44.
[81] Ibid., 45.
[82] Literacy Movement Organization, *The Role and Rights of Women in Islam*, 22.
[83] MoE, *Farsi 1*, 2015, 2, 5; Idem, *Farsi 2*, 2015, 6; Idem, *Farsi 3*, 2013, 20; Literacy Movement Organization, MoE, IRI, *Farsi* (Tehran, Iran: Literacy Movement Organization, 2015), 98. Idem, *Social Studies 3*, 2015, 3–4; Idem, *Social Studies 3*, 2017, 12; Idem, *Social Studies 4*, 1999, 134; Idem, *Social Studies 4*, 2004, 108–9.
[84] Literacy Movement Organization, MoE, IRI, *Social Studies* (Tehran, Iran: Literacy Movement Organization, 2014), 5.
[85] Literacy Movement Organization, *Social Studies*, 5.
[86] MoE, *Social Studies 3*, 2017, 35–42.

the needs of his wife and children.⁸⁷ Imam Khomeini is iconized as the symbol of the perfect father/leader who was attentive to his wife's needs and inclusive of her opinions in all aspect of personal and family issues.⁸⁸

The curricula, moreover, construct the ideal mother as an altruistic individual who shares the pain of her loved ones' defeats. She is a warm-hearted person whose love for her children is unmatched, as she unselfishly puts her children's needs and dreams ahead of her own and considers their successes as her own.⁸⁹ Yet the textbooks highlight that "she must put the needs of the nation ahead of her children, by selflessly influencing her children to become martyred."⁹⁰ These characteristics frame the limits of the discourse of hegemonic motherhood. Curricular knowledge silences the dilemmas mothers face and assumes that the skills associated with being a mother and housewife are universally available and shared. The curricula essentialize and normalize the characteristics of compassion and care and a mother's *īmān* (faith) and unpolluted virtues as important features of emphasized femininity and the cult of domesticity. It is in the context of mothers' efforts to establish cohesive peaceful family environments that their members, as loving persons (a characteristic that is formalized as the rights of all Iranian citizens),⁹¹ are able to be ethically engaged with each other. In such families "children are familiarized with religious deeds, [learn to] respect [their] father[s] and mother[s], and [are introduced to] good morals"⁹² and can learn to respect the rights of each member in cooperative ways. The character formation of a righteous child and his/her right to be cared for is framed in light of her/his *bā-īmānī* and rational parents' correct choice of a moral and an ethical partner⁹³ who consumes and practices *ḥalāl* food and thoughts, as the formative aspects of humanities and natural rights.⁹⁴

It is the responsibility of the ideal pure/Islamic woman/mother to teach her children their religious functions and obligations.⁹⁵ Her main role is to socialize (her) veiled daughter(s). This universal duty of the supreme mother's subjectivity formalizes the ideals of feminine modesty/virtue.⁹⁶ The discourse of *ḥijāb* establishes and regulates who belongs to the category of ideal family/citizen/mother/woman. It is constructed as one of the most important Islamic teachings that plays a significant role in the healthy reproduction of the spirit of men and women.⁹⁷ Consider, for example, how the children of the Hashemi family are described by the principals of their new schools.

---

87 MoE, *Social Studies 6*, 2004, 34, 45.
88 Literacy Movement Organization, *Teaching Literacy 2*, 62.
89 MoE, *Social Studies*, 2004, 54; Idem, *Provincial Studies: Boher Ahmad* (Tehran, Iran: ITPWC, 2016) 59; Idem, *Provincial Studies: Qum* (Tehran, Iran: ITPWC, 2016), 68.
90 Editorial comments by Janet Afary.
91 MoE, *Social Studies 7*, 2017, 3.
92 MoE, *Social Studies 4*, 1994, 134; Literacy Movement Organization, *Social Studies*, 2.
93 Literacy Movement Organization, *Farsi*, 97.
94 Ibid., 97–8.
95 Literacy Movement Organization, *The Role and Rights of Women in Islam*, 12–14; MoE, *Farsi 1*, 2015, 33, 75.
96 Literacy Movement Organization, *The Role and Rights of Women in Islam*, 14; MoE, *Farsi 1*, 2015, 80–1; Idem, *Fundamental Reform Document of Education (FRDE)*, 34.
97 Literacy Movement Organization, *Women's Commandments*, 10; MoE, *Farsi 1*, 2016, 80–1; Idem, *Farsi 2*, 2004.

Ali is described as a good student.⁹⁸ In contrast, Maryam's adherence to *ḥijāb* frames her identity. Maryam is constructed as "a good girl" whom Mr. Hashemi hopes will "be well-mannered and organized in school and studies well."⁹⁹ Ali is portrayed as the ideal male student who will play an important role in the development of Iran. Maryam is the manifestation of the ideal women/citizen who does not question the role of the state in controlling women's bodily dispositions. She represents a well-mannered and organized veiled Muslim woman. As the ideal *bā-ḥijāb* female citizen, Maryam's veil symbolizes her purity and Islamic values. The discourse of *ḥijāb* functions as a historical ideological code and a trace that reaffirms and normalizes patriarchal constructions of gender relations in the narration of nation. However, the discourse of *ḥijāb* also frames women's bodies as pathological spaces that must be protected from the gazes of *nā-maḥrām* men, preadolescent boys, and other immoral women who view the bodies of women as sites of pleasure.¹⁰⁰ The *ḥijāb* functions as a form of heteronormative "symbolic power" that is also a "spectacle of surveillance" of impure and homosexual lust, with the main function of problematizing and identifying unruly bodies.¹⁰¹ It is an "inspecting gaze" that separates insiders from outsiders and celebrates heterosexuality as the sign of a woman's virtue.¹⁰² The *ḥijāb*, as the natural *hexis*, normalizes a *bī-ḥijāb* mother/daughter/sister as undesirable, "impious," and un-Islamic. Although the obligation of women to practice *ḥijāb* and protect themselves from the gazes of outsiders are the main measures in determining the ideal female's level of *īmān* and self-worth, it is contextualized in light of the efforts of exalted male leaders, who, as the main protectors of the moral foundations of the nation, have resisted the West and its internal agent's attempt to unveil and defile women during the reign of Reza Shah.¹⁰³

The obligation of Muslim men to protect women's virtue is normalized as a natural right and a reflection of God's will. The rights of children to be loved and cared for, for example, are narrated in light of the inalienable natural, social, and civil rights of Iranians due to their privileged place in the natural world, which are also protected by the Iranian Constitution. The Iranian Constitution is constructed as the manifestation of (1) the will of God, (2) the continuation of the tradition of the Prophet and Shiʿa Imams, and (3) modern interpretations of Islamic jurisprudence by the Islamic Republic's leadership (the discourse of *Velāyat-e Faqih*).¹⁰⁴ The discourse of rights informs school knowledge in the context of the obligations that Iranian citizens have toward their family members, the nation, and the state. The ideal citizen is one who affirms and follows the rules and laws of the state within the context of alienable rights bestowed upon him/her by the Islamic Republic and its leadership (the discourse of *Velāyat-e Faqih*). These rights are portrayed as universal and applicable to both men

---

[98] MoE, *Social Studies 3*, 2004, 69; Idem, *Social Studies 3*, 2000, 95.
[99] MoE, *Social Studies 3*, 2004, 70; Idem, *Social Studies 3*, 2000, 96.
[100] Literacy Movement Organization, *Women's Commandments*, 11.
[101] See Rebecca Haskell and Brian Burtch, *Get That Freak: Homophobia and Transphobia in High Schools* (Halifax, Nova Scotia: Fernwood Publishing, 2010), 93–4.
[102] See Haskell and Burtch, *Get That Freak*, 94–5, 97.
[103] MoE, *Social Studies 3*, 2000, 96; Idem, *Social Studies 3*, 2004, 70; Idem, *Social Studies 5*, 1993, 176; Idem, *Social Studies 5*, 2004, 124–5.
[104] MoE, *Social Studies 5*, 1993, 214; Idem, *Social Studies 5*, 2004, 135, 140; Idem, *Social Studies 7*, 2017, 1–12.

and women.¹⁰⁵ Citing the Qur'an, the discourse of the children of Adam contextualizes the construction of the natural rights that all Iranians are entitled to: "We cherished the children of Adam.... And [we] made them superior to many other [creations of God]."¹⁰⁶ It is through an anthropocentric approach that humans are framed as the most exalted creations of God and the narration of rights and obligations are recited. Iranians have the right to life, to God's blessings, to work to satisfy their basic needs, to marry and form families, to learn how to choose their paths in life, and to freedom.¹⁰⁷ Although Iranians also have the right to "appropriate" housing, food, and clothing; to be literate and educated; to develop and prosper from their talents; and to be respected and not face bullying/discrimination, these social rights (not civil rights) are framed in light of the responsibilities of parents and their abilities and income levels to properly socialize their children as useful and moral future citizens.¹⁰⁸ The curricula do not account for the effects of structural inequalities on families and their abilities to satisfy them.

The social rights of Iranians and their obligations are narrated through patriarchal discourses of *Velāyat-e Faqih* and Imam's line that situate the Supreme Leader as the representative of God and the Prophet until the coming of Imam Mahdi.¹⁰⁹ The orderly reproduction of Islamic Iran requires (1) the preservation of order within the family and (2) citizens who are well aware of their obligations and duly perform their duties as ethical adults in developing and protecting the Islamic Republic.¹¹⁰ As *bā-īmān (devout)* citizens, children must love and care for their parents, respect their rights, and accept their authority.¹¹¹ Children also have responsibilities toward themselves. They must take care of their bodies, know their talents, and actively improve their aptitudes.¹¹² Societal inequalities and injustices are framed through the discourse of individual pathologies of parents (read mothers) and their children, as reflections of *bī-īmān* individuals who (1) behave based on *ḥarām* thoughts, (2) do not follow the Imam's line, and (3) are irresponsible and unreflective individuals. The rights of children are assumed in the context of a well-functioning and safe family, where parents are fair and attentive to the needs of children. The curricula ignore the effects of violence within the family due to structural factors such as hegemonic patriarchal relations, existing misogynist state policies, and the effects of alcoholism, drug dependency, and/or economic inequalities. The ideal family is constructed as a unified space where pious parents, who are aware of their obligations as *bā-īmān* and loving individuals, will ensure that their children's rights are upheld and protected. The curricula do not present these rights as the civil/

---

¹⁰⁵ MoE, *Social Studies 7*, 2017, 1–12.
¹⁰⁶ Ibid., 2.
¹⁰⁷ Ibid.
¹⁰⁸ Ibid., 4.
¹⁰⁹ Literacy Movement Organization, *Teaching Literacy 1*, 129.
¹¹⁰ Literacy Movement Organization, *Teaching Literacy 2*, 120; MoE, *Farsi 1*, 2004, 100–1; Idem, *Farsi 1*, 2012, 44–7; Idem, *Farsi 3*, 2004, 48–50, 103–4; Idem, *Farsi 4*, 2004, 17–18, 143; Idem, *Farsi 5*, 2004, 42–3; Idem, *Social Studies 3*, 2004, 1–2; Idem, *Social Studies 4*, 1994, 136–8; Idem, *Social Studies 4*, 2004, 108–9.
¹¹¹ MoE, *Social Studies 3*, 2017, 15; Idem, *Social Studies 7*, 2017, 6, 8; Literacy Movement Organization, *Social Studies*, 3; Idem, *Teaching Literacy 1*, 67; Idem, *Teaching Literacy 2*, 10.
¹¹² MoE, *Social Studies 7*, 2017, 7.

political rights of citizens, guaranteed and enforced by the state. It is the institution of the family that is responsible in guaranteeing these rights.

The discursive intersections of the ideological codes of hegemonic motherhood, emphasized femininity, and the cult of domesticity, in the context of paternalistic depictions of rights, obligations, and leadership offer very limited status-positioned categories for women outside the institution of the family. They are mainly depicted as mothers and managers of the household, in the context of family relations, or performing feminized jobs.[113] A mother's daily tasks in the household, whose members are constructed/represented as always cooperating with one another, include "the responsibility of washing the dishes and putting the breakfast items in their specific places."[114] The discourse of cooperation reinforces a gender division of labor within the family, which is considered as central to its reproduction as an orderly institution.[115] For example, in *Provincial Studies: Boher Ahmad*, by reference to a traditional lullaby, the authors essentialize mothers as caring, warm-hearted, and compassionate persons— characteristics that define the discourse of hegemonic motherhood.[116] Despite the fact that such examples are ways of being inclusive of non-Persian cultural mores within Iran, the authors are not interested in the cultural significances and meanings of this lullaby. The inclusion of this information normalizes the dominant view associated with women as mothers of the nation whose main task is to socialize the young as active and healthy members of society. It offers a standardized view of motherhood that does not account for the dilemmas and difficulties mothers face in contemporary Iran. Mothers are portrayed as nonviolent individuals whose perceptions of their children are framed in the context of a natural love and care for infants. Such discursive formations of hegemonic motherhood contradict the assertion that women have the right to achieve the status of *mojtahid* (religious leader),[117] to be elected to parliament, to earn an income, to own property, and to hold some prominent positions in the state.[118] The curricula do not offer any examples of females in such positions. The main occupations for women are teacher, principal, and nurse, two of which elevate them as agents of the state. For example, depending on the edition, Maryam, the daughter of Mr. Hashemi, wants to become either a nurse[119] or a teacher.[120] Her feminized employment choices fit into the constructed image of the ideal woman as a caring and unselfish mother whose main responsibility is the socialization of Iranian youth and the healthy reproduction of the nation.

---

[113] MoE, *Farsi 1*, 2004, 2, 3, 5, 7, 9, 10, 13, 14, 17, 18, 19, 22, 26, 27, 28, 29, 37, 38, 40, 41, 43, 44, 45, 46, 54, 56, 67, 81, 82, 83, 117, 26, 27, 40, 45, 46, 81, 117; Idem, *Farsi 2*, 2004, 7, 12, 15, 21, 26, 29, 30, 38, 41, 53, 55, 57, 82, 84, 103, 106, 130, 131, 138; Idem, *Farsi 3*, 2004, 3, 7, 8, 19, 18, 41, 42, 54, 64, 74, 87, 96, 98, 101, 106, 114; Idem, *Farsi 4*, 2004, 37, 68; Idem, *Farsi 5*, 2004, 35, 86; P6, 2004, 25, 76, 97, 78, 86, 90, 135, 137.
[114] MoE, *Social Studies 6*, 2004, 24–8; Idem, *Social Studies 6*, 1999, 19.
[115] Ibid.
[116] MoE, IRI, *Provincial Studies: Boher Ahmad* (Tehran, Iran: ITPWC, 2016), 59.
[117] Though their fatwā is only binding on themselves and not on others.
[118] Literacy Movement Organization, *The Role and Rights of Women in Islam*, 26–39.
[119] MoE, *Social Studies 3*, 2004, 32.
[120] MoE, *Social Studies 3*, 2000, 3.

The ideological codes of hegemonic motherhood, emphasize femininity, and the cult of domesticity intersect the discourses of cooperation and unselfishness.[121] Additionally, they frame women's rights, roles, obligations, and status from a Persian-centric and an Islamic-centric perspective. The textbooks construct an ideal image of an Iranian that is contrasted to the demonized representation of pre-Islamic (*jaheliyeh*) Arabs. The texts argue that, before the introduction of Islam, Arabs were barbaric pagans who lacked any and all civilization. They treated women violently, did not give them any rights, and considered them as weak and inferior.[122] The standard denigrations of pre-Islamic Arabs maintain that "Islam appeared in the Arabian peninsula among people who lived in ignorance and foolishness."[123] The textbooks argue that it was with the birth of Islam that women achieved their human status since unlike other religions, Islam did not view women in a derogatory and contemptuous way, nor regard them as perpetrators of an original sin.[124] The discourse of leadership also recounts contemporary Iranian women's political and social roles and rights from a revolutionary patriarchal discourse.[125] Following the teachings of Imam Khomeini, some women are idealized as persons who played an important role in encouraging other women's involvement in the decision-making political processes.[126] Women's rights according to Islamic laws and women's eventual participation in the development of Iran are not only considered as gifts from God but also supported by the Supreme Leader of Iran (the discourse of *Velāyat-e Faqih*). It is due to the liberatory politics of the representative of God on earth that Iranian women now have access to cultural and social rights that have resulted, for example, in their increased education. "Today, more than half of university students are females."[127] However, the curricula ignore the opposition of Imam Khomeini to the election of women to the Iranian *Majlis* and the shah's policy that gave them voting rights in local council elections in the early 1960s.[128] In fact, the curricula frame the shah's civil rights reforms as an imperialist agenda to deceive women and the Iranian people.[129] Although the postrevolutionary rights of women are framed through the discourse of the *Imam's line*, the victory of the Iranian Revolution is also credited to women's participation.[130] However, the revolutionary roles of women are celebrated not as leaders but as individuals who guided their men to change the shah's regime.[131] Women are positioned as the managers of the private sphere with influence over the

---

[121] MoE, *Social Studies 6*, 1999, 43; Idem, *Social Studies 6*, 2004, 53–6.
[122] Literacy Movement Organization, *The Role and Rights of Women in Islam*, 1; See also MoE, *Social Studies 5*, 1993, 93–7; Idem, *Social Studies 5*, 2001, 75–7; Idem, *Social Studies 5*, 2004, 76–8.
[123] MoE, IRI, *Social Studies 9* (Tehran, Iran: ITPWC, 2016), 48.
[124] Literacy Movement Organization, *The Role and Rights of Women in Islam*, 2–4.
[125] Literacy Movement Organization, *The Role and Rights of Women in Islam*, 5; MoE, *Social Studies 3*, 2008, 21.
[126] Literacy Movement Organization, *The Role and Rights of Women in Islam*, 15–16.
[127] Ibid., 33.
[128] MoE, *History 8*, 2004, 72; Idem, *History 8*, 2002, 72; Hale Esfandiari, "The Role of Women Members of Parliament, 1963–88," in *Women in Iran: From 1800 to the Islamic Republic*, eds. Louis Beck and Guity Nashat (Urbana, IL: University of Illinois Press, 2004), 138.
[129] MoE, *History 8*, 2002, 72; Idem, *History 8*, 2004, 72.
[130] Imam Khomeini, as quoted in Literacy Movement Organization, *The Role and Rights of Women in Islam*, 19.
[131] Literacy Movement Organization, *The Role and Rights of Women in Islam*, 20–1.

public sphere through the bodies and minds of their husbands and sons. Nonetheless, the curricula situate Iranian women as the envy of all societies and as the symbol of freedom for global Muslim others (the discourse of *Ummat-e Islamī*).[132]

The discourses of *Ummat-e Islamī*, Imam's line, and *Velāyat-e Faqih* converge to offer an idealist depiction of women, one that is devoid of women's contemporary agencies. The economic roles of women are framed through the discourse of cooperation that often emphasize the nonmaterial functions of their localized economic endeavors in terms of social acceptance, mental health, and leisurely activities among women.[133] For example, in exploring the commercial role of the culturally sanctioned ritual of *vāreh* among the Lur people, as an example of cooperation, in which Lur women share in the production and sale of dairy products, the textbook does not examine this practice in light of its empowering consequences and the role of women's agency to organize and reproduce the economic well-being of their families and communities.[134] The curriculum dehistoricizes such practices and ignores the managerial positions of (ethnic) women in the public spheres and in light of the nation-building process. Furthermore, women's participation in the workforce and the income they earn in both rural and urban settings is conceptualized as "helping" and "assisting" their husbands.

> In the family, everyone has responsibility. The father has the responsibility to provide food, clothing, and other necessary household goods for his wife and children. What does the mother do in the family? What else do father and mother do for us? In some families, women also work outside the house. In the villages, women help their husbands in agricultural activities, weaving carpets and milking cows and sheep. In the cities, some women also work in schools, hospitals, factories or offices.[135]

Although women have the right to earn an income and be employed, these civil rights are explored through the discourse of hegemonic motherhood and as expecting and lactating mothers.[136] Their rights to have an income is only discussed through the discourse of a stipend. They have the right to *mehriyeh*, daily maintenance, and inheritance, which reinforce their dependent statuses as wives.[137] Although they receive far less inheritance than men (a sister receives half of her brother's and a wife and mother receives only one-eighth of her husband's estate), this is explained as the result of their due rights to dowry (a father's gift to his daughter at the time of their marriage) and *mehriyeh* (an amount promised to a woman at the time of marriage). Gender inequality, in terms of inheritance, is justified by a reference to Martyr Motahari's interpretation of Islamic jurisprudence. It is through a paternalistic worldview that women's rights and obligations are presented in the curricula. The curricula also frame representations of a family's income from a patriarchal discourse that delineates a

---

[132] Ibid., 17.
[133] MoE, IRI, *Provincial Studies: Luristan* (Tehran, Iran: ITPWC, 2016), 59.
[134] Ibid.
[135] MoE, *Social Studies 4*, 2004, 108–9.
[136] Literacy Movement Organization, *The Role and Rights of Women in Islam*, 35–6.
[137] Ibid., 37–8.

wife's economic role in terms of her responsibility to be considerate of the income and occupational status of her husband when she spends his earnings in her efforts to reproduce a healthy family.[138] In the ideal family, fathers work in white-collar jobs, and mothers stay at home and take care of children. It is as frugal, compassionate, attentive, and caring mothers/wives that veiled adult women are respected.

The ideological discursive formations of women's roles and histories in the Iranian society limit the range of meanings available to social actors to interpret the world from the diverse perspectives and multiple biographies of women based on factors such as race, ethnicity, age, ability, sexuality, political-ideological beliefs, and social class. The silencing of women's issues turn the curricula into regimes of disappearance,[139] that not only erase and displace various categories of women and their histories but also invoke what Beth Richie refers to as the trap of loyalty.[140] It is only as loyal Muslim/revolutionary objects of male leadership that the subjectivity of the ideal woman is acknowledged. Her disloyalty to the revolutionary Islamic leadership is viewed as her lack of modesty as an unveiled woman whose body and mind defies and undermines ḥalāl thoughts and actions necessary for the reproduction of an Islamic-Iranian society.

Shiʿa Leadership, Whiteness, Culture, and Normative Representations of Hegemonic Sameness

An understudied aspect of Iranian curricular materials is the extent to which a racialized image of the ideal family informs school knowledge. This section focuses on the racialization and ethnicization of the family and explores how religion, Islam, gender norms and relations, and rights and obligation are portrayed in Iranian educational textbooks. In these textbooks, religion, language, ethnicity, and race intersect in offering a homogenized/essentialized Orientalist, Persian-centric, and Shiʿa-centric image of the ideal family that reaffirms the importance of the Imam's line in imagining Iran.[141] This is the case even though Iran is represented as an ethnically and racially diverse population, and Iran and the ideal family are celebrated as white, Persian, Aryan, Shiʿa, and urbanized entities.[142] The curricula normalize Persian/Shiʿa identities as quintessential characteristics of the ideal family through the selection of books that the SIF approves. In the first lesson of Persian 1, for example, the ideal family is epitomized as an exclusively Muslim unit of sameness, as implied by the presence of the Qur'an in the collection of books this middle-class nuclear family owns, which simultaneously excludes other "minority" religions as the bases for defining the nation and its heroes (see Figure 4.1). It is, furthermore, a Shiʿa construct, a fact highlighted by the presence of a copy of *Nahj-al-Balaghaheh*, or the sermons of Imam Ali, who

---

[138] Literacy Movement Organization, *The Role and Rights of Women in Islam*, 22–3.
[139] See David Hugill, *Missing Women, Missing News: Covering Crises in Vancouver's Downtown Eastside* (Halifax: Fernwood Publishing, 2010), 22, 52.
[140] Beth E. Richie, *Arrested Justice: Black Women, Violence, and America's Prison Nation* (New York: New York University Press, 2012), 36–7.
[141] MoE, IRI, *Social Studies 4* (Tehran, Iran: ITPWC, 2004), 129, 132.
[142] MoE, IRI, *Farsi 1* (Tehran, Iran: ITPWC, 2015).

Figure 4.1 'Welcome to Our House.' *Source*: MoE, IRI, *Farsi 1* (Tehran, Iran: ITPWC, 2015).

is constructed as the first Shi'a martyr.¹⁴³ This family is also a Persianized family, as indicated by the presence of the *Shāhnāmah* and *Divan-e Hafez* and the fact that there are no non-Persian poetry/literary books included in this collection: The celebrated dominant cultural capital is framed through the discursive formation of Persian literary achievements.¹⁴⁴

These books not only construct and locate the ideal family in the context of the assumed Persian/Aryan heritage of all Iranians and their Shi'a religious affiliation but also objectify and naturalize how historical male leaders/heroes of the nation have protected Iran against its many enemies.¹⁴⁵ The migration of the Aryans and the establishment of the first world empire and subsequent other powerful empires by Pars and Parthian tribes in prehistory are identified as indicators of the birth of

---

¹⁴³ MoE, IRI, *History 6* (Tehran, Iran: ITPWC, 2004).
¹⁴⁴ MoE, IRI, *Farsi 1* (Tehran, Iran: ITPWC, 2016), 2, 5.
¹⁴⁵ MoE, IRI, *Farsi 5* (Tehran, Iran: ITPWC, 2014), 130–4; Idem, *Farsi 2* (Tehran, Iran: ITPWC, 2004), 135–6; Idem, *Farsi 2* (Tehran, Iran: ITPWC, 2016), 77–3; Idem, *History 7* (Tehran, Iran: ITPWC, 2004), 34.

the nation and its rise to global power.¹⁴⁶ In another lesson, in the form of a series of conversational narratives between the Amiri children, their parents, and other extended family members that chronicle the travels of this family to central Iran and the ruins of Persepolis, students read that "Iran means the land or the place of the Aryans. Aryan means honorable and noble."¹⁴⁷ The curricula idealize the fathers of the nation as brave people who resisted and fought various invaders. Students read about Iranians like Aryo Barzan, depicted as a fearless Pars military leader who resisted "Alexander, the Great" and eventually lost his life in protecting the nation against the Greek invasion of Iran.¹⁴⁸ In *Farsi 5*, the love, affection, and the desire to protect and die for the nation is historicized through a narration that depicts Iran as a land of many thousand individuals like Aryo Barzan, who have victoriously sacrificed their lives for Islam and Iran and have chosen martyrdom to ensure all Iranians are free and independent.¹⁴⁹ The textbooks highlight that the Iranian self has never been subdued or dominated by outsiders since an important characteristic of the Iranian (read Persian) consciousness is self-sacrifice, *fadākārī*. The emphasis on martyrdom, as a characteristic of both pre-Islamic and post-Shiʿa Iranians, also highlights the importance of defending Iran against its enemies, not only as the land of the Aryans but also as the site of Islamic power.¹⁵⁰ Ferdawsī, for example, is iconized as the exalted post-Islamic hero who saved the Persian language from obliteration. The textbooks also normalize the *Shāhnāmeh*, as a textual and historical record of the love and passion students must possess and show for the Persian language/literature.¹⁵¹ This affection is presented as a natural and necessary characteristic and obligation of the ideal citizen, which is then used as a justification for the historical desire of Iranians to (1) protect the rich cultural heritage of the dominant Pars group¹⁵² and (2) to preserve the Persian (Parsi) language as the historic language of the nation since the arrival of the Aryans and as the only legally sanctioned language of the country.¹⁵³ The textbooks frame the Persian language as the symbol of the resilience of the ideal citizen, whose main responsibilities are to develop Iran, resist the enemy insiders/outsiders, and defend Islam/Iran.¹⁵⁴ Students read that since the arrival of the Aryans, "Parsi" (Farsi), in both written and spoken forms, and in its historical or contemporary manifestations, has been the language of Iran: "Many writers and poets have written and composed [in this language]."¹⁵⁵ The Persian language is idealized as the language of art/sciences and the linguistic form

---

¹⁴⁶ MoE, IRI, *Social Studies 7* (Tehran, Iran: ITPWC, 2015), 116–17.
¹⁴⁷ MoE, IRI, *Social Studies 4* (Tehran, Iran: ITPWC, 2015), 47.
¹⁴⁸ MoE, *Social Studies 4*, 57.
¹⁴⁹ MoE, IRI, *Farsi 5* (Tehran, Iran: ITPWC, 2014), 130–5, 134.
¹⁵⁰ MoE, IRI, *Social Studies 5* (Tehran, Iran: ITPWC, 2008), 162–4; Idem, *Farsi 4* (Tehran, Iran: ITPWC, 2004), 18.
¹⁵¹ Vaziri Mostafa, *Iran as Imagined Nation: The Construction of National Identity* (New York: Paragon House, 1993).
¹⁵² MoE, IRI, *Farsi 3* (Tehran, Iran: ITPWC, 2015); Idem, *History 6*, 2004; Idem, *Geography 8* (Tehran, Iran: ITPWC, 2004).
¹⁵³ MoE, IRI, *Farsi 3* (Tehran, Iran: ITPWC, 2016), 102–3; Idem, *Social Studies 7* (Tehran, Iran: ITPWC, 2015), 148.
¹⁵⁴ MoE, *Farsi 1*, 2015; Idem, *Farsi 3*, 2016, 51; Idem, *Social Studies 4*, 2004, 129, 132.
¹⁵⁵ MoE, IRI, *Social Studies 7* (Tehran, Iran: ITPWC, 2015), 148.

through which many Iranian scientists have expressed their ideas and communicated their knowledge with the world.[156]

The exclusionary Persian and Shiʿa biases of the textbooks are accentuated by the construction of the ideal family as a revolutionary orderly unit that believes in freedom and supports the Islamic Revolution, the state, and the Supreme Leader.[157] The Islamic Revolution is reproduced through the efforts of exalted Shiʿa families where "children who [are exposed to correct moral upbringing], kindness and good deeds . . . will become useful and responsible individuals."[158] The Hashemi family, for example, represents a quintessential example of a caring ideal family, where their children are socialized in light of the teachings of Imam Khomeini. He is canonized as an anti-imperialist leader who led the Islamic uprising and established a nonviolent and egalitarian society based on universal and essential Islamic moral values (see Figures 4.2 and 4.3).[159]

The Hashemi family proudly displays the pictures of the past and present Supreme Leaders in the living room, highlighting the adoration it has for the revolutionary elite and legitimizing their religiously ordained authority (see Figure 4.3).[160] As a

Figure 4.2 Imam Khomeini during his sermon in Behesht-e Zahrah (The Paradise of Zahrah) Cemetery, in Tehran, Iran in 1978. *Source*: MoE, IRI, *Social Studies 9* (Tehran, Iran: ITPWC, 2016), 106.

---

[156] MoE, IRI, *Farsi 6* (Tehran, Iran: ITPWC, 2012), 25; Idem, *Farsi 3* (Tehran, Iran: ITPWC, 2013), 81.
[157] MoE, *Social Studies 4*, 2004, 130.
[158] Ibid., 108–9.
[159] MoE, IRI, *Social Studies 3* (Tehran, Iran: ITPWC, 2004); Idem, *History 8* (Tehran, Iran: ITPWC, 1999), 86; Idem, *History 8* (Tehran, Iran: ITPWC, 2002), 90; Idem, *History 8* (Tehran, Iran: ITPWC, 2004), 90.
[160] MoE, IRI, *Social Studies 3* (Tehran, Iran: ITPWC, 2009), 1.

خانواده‌ی هاشمی

Figure 4.3 The Hashemi Family. *Source*: MoE, IRI, *Social Studies 3* (Tehran, Iran: ITPWC, 2004), 1.

supporter of the state, this family also visits the shrines of Imam Khomeini and other male revolutionary martyrs of the revolution and the Iran–Iraq War. It is through the efforts of such a dedicated family that believes in the sanctity of the Supreme Leader, as a fair religiously learned male with a well-established vision of a just society, that the country progresses and plays a leadership position among the oppressed (Muslim) nations of the world in defeating Western imperialism and ending global injustices.[161] The curricula maintain that it is only through the actions and deeds of a leader who is rational, pious, and perfect, and is a knowledgeable Muslim scholar, a follower of the commands of Islam in all matters, and aware of the state of affairs of society, that the ideal Islamic society of Iran can be reproduced.[162] As the Hashemi family attends Friday Prayer, led by the current Supreme Leader, the main obligations of the ideal family are reinforced— resisting and destroying internal and external enemies of Iran whose

---

[161] MoE, IRI, *Social Studies 3* (Tehran, Iran: ITPWC, 2008), 32–4, 70–3.
[162] MoE, IRI, *Social Studies 5* (Tehran, Iran: ITPWC, 2004), 140.

aims are to destabilize the state[163] by sacrificing their lives for the goals of the eternal revolution: independence, freedom, and development.[164] As Mr. Hashemi passionately maintains, the role of the ideal citizen is also to free occupied Palestine from control of the enemies of Islam.[165] The ideal citizen has the moral, political, and ethical obligation to show his/her loyalty to the nation and the community of Islam by being prepared to fight the enemies of Islam and Iran and participate in the economic reconstruction of the country (the discourse of *jihād-i sūzandagī*, reconstruction crusade).[166] The discourse of *Ummat-e Islamī* functions as an important criterion in the construction of the ideal family as a transnational entity and the supporter of the Palestinian cause. Although the discourse of Palestine, as an example of the oppressed of the world, offers the ideal Iranian a textual space to affirm his/her liberatory pan-Islamic identity, this is achieved through a homogenized view of the Palestinian Other that ignores religious and political diversity within this category of sameness and difference. The leadership role of Iranians to free disenfranchised members of the *Ummat-e Islamī* is maintained through a Shi'a-centric approach to the discourse of Imam's line that excludes other forms of minority identities and worldviews.[167] Members of the Hashemi family love their religion and country, a message that is pervasive across the curricula.[168] Loving one's family members, loving Iranians and Iran, and caring for the oppressed of the Islamic world converge to produce an image of the ideal citizen that demonizes those Iranians who are critical of the leadership. They are labeled as dangerous insiders who promote outsiders' nefarious goals of destroying Iran and the Islamic-Iranian civilization.

The curricula offer a politicized image of the ideal family whose members' ideology is also defined through patriarchal and Shi'a-centric discourses of leadership, Imam's line, and *Velāyat-e Faqih*. The discourses of independence, freedom, and the Islamic Republic intersect and are also narrated through the voice(s) of the Supreme Leader(s) in depicting Iran as one's home and larger family that need to be protected from "interference by foreign enemies" and be developed to obstruct "foreign penetration inside the country to plunder [Iran's] wealth."[169] The curricula attribute the transfer of power and the administration of the country to the *mārdom* (people) of Iran to the politically conscious efforts and leadership of Imam Khomeini, who is identified as the father of the revolution and nation. Within the context of the curricula, however, the discourse of *mārdom* lumps all non-Persian ethnic groups into a unified and essentialized category of sameness without problematizing the hegemonic roles of Persians in the nation-building process.[170] The Hashemi family is also textually presented as a Persianized family—it is not identified as a Kurdish or Baluch family and has all the characteristics of the Persian cultural entity. They begin their relocation

---

[163] MoE, *Social Studies 3*, 2008, 37–8.
[164] Ibid., 32–4. See also Idem, *Social Studies 3* (Tehran, Iran: ITPWC, 2012).
[165] MoE, *Social Studies 3*, 2004, 57; Idem, *Social Studies 3*, 2000, 75–6.
[166] MoE, *Social Studies 3*, 2008, 56–7; Idem, *Social Studies 3*, 2004, 57; Idem, *Social Studies 3*, 2000, 75–6.
[167] MoE, *Social Studies 3*, 2004, 33.
[168] MoE, *Farsi 2*, 2015, 79; Idem, *Farsi 3*, 2015, 73–4.
[169] MoE, *Social Studies 5*, 132; See also Idem, *Social Studies 8* (Tehran, Iran: ITPWC, 2004), 23–9; Idem, *Farsi 1* (Iran: ITPWC, 2004), 100–101.
[170] MoE, *Social Studies 5*, 2004, 133.

across Iran from the exact geographical space where the founding nation of Iran, the Persian/Aryan tribe, settled the country some 4,000 years ago and established the first world empire[171] and also visit the tombs of celebrated "Persian" poets who are idolized as Iranian cultural artistic/political/scientific contributors of the world.[172]

The normalization and standardization of the desired middle-class Persian cultural capital of the ideal family, as a religiously conscious nuclear family and an urban household with a number of essential consumer items, are also framed through the ideological code of whiteness,[173] which functions as a trace in defining and setting the limits of who belongs to the ideal citizen category. It turns the SIF into an apolitical racialized framework of exclusion through which the Indo-European origin of Iranians is sustained. This is especially the case since (1) non-Persians are always depicted through the discourses of *'ashayir* (nomadic tribes), ethnic clothing, or color of skin (e.g., Afro-Iranians)[174] and (2) Iran, as the symbol of one's macrofamily, is framed as a white Persian-speaking country in representations of racial/linguistic diversity in Asia, where whiteness and Persian language symbolize and affirm Iran's Aryan, Persian, and Indo-European identity (See Map 4.1).[175] Through dehistoricized racialized categories in representing population diversities in Iran, Asia, Europe, Africa, Australia, and the Americas, the curricula associate whiteness with progress, thus superior to other racialized groups,[176] without accounting for its negative racist/chauvinistic consequences for non-Persian/nonwhite Iranians. It is through the discourse of whiteness that curricula authors frame who belongs to the category of the ideal citizen/family. The curricula treats nonwhite Iranians and non-Persians as "colonized subjects" who must come to view themselves based "on the colonizer's terms" of reference[177] and whose homogenized love for the multiracial and

---

[171] MoE, IRI, *Geography 7* (Tehran, Iran: ITPWC, 2004); Idem, *Social Studies 4*, 2004; Idem, *Social Studies 5*, 2004; Idem, *Social Studies 7*, 2015.
[172] MoE, *Farsi 2*, 2016, 80–3; Idem, *Social Studies 3*, 2004, 7; Idem, *Social Studies 3*, 2009, 10, 65–8.
[173] MoE, *Farsi 1*, 2015, 1–6; See also Idem, *Social Studies 3*, 2004, 1–3.
[174] MoE, *Farsi 1*, 2004, 48; Idem, *Farsi 1*, 2016, 44, 47, 65, 67, 79; Idem, *Farsi 3* (Tehran, Iran: ITPWC, 2004), 106; Idem, *Farsi 3*, 2016, 55; Idem, *Farsi 5* (Tehran, Iran: ITPWC, 2004), 179–80; Idem, *Social Studies 3*, 2004, 12–14; Idem, *Social Studies 4* (Tehran, Iran: ITPWC, 1999), 137; MoE, *Social Studies 5*, 1993, 214; MoE, *Social Studies 6* (Tehran, Iran: ITPWC, 2004), 22.
[175] See "The Map of Racial Diversity in Asia," in MoE, *Social Studies 5* (Tehran, Iran: ITPWC, 1993), 67; "Illustrations 27, 28, 29," in Idem, *Social Studies 5* (Tehran, Iran: ITPWC, 2001), 50; "The Map of the Distribution of Languages and Races in Asia," in Idem, *Geography 7* (Tehran, Iran: ITPWC, 2009), 16; Idem, *Social Studies 7* (Tehran, Iran: ITPWC, 2014), 115.
[176] See Amir Mirfakhraie, "Racialization of Asia, Africa and the Americas, and the Construction of the Ideal Iranian Citizen: Local and Global Representations of Colonialism, Geography, Culture and Religious Diversity in Iranian School Textbooks," in *Africa's Many Divides and Africa's Future: Pursuing Nkrumah's Vision of Pan-Africanism in an Era of Globalization*, eds. Charles Quist-Adade and Vincent Dodoo (Newcastle upon Tyne, UK: Cambridge Scholars Publishing, 2015), 217–53; Idem, "Constructions of Phobias, Fractured and Stigmatized Selves, and the Ideal Citizen in Iranian School Textbooks," in *Manufacturing Phobias: The Political Production of Fear in Theory and Practice*, eds. Hisham Ramadan and Jeff Shantz (Toronto, ON: University of Toronto Press, Scholarly Publishing Division, 2016), 69–115; Idem, "A Social Justice Approach to Iranian School Textbooks as Racist Frameworks of Othering and a Critique of the Imperialism of Anti-Imperialism," in *Iran's Struggles for Social Justice: Economics, Agency, Justice, Activism*, ed. Peyman Vahabzadeh (New York: Palgrave Macmillan, 2017), 99–125.
[177] Alireza Asgharzadeh, *Iran and the Challenge of Diversity: Islamic Fundamentalism, Aryanist Racism, and Democratic Struggles* (Gordonsville, VA: Palgrave Macmillan, 2007), 37.

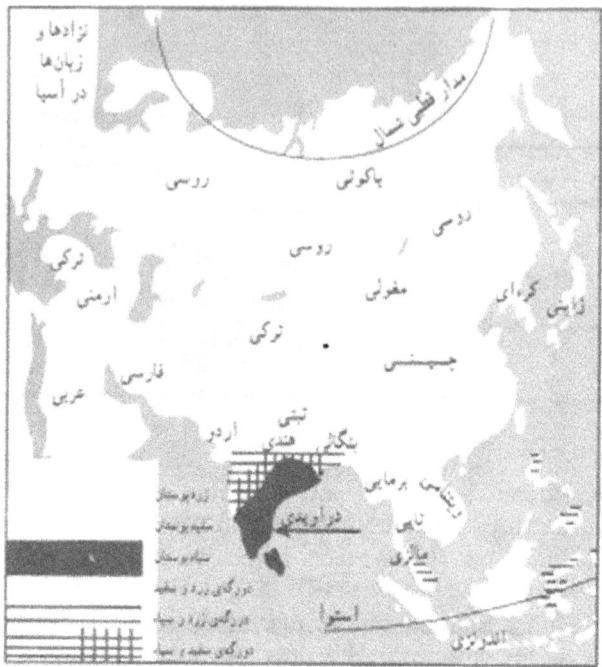

Map 4.1 "The Map of the Distribution of Races and Languages in Asia." In this map, the color *yellow* is used to represent the yellow race, *white* is used for the white race, and *black* for the black race. An example of the black race is the Dravidian group in India (see the arrow on the map). Arabs and Iranians are constructed as white-skinned. Iranians are also constructed as belonging to the Indo-European category, whose language is Persian. Sources: MoE, IRI, *Geography 7* (Tehran, Iran: ITPWC, 2004), 16; MoE, IRI, *Social Studies 8* (Tehran, Iran: ITPWC, 2017), 115.

multicultural Iranian nation is normalized through the discourses *Īrān-dūstī* (loving Iran) and caring (e.g., showing affection for one's family member) that require all Iranians to cherish and embrace the Aryan heritage/Pars cultural/linguistic artfacts, as its quintessential defining characteristics. For example, in a lesson titled, "Our Country," the ideological and political message is reiterated that "Iran belongs to all [students]" and they are all Iranians regardless of where they live.[178] This discourse of loving Iran is imagined in light of other representations of Iran, such as "*khāk-i pak Iran*" (the pure soil of Iran)[179] and the "land of purities and heroism,"[180] that assume Iran has been untouched by foreign invasions and their cultural influences. In such lessons, students are constructed as both the subjects and objects of the lesson: "We like (*dūst-dārīm*) Iran and Iranians."[181] However, the subject "we" does not textually

---

[178] MoE, *Farsi 1* (Tehran, Iran: ITPWC, 2004), 118.
[179] MoE, *Farsi 1*, 51.
[180] MoE, *Farsi 3* (Tehran, Iran: ITPWC, 2004), 104.
[181] MoE, *Farsi 1*, 118.

include the historical memories of all Iranians, especially those ethnic minorities that view themselves as exploited and discriminated against. Despite the fact that the unquestionable universal love by students for their nation and country is portrayed in light of the construction of Iran as an ethnically and a racially diverse society, the category "we" is an exclusive marker that is informed by cultural practices, language, religion, and value system of the Persian "majority." For example, in the lesson, "Iran," children of different racial backgrounds (white, brown, and black) dressed in different ethnic clothing represent Iran as a peaceful and happy multiracial and multicultural country. This seemingly inclusive image of Iranian cultural and racial diversity frames a homogenized/essentialized and exclusive understanding of the "we" category that does not critically reflect on the history of cultural, racial, religious, and ethnic inequalities and validate such oppositional voices.[182] Regardless of students' racial and cultural backgrounds, the ultimate roles of the ideal citizen and his/her obligations to the country and the state are narrated for student early in their education: "*Ābād* [prosperous], *Ābād, Iran Ābād, Bīdār* [vigilant], *Bīdār, Iranī Bīdār.*"[183] The curricula institutionalize the act of protecting Iran against invasion by outsiders as an important function of the ideal family and citizen, a message that also informs the content of the lesson, "Soldier," in *Farsi 1*: "Iran, Iran, perpetual and lasting, with the combatant soldier."[184]

The curricula normalize and narrate the desired ideal cultural, religious, and ideological capital through an approach to the historiography and political economy of Iran that frames the transformation of Iran in light of four major epochs: (1) the birth of the nation after the migration of the Aryans from Central Asia, (2) the rebirth of Iran after the introduction of Islam, (3) the reawakening of Muslim Iranians as followers of Shiʿa Imams, and (4) the final rebirth of Iran during/after the establishment of the Islamic Republic.[185] The ideal middle-class, Persian(ized), Shiʿa, and revolutionary family functions as an evaluative criterion of sameness and difference and institutionalizes the ideological codes of leadership, *Velāyat-e Faqih*, the Aryan thesis, freedom, independence, martyrdom, and Shiʿa and Pars identities that, in turn, sanitize the diversity of the social, political, and economic structures of power and family formations into manufactured homogenized entities. These ideological codes perpetuate and formalize a monolithic bias through which the ideal family is celebrated as the only essential reflection of "normalcy."

Conclusion

The Standard Iranian Family is an idealized patriarchal, Islamic-centric, Persian-centric, rights-oriented, orderly, cooperative, and compassionate unit of sameness

---

[182] MoE, *Farsi 1* (Tehran, Iran: ITPWC, 2015), 44.
[183] MoE, *Farsi 1*, 44; Idem, *Farsi 1* (Tehran, Iran: ITPWC, 2004), 48.
[184] MoE, *Farsi 1*, 49.
[185] See Mirfakhraie, "Racialization of Asia, Africa and the Americas"; Idem, "Constructions of Phobias, Fractured and Stigmatized Selves"; Idem, "A Social Justice Approach to Iranian School Textbooks."

through which the nation, country, and *Ummat-e Islamī* are discursively reproduced as imagined macrofamilies. Love and care for family members, the nation, and the Iranian leadership are narrated as universal and necessary components of a healthy family and as preconditions for its members to accomplish their collective responsibilities and to achieve their various predetermined gendered tasks.[186] The ideal family is a socio-ideological-political discursive formation that constructs the ethno–racially–religiously diverse student body into a monotony of characteristics. It is a Persian-centric and Shiʿa-centric perspective that ignores or downplays the differences and power differentials that separate them into unequal subject-positions based on conflicting factors of race, class, ethnicity, language, ability, age, sexuality, gender, and religion. The SIF is informed by the racialized Orientalist discourse of the *Aryan*. The Aryan discourse intersects with other conflicting ideological codes of *Ummat-e Islamī*, ḥijāb, marriage, whiteness, tribes, ethnic clothing, color of skin, martyrdom, development, independence, freedom, caring, and *Velāyat-e Faqih*. The textbooks, further, frame these ideological codes in light of other patriarchal discursive formations such as hegemonic motherhood, cult of domesticity, self-sacrifice, and unselfishness. Monolithic, microstructural, conservative, racist, classist, ableist, and heterosexist biases intertextually and discursively assume and objectify how superior the ideal Persian, Shiʿa, and male self is in relation to various forms of internal and external otherness. The curricula construct the ideal family as a Persian, white, Aryan, Shiʿa, middle-class, patriarchal, rational, able-bodied, and heterosexual subject-position whose main obligations are to defend the boundaries of Islamic Iran; promote its industrialization, progress, and economic growth; and establish a cohesive Mahdavi society.

Iranian school textbooks, as (trans)national ideological discursive units, provide students with ethical and politicizing pedagogies[187] that situate them not as subjects with conflicting agencies but as transnational homogenized Muslim objects who are the followers of the Imam's line. As consent-producing discursive formations of power, they do not reflect the varied historical memories of women, ethnic and religious minorities, people with disabilities, working classes, elderly, and certainly not gay, lesbian, and transgendered individuals and families. The curricula do not offer students critical and multicentric standpoints outside the dominant Islamic-Iranian ideological codes.[188] They legitimate, normalize, and justify patriarchal, racialized, heteronormative, ableist, and sexist ruling ideas about the family and gender relations that reinforce the power of the Islamic leadership. To develop effective anti-oppressive, -sexist, -ageist, -classist, -ableist, and -hegemonic and decolonizing subaltern forms of knowledge, Iranian curricula writers need to account for how they exclude and silence the historical memories of diverse forms of families, women, and men in constructions of difference and the narration of the ideal family and the nation.

---

[186] Literacy Movement Organization, *Social Studies*, 6.
[187] Henry Giroux, *Neoliberalism's War on Higher Education* (Chicago, IL: Haymarket Books, 2014), 43.
[188] Hillary Janks, *Literacy and Power* (New York: Routledge, 2010), 22.

Part Two

Online Dating, Hymenoplasty, and Assisted Reproductive Technologies

5

Negotiating Intimacy through Social Media

Challenges and Opportunities for Muslim Women in Iran

Vahideh Golzard and Cristina Miguel

Introduction

Over the past decade, social media have dramatically altered interactions in Iran. For Iranian women, social media have allowed a space to exchange information and participate in an online, globalized world. For many urban Iranian women, social media have opened up new ways to engage in a wider public sphere that might not have been possible in offline spaces. Social media platforms have also been used by Iranian women as a "method of education that would bring creativity and inter personal relationship strength."[1] As Akhavan states "the internet has not only created a unique opportunity for the missing participation of Iranian women to engage in the public sphere, but it has also allowed them to be active in society as journalists, filmmakers, and scientists."[2]

Globalization and the new media are both playing significant roles in the emergence of ideas and discourses in the public sphere, and in reshaping ideas about women's participation in society.[3] Global changes in communication technologies have also contributed to a new flexibility for women's voices and spaces. In particular, the internet has played an especially important role in the economic, social, cultural, and intellectual empowerment of women who had previously been denied access to knowledge. The emergence of globalization at around the time of the 1979 Islamic Revolution has transformed the social lives of Iranian women in multiple ways. During the revolution, many of them joined the revolutionary movement under the leadership

---

[1] Mohtasham Ghaffari, Sakineh Rakhshanderou, Yadollah Mehrabi, and Afsoon Tizvir, "Using Social Network of Telegram for Education on Continued Breastfeeding and Complementary Feeding of Children Among Mothers: A Successful Experience from Iran," *International Journal of Pediatrics* 5, no. 7 (2017): 5275–86.
[2] Niki Akhavan, "The Iranian Internet: Interventions in New Media and Old Politics" (PhD, Santa Cruz, 2007).
[3] Loubna H. Skalli, "Communicating Gender in the Public Sphere: Women and Information Technologies in the MENA," *Journal of Middle East Women's Studies* 2, no. 2 (2006): 35–59.

of Ayatollah Khomeini. Since then, the participation of women as important social and political agents in the Iranian society has been remarkable. Despite the imposition of regressive laws against them, such as gender segregation in public spheres (e.g., universities and schools) and compulsory *ḥijāb* (veiling), the Islamic government has encouraged women and girls to get an education and participate in society while remaining within the bounds of Islamic practices.[4] With the increase in female education, magazines such as *Zanan* (Women) have played a crucial role in raising women's awareness while also increasing their visibility and access to equal rights in both public and private spheres.[5] In 2001, the activities of female bloggers increased the visibility of Iranian women, including Tehran-based journalists and activists. Weblogs became popular among urban-educated Iranians and enabled Iranian middle classes to talk openly about social, cultural, and political issues, as well as their personal lives and aspirations.[6] In recent years, female bloggers have played a significant role in giving prominence to women's voices. Micheal Keren suggests that blogs may help to build the recognition for Muslim Iranian women that they miss in ordinary public life: "It is their window to liberty."[7]

In the context of Iranian society, Amir-Ebrahimi has argued that, even with government censorship, young Iranians have increasingly used social media platforms—mainly blogs and Facebook—to meet new people online: "Despite effective filtering of the Internet, self-disclosure through social media has permitted [the] younger generation to slip beyond the visible boundaries of the religious social community, encountering other people with different points of view, including members of the opposite sex, [and] to know one another."[8] Some studies[9] show that a remarkable amount of internet use in Iran involves intimate heterosexual relationships. This means that in Iranian society, where the level of control and surveillance is very high and interaction between males and females is strictly controlled, people are eager to search for partners online.[10]

In recent years, most research into practices of online intimacy has been conducted in the United States, Australia, or the United Kingdom. Some studies have focused on teenagers or college students,[11] while others have investigated the use of social media

---

[4] Asemeh Ghasemi, "Women's Experiences of Work in the Iranian Broadcast Media (IRIB): Motivations, Challenges, and Achievements," *Feminist Media Studies* 13, no. 5 (2013): 840–9.
[5] Azadeh Kian, "Women and Politics in Post-islamist Iran: The Gender Conscious Drive to Change," *British Journal of Middle Eastern Studies* 24, no. 1 (1997): 75–96.
[6] Masserat Amir-Ebrahimi, "Transgression in Narration: The Lives of Iranian Women in Cyberspace," *Journal of Middle East Women's Studies* 4, no. 3 (2008): 89–111.
[7] Michael Keren, *Blogosphere: The New Political Arena* (Plymouth: Lexington Books, 2006).
[8] Masserat Amir-Ebrahimi, "Blogging from Qom, Behind Walls and Veils," *Comparative Studies of South Asia, Africa and the Middle East* 28, no. 2 (2008): 235–49.
[9] Ehsan Shahghasemi, Hosna Masoumi, Manijeh Akhavan, and Bijan Tafazzoli. "Liquid Love in Iran: A Mixed Method Approach," *Mediterranean Journal of Social Science* 6, no. 1 (2015): 138–44.
[10] Ibid.
[11] Sonia Livingstone, "Taking Risky Opportunities in Youthful Content Creation: Teenagers' Use of Social Networking Sites for Intimacy, Privacy and Self-Expression," *New Media & Society* 10, no. 3 (2008); Danah Boyd, *It's Complicated: The Social Lives of Networked Teens* (New Haven: Yale University Press, 2014).

for intimate relationships among adults.[12] The predominance of research focused on these countries has led Baym to argue that there is a need for additional studies on the use of social media by adults from different countries.[13] This chapter is intended to fill this gap with regard to the Iranian social media landscape. In particular, it aims to offer insights into the ways in which Muslim women use social media platforms (blogs, Facebook, and dating sites) to overcome the boundaries of physical space and to create intimate relationships online. We consider both the challenges and the opportunities that different social media platforms offer to Muslim Iranian women as a way to negotiate their personal relationships. The ethnographic fieldwork was conducted in August and September 2011, in Tehran, where the internet is popular among educated and middle-class urban Iranians, who can afford the cost of its regular use. We examined digital intimacy from the point of view of Tehrani women, who have more opportunities to access the internet than women who live in rural areas with less internet access. Although the internet has opened up new forms of visibility and networks for Iranian women, this opportunity is only available to affluent families and those with high incomes and "sufficient cultural resonance."[14] Access to the internet requires some basic elements, such as a computer, the ability to use it (computer literacy), and access to telecommunication systems. These elements are not equally available to the diverse groups of Iranian women. This research is based on online participant observation, and ten semistructured interviews with female Muslim users of social media between the ages of eighteen and forty. Participants were identified as users of Facebook, blogs, or dating sites and were selected by the snowballing sampling technique. The study analyzes and compares participants' online activities on these different social media platforms. The fact that interviewees were contacted through common friends helped us establish trusting relationships with them.

Being trusted by the interviewee, as Kember and Zylinska note, is essential to developing rapport, and the private environment of the interview also encourages participants to open up: "The intimacy of one-on-one interviews can also provide informants permission to speak about subjects they may not feel comfortable discussing with other group members."[15] The semistructured interviews allowed interviewers to access the participants' mindsets and provided insight into their attitudes and experiences. We analyzed the qualitative data collected through participant observation and semistructured interviews by using thematic analysis, which allowed us to identify key themes and create connections among the ideas gathered by different data-collection techniques. "By using Thematic Analysis, it is possible to link the various concepts and opinions of participants and compare them with the data that has been gathered in different situation[s] at different times from other or the same

---

[12] Millsom Henry-Waring and Jo Barraket, "Dating & Intimacy in the 21st Century: The Use of Online Dating Sites in Australia," *International Journal of Emerging Technologies & Society* 6, no. 1 (2008); Nancy K. Baym, *Personal Connections in the Digital Age* (Cambridge: Polity, 2010); Alexander Lambert, *Intimacy and Friendship on Facebook* (Houndmills: Palgrave Macmillan, 2013).
[13] Baym, *Personal Connections in the Digital Age*.
[14] Barbara M. Kennedy and David Bell, *The Cybercultures Reader* (London and New York: Routledge, 2000).
[15] Sarah Kember and Joanna Zylinska, *Life After New Media: Mediation as a Vital Process* (Cambridge: MIT Press, 2012).

participants during the project."[16] After identifying the main themes, we initiated the data reduction process. Following Miles and Huberman,[17] Alhojailan has explained that data reduction, the first step in analyzing data, includes three processes: "selecting, simplifying and transforming the data."[18] After reducing the data, we chose the interview extracts that in our view best represented the key themes. Finally, we made connections among the themes and interpreted the data.[19]

We have examined our interviewees' attitudes about social media activities to understand the extent to which Facebook, blogs, or dating sites empower them in the context of their intimate relationships. Experiencing intimacy is paramount to one's sense of well-being.[20] Participants in this study reported that their use of social media increased their emotional well-being, because these platforms allowed them to express themselves and create new friendships with like-minded people. A few participants even found their partners through dating sites. In their opinion, such platforms were more effective for finding a partner than face-to-face dating because they offered more options from which to choose a compatible partner. However, this freedom comes with certain restrictions due to censorship: internet users can face problems accessing banned social media services (e.g., Facebook, YouTube, and Twitter). In fact, since the disputed presidential elections in June 2009, the Iranian government has been trying to control oppositions' websites and blogs. There are also other barriers, such as security issues, computer illiteracy, and lack of knowledge, all of which reinforce the exclusion of women from social media. In the next section, we examine how social media platforms have emerged as tools for both control and agency for Muslim Iranian women.

Social Media Use by Iranian Women

After the 1979 Islamic Revolution, the visibility of Iranian women was reshaped through a set of conservative norms and a legal system that created a new form of public space for them. Following the changes in the social and political situation in Iran and the Islamization of society after 1979, Sadeghi explains that the Islamic government restricted aspects of women's public and private lives.[21] Mohammadi highlights how the Islamic government created boundaries between men and women as soon as it was

---

[16] Mohammed I. Alhojailan, "Thematic Analysis: A Critical Review of Its Process and Evaluation," *West East Journal of Social Sciences* 1, no. 1 (2012): 39–47.

[17] Matthew B. Miles and A. Michael Huberman *Qualitative Data Analysis: An Expanded Sourcebook* (London: Sage, 1994).

[18] Alhojailan, "Thematic Analysis: A Critical Review of Its Process and Evaluation" (2012).

[19] As Bazeley (2009) asserts, the most important phase of thematic analysis is contextualizing and connecting the themes, identifying patterns emanating from the data and building a coherent argument. Pat Bazeley, "Analysing Qualitative Data: More than 'Identifying Themes,'" *Malaysian Journal of Qualitative Research* 2, no. 2 (2009): 6–22.

[20] Lynn Jamieson, *Intimacy: Personal Relationships in Modern Societies* (Cambridge: Polity Press, 1998).

[21] Fatemeh Sadeghi, "Negotiating with Modernity: Young Women and Sexuality in Iran," *Comparative Studies of South Asia, Africa and the Middle East* 28, no. 2 (2008): 250–9.

established: "Males and females were separated in higher education classes where [as] the classes had been mixed before, females were barred from some professions, such as the judiciary and singing, women were forbidden to participate in some sports and disallowed to watch men on the sport fields."[22]

Premarital sexual relations were banned. Iranian authorities, who follow strict Islamic laws, encouraged marriage both as a matter of social prestige and to prevent premarital sexual intercourse. Two types of marriages were legitimate under Islamic law: formal marriage (*nekāh*) and temporary marriage (*sigheh*). Traditionally, formal marriages are arranged through negotiations between families of prospective brides and grooms.[23] Unlike formal marriage, temporary marriage is a contract between a man and an unmarried woman (because only men can marry more than one partner under Islamic law), for a specified length of time.[24] As Ghodsi explains, after the Islamic Revolution (1979), the government promoted temporary marriage as a way of controlling people's sexual practices.[25] Although this type of marriage is legal and religiously allowed, Iranian society does not culturally accept it as a good social practice: "Iranian people commonly reject it as illegitimate and morally reprehensible."[26]

Over the past few decades, dramatic changes have occurred in patterns of marriage. Although the legal age of marriage in Iran is thirteen for girls and fifteen for boys, in the last few years, the average age at marriage has increased to twenty-two for women and twenty-seven for men due to high unemployment rates and soaring housing prices. In addition, more than 22 percent of marriages among Iranians end in divorce—a very high rate compared to the past—and the rate is even higher in Tehran.[27] According to Hatam, these changes are due to transformations of relationships between generations and between men and women; rapid urbanization; better access to education, especially for girls (nearly 60 percent of university students are female); the emergence of new options regarding marriage; and changes in marriage and divorce laws.[28] Because of the increase in the median age of marriage and the high divorce rate, the government has launched officially sanctioned dating sites. The purpose of these websites is not only to reduce the divorce rate but also to encourage young Iranians to find compatible partners within the framework of traditional religious values. For instance, Tebyan is a religious, state-run dating site that promotes marriage according to Islamic rules. Tebyan users enter their personal information, and their profiles can then be matched with compatible partners. According to the policy of this website, a cleric intervenes in the first meeting to give an assessment. If the meeting is successful, the

---

[22] Ali Mohammidi, *Iran Encountering Globalization: Problems and Prospects* (London: Routledge, 2003).
[23] Shahla Haeri, *Law of Desire: Temporary Marriage in Shi'i Iran* (New York: Syracuse University Press, 1989).
[24] Soraya Tremayne, "Modernity and Early Marriage in Iran: A View from Within," *Journal of Middle East Women's Studies* 2, no. 1 (2006): 65–94.
[25] Tamilla F. Ghodsi, "Tying a Slipknot: Temporary Marriages in Iran," *Michigan Journal of International Law* 15, no. 2 (1994): 645–86.
[26] Ibid.
[27] Nassim Hatam, "Iran: Internet Dating Website Launched by State," http://www.bbc.co.uk/news/world-middle-east-32833363.
[28] Ibid.

family is later involved in the marriage arrangement.[29] During the last decade, despite censorship, the growth of internet usage in Iran has introduced new possibilities to the younger generation. Iranian women have become increasingly active bloggers and Facebook users. According to Shirazi, since the emergence of the first blog in Iran in September 2001, women have become an important part of the Iranian blogosphere, the so-called *Weblogestan*.[30] The number of female bloggers is less than male bloggers. However, their personal writing has given value to their blogs, where they usually talk about their inner thoughts and their everyday life.[31] Blogs and Facebook offer young, middle-class women a new environment to voice their opinions and to seek new kinds of friendships. Amir-Ebrahimi argues that despite the political and sociocultural restrictions in Iran, gender boundaries, and conflicts between cultural tradition and modernization, women can write about their personal and private lives in their blogs.[32] They can write under a pseudonym or a constructed identity in anonymous blogs, which allows them more freedom for self-expression and enables them to create meaningful relationships without any fear of "real world" consequences, including persecution. Nevertheless, Graham and Khosravi have noted that "not all private details are cloaked in anonymity,"[33] insofar as people usually display their real identities on Facebook. Graham and Khosravi observe how social media platforms permit access to one's private life:

Some Iranians have written about their lives and scanned in their family photo albums. It is unusual for Iranians to show family albums to complete strangers. Indeed, one conspicuous feature of Iranian houses is the clear spatial distinction that creates relative degrees of privacy. The private space in urban Iranian homes emphasizes looking inward. In traditional Iranian architecture, the house is divided into a private space, *andaruni* (the family quarter), and a semiprivate *biruni* (where nonfamily members are entertained). The internet is allowed to enter the *andaruni* like kin or close friends.[34]

The separation of the private and public spheres is deeply embedded in the culture and history of Iran. However, the lives of Iranians after the Islamic Revolution have been significantly affected by a set of conservative rules based on "commanding what is just and forbidding what is wrong (*amr-e be ma'ruf va nah-ye az monker*), a basic tenet of Islamic jurisprudence and a moral obligation for every Muslim."[35] With the establishment of the Morality Bureau in 1979, the Islamic government enforced a special conservative Islamic code of behavior in the public sphere. But with the advent of the internet in Iran in the 1990s, and as Iranians gained access to a wider and more

---

[29] Ibid.
[30] Farid Shirazi, "Free and Open Source Software Versus Internet Content Filtering and Censorship: A Case Study," *Journal of Systems and Software* 85, no. 4 (2012): 920–31.
[31] Ibid.
[32] Amir-Ebrahimi, "Transgression in Narration: The Lives of Iranian Women in Cyberspace."
[33] Mark Graham and Shahram Khosravi, "Reordering Public and Private in Iranian Cyberspace: Identity, Politics and Mobilization," *Identities: Global Studies in Culture Power* 9, no. 2 (2010): 219–46.
[34] Ibid.
[35] Azam Khatam, "The Islamic Republic's Failed Quest for the Spotless City," *Middle East Report* 250 (2009): 44–9, https://merip.org/2009/03/the-islamic-republics-failed-quest-for-the-spotless-city/. Retrieved on September 25, 2020.

open public sphere, policies designed to enforce moral behavior gradually became ineffectual. For this reason, together with the desire for political control over virtual space, the Iranian government took measures to censor internet usage.

Internet service providers (ISPs) do not have unmediated access to the internet. Access is possible only through proxy servers, which are maintained by government-controlled telecommunication companies.[36] Goldstein and colleagues have noted that the government can use these proxy servers for surveillance: "A proxy server can be used by the authorities to track which computer terminals are accessing which websites and for how long."[37] Iranian authorities filter materials that promote Western culture and values, because they consider them harmful to public morality. The authorities have serious concerns about websites they call "illegal and immoral" because they believe such websites encourage sex before marriage, which is unlawful under Iranian-Islamic law.[38] The government also pressures web publishers to remove and impose limits on "blasphemous" and "immoral" content, such as information about women's rights and gay and lesbian issues.[39] In Iran, conservative Islamic views and notions about gender roles are a significant barrier to internet access. This censorship has consequences for Iranian society, especially for people who lack sufficient resources, because wealthier people can afford to buy professional devices to defeat censorship and have the advantage of greater computer literacy.[40] They also know the techniques of using proxy servers to visit blocked websites. Many social media services (e.g., Facebook and Twitter) are blocked in Iran; internet users have to access their accounts through illegal proxies. Blogs and dating sites need to obtain an authorization for publishing, and specific laws regulate their content.[41]

In addition, Iranian women face online harassment when interacting with strangers. Potential interpersonal harms have been associated with self-exposure on social media platforms.[42] According to Halder and Jaishankar, after children, the most vulnerable targets on the internet are women, especially in social networking sites (SNSs), which are one of the most notorious places for harassment. Leung and Lee argue that, in comparison to anonymous blogs, SNSs are most likely to be used by harassers to target women, because female users spend more time on SNSs. Online harassers often ask victims to disclose personal information; as Leung and Lee explain, women often "encounter a lot of unwelcome solicitation of personal or private information such as names, pictures, and

---

[36] Eric Goldstein, *The Internet in the Mideast and North Africa: Free Expression and Censorship* (Washington, DC: Human Rights Watch, 1999).
[37] Ibid.
[38] Hatam, "Iran: Internet Dating Website Launched by State."
[39] Ian Brown, "Internet Censorship: Be Careful What You Ask For," *Social Science Research Network* (2008).
[40] Farid Shirazi, "The Contribution of ICT to Freedom and Democracy: An Empirical Analysis of Archival Data on the Middle East," *The Electronic Journal of Information Systems in Developing Countries* 35, no. 1 (2008): 1–24.
[41] Babak Rahimi, "Censorship and the Islamic Republic: Two Modes of Regulatory Measures for Media in Iran," *The Middle East Journal* 69, no. 3 (2015): 357–78.
[42] Debarati Halder and Jaishankar Karuppannan, "Cyber Socializing and Victimization of Women," *The Journal on Victimization* 12, no. 3 (2009): 5–26.

phone."[43] In what follows, we explore how Tehrani women we met use social media to create intimate relationships and how they deal with the potential risks they face online.

Risks and Barriers in the Search for Intimacy Online

According to our findings, Iranian women have shown an increasing interest in social media, mainly Facebook and blogs. However, a number of barriers limit their participation online. These barriers range from economic restrictions to internet access and security issues, such as fear of online harassment. The least expensive computer in Iran costs around 4,500,000 rials (US $450), and the average monthly cost for internet access without a telephone line is 350,000 rials (US $35), while the average annual urban household income is 25,831,527 rials (US $2,583 annually or US $215 per month).[44] Thus, lack of resources to access a good internet connection is one of the issues most emphasized by participants as a barrier to social media use. For example, Mahsa, age thirty-six, Facebook user said, "The high cost of Internet subscription has led me to use the internet less frequently. I spend one hour per week online and I use low-speed Internet service, which is much cheaper." Low-speed internet service and regular disconnections from the internet provider significantly discourage Mahsa from developing a profound interest in the regular use of this modern technology. In Iran, the Asymmetric Digital Subscriber Line (ADSL) service is not available in all areas and is more expensive than dial-up connections. Due to poor infrastructure and technical problems in some areas, there is no cable for the ADSL system. The low speed of the internet means that some women who participated in this study were not able to spend a substantial amount of time online.

In addition, some participants argued that privacy is difficult to maintain for those who use popular social media services. Participants often reported their fear of online harassment. Some participants complained about receiving abusive posts and personal messages after they befriended unfamiliar people with the aim of developing new friendships. Sahar (age twenty-three, Facebook user), who shares her thoughts on her Facebook wall, and Mahshid (age forty, a blogger and Facebook user), who writes about her emotions in her blog, said that they received threatening comments from some readers, making them concerned for their safety. Online harassment in the form of unpleasant comments and misbehavior were the main challenges for Shirin (age thirty-seven, Facebook user with a master's degree) and Sahar, both of whom were single and frequent Facebook users. For instance, Shirin explained that someone harassed and blackmailed her. Shirin and Sahar added that online harassment discouraged them from sharing their feelings and personal information such as photos or videos. In particular, some participants reported that they had experienced online sexual harassment. Mehri (age twenty-nine, Facebook user), a single mother who works as a secretary, noted that although Facebook had a positive impact on her social life, it was not a completely safe environment. Mehri started using social media ten

---

[43] Louis Leung and Paul S. N. Lee, "The Influences of Information Literacy, Internet Addiction and Parenting Styles on Internet Risks," *New Media & Society* 14, no. 1 (2012): 1–21.
[44] Gholam Khiabany, *Iranian Media: The Paradox of Modernity* (New York: Routledge, 2009).

years ago to access reliable information and connect with other people. She said she had received messages on Facebook inviting her to participate in erotic discussions. Mehri also noted that she had received unwelcome propositions to have sexual relations. Receiving sexual photographs and pornographic images from strangers and, in some cases, even threats of a sexual nature, were some of the problems that participants faced. To prevent online harassers from approaching them, these women engaged in self-censorship and tried to categorize and select their audiences in the online environment. Most of them explained that they only allowed close and intimate friends to access shared personal information. As Sahar said, "I always decide with whom I can share Facebook posts." Likewise, Shirin, who usually spends around twenty-five hours a week on Facebook, is vigilant when sharing personal information, such as photos and videos, because she fears being blackmailed. Shirin has learned to customize the privacy of her posts and photo albums using friends' lists on Facebook:

> Each time I manage to control my privacy settings while posting any comments or photos, as most of the time I wish to send my posts only to certain people not to all my Facebook friends. By this method, I can reduce the chance of becoming a victim of online abuse and cybercrime.

Participants have learned that self-censorship and privacy settings can prevent wider audiences from accessing their content and thus avoid receiving unwelcome comments from strangers or being blackmailed. Apart from the lack of adequate resources to purchase a fast internet connection (as they all access the internet from home), online sexual harassment was the main issue that affected women's regular participation in social media services. Despite that, many embraced social media as an opportunity. In the following section, we discuss the impact of social media interaction on the psychological well-being of Iranian women, insofar as social media platforms allowed them the opportunity to express their thoughts and feelings, communicate with friends at a deeper level, and create friendships with like-minded people who can support them in their everyday struggles.

Online Intimacy in Iran: The Digital *Andaruni*

Mahshid, a forty-year-old single woman, is a teacher at a school in Tehran. She is an active, anonymous blogger who uses a pseudonym, but she uses her real identity on Facebook. On her blog, Mahshid was eager to write about sensitive issues such as discriminatory laws against women, inequality, as well as men's privileged position in society and the problem of drug addiction among young Iranians caused by high unemployment rates and poverty. Mahshid stressed that the blogosphere was a great place to interact with people from different backgrounds and learn about their experiences. In Mahshid's view, the blog was a tool to express feelings and personal desires that were not allowed or tolerated in the "real" world. She explained how she used her blog to overcome governmental constraints and talk about women's issues in public:

> Due to the patriarchal culture and governmental restrictions in Iran, talking and writing about women's lives and such matters in public space is not tolerated.

Therefore, the blog, more than other forms of media, provides an opportunity to write about women's issues.

Most participants stated that blogs allowed them to voice their own opinions and share their feelings and interests with close friends. For example, Nafiseh (age twenty-seven, blogger and Facebook user) indicated that her blog had made her visible. For four years Nafiseh, who is unemployed, had used a blog to express her concerns, aspirations, and desires. She pointed out that her blog allowed her to receive feedback about her thoughts: "I am able to express my feeling of frustration and discuss social problems which arise as a consequence of poverty and then to get public opinions about them." Blogging also helped Simin (age twenty-six, a blogger and a teacher) to express herself and develop meaningful relationships with other people. She reported that her blog allowed her to expose her inner feelings: "In my blog I write about my everyday life issues, about my happiness and sadness, and it is a way to feel positive once I gain comments from the readers." These two narratives showed that blogs can be meaningful tools that support women and allow them to express and share different aspects of their personalities and receive feedback from others. Simin reiterated this point by stating that "it is very delightful when I post my stories and then [there is] collaboration and comments about the topic between the readers and me." As noted earlier, both Simin and Mahshid used pseudonyms and were eager to share some aspects of their lives and relationships, along with tales of their experiences, in their pseudonyms, which reduced the risks of self-disclosure and allowed them to feel safe in disclosing intimate information. Anonymity protects their identity, helps women achieve visibility, and allows them to become dynamic members of the society through sharing and exchanging information.

Similarly, our interlocutors used Facebook to express personal feelings and emotions, but they used their real names instead of pseudonyms to communicate with friends and family more efficiently. For example, Nahid (age twenty-nine, Facebook user), a computer programmer, stressed that Facebook had empowered her emotionally: "Using Facebook has empowered me psychologically and intellectually, as I have the opportunity to access a space where I can have a voice and express my feelings." For Nahid, who recently divorced her husband, using social media has helped reduce her feelings of loneliness and cope with the breakup of her marriage. She used Facebook mainly to chat and keep in contact with people. The intimate relationships she developed through Facebook improved her self-confidence, and she claimed to feel happier. Sharing personal photos and videos with friends also helped her maintain ongoing relationships with her Facebook friends.

Almost all participants valued Facebook because, through Facebook groups, they were able to meet like-minded people who provided them with support, as indicated by the following quotations:

- Facebook has opened an opportunity to create a group of close friends who are sympathetic and supportive towards me. They have positively energized me, and I have never experienced this in the "real world." (Mehri, age twenty-nine, Facebook user)

- Online interactions have assisted me to make friendships with like-minded people and contributed to the development of my self-confidence and emotional well-being. (Shirin, age thirty-seven, Facebook user)
- Through Facebook I could find some friends who have experienced a similar situation in their lives. Through Facebook chat we share our feelings and concerns, so that I am no longer lonely and isolated. Even our children are benefiting from this kind of friendship. They have so many common things to share, such as growing up with a single parent. (Nahid, age twenty-nine, Facebook user)

Nahid spends forty hours online weekly and relates that Facebook helped her develop relationships with people who have had similar life experiences as single parents. She found very good friends through Facebook groups, later met them face-to-face, and went with their children to the cinema or leisure centers.

Mehri is also a heavy social media user: she spends thirty-five hours a week online. Facebook changed her life significantly, because it allowed her to reach out to a community of internet users who could empathize with her. She was also able to create new friendships through common friends.

In our interlocutors' experiences, Facebook emerged as a site that helped create and develop new friendships among like-minded people, thereby enhancing their emotional well-being. Tehrani women celebrated Facebook and blogs, which allowed them the opportunity to overcome social, cultural, and political limitations in Iranian society. In the next section, we analyze how dating sites open new opportunities for internet users to find partners.

Online Dating

Two participants in this study, Rahele (age thirty-seven, Facebook and dating sites user) and Fataneh (age thirty-eight, Facebook and dating sites user), met their husbands through dating sites. Online dating has different implications for social and cultural constructions in traditional societies such as Iran where semiarranged marriages are still an important component of family structure and relationships. These two women were in their mid-thirties when they started to look for partners online (in Iran, this is quite late, as the average age of marriage is twenty-two for women and twenty-seven for men).[45] For these participants, dating sites served as powerful tools to look for marriage partners, to take control of their lives, and to make their own decisions. Indeed, dating sites enabled them to initiate their marriages without control and interference from their families.

In 2015, there were around three hundred dating sites in Iran,[46] including those that specialized in temporary and formal marriages. One of these dating sites is Amin

---

[45] Mardomsalari, "Average Age of Marriage in Iran," http://mardomsalari.com/template1/News.aspx?NID=174830.
[46] Hatam, "Iran: Internet Dating Website Launched by State."

Institute for Finding a Spouse, a nongovernmental dating site launched in 2000. The main goal of this site is to facilitate formal marriage, maintain and enhance the identity of family, and open a new framework for marriage by taking advantage of the internet. There are also some nongovernmental dating sites, such as Hafezun, that are designed to assist people who are interested in temporary marriage. On independent dating sites, there are no intermediaries, and users are responsible for searching the database and finding compatible partners.[47] Rahele and Fataneh used nongovernmental dating sites, such as Amin Institute, to look for potential husbands for formal marriages. Dating sites claim to promote better romantic outcomes than conventional offline dating. Both Rahele and Fataneh believed that dating sites were more effective in finding a partner than face-to-face dating, because dating sites offered more options and unprecedented levels of access to potential partners. For this reason, Fataneh decided to look for her partner online because in her social environment she was not meeting anyone new:

> This method was successful for me because I found it hard to find a compatible partner in the real world. Moreover, my socializing was limited to a few friends and relatives. Apart from this, I am unemployed, and I did not have the chance to see different people at my workplace. Therefore, online dating was an alternative option. (Fataneh, age thirty-eight, Facebook and dating sites user)

However, searching for partners online took time. Rahele and Fataneh spent almost two years looking for partners online before they finally met the men who became their husbands. Rahele explained that after she received the results of the compatibility test, communication took place through Yahoo messenger. She spent a good deal of time every day interacting with potential partners to gather enough information to lower the risks of interacting with strangers online:

> To avoid the potential risks of online dating, such as harassment and cyberbullying, I had to spend a few hours online each day at home chatting to different people in order to gather more information and monitor the behavior of those people to minimize the risks of online activities (Rahele, age thirty-seven, Facebook and dating sites user).

Rahele and Fataneh also noted that after chatting with people they were interested in, they could receive refusals online. They emphasized that patience and good self-esteem were important qualities when looking for a partner online. For these participants, online dating sites were an effective tool for finding compatible partners. They expressed a common concern about the limited opportunities to meet new people for those who have fewer social connections, and they stressed that it was important to have more options to choose a compatible partner. Online dating sites have opened a new framework for marriages and have become more acceptable to Iranian youth, whose common view seems to be that "traditional and arranged marriage is collapsing."[48]

[47] Hafezun, "*Dating Site for Temporary Marriage*," http://haroo.ir/.
[48] Hatam, "Iran: Internet Dating Website Launched by State."

Today, young people are eager to choose partners outside of their traditional social networks of relatives, friends, or people from their workplaces.

New social media platforms such as Instagram have also opened a wide range of dating opportunities for Iranian youth in recent years. In January 2018, Iranians were among the most active participants on Instagram, making Iran the seventh biggest market in the world for the photo-sharing app. According to Statista (2017), 30 percent of the population in Iran use Instagram, which is the second most popular social media network after the messaging app Telegram.[49] This platform offers its users a range of interactions and allows them to express their feelings and share interests through likes and comments and to connect in private chats. Instagram comments through pictures are a new way for young Iranians to establish relationships.[50] Dating apps, such as Tinder, BeeTalk, or Badoo, have also been welcomed in Iran. These applications allow young Iranians to explore "dating on their own terms, entirely free of the strict regulations."[51] Through dating apps, some users receive invitations to underground parties in private homes, where they can experience more intimate relationships.[52] These technologies have also had a significant impact on youth dating culture. The dating sites have partially displaced the role of traditional sites for meeting singles, such as schools, universities, and workplaces. They allow people the opportunity to meet and form relationships with individuals with whom they have no previous social connections.[53]

Conclusion

Blogs, Facebook, and dating websites have transformed the daily lives of Tehrani women by providing them with new opportunities and challenges. Social media are used for self-expression, to combat loneliness, and to create meaningful relationships with like-minded people. In online public spaces, female social media users minimize the constraints imposed on them by conservative Iranian social laws and strict religious norms. They are eager to defy traditional patriarchal gender roles by disclosing their thoughts and inner feelings online. However, social media are only available to affluent families whose income enables them to access the internet regularly. Tehrani women also participate in social media to overcome the boundaries of physical space, including segregation and gender inequalities imposed by the state. Social media platforms, in their view, have the potential to empower and liberate women, because they allow them to express themselves openly. Social media platforms also allow them to meet

---

[49] *Financial Tribune*, "Iran Ranked World's 7th Instagram User," https://financialtribune.com.
[50] Maryam Mirza, "Internet Difficulty in Iran," DW, https://www.dw.com/fa-ir/-دشواری-زوجیابی-اینترنتی/a-19061799 در-ایران.
[51] React Cornell Student Articles on Topical Affairs, "Iran's Youth Find Their Unconventional Way to Romance Amid Strict Dating Laws," Cornell University (2019), https://blogs.cornell.edu/react/2019/01/28/irans-youth-find-their-unconventional-way-to-romance-amid-strict-dating-laws/. Retrieved on September 25, 2020.
[52] Gus Serendip, "Exploring the Real Iran, with Social Media as Your Guide," *The Guardian*, 2016.
[53] Mitchell Hobbs, Stephen Owen, and Livia Gerber, "Liquid Love? Dating Apps, Sex, Relationships and the Digital Transformation of Intimacy," *Journal of Sociology* 53, no. 2 (2017): 271–84.

like-minded people who offer them emotional support. Most participants reiterated that blogs and Facebook helped them create new friendships, and a few even found partners outside traditional, semiarranged marriages by using the services of dating sites. The anonymity and flexibility of online services allowed them to find suitable partners. These women also stated that social media platforms contributed to the development of their self-confidence and emotional well-being. Thus, social media platforms play a very important role in the participants' lives by allowing them, at least to some degree, to escape the constraints of strict social norms and laws imposed by the current Iranian regime. Several key barriers, however, limited participants' online intimacy, including censorship imposed by the theocratic regime and fear of online harassment. Tehrani women consciously navigate social media platforms to take advantage of the opportunities that these services offer them, while trying to avoid the potential risks involved with digital communication. Hence, it is crucial for them to become knowledgeable about how to use anti-filter software and to learn a variety of methods to protect themselves online to enjoy the possibilities that social media afford for the development of intimacy. Social media platforms and dating apps have been credited with facilitating intimate relationships among Iranian women and men and allowing them to explore and develop different intimacies.

6

Recreating Virginity in Iran

Hymenoplasty as a Form of Resistance

Azal Ahmadi[1]

Hymenoplasty basically builds a corporeal appearance of virginity in women by surgically restoring the hymen, the membrane cross-culturally equated with female virginity. Although scholarly literature about hymenoplasty remains sparse, media accounts suggest that demand for this controversial surgery is increasing worldwide, notably in countries where women's virginity shapes social conceptions of honor.[2] Iranian women who undergo hymenoplasty have often broken the taboo of premarital sex and seek to reinstate an anatomical marker of virginity to help secure a suitable marriage partner.

Failure to present oneself as virginal for marriage risks the defilement of honor and may entail serious ramifications for women in Iran, including divorce, ostracism, and violence. While no statistics exists regarding the rate of "honor killings" in Iran,

---

[1] Acknowledgments: I thank my advisers at the University of Oxford, Drs. Soraya Tremayne and Stanley Ulijaszek, for providing me with guidance during my research. The University of Oxford, St. Cross College, provided me with a Student Academic Travel Grant to help fund my fieldwork in Iran. Finally, I am deeply indebted to the women I interviewed in Iran, who trusted me, sharing with me the most personal aspects of their lives.

Editor's note: Tragically, Azal Ahmadi passed away in 2016. She received her BA in Philosophy from Wellesley College and master's in Medical Anthropology from the University of Oxford. Her dissertation research focused on migrant female sex workers living with HIV in Senegal. This article is published here with the permission of the editors of Medical Anthropology Quarterly, where the article first appeared. It has been slightly edited to fit the requirements of this volume.

[2] Janet Afary, *Sexual Politics in Modern Iran* (Cambridge: Cambridge University Press, 2009); Marrie H. J. Bekker, Jany Rademakers, Ineke Mouthaan, Milleke De Neef, Wouter M. Huisman, Helma Van Zandvoort, and Anne Emans, "Reconstructing Hymens or Constructing Sexual Inequality? Service Provision to Islamic Young Women Coping with the Demand to Be a Virgin," *Journal of Community & Applied Social Psychology* 6, no. 5 (1996): 329–34; Dilek Cindoglu, "Virginity Tests and Artificial Virginity in Modern Turkish Medicine," in *Women's Studies International Forum*, vol. 20 (Elsevier, 1997), 253–61; Thomas Eich, "Constructing Kinship in Sunni Islamic Legal Texts," in *Islam and Assisted Reproductive Technologies: Sunni and Shia Perspectives* (New York: Berghahn Books, 2012), 27–52; Birgitta Essén et al., "The Experience and Responses of Swedish Health Professionals to Patients Requesting Virginity Restoration (Hymen Repair)," *Reproductive Health Matters* 18, no. 35 (2010): 38–46; Fatima Mernissi, "Virginity and Patriarchy," in *Women's Studies International Forum*, vol. 5 (Elsevier, 1982), 183–91.

reports even document cases in which women were killed by relatives for engaging in premarital sex.[3]

In this chapter, I present an ethnographic analysis of hymenoplasty in Iran through the critical medical anthropological lens of resistance. This lens links hymenoplasty to conceptions of power dynamics, medicalization, social control, and gender in Iranian society. I argue that hymenoplasty functions as a covert form of resistance to the prevailing sociocultural order in Iran, which forbids young women from freely engaging in their sexuality and permits sex solely under state-sanctioned marriage. My analysis draws on Michel Foucault's[4] notion of "reverse discourse" and Judith Butler's[5] theory of gender as "performativity."

Power, Medicalization, and Social Control

Hymenoplasty underscores the conflict between the sexual disciplining of women's bodies through medical and sociocultural discourses and women's desire to engage freely in sexuality prior to marriage. Foucault's[6] conceptions of societal power relations, medicalization, and social control help us understand how some women negotiate this conflict.

Foucault describes biopower as the exercise of regulatory power to manage populations and disciplinary power to manipulate individual human bodies. The spread of disciplinary power can be attributed to both regulatory discourses, which are forms of knowledge and disciplinary techniques, including surveillance, examination, and normalization. As disciplinary power is exercised throughout heterogeneous social networks, individuals internalize the invisible and the productive power of the subtle gaze, thus rendering subjected and self-policing docile bodies,[7] conforming to societal conceptions of normalized, nondeviant dispositions.

Foucault highlights the notion of medicalization to describe how medical discourse delineates normal from abnormal bodies and contributes to the diffused, disciplinary gaze. Medicalization is the process through which medicine expands its jurisdiction and dominance in areas of society that were originally deemed as nonmedical and social, with medical ideologies regulating acceptable looks, behavior, and states of being.[8] The construction of deviant and nondeviant bodily forms functions as a source of social control via normalization. People internalize expert medical knowledge of

---

[3] Landinfo (The Country of Origin Information Centre), "Honour Killings in Iran," 2009, http://www.unhcr.org/refworld/docid/4a704f352.html.
[4] Michel Foucault, *The History of Sexuality: An Introduction, Volume I*, trans. Robert Hurley (New York: Vintage 95, 1976).
[5] Judith Butler, *Gender Trouble: Feminism and the Subversion of Identity* (New York: Routledge, 2011); Judith Butler, *Bodies That Matter: On the Discursive Limits of 'Sex'* (New York: Routledge, 1993).
[6] Foucault, "The History of Sexuality: An Introduction, Volume I"; Michel Foucault, *Discipline and Punish: The Birth of the Prison* (New York: Vintage, 1975).
[7] Foucault, *Discipline and Punish: The Birth of the Prison*.
[8] Peter Conrad, *The Medicalization of Society: On the Transformation of Human Conditions into Treatable Disorders* (Baltimore: Johns Hopkins University Press, 2007).

categorical boundary markers, classifications, and ideologies and strive to adjust their corporeal makeup.

Resistance

In his later work, Foucault acknowledges that individuals are not mere effects of power relations. Resistance is possible due to the dynamics of the social field, which entails perpetual sites of power contestation and struggle. Foucault describes a relational interdependency of power and resistance; the dense network of power relations necessarily entails and depends on the existence of multiple resistance loci. A plethora of resistance possibilities emerge due to the ephemeral and unstable operative nature of power relations within social fields, which are constantly shifting.

Resistance, thus, undermines the status quo by mobilizing populations, transposing power relations, and enacting social change.

Resistance to power is generated through reverse or "alternative discourses,"[9] which may transform prevailing truths, generating novel forms of knowledge and power. Based on Foucault's model of strategic power, the prevailing discursive elements may be manipulated for alternate aims, thus generating tactical reverse discourse. For instance, the nineteenth-century European medical discourse labeled homosexuality as deviant and attempted to suppress it. Such suppression, ironically, enabled resistance by homosexuals who took advantage of the medicalization of homosexuality to legitimize their sexuality.[10]

Sawicki situates Foucault's theories within a feminist framework, demonstrating how feminism and Foucauldian thought are not mutually exclusive. She argues—in what may be deemed a pragmatic approach, as opposed to an ideological one—that total freedom from power is impossible. The oppressed can never completely be freed from power, which circulates continually through the social body. Women function as both "victims and agents"[11] in society, as a power-free society is an unrealistic and abstract conception. However, while Foucault "lacks a particular Utopian vision,"[12] women can strategically adjust power's grip and progressively advance social change, albeit within the existing power constraints.

Further building on a Foucauldian analysis of subjection, Butler (1993) articulates a notion of gender as "performativity," arguing that the sexed body is socioculturally constructed, constituting reality via repeated stylized actions, performative mechanisms and dispositions. Gender, a "free-floating artifice,"[13] as opposed to a static identity, allows women to introduce newly constructed stylized repetitions or to discontinue a currently existing performative style. "Gender trouble,"[14] or

[9] Foucault, "The History of Sexuality: An Introduction, Volume I."
[10] Ibid.
[11] Jana Sawicki, *Disciplining Foucault: Feminism, Power, and the Body* (Hove: Psychology Press, 1991).
[12] Ibid.
[13] Donn Welton and B. H. Blackwell, *Body and Flesh: A Philosophical Reader* (Oxford: Blackwell, 1998).
[14] Butler, *Gender Trouble: Feminism and the Subversion of Identity*.

resistance to established gender norms, involves performative acts that run counter to those expected, producing "resignification" of gendered meanings and alternate gender configurations.[15] Consistent with Foucault, Butler also argues that gender and subversive transformation of gendered scripts are constrained by the existing sociocultural order. Although full autonomous subjectivity may not be possible, through resistive performativity, women's agency may gradually adjust the dynamics of the social field, enacting social change and altering gendered identity.

I will now describe how virginity is medicalized in Iran, which, as the ethnographic research will show, enables women to resist sociocultural mores surrounding femininity.

Medicalization of Virginity in Iran

Virginity is medicalized in Iran by equating it with the possession of a hymen, thus reducing it to a physical reality under surveillance by clinicians. This discourse persists although the hymen is not a reliable indicator of past sexual experience[16] (Edgardh and Ormstad 2002; Emmans et al. 1994; Essen et al. 2010; Goodyear-Smith and Laidlaw 1998; Sloane 2002). While an intact hymen may bleed at first coitus, a lack of bleeding is common. Some women lack a hymen at birth,[17] and the hymen can be torn for reasons other than sexual intercourse, including strenuous exercise or an injurious fall. Nevertheless, some Iranian women opt for hymenoplasty to prove their virginity. Practiced covertly, hymenoplasty (also known as hymenorrhaphy or hymen reconstruction/repair surgery) reconstructs or synthetically reproduces the hymen, aiming to mimic the virginal state and induce bleeding (sometimes by inserting a gelatin capsule containing a blood-like substance) when the membrane is torn.

Iran and Virginity

The sociopolitical and religious dynamics of Iran have continued to transform since the 1979 Shi'a Islamic Revolution, but there remains a deeply rooted preference for a virgin bride.[18] *Bekarat* (virginity) and *nejabat* (purity) are qualities that many

---

[15] Anna Carline, "Resignifications and Subversive Transformations: Judith Butler's Queer Theory and Women Who Kill," *Liverpool Law Review* 27, no. 3 (2006): 303–35.

[16] Karin Edgardh and Kari Ormstad, "The Adolescent Hymen.," *The Journal of Reproductive Medicine* 47, no. 9 (2002): 710–14; S. Jean Emans, Elizabeth R. Woods, Elizabeth N. Allred, and Estherann Grace, "Hymenal Findings in Adolescent Women: Impact of Tampon Use and Consensual Sexual Activity," *The Journal of Pediatrics* 125, no. 1 (1994): 153–60; Essén et al., "The Experience and Responses of Swedish Health Professionals to Patients Requesting Virginity Restoration (Hymen Repair)"; Felicity A. Goodyear-Smith and Tannis M. Laidlaw, "What Is an 'Intact' Hymen? A Critique of the Literature," *Medicine, Science and the Law* 38, no. 4 (1998): 289–300; Ethel Sloane, *Biology of Women* (Cengage Learning, 2002).

[17] Essén et al., "The Experience and Responses of Swedish Health Professionals to Patients Requesting Virginity Restoration (Hymen Repair)."

[18] Shideh Hanassab, "Sexuality, Dating, and Double Standards: Young Iranian Immigrants in Los Angeles," *Iranian Studies* 31, no. 1 (1998): 65–75; Pardis Mahdavi, *Iran's Sexual Revolution:*

Iranian men seek in a suitable spouse[19] although alternative views exist. A woman's premarital sexual activity may be construed as a "sexual awakening,"[20] insinuating that she is promiscuous and, hence, nonmarriageable. Prospective grooms, their families, and sometimes the families of the bride may request a *govahiye bekarat* (virginity certificate) to prove the woman's virginal status prior to the wedding, which may be obtained from *pezeshke ghanooni* (legal forensic medical examiners) or gynecologists. Prevailing norms mandating female bridal virginity are at odds with the increasing sexual liberalization of urban youth. Studies suggest that premarital sex is becoming more common in contemporary Iran, especially in urban locales.[21] Research also shows that premarital sex has been on the rise in Iran since the 1979 Islamic Revolution.[22] There are no official statistics regarding hymenoplasty in Iran, but limited literature and recent media reports indicate that it mostly takes place in major cities, such as the capital.[23]

Per Iran's Islamic penal code, which regulates acceptable moral conduct, sex outside the confines of legal, heterosexual marriage remains a criminal offense.[24] However, while Islamic teachings advocate modesty, no explicit requirement for female marital virginity exists in Islamic doctrine.[25] Minority Iranian religious groups, such as Jews and Zoroastrians, also revere female bridal virginity. And the Avesta, the holy book of the pre-Islamic Persian religion of Zoroastrianism, also extols the virginity of a bride.[26]

By criminalizing premarital sex, Iran's Islamic government adds a subtle, legal level of control regarding the demand for female virginity, amplifying the surveillance of women's sexuality already enforced by deeply rooted historical and sociocultural discourses. While Iran's Shi'a law does not directly impose penalties on women who are not virgins when they marry, virginity can be mentioned as a condition of marriage in an Iranian marriage contract.

As in other societies where bridal virginity is valorized, female sexuality functions as a regulated commodity in Iran. As "consumers of female sexuality" (Moghadam 1994:85), a groom often promises to pay a predetermined amount of money to his

---

Passionate Uprising (Stanford: Stanford University Press, 2009); Haideh Moghissi, "Away from Home: Iranian Women, Displacement Cultural Resistance and Change," *Journal of Comparative Family Studies* 30, no. 2 (1999): 207–17; Nayereh Tohidi, "Iranian Women and Gender Relations in Los Angeles," *Irangeles: Iranians in Los Angeles* (1993): 175–217.

[19] Mohammadreza Hojat et al., "Premarital Sexual, Child Rearing, and Family Attitudes of Iranian Men and Women in the United States and in Iran," *The Journal of Psychology* 133, no. 1 (1999): 19–31.

[20] Eliz Sanasarian, "The Politics of Gender and Development in the Islamic Republic of Iran," *Journal of Developing Societies* 8 (1992): 56.

[21] Afary, *Sexual Politics in Modern Iran*; Willem M. Floor, *A Social History of Sexual Relations in Iran* (Washington, DC: Mage Publishers, 2008); Mahdavi, *Iran's Sexual Revolution: Passionate Uprising*; Behzad Yaghmaian, *Social Change in Iran: An Eyewitness Account of Dissent, Defiance, and New Movements for Rights* (Albany: SUNY Press, 2002).

[22] Mahdavi, *Iran's Sexual Revolution: Passionate Uprising*.

[23] Afary, *Sexual Politics in Modern Iran*; Mahdavi, *Iran's Sexual Revolution: Passionate Uprising*.

[24] Vanja Hamzić and Ziba Mir-Hosseini, *Control and Sexuality: The Revival of Zina Laws in Muslim Contexts* (London: Women Living Under Muslim Laws, 2010).

[25] Alia Imtoual and Shakira Hussein, "Challenging the Myth of the Happy Celibate: Muslim Women Negotiating Contemporary Relationships," *Contemporary Islam* 3, no. 1 (2009): 25–39.

[26] Fataneh Farahani, "Diasporic Narratives of Sexuality: Identity Formation Among Iranian-Swedish Women" (Acta Universitatis Stockholmiensis, 2007).

bride, known as the *mahriyeh* (bride price), in return for her sexual services. The *mahriyeh* is often proportional to the woman's social worth, attractiveness, and virginity, which collectively increase the male's social utility. Honor and shame are also heavily associated with female virginity in Iran. Women, in conforming to acceptable social mores by abstaining from premarital sex, are expected to uphold the honor of men, the family, and their community.[27] As Mernissi states, these concepts "locate the prestige of a man between the legs of a woman."[28] Female family members also function as collaborators in preserving family honor, advising female relatives to adhere to social norms dictating female sexual restraint. Shame is brought to the family by deviation from culturally mandated gender roles, putting the family's honor at risk.

Although Foucault's theories of surreptitious power have been criticized for their gender neutrality,[29] they still help elucidate how the medicalization of virginity functions as female social control in Iran. Virginity examinations, a "mechanism of surveillance deployed by the modern state,"[30] are a medically sanctioned procedure enforced through institutionalized medicine in Iran. Women are classified as virginal and normal if they possess a hymen or as nonvirginal and deviant if they do not. Women's subjugation to the expert judgment of medical examiners is a classic illustration of "normalizing judgment" and "hierarchical observation" as disciplinary techniques.[31]

Foucault argues that linguistic discourse also plays a role in reproducing the normalizing gaze and systems of knowledge. Indeed, the Persian language exhibits linguistic forms that mandate female sexual passivity and a chaste, premarital body as part of gender norms. The *pardeh-ye bekarat* (hymen), literally, the "curtain of virginity," implies that the hymen serves as an entrance for penetration.[32] The words for girl/virgin and woman/nonvirgin are iconic:[33] To refer to a female as either *dokhtar* (girl) or *zan* (woman) implies that she is a virgin or nonvirgin, respectively. *Zan* is also synonymous with wife, reinforcing the notion that a female gives up her *dokhtari* (girlhood or virginity) upon marriage.[34] Such linguistic discourses normalize premarital virginity of a woman's body,[35] thus reinforcing Foucauldian disciplinary techniques. As women internalize these messages, they may take measures to safeguard their hymens to fit norms of proper feminine behavior.

---

[27] Afary, *Sexual Politics in Modern Iran*; Cindoglu, "Virginity Tests and Artificial Virginity in Modern Turkish Medicine"; Eich, "Constructing Kinship in Sunni Islamic Legal Texts"; Essén et al., "The Experience and Responses of Swedish Health Professionals to Patients Requesting Virginity Restoration (Hymen Repair)"; Mernissi, "Virginity and Patriarchy."
[28] Mernissi, "Virginity and Patriarchy."
[29] Sandra Lee Bartky, *Femininity and Domination: Studies in the Phenomenology of Oppression* (Routledge, 2015); Nancy Hartsock, "Foucault on Power: A Theory for Women," *Feminism/Postmodernism* 162 (1990).
[30] Ayse Parla, "The "Honor" of the State: Virginity Examinations in Turkey," *Feminist Studies* 27, no. 1 (2001): 65–88.
[31] Foucault, *Discipline and Punish: The Birth of the Prison*.
[32] Farahani, "Diasporic Narratives of Sexuality: Identity Formation among Iranian-Swedish Women."
[33] Parla, "The "Honor" of the State: Virginity Examinations in Turkey."
[34] Farahani, "Diasporic Narratives of Sexuality: Identity Formation among Iranian-Swedish Women."
[35] Afsaneh Najmabadi, "Veiled Discourse-Unveiled Bodies," *Feminist Studies* 19, no. 3 (1993): 487–518.

Setting and Methods

During two visits in 2010–11, I conducted ten weeks of ethnographic research on hymenoplasty in Tehran. Results from the first visit are presented here; those from the second visit are analyzed elsewhere.[36] I chose northern Tehran as the primary research site due to its secularity and affluence relative to the south. Previous reports suggested that hymenoplasty, which cost between $500 and $1,500 as of 2012, is more common in the richer, more secular areas of urban Tehran.[37]

I conducted in-depth, semistructured interviews in Persian with five young women who had undergone hymenoplasty, ten women who had not, and five physicians who perform the procedure. Here, I focus on the stories of physicians who performed and women who obtained hymenoplasty, as their experiences are not well documented. I recruited women and physicians using a snowball sampling technique in which initial participants nominated women who had undergone hymenoplasty and physicians who performed the surgery. This method was appropriate because of the secretive, sensitive nature of the topic and the widespread perception that hymenoplasty is illegal. To maximize comfort and gain trust, I conducted interviews with women who underwent hymenoplasty in the protective space of a women's organization in Tehran. I interviewed physicians in private offices in hospitals and clinics. All names have been fictionalized to preserve the anonymity and safety of the interviewees. The University of Oxford's Research Ethics Committee approved this study.

During my fieldwork, I often found myself balancing the roles of an outsider and insider: I was both a foreign academic researcher and a Persian-speaking woman who had to obtain the trust of my interviewees.[38] My "in-between position"[39] sometimes hindered and sometimes accelerated my progress. For instance, one physician stated that, due to my Persian accent, I was clearly a *khareji* (foreigner), and thus he could not help me. Other physicians said that it was precisely due to my position as a foreigner that they were able to disclose sensitive information on the surgery to me. Similarly, a few women I interviewed said, "I can only tell you these things" because they perceived me as a *khareji*.[40]

The short duration of the fieldwork and the sensitive nature of hymenoplasty posed challenges in locating women and physicians who were prepared to talk to me about their experiences with the surgery. Since participants did not consent to have the interviews audio recorded, I also had to rely on detailed notes to reconstruct participants' experiences. Last, while interviewing men would have produced a more holistic understanding of virginity in Iran, it was impossible to do so because of my status as a single Iranian female traveling solo, the sensitivity of the research topic,

---

[36] Azal Ahmadi, "Ethical Issues in Hymenoplasty: Views from Tehran's Physicians," *Journal of Medical Ethics* 40, no. 6 (2014): 429–30.
[37] Afary, *Sexual Politics in Modern Iran*; Mahdavi, *Iran's Sexual Revolution: Passionate Uprising*.
[38] Farahani, "Diasporic Narratives of Sexuality: Identity Formation Among Iranian-Swedish Women."
[39] Halleh Ghorashi, *Ways to Survive, Battles to Win: Iranian Women Exiles in the Netherlands and United States* (New York: Nova Publishers, 2003).
[40] Ghorashi; Hammed Shahidian, "'To Be Recorded in History': Researching Iranian Underground Political Activists in Exile," *Qualitative Sociology* 24, no. 1 (2001): 55–81.

and suspicions it would have aroused to interact with *na-mahram* (unrelated) males. Despite such limitations, this ethnographic investigation provides unique insight into a secretive and highly understudied topic.

Narratives and Discourses Surrounding Virginity

I interviewed two male gynecologists, two female gynecologists, and a male neurosurgeon to ascertain their personal experiences performing hymenoplasty, their views on ethical issues, and demographic information about women who seek the procedure. They stated that clinicians from all medical specialties (including midwives) perform hymenoplasty and are known in slang as Dr. *Khayyat* (Dr. Tailor). While all five physicians reported performing the surgery out of moral obligation to women requesting it, with some even performing it for free; they also described their personal conflict with the surgery, viewing themselves as accomplices to deception.[41]

According to the physicians, women who undergo hymenoplasty tend to represent a particular socioeconomic and religious stratum of Iranian society. Physicians drew on their own experiences and that of others they knew who performed the surgery. They stated that most women who first undergo this surgery are between 18 and 25 years old, have recently found a *khastegar* (suitor), are mostly educated (either in university or have obtained a university degree), and often come from families residing in the more prosperous areas of Tehran. They also confirmed that hymenoplasties are more common in northern Tehran, with some women traveling from other major cities throughout Iran to obtain the surgery. Two of the physicians reported performing the surgery on socioeconomically disadvantaged women, who sometimes offer goods or sex in exchange to cover the costs of this expensive surgery. While all the physicians reported that many women who seek hymenoplasty are secular, they also served religious women, some of whom had traveled from Qom, one of the holiest cities in Iran, to obtain the surgery secretly.

The interviews confirmed that the concept of recreating virginity is not novel, as women have historically undertaken nonsurgical procedures to imitate the rupturing of a torn hymen on the wedding night.[42] Physicians reported that less-affluent women who cannot afford hymenoplasty might resort to cutting herself or using animal blood on the sheets on the wedding night. In Mahdavi's fieldwork on sexual practices in Iran, one physician reported that some women insert capsules of goat blood, sold on the black market in Tehran, into the vagina on their wedding night.[43] In my interviews, young women also described how some women strategically schedule weddings to coincide with their menstrual cycle or how others manipulate the use of oral contraceptives so that they bleed on the wedding night. While these more primitive solutions may mimic virginity loss, the more sophisticated reproductive health technology of hymenoplasty effectively recreates virginity itself.

[41] Ahmadi, "Ethical Issues in Hymenoplasty: Views from Tehran's Physicians."
[42] Mernissi, "Virginity and Patriarchy."
[43] Mahdavi, *Iran's Sexual Revolution: Passionate Uprising.*

Five Young Women

Susan, a 24-year-old originally from Shiraz, underwent three hymen repairs. After having premarital sex with a few men, she underwent her first hymenoplasty when her family found her a *khastegar*. However, this engagement failed because the fiancé was abusive. Afterward, Susan had a few additional boyfriends with whom she had sex. She underwent the second hymenoplasty after another suitor was found, with whom she also had sex. This second *khastegari* (marriage proposal) also failed due to family tensions. She underwent her third and final surgery to marry another suitor, with whom she was "deeply in love." All three surgeries, for which she paid herself the equivalent of $500 each, were performed at her house by a female gynecologist, who she "greatly trusted" and who was recommended to her by one of her sister's friends.

Susan stated that not being a virgin was causing her substantial "stress." Throughout her narrative, Susan, who recently completed her degree in chemical engineering and comes from an affluent family, emphasized that I was one of the few people who was aware that she had undergone hymenoplasty. When asked about her religious status, she said she was Muslim but did not "actively practice" Islam. She recounted how the first surgery was especially painful but that she did bleed during the three subsequent sexual encounters, implying that the surgeries were successful in mimicking the bleeding of a ruptured hymen. She received a virginity certificate for her final *khastegar*. Throughout her narrative, Susan was very enthusiastic, giving long-winded answers, stating that "everyone is doing this" (obtaining hymenoplasty), and that "boys here just want to use women who do not have a hymen."

Maryam, twenty-seven years old, is from Tehran and has a degree in art. She is a housewife in an affluent neighborhood in northern Tehran and underwent hymenoplasty three years ago before her current husband asked for her hand in marriage. She describes herself as "believing in God," but, like Susan, does not fast or perform the obligatory Islamic prayers. Maryam had dated one of her former boyfriends for three years. Everyone in the family knew about this relationship except her father. When this former boyfriend eventually came to ask for her hand in marriage, Maryam's father forbade it because the suitor was a divorcé. Maryam stated that she loved him and had sex with him because she thought that they would eventually get married. After obtaining hymenoplasty, Maryam had to immediately leave the private clinic so that her parents would not find out, resulting in some pain for about a week afterward.

Before marrying her current husband, Maryam dated a few other men but did not allow any of them to have vaginal sex with her; she permitted only anal sex. Before her marriage, Maryam went to a *pezeshke ghanooni* to obtain a virginity certificate for her groom's family. She was aware that her husband was not a virgin when they married, recounting how he went to see a masseuse during a trip to Thailand, where he had sex for the first time. While dominating discourses do not require male virginity, she knew how important it was for her to present herself as a virgin upon marriage, describing how her husband would most certainly divorce her if he found out she had premarital sex. When she got married, she had to pretend to be a virgin on her wedding night, despite her sexual experience, which she said was especially bothersome. When asked if she was satisfied with the results of the surgery, Maryam enthusiastically responded that she was very satisfied since her husband did not suspect anything on their wedding night.

Niloofar, thirty years old, has a bachelor's degree in management and is from a middle–upper-class background. She works as a governmental employee and is married to a religious husband. She believes it is important to have sexual experience prior to marriage. In 2002, through one of her friends, Niloofar located a midwife who restored her hymen for approximately $600. She emphasized that she found this midwife through trusted social networks, as she "didn't want to tell this [her desire to undergo hymenoplasty] to anyone." It took her a "very long time" before she was able to find someone trustworthy who was willing to perform the procedure. Niloofar's operation was particularly difficult, as she succumbed to an infection, was unable to rest after the surgery due to work commitments, and had to tolerate the midwife's "offensive" language for having premarital sex. Niloofar attributed her infection to the fact that she promptly returned to work after undergoing the operation and thus was unable to obtain sufficient rest for recovery. Throughout her narrative, Niloofar often blamed herself for having sex outside of marriage. Despite her troubles, she was satisfied with the surgery, as she obtained a virginity certificate from a gynecologist and bled on her wedding night.

Married in 2009, Shaghayegh, twenty-two years old, is a university student studying arts. She stated that choosing to have sex with her former boyfriend was a difficult decision, explaining how she was very attracted to him but also was aware of the consequences that may ensue if her family discovered that she was not a virgin upon marriage. Shaghayegh wanted to marry her former boyfriend, but her father did not approve. Through her friends, Shaghayegh located a gynecologist who performed hymenoplasty for the equivalent of approximately $500 at a private clinic in Tehran, for which her former boyfriend paid. Shaghayegh underwent hymen repair both to satisfy the requirement of her family and that of her groom's that she be a virgin at marriage and also to prevent communal gossiping and shame about her virginal status. She experienced no pain during the surgery or afterward. Laughing, she recounted how happy she was that she had the surgery, explaining how she easily obtained her virginity certificate and subsequently bled a lot on her wedding night. Shaghayegh recounted her sexual encounters prior to her marriage in great detail and resorted to hymen repair surgery to not "ruin her chances" of marriage.

Negar, twenty-seven years old, married in 2009. She reported having over ten boyfriends prior to undergoing hymenoplasty, laughing that "this number may be even higher." She proceeded to explain how she "enjoys sex" and that it is "natural" to have sexual relations prior to marriage. She also mentioned how "none of her close female friends are virgins." When it came time for her to marry a suitor that her father chose for her, one of her close friends recommended an experienced male gynecologist who performed the surgery for free in a private clinic in Tehran (even though she offered to pay for it). When Negar did not bleed on her wedding night, her husband questioned her virginity the next day. Fearing physical violence from her husband, she managed to assure him that she was a virgin (she had received a virginity certificate prior to her marriage from a local gynecologist), explaining that "not all women bleed" when they lose their virginity. He did not bring up the subject again. She reported being "very nervous" on her wedding night and acting "inexperienced" to deceive her husband into thinking that she was a virgin. Negar stated that on her wedding night, her husband was very sexually experienced, and assumed that he had multiple sexual partners prior to marrying her.

Themes in the Narratives of Virginity

The women I interviewed manipulated the medicalization of virginity to assuage fears that a suitor would discover past sexual histories and to maximize chances of finding a suitable marriage partner. One young woman who had not yet undergone the surgery bluntly described this instrumental use of hymenoplasty when I interviewed her at a social event: "Here, you want a hymen? Here it is." Susan stated that she would become *badbakht* (unfortunate) if she did not undergo the surgery since she knew that her *khastegar* was expecting a *dokhtare najeeb* (pure girl). Maryam explained how a nonvirgin girl would still be able to marry, but that a virgin girl, viewed as a commodity, could greatly maximize her social utility by marrying a man who was well established professionally and financially. Niloofar stated that she had "peace of mind" prior to going to the gynecologist for her virginity certificate since she had undergone hymenoplasty a few months prior. Shaghayegh explained how she obtained the surgery so that she would not "wreck her future." Another woman who had not undergone hymenoplasty stated that "we women are smart as well" and that "we can only survive in this country by doing such things." Taking advantage of virginity's medicalized state by reconstructing their hymens, ensuring acquisition of a virginity certificate, and maximizing their chances of bleeding on the wedding night, offered these women assurance that their previous sexual activity would not hinder them from maximizing their marital social utility.

Women often spoke of the desire for *azadi* (freedom) or, more specifically, sexual freedom. Susan stated that she simply "wants to be free." She talked about her sexual escapades with her previous boyfriend, stating that she was "in love" with him and wanted to freely express her sexuality. Maryam described how "boys are free" and that throughout her previous relationships, she simply wanted to "do what [she] wants [sexually]," by freely engaging in premarital sex without stigmatization. Negar elaborated on this lack of freedom: "We don't have freedom of speech. How can we have freedom over our own bodies?" Here, she lamented the restrictions placed on Iranian women and their bodies, placing such loss of freedom within the larger social context of the restricted liberties in modern-day Islamic Iran.

The issue of freedom was discussed in conjunction with women's understanding of the sociocultural sexual mores that frown on female sexual liberty but encourage that of their male counterparts. Negar acknowledged that hymenoplasty is deceptive but attributed the cause of such deception to "cultural pressures." Niloofar explained how men often have multiple girlfriends, but when it came to marriage, they "want a girl who has not been touched." Another woman interviewed at a social event angrily questioned why "men can do whatever they want and we cannot." A few other women stated that when they were younger, their female relatives told them to remain "pure" and not to "jump up and down," lest they tear their hymens.

In describing societal pressures that drive females to obtain hymenoplasty, the interviewees attributed such pressures to traditional Iranian norms advocating female purity, as opposed to Islamic factors. The five women who underwent hymenoplasty described themselves as nonreligious. Susan, Maryam, and the female gynecologists explicitly stated that the requirement for virginity has no relevance to Islam. Rather, the Iranian conception of *gheyrat* (honor or zeal), involving one's female relationships, sometimes surfaced in the narratives. A male exhibiting *gheyrat* would display assertive masculinity by zealously guarding and controlling his female partner's sexual conduct, viewing her previous sexual escapades as threatening to his masculinity and honor. One woman stated that Iranian men simply "cannot accept" that their wife is not a virgin and that this is "just how Iranian men are." Maryam further explained how men may "humiliate" a woman who was not a virgin.

Women used dichotomies such as pure/impure and virgin/nonvirgin, which reinforce sexual norms of female purity and passivity. For instance, Negar insisted that she obtained a hymenoplasty so that she could come across as a *dokhtare khoob* (good girl), not an unmarriageable *zane kharab* (literally "defective woman," or figuratively a "loose, lewd woman"), insisting she was not the latter. When asked why she underwent the surgery, Susan insisted that she had to "preserve her purity" to get married and to not be viewed as impure.

Hymenoplasty as Resistance

The virginity narratives demonstrate how affluent Iranian women in northern Tehran who willingly engage in premarital sex are covertly and unintentionally defying hegemonic sociocultural discourses that mandate female premarital virginity. Despite restrictions on premarital sexual expression, these women covertly explore their sexuality until a suitable *khastegar* is found. They do not conform to the double standard that condones premarital sex for men but denies it for women. As they transgress the normalizing standard of female sexual restraint, these women inadvertently embody resistance toward the dominant discourses that aim to control their sexuality.

Women were physically intimate with their partners simply due to sexual and emotional attraction, which many described as *eshgh* (love). The interviews suggest they were acting on desire, rather than intentionally setting out to challenge inegalitarian gender norms. While the women who underwent hymenoplasty were indeed aware of the gender mores restricting them to the social sphere of premarital chastity, their narratives gave no indication that they intentionally engage in premarital sex or underwent hymenoplasty to resist or undermine specific political, religious, or sociocultural norms. Thus, resistance via hymenoplasty operates on a structural, rather than individual level. As the actions of individual women who undergo hymen repair surgery are (ideally) publicly undisclosed, it is women's collective election of this surgery that engenders the unintended structural effect of covert resistance and the subsequent erosion of sociocultural norms.

Women's Manipulation of the Medicalization of Virginity

While the medicalization of virginity seeks to regulate and restrain the sexual conduct of women, it is paradoxically through this process of medicalization that women establish some control over their lives. Through hymenoplasty, women are empowered to explore their sexuality prior to marriage and to "combat the patriarchal expectations of family and society"[44] without compromising their social worth, which is deeply contingent on successful marital relations. In Iran, a successful marriage is vital to a woman's financial security, social standing, and overall communal respect. The "social safety of girls," therefore, "is strongly influenced by how they choose to manage their sexual bodies and sexual practices."[45] Thus, the possession of a hymen is a form of physical capital that women can exchange for symbolic and socioeconomic capital.[46]

On a structural level, hymenoplasty is a form of Foucauldian reverse discourse against the prevailing gendered power dynamics in Iranian society. Similar to how men used the medicalized state of homosexuality in nineteenth-century Europe to legitimize their sexual orientation, young Iranian women take advantage of the dominating medical discourse surrounding virginity to engage in premarital sex without risking social consequences. The medicalization of virginity seeks to produce women who conform to the normalization of female premarital sexual restraint by internalizing the gaze. Yet women inadvertently resist by manipulating the existing medical discourse for an opposing strategy: to appear compliant with sociocultural norms mandating female purity. Thus, although they have internalized the importance of virginity, these women do not represent Foucauldian docile bodies as they resist disciplining of their bodies through reverse discourse. By undergoing a secretive and subversive surgery, women explore their sexuality and collectively and unintentionally thwart the repressive discourses that seek to inhibit female premarital sexual expression.

Femininity and Resignification

The cultural paradigm that equates female virginity with purity assumes an unchanging essence of femininity.[47] Women who restrain their sexuality and maintain their hymen prior to marriage are continuously pure; those who have premarital sex and compromise their hymen are continuously impure. This dichotomy is evident, for instance, in Negar

---

[44] Cindoglu, "Virginity Tests and Artificial Virginity in Modern Turkish Medicine."
[45] Marie Rosenkrantz Lindegaard and A. Henriksen, "Sexually Active Virgins: Negotiating Adolescent Femininity, Colour and Safety in Cape Town," *Transgressive Sex: Subversion and Control in Erotic Encounters* (New York: Berghahn Books, 2009), 25–45.
[46] Pierre Bourdieu, *Outline of a Theory of Practice*, vol. 16 (Cambridge: Cambridge University Press, 1977).
[47] Eich, "Constructing Kinship in Sunni Islamic Legal Texts."

and Susan's insistence that they must possess a hymen to be classified as marriageable, as opposed to not possessing a hymen and being nonmarriageable. Such a view "is linked to inherently inflexible concepts of a fixed, unchangeable nature of women, who naturally fulfill only certain social roles."[48] No intermediary position exists in between these two polarities, with women naturally categorized as deviant or nondeviant based on presence of the hymen.

Women who undergo hymenoplasty position themselves between two seemingly incompatible social roles: the deviant, socially prohibited role of a sexually liberated young woman who freely expresses her sexuality prior to marriage and the normal, socially expected role of the chaste young woman who presents herself as a virgin bride. Occupying this intermediary position covertly resists the prevailing sociocultural order that seeks to confine women to premarital chastity. These women inhabit "two social roles within one life itinerary."[49] Contra to the static role of women as indicated by Iranian medical and sociocultural discourses surrounding virginity, women who undergo hymenoplasty operate fluidly between these two polarities, carving out a social space for premarital sexual fulfillment without compromising future marital stability.

These women also collectively resist stoic gendered categorizations, which the prevailing medical and sociocultural discourses proclaim as natural in the construction of a woman's feminine identity. For instance, the male gynecologists maintained that all females are born with hymens and that if the hymen is not intact, she is not a virgin—an essence of her femininity. Yet women who undergo hymenoplasty construct their own fluid, feminine identities, deviating from a fixed, natural notion of gender embodiment. In deviating from the expected performance of premarital sexual restraint, women who undergo hymenoplasty thus re-signify sociocultural concepts of proper feminine dispositions, resisting fixed norms of gender via performativity.[50] These women undermine the dichotomy between virgin and nonvirgin as normal and abnormal, respectively, because they encompass both domains. They conform to a medicalized ideal of virginity because they have hymens, but they do not adhere to the social definition as they have indeed had sex.

Hymenoplasty constitutes a unique form of resistance within this context. Nonsurgical techniques that imitate virginity loss through bleeding do not challenge the prevailing Iranian sociocultural order in the same way because bleeding in and of itself does not signify virginity. By contrast, the hymen is necessary and sufficient to signify virginity in Iranian medical, legal, linguistic, and sociocultural discourses. As the narratives demonstrate, women who undergo hymenoplasty acquire virginity certificates to attest to the presence of a hymen prior to marriage. Even though Negar failed to bleed on her wedding night, the virginity certificate she acquired through hymenoplasty was enough to alleviate her husband's suspicions about her virginal status. Thus, hymenoplasty corroborates a woman's claim to purity in a way that

---

[48] Ibid.
[49] Ibid.
[50] Butler, *Bodies That Matter*.

primitive forms of faux virginity loss cannot. It does so by co-opting a medicalized, hegemonic discourse that would otherwise defile her as impure.

Some argue that obtaining hymenoplasty ultimately reproduces repressive gender norms, even though it facilitates premarital sexual exploration.[51] Yet in the context of prevailing social constraints and discourses, hymenoplasty can be seen as a pragmatic form of resistance.[52] The expectation of female virginity at marriage is deeply embedded in Iranian history and society, and women who are found not to be virgins prior to marriage may face severe consequences.[53] In this context, the subtle resistance of Iranian women who undergo hymenoplasty may gradually transform the discourse via the resignification of gendered constructs.

This potential is beginning to take shape in changing public and private discourses surrounding virginity in Iran. Qom-based Islamic cleric Ayatollah Rouhani issued a 2006 fatwā (religious ruling) clarifying that hymenoplasty is permissible under Iran's Islamic law, stating that there is "no difference between a real or a fake hymen."[54] Men also often joke that "there are no real virgins" remaining in Iran.[55] In a recent radio report, a journalist also reported that the Iranian government sent a memo to legal forensic medical examiners advising that they not be so strict with regard to differentiating between an original hymen and one suspected to be reconstructed if a woman is sent in for a virginity examination.[56] One physician who was interviewed stated that, after healing, it is difficult even for clinicians to distinguish a reconstructed from an original hymen. Furthermore, while I was unable to interview men in this study, some women suggested that young men are gradually shunning sexually inexperienced women as marriage partners, thus rejecting dominant discourses espousing female premarital virginity.

As these developments are relatively recent, it is difficult to know whether they reflect substantial changes in discourses pertaining to sexuality and virginity in Iran. In the meantime, hymenoplasty is blurring borders between virgin and nonvirgin, which may gradually minimize the value attributed to virginity and the hymen.[57] This possibility paves the path for social transformation, a "future horizon that values bodies differently."[58]

---

[51] Marrie H. J. Bekker, Jany Rademakers, Ineke Mouthaan, Milleke de Neef, Wouter M. Huisman, Helma Van Zandvoort, and Anne Emans, "Reconstructing Hymens or Constructing Sexual Inequality? Service Provision to Islamic Young Women Coping with the Demand to Be a Virgin"; Ihab Usta, "Hymenorrhaphy: What Happens behind the Gynaecologist's Closed Door?" *Journal of Medical Ethics* 26, no. 3 (2000): 217–18.

[52] Butler, *Bodies That Matter*; Foucault, "The History of Sexuality: An Introduction, Volume I"; Sawicki, *Disciplining Foucault: Feminism, Power, and the Body*.

[53] Landinfo (The Country of Origin Information Centre), "Honour Killings in Iran"; Mahdavi, *Iran's Sexual Revolution: Passionate Uprising*.

[54] Negar Farshidi, *Virginity Still a Commodity in Iran*, 2015.

[55] Afary, *Sexual Politics in Modern Iran*.

[56] R. Karimi, "The Hymen Restoration Operation: The Fashion in Iran," *Radio Farda*, (January 20, 2011): 2009.

[57] Farahani, "Diasporic Narratives of Sexuality: Identity Formation among Iranian-Swedish Women."

[58] Susan Bordo, *Unbearable Weight: Feminism, Western Culture, and the Body* (Berkeley: University of California Press, 2004).

Conclusion

These findings apply to affluent northern Tehrani women who choose to explore their sexuality prior to marriage. They do not represent the heterogeneity of Iranian women's experiences with virginity and hymenoplasty. The limited literature and media reports available on hymenoplasty indicate that socioeconomically disadvantaged and religious women, even former sex workers, divorcees, and rape victims, also undergo the procedure.[59] Additional research is needed to provide insight into the diverse experiences of Iranian women who undergo hymenoplasty and to elucidate its cross-cultural implications.

As the case of hymenoplasty in Iran demonstrates, socioculturally sanctioned rules and expectations are often inscribed on a woman's body. It is a locus of resistance, conformation, intervention, and transformation of hegemonic norms. Hymenoplasty demonstrates that, despite the constraints of the prevailing social order, some women are able to employ clandestine tactics to negotiate governing discourses that restrict their freedom and confine them to gendered, socially prescribed spaces. Thus, "what can no longer be spoken is repeated in behavior."[60] Women may not be able to freely navigate outside the constraining social forces, but they engage in covert resistance—silently and gradually destabilizing inequalities in rough yet fluid social terrains.[61]

---

[59] Henrietta L. Moore, *A Passion for Difference: Essays in Anthropology and Gender* (Bloomington: Indiana University Press, 1994).
[60] Ibid.
[61] Henrik Vigh, "Motion Squared: A Second Look at the Concept of Social Navigation," *Anthropological Theory* 9, no. 4 (2009): 419–38.

7

Whither Kinship?

Assisted Reproductive Technologies and Relatedness in the Islamic Republic of Iran

Soraya Tremayne

I met Mohsen at one of the private in vitro fertilization (IVF) clinics in Tehran. He told me that he had been married for five years but had no children and added, "My wife is infertile, which is why we have come here. With God's will she will conceive." Mohsen seemed very positive about his wife's chances of becoming pregnant. When I queried the doctor about Mohsen's optimistic outlook, he smiled and refrained from commenting, but said, "It is better if you talk to Mohsen yourself." I returned later to the clinic to meet Mohsen to find that he was leaving without speaking to me but had a friendly expression and a smile on his face. The doctor said, "Mohsen does not wish to talk to you directly, but he knows that you are carrying out research and has agreed that I can tell you his story, in strict confidence." The doctor then told me that it was Mohsen, and not his wife, who was infertile but, on finding out, he had begged the doctor not to tell his wife the truth and had brought his brother to the clinic to use his sperm to fertilize his wife's egg. The doctor had agreed, and the fertilization had proceeded without the wife's knowledge or consent. The treatment proved successful, and to date, she had not even suspected that it was her brother-in-law's sperm that had impregnated her. For Mohsen, the gain was total, because not only had he been seen to be fertile, but he had also succeeded in keeping his lineage intact by using his brother's sperm. Furthermore, this donation had brought him even closer to his brother.

Mohsen's case raises several questions, ranging from the ethical aspects of the doctor's action to the persisting stigma of male infertility and the gender dimension of how men and women perceive and respond to infertility and its treatment. However, the focus of this chapter is on a different aspect of third-party gamete donation; namely, that of kinship, and the way assisted reproductive technologies (ARTs) have become instrumental in the hands of infertile individuals, who tend to use them to perpetuate their lineage and forge new bonds with their kin group, who are the donors or recipients of gametes.

Family and kinship are foundational, sacrosanct institutions in Iranian culture, acting as guiding principles of social organization. Their significance has not diminished in the face of the major changes that have taken place in all aspects of reproductive life in Iran during the past few decades. Islamic laws and practices, which are intensely focused on the protection of family and its perpetuity, and which define the parameters of relatedness predominantly through biological lineage, further frame and strengthen cultural values and norms in relation to family and kinship. To ensure the continuity of the family and lineage, pressure on individuals to reproduce is intense, and infertile individuals are often marginalized and have to carry the burden of their barrenness. However, even for fertile individuals, reproducing per se is not unconditional or sufficient to make them welcome or full members of their kin group. The unity of the family being the ultimate priority, individuals who have no biological link with the family or the kin group are rarely welcome members of the group.

As infertility is such a major stigma, it is understandable that when ARTs were first introduced to Iran, a theocratic Islamic state, they were received with open arms and legitimized in a relatively short time, with the full endorsement of leading Shia scholars.[1] The ARTs' contribution to procreation went even further than just offering a cure for infertility. ARTs became instrumental in allowing infertile individuals to interpret the rules, which gave ARTs legitimacy in the first place and to use them to meet their understanding of what constitutes kinship and to maintain the integrity of their lineage.

Methodology

The data presented in this chapter are part of a larger study, which began in 2004 and continues to date. The sites of the study are Tehran and Yazd in Iran, and in the UK, where I worked with Iranian women who were asylum-seekers and refugees. A total of 130 infertile couples were interviewed, one-third of whom remain part of the longitudinal study. The main method used is that of participant observation and in-depth interviews with infertile couples, as well as the donors of gamete, and the medical personnel in various public and private clinics. Data in this chapter include only the infertile individuals, not the donors. In Yazd, I worked in the city's oldest maternity hospital, Mojibian, which has an infertility treatment clinic, where I carried out in-depth interviews with infertile couples, through whom I was able to meet a larger number of infertile individuals and their wider kin groups. I also had extensive interviews with the leading medical practitioners in the clinic. Thirty-five infertile couples were interviewed: twenty-four of them were approached in the clinic, and eleven were friends or relatives of those interviewed or were relatives of my host family. In Tehran, between 2004 and 2011, I carried out in-depth interviews with sixty-two infertile couples in three public hospitals, two private clinics, and one specialized infertility treatment center set up to treat infertile war veterans, who had suffered spinal injuries during the Iran–Iraq War. In addition, I interviewed doctors, bioethicists, psychologists, and midwives, in and out of the clinics. Through personal

---

[1] Soraya Tremayne, "Law, Ethics and Donor Technologies in Shia Iran," *Assisting Reproduction, Testing Genes: Global Encounters with New Biotechnologies* 18 (2009): 144.

contacts, I studied an additional ten couples. In the UK, I provided expert reports for courts for twelve female Iranian asylum-seekers who had to flee the country because of pending court cases and the extreme violence inflicted on them by their husbands, who had initially agreed to resort to third-party gamete donation and later had accused them of adultery.[2] The majority of the individuals in the study come from conservative and religious groups. They have varying levels of education, and a considerable number belong to middle- or low-income groups.

ARTs, Kinship, and Islam

The social and cultural implications of ARTs on family and kinship have been the subject of great interest to anthropologists from the start, and a substantial body of literature exists on them.[3] As these studies have shown, the impact of ARTs on family forms and kinship is greater than on any other institution in society. However, scholars were initially divided on the impact of ARTs on kinship. For example, Strathern argued that the ability of users of ARTs to have a choice in the area of human reproduction has "destabilized" the understanding of kinship, which the English worldview perceived as natural rather than socially constructed. She explained that the availability of these technologies forced the perception of kinship as social construction and as a choice. Susan Kahn's studies of Israel, on the other hand, argued against the idea that ARTs necessarily displaced a culture's foundational assumptions about kinship.[4] In Parkin and Stone's view, ARTs have resulted in the emergence of "a tension between kinship as a choice and social construction and the older cultural conception of kinship as rooted in biological reproduction." Referring to these divergent views, Parkin and Stone point at a different outcome by stating that although "new constructions of kinship are occurring in European and American society and in this process choice is playing a larger role, there is at the same time a counter-current drawing Americans

---

[2] Marcia C. Inhorn and Soraya Tremayne, *Islam and Assisted Reproductive Technologies: Sunni and Shia Perspectives*, vol. 23 (New York and Oxford: Berghahn Books, 2012).

[3] see, for example, Faye Ginsburg and Rayna Rapp, "The Politics of Reproduction," *Annual Review of Anthropology* 20, no. 1 (1991): 311–43, Faye Ginsburg and Rayna Rapp, "Introduction: Conceiving the New World Order," in *Conceiving the New World Order: The Global Politics of Reproduction* (Berkeley: University of California Press, 1995); Marilyn Strathern. *After Nature: English Kinship in the Late Twentieth Century*, vol. 1989 (Cambridge: Cambridge University Press, 1992); Marilyn Strathern, *Reproducing the Future: Essays on Anthropology, Kinship and the New Reproductive Technologies* (Manchester: Manchester University Press); H. Ragone, *Surrogate Motherhood: Conception in the Heart* (Boulder: Westview Press, 1994); Sarah Franklin *Embodied Progress: A Cultural Account of Assisted Conception* (London: Routledge 1997); Janette Edwards, "Explicit Connections: Ethnographic Enquiry in North-West England," in J. Edwards, S. Franklin, E. Hirsch, F. Price, and M. Strathern (eds.), *Technologies of Procreation: Kinship in the Age of Assisted Conception* (London: Routledge, 1993); J. Carsten (ed.), *Cultures of Relatedness: New Approaches to the Study of Kinship* (Cambridge: Cambridge University Press, 2000); Janet Carsten (ed.), *Cultures of Relatedness: New Approaches to the Study of Kinship* (Cambridge: Cambridge University Press, 2000); R. Parkin and L. Stone (eds.), *Kinship and Family: An Anthropological Reader* (Oxford: Blackwell Publishing, 2004).

[4] Susan Martha Kahn, Judith Farquhar, and Arjun Appadurai, *Reproducing Jews: A Cultural Account of Assisted Conception in Israel* (Durham: Duke University Press, 2000).

back to biogenetic conceptions of kinship."[5] Inhorn's and Clarke's more recent studies of ARTs in the Muslim Middle East throw a different light on what constitutes kinship in Islamic societies.[6] For example, Clarke argues that "[a]ccording to the vision of the Islamic legal establishments, relations of filiation (*nasab*) are not mutable or fluid, but are given paradigmatically—but not exclusively—through procreation."[7] Clarke's analysis clearly distinguishes Islamic notions of relatedness from the Euro-American ones and their place in relation to the application of ARTs.[8]

Following from these discussions, the case of Iran provides fertile ground for an examination of whether and to what extent ARTs have redefined the "filial" relations by providing a choice for their consumers. In what follows, I argue that the responses of the users of ARTs to third-party gamete donation have evolved from initial resorts to their kin group for gamete donation. Gradually, ART users are moving away from seeking help from relatives and are, wherever possible, secretly resorting to strangers' gametes to be able to claim biological parenthood and thus prove their own reproductive ability. The history of the legitimization of ARTs in Iran is well documented.[9] ARTs were introduced to Iran soon after they were first used in the West, and they are currently offered in all their forms, from in vitro fertilization (IVF) to

---

[5] Robert Parkin and Linda Stone, *Kinship and Family: An Anthropological Reader* (London: Blackwell, 2004).

[6] Marcia C. Inhorn, "Making Muslim Babies: IVF and Gamete Donation in Sunni versus Shi'a Islam," *Culture, Medicine and Psychiatry* 30, no. 4 (2006): 427–50; Marcia C. Inhorn, "Defining Women's Health: A Dozen Messages from More than 150 Ethnographies," *Medical Anthropology Quarterly* 20, no. 3 (2006): 345–78; Morgan Clarke, *Islam and New Kinship: Reproductive Technology and the Shariah in Lebanon*, vol. 16 (New York and Oxford: Berghahn Books, 2009).

[7] Clarke, *Islam and New Kinship: Reproductive Technology and the Shariah in Lebanon*. (New York and Oxford: Berghahn Books, 2009).

[8] See also, Thomas Eich, "Constructing Kinship in Sunni Islamic Legal Texts," in *Islam and Assisted Reproductive Technologies: Sunni and Shia Perspectives* (New York and Oxford: Berghahn Books, 2012), 27–52.

[9] For example, see M. A. Akondi (ed.), *Modern Human Reproductive Techniques from the View of Jurisprudence and Law* (in Persian). The Avicenna Research Institute in association with the Academic Publishing House for the Social Sciences, 2001; M. A. Akondi, *Essays on Gamete and Embryo Donation in Infertility Treatment: From Medical, Theological, Legal, Ethical, Psychological and Sociological Approaches*. The Avicenna Research Institute in association with the Academic Publishing House for the Social Sciences, 2006; M. C. Inhorn, *Local Babies, Global Science: Gender, Religion, and In Vitro Fertilization in Egypt* (New York: Routledge, 2003); M. C. Inhorn, "Right to Assisted Reproductive Technology: Overcoming Infertility in Low-Resource Countries," *International Journal of Gynecology and Obstetrics* 106 (2009): 172–4; M. C. Inhorn, *The New Arab Man: Emergent Masculinities, Technologies, and Islam in the Middle East* (Princeton, NJ: Princeton University Press, 2012); Soraya Tremayne, "Not All Muslims Are Luddites," *Anthropology Today* 22, no. 3 (2006): 1–2; Tremayne, "Law, Ethics and Donor Technologies in Shia Iran"; Soraya Tremayne, "The 'Down Side' of Gamete Donation: Challenging 'Happy Family' Rhetoric in Iran," in *Islam and Assisted Reproductive Technologies: Sunni and Shia Perspectives* (New York: Berghahn, 2012); J. Abbasi-Shavazi, H. B. Razeghi, Z. B. Ardekani and M. N. Akhondi, "The Socio-cultural Aspects of Gamete and Embryo Donation in Infertility Treatment," in *Essays in Gamete and Embryo Donation in Infertility Treatment: From Medical, Theological, Legal, Ethical, Psychological and Sociological Approaches*, ed. M. A. Akondi (Tehran: Centre for Research and Development in Human Sciences (Semat), 2006); J. Abbasi-Shavazi, M. Inhorn, H. B. Razeghi-Nasrabad and G. Toloo, "The 'Iranian ART Revolution': Infertility, Assisted Reproductive Technology, and Third-Party Donation in the Islamic Republic of Iran," *Journal of Middle East Women's Studies* 4, no. 2 (2008): 1–28; Morgan Clarke, *Islam and New Kinship: Reproductive Technology and the Shariah in Lebanon* (New York and Oxford: Berghahn Books, 2007).

third-party donation of sperm, egg, and embryo, to surrogacy and sex selection. Stem-cell research is carried out too but is limited in its application. When IVF was first introduced, it went unnoticed by those outside the medical world, as it was considered a medical technology, and its practice was limited to married couples only. However, with the introduction of third-party donation of sperm and egg, and later embryo and surrogacy, the question of their legitimate practice extended beyond that of the medical sphere and required endorsement from legal and ethical regulatory bodies. Because Iran is a theocracy, the legalization of ARTs became the responsibility of the leading Muslim scholars, who took great interest in finding ways of legitimizing them and did so in a relatively short time. As Inhorn and Tremayne discuss, in the context of the role played by religious leaders in Muslim countries of the Middle East,

> Initially, these scholars returned to early Islamic texts, in order to examine and better understand the basis upon which kinship and family relations are formed. At first, both Sunni and Shia scholars shared the view that the treatment of infertility and use of ARTs should be limited to married couples, with no third party involved in this process. The rationale behind this argument was the protection of the purity of lineage (*nasab*), which the intrusion of a third party would destroy and which would lead to biological and social confusion.[10] The effects on kinship and family relations, and the consequent social disorder, were considered profound.[11]

The Sunni religious leaders, therefore, banned all forms of third-party donation. Their Shi`i counterparts, however, subsequently allowed third-party donation, by resorting to independent reasoning (*ijtihad*), which allows senior clerics, faced with new questions, to interpret the Qur'an and come up with new answers. It was the involvement of some of the more liberal religious leaders, who approved of third-party donation, which opened the way for these practices.[12] As Inhorn and Tremayne explain:

> To understand the process by which ARTs were legitimized with relative speed and ease in Iran, it is necessary to understand two fundamental aspects of Shi`i Islam: first, the nineteenth-century development of the concept of 'sources of emulation' (*marja' al-taqlid*), or Shi`i religious scholars who are to be followed for their learnedness; second, the Shi`i emphasis on independent reasoning (*ijtihad*) to find new answers to arising problems.[13]

---

[10] Marcia C. Inhorn, "Global Infertility and the Globalization of New Reproductive Technologies: Illustrations from Egypt," *Social Science & Medicine* 56, no. 9 (2003): 1837–51; Clarke, *Islam and New Kinship: Reproductive Technology and the Shariah in Lebanon*.
[11] Inhorn and Tremayne, *Islam and Assisted Reproductive Technologies: Sunni and Shia Perspectives*.
[12] Inhorn, "Making Muslim Babies: IVF and Gamete Donation in Sunni versus Shi'a Islam"; Clarke, *Islam and New Kinship: Reproductive Technology and the Shariah in Lebanon*; Inhorn and Tremayne, *Islam and Assisted Reproductive Technologies: Sunni and Shia Perspectives*.
[13] Inhorn and Tremayne, *Islam and Assisted Reproductive Technologies: Sunni and Shia Perspectives*; Morgan Clarke, "Islam, Kinship and New Reproductive Technology," *Anthropology Today* 22, no. 5 (2006): 17–20.

Unlike their Sunni counterparts, Shi'i scholars remain reluctant to engage in formal collective *ijtihad* deliberations on issues of global importance. Instead, they rely on individualistic, independent reasoning, which has led to a diversity of opinions among Shi'i *marāje'*, who, in fact, take opposing views on the interpretation of the Qur'an. Such a great scope of opinions has led to considerable "flexibility" for the Shi'i *marāje'* in allowing the introduction of scientific and other innovations. It is the individualistic practice of *ijtihad* that has paved the way for the Shi'i to engage dynamically with most forms of biotechnology.

Once the use of ARTs was approved by some *marāje'*, the disapproval of other *marāje'*, of equal or more senior standing, had a minimal impact and remained limited only to the followers of those particular *marāje'*. Besides, many infertile couples, whose *marja'* did not approve of third-party donation, changed their *marja'* and joined one who did endorse it.

In addition to examining Islamic texts, the leading Shi'i scholars also engaged with scholars from other disciplines, such as medical experts, jurists, lawyers, psychologists, and bioethicists, to explore the full implications of third-party donation. The history of the engagement of the leading clerics with the specialists is documented elsewhere.[14] The result of these intense debates was that donation of gametes could only take place between a married couple, but the practice of temporary marriage (*sigheh* or *mut'a* marriage) was used to legitimize donation between any willing pair. However, temporary marriage, in this case, did not allow bodily contact between the donor and the recipient; the sole purpose was for the infertile party to legitimately receive the gamete donated by his or her temporary spouse. The rules also specified that egg donors should be widows or divorcees, ideally with children of their own, as one woman could not be married to two men at the same time.[15] In the late 1990s, Ayatollah Khameini, the Supreme Religious Leader of Iran, was asked for his opinion on the legitimacy of third-party donation. His approval, which did not refer to temporary marriage, specified that "donation was allowed as long as no touch or gaze took place." This endorsement remains open to interpretation to date, but it paved the way for infertile partners to freely choose donors of sperm or egg—a choice that invariably turned out to favor their siblings or other relatives. While gamete donation by siblings and relatives is practiced in many parts of the world,[16] under the Islamic rules, this would constitute incest or adultery. Under these rules, men and women are divided into two categories, *mahrams* and *na-mahrams*, which define and determine their social and sexual relationship with each other.[17] The *mahrams* are relatives, who are not potential marriage partners, and

---

[14] For example, see Akondi, *Modern Human Reproductive Techniques from the View of Jurisprudence and Law*; Tremayne, "Law, Ethics and Donor Technologies in Shia Iran."

[15] Tremayne, "Law, Ethics and Donor Technologies in Shia Iran"; Soraya Tremayne, "Not All Muslims Are Luddites," *Anthropology Today* 22, no. 3 (2006): 1–2.

[16] For example, see E. F. S. Roberts, "The Traffic Between Women: Female Alliance and Familial Egg Donation in Ecuador," in *Assisting Reproduction, Testing Genes: Global Encounters with New Bio-technologies*, eds. Daphna Birenbaum-Carmeli and Marcia Inhorn (New York and Oxford: Berghahn Books, 2009).

[17] Men and women who are related by blood or through fostering, and who are thus not potential marriage partners, are *mahrams*. Women who are *mahram* to a man include his mother, grandmother, daughter, granddaughter, sister, aunt, grandaunt, niece, grandniece, his father's wife,

any sexual relationship with them constitutes incest. *Na-mahrams*, on the other hand, are potential marriage partners; however, no social or sexual contact or relationship between them is permitted outside marriage. Any transgression from these rules is punishable under the shari'a.

The legitimization of third-party donation, while removing the prohibition of donation between any two parties, raised many questions concerning cultural norms and values and religious and legal practices. For example, from what precedes, it is clear that when an infertile woman's sister donates her egg and this is fertilized with her brother-in-law's (the infertile woman's husband's) sperm, this constitutes adultery, as a man cannot impregnate his wife's sister. The reverse, in the case of an infertile man using his brother's sperm to impregnate his infertile wife, also applies, and both are forbidden (*haram*). However, the infertile parties typically do not see the donation by a close relative in this light. Their understanding of incest and adultery is that of the sexual contact taking place, whereas making an embryo on a petri dish is viewed as a technology, which allows them to conceive.[18] In choosing a close relative as a donor, the ultimate concern is to try and keep the donation "all in the family," and to avoid mixing one's blood with that of a stranger. In his examination of the significance of "substance" in Islamic kinship, Clarke argues that, "for the European or American reader, the substance most naturally associated with the idea of kinship is blood, and Arabic and Islamic concepts are often so translated: *nasab* as 'blood' relationship, for example." Clarke's observations during his fieldwork in Lebanon confirm that blood was commonly used as a symbol of kinship. During my fieldwork, the term *hamkhouni*,[19] or "sharing the same blood," meaning "consanguinity," was one that I heard most frequently from donors and recipients, who used their siblings' gametes, as they explained why they preferred donation from relatives: "We are from the same blood and flesh, and it is obvious that we should help each other maintain our *hamkhouni*." In their view, the "best" gamete "naturally" comes from one of their close relatives. It is clear that "best" in this case did not mean the healthiest in genetic or medical terms, but implied "desirable," in that it ensured retaining the continuity of their biological links with their lineage. Interestingly, growing research shows that consanguinity and marriage between cousins or other blood relatives are contributing factors to male

---

his wife's daughter (i.e., a step-daughter), his mother-in-law, his foster mother, foster sisters, and any foster relatives that are similar to the aforementioned blood relatives. *Mahram* men are a woman's father, grandfather, son, brother, uncle, granduncle, nephew, grandnephew, foster brothers, and any other foster relatives (see also Clarke, *Islam and New Kinship*).

[18] The various parties at the clinics with whom I discussed ARTs were unanimous in believing that donation of a gamete did not hint at any sexual act. See also Mohamad Jalal Abbasi-Shavazi, H. B. Razeghi, Z.B. Ardekani, and M. N. Akhondi, in M. A. Akhondi (ed.), *Essays in Gamete and Embryo Donation in Infertility Treatment: From Medical, Theological, Legal, Ethical, Psychological, and Sociological Approaches*. (Tehran Centre for Research and Development in Human Sciences: Semat): 371–91; Mohamad Jalal Abbasi-Shavazi, Marcia Inhorn, H. B. Razeghi-Nasrabad, and G. Toloo " 'The 'Iranian ART Revolution'": Infertility, Assisted Reproductive Technologies, and Third-Party Donation in Islamic Republic of Iran, *Journal of Middle East Women's Studies* (2008).

[19] On the question of the significance of blood as the substance that constitutes kinship, both Inhorn (2012) and Clarke (2009) have extensively discussed the question of substance in kinship. In this chapter I do not elaborate on the issue of which substance is the basis of relatedness, but refer instead to the perceptions and beliefs of infertile individuals about which substance is the basis of relatedness, which, for them, is blood.

infertility, which is transmitted down the male line from fathers to sons. Research also reveals the high prevalence of male infertility in the Middle East, where the number of consanguineous marriages is high.[20] Islamic encouragement of marrying one's blood relatives, especially one's first cousins, is significant in perpetuating cousin marriages too. In her seminal book, *The New Arab Man: Emergent Masculinities, Technologies, and Islam in the Middle East*, Inhorn devotes an entire chapter to what she terms "consanguineous connectivity" (2012, 123–61), in which she explains the prevalence and importance of marrying "blood" relatives, which is shown to be high, ranging between 16 and 78 percent. Of the 220 cases of infertile men who appear in Inhorn's samples and were from various parts of the Middle East, 20 percent had married their cousins (137).[21] Cousin marriages also occur extensively among Iranians, who believe that the Prophet has recommended marriage between children of two brothers as "having been arranged in the sky" (meaning in heaven).

To return to third-party gamete donation between close relatives, this form of donation, inevitably, breaks the very rules that allowed it in the first place. For example, on the question of married women not being allowed to donate eggs, most relatives are married and pay no attention to the rule. Furthermore, if the format of temporary marriage were to be applied in cases of sibling donation, this would be another breach of the *mahram/na-mahram* rules, as a man cannot marry his infertile wife's sister, even temporarily, while he is married to his own wife to receive the sister-in-law's egg, nor can a woman receive her infertile husband's brother's sperm. Both cases would constitute adultery.

The degree of closeness is also an important factor in the choice of the donors. Infertile individuals seem to have an order of priority as to who the donor should be. For example, if an egg donor cannot be found among the blood relatives, usually one of the women married to a blood relative is selected. In one clinic, an infertile woman told me that "my husband's brother's wife is going to donate an egg to me. She is married to my brother-in-law and therefore can be considered as a 'remote' blood relative." The terms *nazdik* (close) and *dur* (remote) are often heard in conversations between women in the waiting halls of infertility clinics. The infertile women seem to measure carefully the degree of their affinity with the donor. Some of the women, who had traveled from afar, mentioned that when they returned for the actual treatment, they intended to bring their donor, who is a *qowm o khish* (*qowm* denoting the ethnic group and *khish* the member of the kin group), which implies how important it is that the donor, while perhaps not a direct or close relative, be chosen from among the members of their own kin or ethnic group.

For infertile men, too, the first choice of a donor is their brother. However, one of the interesting aspects of third-party donation is the difference in the way infertile men and women resort to gamete donation. In general, sperm donation does not come to public attention as much as egg donation, because only private clinics practice sperm donation, and they are more discreet than is the case with egg donation. Similar to

---

[20] Personal communication from the Head of the Embryology Unit, University of Oxford, UK
[21] Marcia C. Inhorn, *The New Arab Man: Emergent Masculinities, Technologies, and Islam in the Middle East* (Princeton: Princeton University Press, 2012).

the way ARTs have highlighted the persistent kinship preferences among infertile individuals, they have also made gender differences, in relation to infertility, strikingly obvious. Male infertility is more stigmatized than female infertility, and men try to hide their infertility whenever possible, as was shown in Mohsen's case. A study by Abbasi-Shavazi et al. (2008) conducted in clinics in Tehran also confirms that infertile men ask their wives to take the blame for infertility or face divorce. As I have already discussed elsewhere, even when men resort to sperm donation, especially if the sperm belongs to a stranger, they do their utmost to keep it a secret, so that the child is seen as their biological offspring.[22] While donations from blood relatives remain common, this situation is gradually changing as infertile couples increasingly choose to accept gametes from strangers, as discussed later in the chapter.

Another outcome of legitimizing third-party donation has been the emergence of donation between siblings of opposite sex, with brothers donating sperm to their sister's infertile husbands.[23] This results in an embryo formed with a brother and sister's gametes. Biological and genetic concerns notwithstanding, this would be incest from a cultural and religious perspective. The idea of incest associated with the practice of ARTs is not unique to the Islamic world. Edwards' study of women in the north of England provides an interesting example of the deeply rooted fear of incest. Women interviewed by Edwards were asked whether they would use third-party donation; they replied that they would not, because they were not sure whose sperm they would be using. It could be their father's or that of their boyfriend's father or some other relative. As Edwards discusses, what provoked such a reaction by these women was the abhorrence of committing incest by receiving an anonymous donor sperm, which could turn out to be that of a relative.[24] The reactions of Iranian recipients of gametes, as mentioned earlier, are quite different. Even those infertile couples who were not aware of the religious endorsement did not consider gamete donation an act of incest or adultery as was also observed by Abbasi-Shavazi et al.[25] As one woman told me, "This all happens outside my body."

Finally, in cases of surrogacy, we find the same pattern of preference for using relatives as surrogates. In the early days of surrogacy, very few women were prepared to act as surrogate mothers. Because of cultural constraints, they did not want to be seen carrying another couple's child. At that time, in 2004, only family members were prepared to act as surrogates. Since then, as the practice has become better known, an increasing number of commercial surrogate mothers have come forward, and currently, hundreds of women act as surrogate mothers. Once more, the endorsement of religious leaders has made the practice acceptable. However, in her study of surrogacy in Iran,

---

[22] Tremayne, "The 'Down Side' of Gamete Donation." also see Abbasi-Shavazi et al., "The Sociocultural Aspects of Gamete and Embryo Donation in Infertility Treatment," 383–4, on secrecy.
[23] Shirin Garmaroudi Naef, "Gestational Surrogacy in Iran: Uterine Kinship in Shia Thought and Practice," *Islam and Assisted Reproductive Technologies: Sunni and Shia Perspectives*, 2012. also personal communication
[24] Jeanette Edwards, "Incorporating Incest: Gamete, Body and Relation in Assisted Conception," *Journal of the Royal Anthropological Institute* 10, no. 4 (2004): 755–74.
[25] Mohammad Jalal Abbasi-Shavazi and Peter McDonald, "Fertility Decline in the Islamic Republic of Iran: 1972–2000," *Asian Population Studies* 2, no. 3 (2006): 217–37.

Garmaroudi shows the strength of the bonds between relatives, who continue to act as surrogates for their kin group, especially the siblings.[26]

The involvement of the infertile couples' kin group does not stop at donation between relatives. Reproduction is still a matter for the entire kin group, especially the husband's side of the family, regardless of whether he is the infertile party or not. The motivation for the man's kin group stems from the fact that he has the ownership of the child, hence his family's greater interest in the matter. In cases of female infertility, often one or more members of her husband's family, the mother-in-law or brother-in-law, accompany her and get involved in discussions with the medical staff. If the husband has an older brother, he lets his older brother take charge of the negotiations with the clinic. I have witnessed scenes in which relatives' tempers rise, rows break out, and fists are banged on tables in attempts to make doctors agree to the demands of the family. In one case, reported by Abbasi-Shavazi et al., the infertile woman mentioned that she and her husband were trying to keep the treatment secret from their relatives

> because every time we go to the clinic, my mother-in-law and sister-in-law telephone me and tell me to be careful that the clinic does not use somebody else's gamete on us. My brother-in-law told us today, that "you are busy with other matters and are not paying enough attention to what the clinic is doing and they may use another person's gamete for you. Therefore, I am going to accompany you in future, so that you are not cheated."[27]

Effectively, one person's infertility becomes the "kin group's infertility."

In addition, the drive for conception is so strong that even couples who cannot afford the costs of the private treatment try to use the private clinics. This is especially so in the case of sperm donation, a service that the public clinics do not offer. In such cases, relatives may join in to raise the necessary funds by selling their car or mortgaging their house to pay for the cost of treatment. The financial contribution of the kin group toward the fertility treatment in other Muslim countries in the Middle East is also confirmed by Inhorn's study.[28] As extended families get involved, the clinics, especially the private ones, have encountered regular conflicts arising between relatives, mainly over the ownership of the children born as a result of third-party donation. Some clinics have taken the choice of the donor into their own hands, selecting suitable donors from their own data bank, and keeping their identity confidential from the recipients of gametes. In the process, they inevitably break the very rules that permit the donation—namely, that the child should inherit from his biological parent. So, as the use of ARTs continues and new problems arise, medical practitioners are forced to find new solutions and redefine the boundaries of what is permitted in terms of interaction between the donors and the recipients of gametes. As a result, ARTs are increasingly controlled by the medical practitioners; this means that fewer infertile couples may be able to resort to their relatives for donation in the

---

[26] Naef, "Gestational Surrogacy in Iran: Uterine Kinship in Shia Thought and Practice."
[27] Abbasi-Shavazi and McDonald, "Fertility Decline in the Islamic Republic of Iran: 1972–2000."
[28] Inhorn, *The New Arab Man: Emergent Masculinities, Technologies, and Islam in the Middle East.*

long run. Interestingly, as ongoing research is beginning to reveal the unrelenting interference by the kin group at all stages of the treatment is forcing infertile couples to try to minimize the involvement of their relatives by withholding information from them, and even seeking gametes from strangers to keep the relatives out. These couples realize that once a child is born through third-party donation, they can claim to have had their own biological child, and nobody needs to know that they have resorted to using a stranger's gametes. However, secrecy is not possible for every couple; only those who live in larger cities are able to avoid daily contact with their close relatives and seek treatment without their knowledge.

The findings of this study have also brought to the fore the gender dimensions of third-party donation and the ways men and women relate to a donor child (born from a donor gamete). For women, infertile or not, the process of procreation remains the same. From gestation to breastfeeding, women are able to develop the bonds they need to establish "real" kinship with the child who is conceived through a donated egg. Breastfeeding itself constitutes the milk kinship, which in Islam follows the same rules as biological kinship. For the infertile men in this study who resorted to stranger's sperm, the fact that they played no part in the creation or the gestational phase left them passive and isolated. Their roles as biological fathers had vanished, and they considered themselves "merely" the social fathers. As I have discussed elsewhere, being merely a social father has provoked a range of reactions among men, from depression to violence.[29] My findings were confirmed through the interviews I carried out with several counselors and psychologists who had treated these social fathers. However, the real insights into infertile men's behavior have come from my work with female Iranian asylum-seekers in the UK, whose husbands had rejected the donor children and turned violent toward their wives and children. The data also show that donor children who were conceived with the gametes of relatives were treated with more warmth and were welcomed as "real" members of the family, regardless of the fact that their biological and social parents may have had arguments and disagreements over them. Although information on donor children among families who have used anonymous gametes is scant, it is clear that these children, especially if they are the result of sperm donation, had not necessarily brought the anticipated stability to the family.[30] However, this aspect needs further research.

Conclusion

This chapter began with the case study of Mohsen to illustrate the importance of biological relatedness and the lengths to which infertile individuals will go to ensure the continuity of their lineage. Mohsen's case is not an isolated one, and abundant evidence substantiates the ingrained belief in biological connection, providing the

---

[29] Tremayne, "The 'Down Side' of Gamete Donation: Challenging 'Happy Family' Rhetoric in Iran"; Tremayne, "Law, Ethics and Donor Technologies in Shia Iran."
[30] Tremayne, "The 'Down Side' of Gamete Donation: Challenging 'Happy Family' Rhetoric in Iran."

basis for family and kinship across the Muslim Middle East.[31] In this study, the wish of couples to have their own biological child is not only expressed among the infertile couples themselves but also confirmed in the examples recounted by doctors and practitioners in the clinics. The introduction of third-party gamete donation in Iran initially provided the perfect solution for infertile individuals. They swiftly realized that not only could these technologies allow them to have children who belonged to their own blood and lineage but they could also become instrumental in consolidating their bonds with their kin group through the exchange of gametes. A few years into the use of third-party gamete donation, these technologies proved the perfect solution to achieving the ideal model of reproduction for the infertile party, in that the secret gamete donation could make them appear as the "biological" parents of the children conceived through donation. The question arises whether and to what extent, in the long run, the balance of infertile individuals' reliance on their kin group for gamete donation will hold or shift against that of secretly resorting to strangers' gametes. Whatever the choice, the results point to the fact that ARTs "do not necessarily displace a culture's foundational assumptions about kinship";[32] indeed, they can become the perfect way for infertile individuals to achieve their metaphysical and cosmological ideals of reproduction.

Finally, there is abundant literature on the innovative ways that consumers have made global technologies fit into local cultural molds. For example, as Unnithan-Kumar, in her study of female-selected abortion in India observes, "It is not the technologies that bring about social transformation but it is in how they are made socially meaningful that their power lies."[33] Horst and Miller's prolific studies of digital technologies in various cultures are further examples, as is the study of the interface between modernity and tradition, which questions "to what extent traditions themselves are exploiting modernity in creative ways, in the interest of their own further developments."[34]

Acknowledgment

An earlier version of this chapter was published in *Assisted Reproductive Technologies in the Third Phase: Global Encounters and Emerging Moral Worlds*, 2015, Hampshire, K., Bob Simpson (Eds.), (New York and Oxford: Berghahn Books, 2015).

---

[31] See also Inhorn, *The New Arab Man: Emergent Masculinities, Technologies, and Islam in the Middle East*; Clarke, *Islam and New Kinship: Reproductive Technology and the Shariah in Lebanon*.
[32] Kahn, Farquhar, and Appadurai, *Reproducing Jews: A Cultural Account of Assisted Conception in Israel*.
[33] Maya Unnithan-Kumar, "Female Selective Abortion–Beyond 'Culture': Family Making and Gender Inequality in a Globalising India," *Culture, Health & Sexuality* 12, no. 2 (2010): 153–66.
[34] Heather Horst and Daniel Miller, *The Cell Phone: An Anthropology of Communication* (Berg, 2006); James Wilkerson and Robert Parkin (eds.), *Modalities of Change: The Interface of Tradition and Modernity in East Asia* (New York and Oxford: Berghahn Books, 2012).

Part Three

Reconstructing Hierarchies: Rural and Tribal Marriages

8

How Marriage Changed in Boir Ahmad, 1900–2015

Erika Friedl

Introduction

In the absence of detailed documents for pre-literate Boir Ahmad communities, I base this chapter on oral histories and ethnographic research that I conducted during a total of seven years in that region between the years 1965 and 2015.[1] As a result of my observations and discussions there I conducted in this fifty-year period, I have come to see local marriage issues mostly as a function of socioeconomic and political conditions that involve strong androcentric and misogynistic assumptions. Providing an ethnographic sketch, I follow these factors through three periods, roughly between 1900 and 2015.

Period 1. Local people's recollections of traditional life point to long-standing and pervasive androcentric customs of the past that have strong echoes in the present. Historical living conditions were marked by toil, dearth, and duress, by aggression and defense, banditry and rivalry, and, on the idea-plane, by idealization of heroic violence. "It was a world of men," local people say, and the difficult gender relations of the time fit this socioeconomic scenario. Autocratic, tribal political leaders' heavy demands for servitude from tribal people fostered exploitative relations in general, including in marriage. Tribal leaders tended to represent themselves as benevolent leaders and as first among equal tribesmen.[2]

---

[1] Reinhold Loeffler and I stayed mostly in the large village/small town of Sisakht, in the tribal Province Kohgiluye/Boir Ahmad in southwest Iran. Local people speak Luri and identify with Twelver-Shi'ism. For the history and general ethnography, see Reinhold Loeffler, "Boir Ahmadī I: The Tribe," in Ehsan Yarshater (ed.), *Encyclopaedia Iranica* IV/3 (1989): 320–4; Reinhold Loeffler, "The World of the People of Deh Koh," in *The Nomadic Peoples of Iran*, eds. Richard Tapper and Jon Thompson (London: Azimuth Editions, 2002), 134–43. To the best of my knowledge, Mary Elaine Hegland's prolific writings about "Aliabad," a large village in Fars Province adjacent to Boir Ahmad, and our work constitute the most comprehensive longitudinal published studies of rural settlements in Iran.

[2] This positive self-image emerged in my talks with expatriate khans in Paris, France (1991), and with members of the last khan's kin group in Yasuj, Iran (2015). A local amateur historian called it "the khans' nostalgic mythmaking." For exceptions and the khans' positive contributions to their realms,

Period 2. Modernity started to seep into Boir Ahmad in the late 1920s. Reza Shah Pahlavi (r. 1925–41) tried to curb the khans' efforts to obstruct his reforms by asserting his own and his government's authoritarian-paternalistic powers. Men's lives continued to be structured by the heavy burden of family responsibilities amid violence and poverty, and women's lives by misogynistic traditions, work, high fertility, and lack of resources. Under Mohammad Reza Shah (r. 1941–79), socioeconomic change accelerated, and gender expectations shifted, but they did so only slowly, because the Pahlavi government's paternalistic-autocratic bias was similar to that of the tribal chiefs it replaced.

Period 3. Aspirations to a global lifestyle have been ubiquitous in Iran since before 2000. Only the nouveau riche can realize them, but aspirations nevertheless drive up normative expectations about marriage even in Boir Ahmad, where people's survival-oriented subsistence economy has changed only recently. Structural macrosocial developments in Boir Ahmad parallel changes in urban Iran and in the country's leadership, which supports androcentric customs and their philosophical underpinnings that are considered "normal" in Boir Ahmad and elsewhere.[3] Young people's dissatisfaction with autocratic leadership parallels their problems with marriage.

A Brisk Walk through Time

People's earliest recollections reach back to the nineteenth century, when small, transhumant kin groups in the Zagros valleys replaced earlier village and tribal communities more or less forcefully. The violent past fostered a heroic tribal identity supported by an ideology valorizing strength, physical daring, and competition.[4]

By all accounts, the local transhumant-pastoral farming economy was labor-intensive for everybody, involving complementary activities and responsibilities for both men and women, and exploiting environmental niches for fields and pastures for sheep and goats. Place names and memories point to bitter disputes over pastures and migration routes. Some disputes continue in the present.

Tribal/subtribal groups were patrilineal. Their chiefs *(khan, kadkhodā)* fought over land, status, and influence. These internecine hostilities and pressures from the rising population made local people insecure, fearful, poor, and ready for defense and aggression "day and night," as many recall. Domestic and economic activities were

---

see Loeffler, "Boir Ahmadī I: The Tribe." For khans in a neighboring tribe, see Pierre Oberling, *The Qashqa'i Nomads of Fars* (Berlin: De Gruyter Mouton, 2017).

[3] For comparison, see Mary Elaine Hegland in this volume and Mary Elaine Hegland, "Wife Abuse and the Political System: A Middle East Case Study," in *Sanctions and Sanctuary: Cultural Perspectives on the Beating of Wives*, eds. D. A. Counts, J. K. Brown, and J. C. Campbell (Boulder, CO: Westview Press, 1992), 203–18.

[4] Erika Friedl and Reinhold Loeffler, "Archaeology and Cultural Memory in Boir Ahmad, Southern Zagros, Iran," *Archiv für Völkerkunde*, 61–62 (2013): 138–231.

interrupted by raids, robberies, the khans' demands for goods, labor, and soldiers. Images of rifles and fighters on old gravestones tell of battles and hunting prowess.[5]

Under these circumstances, positive economic developments were few and slow. Hostile neighbors destroyed each other's fields and experimental orchards, and after the 1940s, the overgrazed pastures degraded. Until the end of the twentieth century, people were indebted to outside merchants who bartered a few necessities for their wool and milk products in exploitative arrangements. Life expectancy was low. Celibacy was a blemish, not a virtue; nearly everybody got married as early as possible, and widowed people remarried soon. Memories of dearth and hunger were interspersed with nostalgic images of herds of animals in idyllic camps in the high mountain pastures, of music and dances at colorful weddings, of men's hunting adventures in the oak forests, and of parties of women collecting plants that provided a precarious base of staple foods.[6] Looking back, people said their hard work "broke their backs"; they had "nothing," yet they were good, generous Muslims, even though their survival needs forced them to neglect some ritual aspects of their religion.

The "times of the khans," as people call the past, ended in 1963 with the last paramount khan's assassination for his violent resistance to the Pahlavi government's interference in tribal affairs, including the land reform.[7] The shah's army pacified the area, gendarmes replaced the khans' riflemen, security increased, and raids and hostilities diminished. People were still very poor, though, dependent on subsistence agriculture, and governed by an army general. Wages from work in Kuwait made life possible, despite diminishing agricultural resources. After the mid-twentieth century, Iran's oil income financed infrastructure projects. The national government replaced the khans, but authoritarian hierarchies were still in place, only less personal now.

Over the next generation, pressures on resources forced men to find income from other sources than agriculture. Fertility and child-survival rates rose when development brought "progress" in health care. Settlements with "good progress" grew fast: Sisakht, established around 1890 as a fortified village by a few families from a nearby hamlet, grew from about three hundred people in the 1940s to more than seven thousand by 2015. It became the administrative center of newly established Dena County, named after the majestic mountain that gives people a sense of belonging and identity. The town has government offices, religious buildings, a health clinic, schools, bank, and bazaar, and tourists from all over the world. As of 2017, it was still growing although emigration of young people was accelerating. All these features have influenced marriage practices.

---

[5] Folk songs provide glimpses of those times, both praising and disparaging heroic young fighters' daring and deaths. Erika Friedl, *Folksongs from the Mountains of Iran. Culture, Poetics and Everyday Life* (London: I. B. Tauris, 2018).

[6] Erika Friedl, "Women's Spheres of Action in Rural Iran," in *Shifting Boundaries: Women and Gender in Middle East History*, eds. Nikki Keddie and Beth Baron (New Haven, CT: Yale University Press, 1992), 195–214.

[7] Khans had no legal titles to tribal land; the "White Revolution" (1963–79) was less traumatic here than elsewhere although the khans resented its anti-feudal aspects. See Ervand Abrahamian, *A History of Modern Iran* (Cambridge: Cambridge University Press, 2008); Mary Elaine Hegland, *Days of Revolution: Political Unrest in an Iranian Village* (Palo Alto, CA: Stanford University Press, 2014).

Marriage in the Distant Past

In the "old days" the khans' politics, defense, and aggression, and a strict division of labor defined people's lives. People needed local chiefs' permission for any enterprise, including marriage; khans frequently were marriage brokers. Gender differences were placed within a hierarchy of authority, with a man being his family's "khan." Marriage and procreation were seen as part of God's order, self-evident and natural as is food, and as absolutely necessary to fulfill survival needs. People addressed male/female interdependence and relationships from the perspective of an androcentric, even misogynistic, gender philosophy, despite a strong ethos of "being human" (*ensāniat*) that included calm cooperation and polite hospitality. A woman's married life was said to be "written on her forehead" (*pishuni neveshte*), her inescapable "fate"; whether her husband was a kind or cruel "khan" was outside her agency. In contrast, a man's married life rarely was called his "fate"; it was God-willed but flexible, because a man had choices. A girl grew up knowing that she "had to go," that "they would come and get her," that her parents would "give her away," that she would be "sold," usually at a very young age and against her will. A boy grew up knowing he would get a wife from his father.

The desire for children (*bacce*) concentrated on sons; one wished for boys, but girls came anyway, "unbidden," people said. Women were needed to perpetuate a lineage and for the domestic life of men, but "being needed" did not in itself confer power or status. A father likely considered his daughter a costly liability, because as soon as she was "useful," not he but her husband's patrilineal group benefited from her work and her womb. To get a "useful" woman, a man had to pay. Most fathers used some of the bride price to buy household items for their daughters' new household; others kept most for themselves or spent more on acquiring wives for sons. Cases of girls given in lieu of blood money to settle feuds were known until the 1980s.

These structural features led to the so-called benign neglect of girls, to high female-infant mortality and a subsequent shortage of women, which, in turn, led to child marriages for girls, while men generally married in their late twenties. As elsewhere in Iran, child-marriage arrangements and teen pregnancies were considered normal. Shortages of women also led to increases in the bride price: when a father had to pay more for his son's wife, he raised the bar for his own daughter.

Authority within an extended family correlated with sex and age: young female children had the lowest status. Brothers usually wielded more authority over their sisters than a father who had a "soft heart" for his daughters.[8] Yet brothers' demands were often challenged by sisters, who created power in the family through their personalities, their work competence, and their emotional attachments. A favorite (or the eldest) brother became his well-liked sisters' ally in potential marital disputes or future existential needs. Yet, informal power was not the same as authority and, in serious disputes, sisters had to give in to their brothers' demands. In matters of marital

---

[8] Tradition (and religious law as understood locally) accords males over the age of nine authority over female members of the household. Boys learn that they can yell at their sisters unchallenged, order them around, and hit them if they disobey.

arrangements, brothers treated sisters like objects they could use for their own benefit.[9] Furthermore, in tribal law, a man's land and property went to his sons; daughters did not inherit anything of value and, thus, were completely dependent on men for their livelihood.

The prime parental duty, to secure spouses for one's children, was tough because of the shortage of women. Boys and men had some say in their spouse-selection; religious law allowed a girl the right to object to a suitor but not to voice her preference. In most cases, though, her objection had no chance to be uttered if for no other reason than that the girl was too young to understand what was going on. Without marital choice, the inevitable commodification led to women being "sold" and "bought," much like slaves. Together with lack of access to resources such as inheritance, it also meant that women lacked authority in their fathers' and husbands' families. The terms I am using here, "buying," "selling," "servant," and even "slave" are terms that are actually used by local people, especially by women themselves. They show quite a realistic assessment of traditional marital transactions.[10]

A suitor's family needed the chief's permission to propose. When a father asked for an absurdly high bride price for his daughter, he is implicitly refusing the proposal, but he, too, had to answer to the chief. Fathers and respected male elders in both families discussed the marriage contract, including the bride price (*shirbahā, bashlyk*), with informal input from female relatives. Acceptance of the proposal triggered expectations from the family of the bride that the groom would demonstrate subservience and allegiance to the family of the bride and culminated in the writing of the marriage contract (*aqd nāmeh*). The contracts were short and simple, often dismissing severance pay for the wife (in case of divorce) by stipulating "a copy of the Qur'an," for example, as compensation. Divorce among common people was rare. People tried to make wedding feasts as big as they could afford without attracting the greed of chiefs, who might demand more tribute if the party was lavish, but most could only arrange small parties, while the khans' weddings stretched over several days with many guests, music, and dances.[11] The new wife was called "bride" (*arus*) in her in-laws' family. Altogether, arranging and facilitating a marriage was an expensive social affair, especially for the groom's family: they received a bride and had to pay for it.

In her husband's house, the young bride lacked both power and authority (defined as the legal use of power). She had to obey everybody while working to create her own power base in the women's circle. The mother-in-law might support her kindly but was

---

[9] This is expressed in a proverb from Afghanistan, where similar relationships prevail: "When sisters are sitting together they are always praising their brothers. When brothers are sitting together they are selling their sisters to others." Eliza Griswold, "The 22 Syllables That Can Get You Killed." *BBC*, November 16, 2016. Available at www.bbc.com/culture/story/20161116 (accessed November 20, 2017).

[10] In 1998, UNICEF described conditions of child-bride marriages for Kurdistan as a form of slavery; these marriages are like those in traditional Boir Ahmad. See Anonymous, "Iran: Human Rights Abuses Against the Kurdish Minority," *Amnesty International*, July 2008, 1–58 (see especially p. 22). Available at www.amnesty.org/download/Documents/MDE130882008ENGLISH.pdf (accessed June 27, 2018).

[11] Tribal dances were gender-segregated: there were women's round dances and men's "stick dances," all accompanied by musicians on drums and oboe. Everybody could participate and watch except the mullah and his household: for them, dance and music were declared *harām*, religiously unlawful.

not obliged to do so. The young wife saw little of her husband, was properly "shy" in his presence, and hardly ever addressed him directly. In disputes in the house, he mostly sided against her. Under these circumstances, it was more consequential for her to have good relations with the women and elders in the house than with her husband.

Nearly three-quarters of marriages were within the bilateral kin group, which was as much a function of the small marriage pool as a matter of preference. People said that the kin group would support the marriage; a mother could stay closer to her married daughters if she lived next door rather than in another village; as in-laws, relatives would treat each other's daughters better than strangers would; and it would strengthen the kin group's cohesion. Such marriages were also cheaper: two related families even might exchange daughters without a bride price, reducing the expenses of the receiver's family to gifts of clothes and food, a small wedding feast, and an obligatory gift (such as honey or a lamb) for the chief. In cousin marriages, when a young wife moved in with her aunt or uncle, she only needed to bring bedding.

In 1994, a local woman described her life in the year 1940 when she was "very young."

> Every family had one room (*tu*) in a stone-and-mud house with a veranda in front with a fireplace for cooking. The room had a wooden storage platform (*tavareh*) at one short end, a big clay vessel (*tapu*) for grain in a corner to keep mice out, and another fireplace. In some old houses this was in the center, with a smoke-hole in the flat roof. Stoves and windows in mud-brick houses with hollow walls for storing wheat came much later. At night we rolled out a rag rug or a felt-mat on the dirt floor. The cover was another rug. When a son got married, for three days and nights he and his bride stayed in a separate place, usually in somebody's storage room (*ānbār*). Their mothers cooked for them. After that, they belonged to his father's house. Everybody slept in one room, young and old, sick and healthy, everybody. The groom had to do his business with his bride quickly and quietly. I was married very young—what did I know what "marriage" meant? I just thought I would get new clothes and live with my aunt. I had three miscarriages. We moved into our own room after I had my first child. Of my twelve pregnancies, five children made it into adulthood. Many women had miscarriages. They married too soon.

Under these circumstances, sex for newlyweds was difficult for both, and there are stories about inexperienced husbands having trouble performing as expected. Defloration and producing a pregnancy were the signs of successful sex and were watched over by the older women in the house.[12]

Even after the husband had built a room next door to his father's, cooking and living were shared. Women spent most of their time with the other women in the courtyard.

---

[12] Sex was seen as a God-ordained, natural necessity, a health issue even, especially for men, to be facilitated in marriage. Illegitimate sex and pregnancy are unlikely in child marriages but are a motif in folktales, ending with the killing of the mother and the child. Extramarital sex was rare and likely hushed up so as to avoid a tragedy, such as children losing their mother upon divorce.

While their husbands were closely related, the women might be strangers to each other. Ideally, they were cooperating in the many chores that filled their days and half their nights, especially in the summer outposts in the mountains.[13] Men were in the fields and pastures most of the day and were entitled to a meal (and sex) upon coming home. All work was done by women, including pregnant and nursing women, without adequate food. Physical weakness, expressed in the inability to perform chores quickly and satisfactorily, along with interference in each other's affairs or work habits, control of the children, accusations of neglect or unreasonable demands, and personality differences that disturbed the peace among women inevitably became problems for the husbands, too, while frictions among brothers (usually about economic matters) also caused frictions among their wives. Most husbands beat "disrespectful" wives. Anecdotes about enmities among women and about strategies of manipulation by both men and women to keep their places in the domestic status hierarchies outnumber happy memories, although there were also stories of friendships, of warm feelings, and of good times in the crowded courtyards.

For an adult woman, every new daughter-in-law was primarily a "servant" (*kolfat*). The younger she was, the easier she was to supervise and to turn into a "good bride," one who was less likely to challenge her mother-in-law later. The disadvantage for the older woman was that in the beginning, the "girl" (*duar*) had to be taken care of as the unhappy child she was, and that she might not get pregnant for quite a while because her mother might have put a penis-spell (*kirrband*) on the husband to prevent him from having sex with her. Although "everybody" knew that forced sex traumatized many child-wives and their husbands and that sexually demanding husbands were bad for "unripe" girls, sex and pregnancy were a woman's reason for existence. Child-wife pregnancies before menarche happened occasionally.[14] In old women's memories, their early years of marriage were "difficult" or even "very bad," with suffering caused by unwanted sex and by pregnancies, as well as by incompatible women in the house and a husband's violent outbursts. Stories of suicides and routine reports of young brides running back home and threatening suicide rather than rejoining their husbands attest to these difficulties.[15]

The wife of the youngest son was the most consequential for a mother-in-law, because ultimogeniture required the youngest son to stay with his parents and to take care of them in old age. His compensation was the father's house and an extra share of the expected inheritance. The day-to-day care of old people, though, fell on the

---

[13] Chores included housekeeping and childcare; procurement of water in heavy goatskin bags and of firewood; milking goats and processing milk into yogurt and butter(fat); gathering and drying wild vegetables, berries, fruits, and acorns; baking bread, weeding fields, and harvesting lentils; spinning wool and weaving rugs and textiles on the horizontal loom. See Friedl, "Women's Spheres of Action in Rural Iran."

[14] Menarche is the onset of menstruation. This means the girl got pregnant with her very first egg and before she menstruated.

[15] For such conditions, see also Sana Safi, "Why Female Suicide in Afghanistan Is So Prevalent," *BBC News*, July 1, 2018. Available at www.bbc.co.uk/news/world/asia/44370711 (accessed August 18, 2018). The reasons given are the same as in Boir Ahmad, but suicide attempts in Boir Ahmad have declined as socioeconomic and cultural conditions for women changed for the better. Statistics for Boir Ahmad, such as are available, are unreliable.

daughter-in-law. If she got on well with the in-laws (and in many households they did get on well), the house was in peace. But if the young woman was "arrogant, uppity, disrespectful, lazy," or if the mother-in-law was "a tyrant," life in the house quickly turned into drama, the men were dragged into the fights, and marriages became battlefields. Suicide attempts by young women in such households were frequent.

Most marriages were monogamous. Polygyny was a sign of elevated social and economic status befitting the tribal upper class. Many khans over their lifetime had more than the four wives simultaneously allowed by sharia law—Sisakht's famous chief had twelve—and some simply "took" other men's wives they fancied. An old joke is about a man with an uncommonly plain wife, whom the khan asked how he could live with such ugliness. "That's not half as difficult as was finding a wife I could keep to myself," the man said. When a commoner took a second wife, people thought he was "crazy" *(mās, kelu)* over a particular woman or had unfulfilled sexual desire. Love-craze was taken as a disruptive, regrettable condition, especially of men, driving them toward depression and violence. By contrast, a khan, besotted by his wife's beauty, might wax poetic. Among common folk, no level-headed man took a second wife unless his first was childless or a dead brother's widow needed a husband. Such levirate marriage made sense. The woman stayed in the family that had bought her already and who owned her children anyway. Failing such arrangement, she had to go back to her father, leaving her children behind. This, too, was the case in divorce, which a husband could initiate easily, making a woman with children "not even think" of giving him reason for dismissing her. Initiating divorce was not a realistic option for women in Boir Ahmad at the time. Tolerance, interdependence, care of children, and loyalty often led to liking and devotion in couples, but amiable intimacy was not taken for granted. A couple's purpose was to fulfill their respective gender responsibilities smoothly and dependably.

In the life cycle of marriages, a couple's life got easier as growing children provided assistance. Mothers had help from their daughters and could count on their sons' support in disputes with their husband or later with daughters-in-law. The mother-in-law was the mistress in the house, responsible for everybody, and managing everything her husband brought home. A wife's position changed again when she lost the emotional support of her daughters who moved away upon marriage and left their mother surrounded by daughters-in-law. Most older women, especially widows, said they preferred to live with a daughter or else alone, and many an elderly widower wished for a wife to take care of him in place of his son's unconcerned wife. Such arrangements were discouraged by relatives, however, because they signaled neglect in the son's house. While ailing old people were a heavy burden on caretakers, the elders' weakness gave daughters-in-law who had suffered under them earlier, a chance to more or less openly dislike the "old, ugly" ones in the house.[16]

Until old couples were relegated to "sit" (rather than work and give orders), the gender division of labor held into old age. This meant that an aging, aching wife

---

[16] Dim memories of occasional placement of senile, infirm old people in a nearby cave in the distant past (before the village of Sisakht had been founded) or of keeping them in baskets hung from a house-beam surfaced in conversations as late as the turn of the twenty-first century

continued to take care of her even older husband who, however, no longer did men's work and was at permanent leisure. Many elderly wives bemoaned their own health and their lot as caretakers, which led to the popular verdict that old women's characters deteriorated, making them cantankerous and unpleasant.

These assumptions and the socioeconomic structures within which marriages existed were challenged by modernity and the introduction of "progress."[17]

Marriage under Pahlavi Modernity

As locally understood, modernity meant progress (*pishraft*) and was a good thing, promising health and a better life. It came to most tribal areas after the khans' authority was broken, when news came from surrounding cities about new crops and farming methods, about how a cash economy worked, and about better houses, education, and medicine. The Pahlavi government started secular schools in the area around 1930 over the objections of religious and tribal leaders. The idea of education as a path—for many, the only path—to an easier life took hold in Sisakht, especially among men, who realized that their sons needed new skills to fulfil their duties when the land no longer sustained the rising population.

After the last paramount khan's death (in 1963), the autocratic rule of many smaller khans weakened. However, people's lifestyle and expectations of the new overlords—the shah's gendarmes, an army general, and administrators in Boir Ahmad—changed only slowly. People continued to be poor, hardworking, in ill health, malnourished, indebted to outside moneylenders, and dependent on authoritarian structures. Infant mortality decreased slowly. Due to continuing mortality imbalances between males and females, women continued to be scarce, marriages continued to be more or less arranged, life continued to be gender-segregated and complementary, including in work routines and work spaces, all within a social hierarchy that assigned males near total authority over women. However, people—and especially women—gradually became aware of the differences in lifestyle and levels of comfort and security that were appearing in many outside communities and started to lift their expectations for living.

Within the continuing constraints, marriages did not change much either— they just got more expensive. Bride price and other demands on a suitor's family increased: rather than accepting viri-patrilocal (also known as virilocal) residence, a young couple (or the bride's relatives) demanded a *dastgah*—a room, fireplace, porch of their own with the necessary household goods (and *necessary* was an elastic term). Social status differences increased with wealth as well as education, and status negotiations became embedded in marriage politics. For example, a father who spent more money on expensive household goods for the young couple than he had received as bride price showed thereby that he put himself socially above the groom's people. In the future, he might dare to interfere in his daughter's treatment by her in-laws or become overly demanding in requests for assistance from his son-in-law. Engagements, the formal

---

[17] "Progress" is a key concept in contemporary Boir Ahmad. See Reinhold Loeffler, "The Ethos of Progress in a Village in Iran," *Anthropology of the Middle East* 6/2 (2011): 1–13.

signing of a marriage contract, and weddings became elaborate, expensive gatherings modeled on the chiefs' parties.

However, in the process of individuation that accompanied literacy and modernity, young people started to speak up, and it became "normal" for parents to listen to their children's opinions about potential spouses. A girl, who might have been beaten up by her parents or brothers if she refused a suitor a generation earlier, now felt much less pressure to accept the next best guy's offer to become a "maid" in his house.[18] Spousal choice came to be seen as an acceptable feature of progress even though there was much hand-wringing over a son's or daughter's "wrong" choice. Indeed, men chose so often on whimsical grounds (such as seeing a girl walk to and from school a couple of times) that a new proverb showed parents' predicament: "You burn on your own!" (*sokhtesuzet tei khote*), meaning, "Don't ever blame me if you suffer with your spouse." Young men started to complain about the difficulty of meeting young women, because girls were always "sticking together" and in public were "moving in flocks." Young women had even fewer chances to meet potential spouses and were on the defensive, hoping and praying that no "old, ugly, good-for-nothing pauper" would come for them. Gender-segregated peer groups now relayed information on potential spouses via siblings and relatives. However, feeble as this choice was, it made the assumption that early marriage was a God-ordained, inevitable, and common-sense institution debatable.

The lack of arable land made it necessary, particularly for younger sons, to seek employment and income outside their own town: as elsewhere in Iran (and in other poor regions in Asia), men left their wives and children for months to work in the Gulf States. Their "unguarded" wives back home had to be especially careful about their reputations. Unless their sons were old enough—and willing—to work with their hands, women had to take on some male tasks, such as clearing snow from dirt roofs or even, clandestinely, ploughing or harvesting to avoid being entirely dependent on their in-laws' help.[19] Help with these chores from brothers-in-law might be given willingly, but there was the danger that the helpers might later make claims to the produce of the land they had cultivated for the absent brother: usufruct right was an old tribal law that became relevant in these new work situations.

Although absent husbands were problematic for wives, women realized they could, indeed, make it on their own, especially where a "little progress," such as a water faucet in the courtyard, a gas cooking range, a convenient new shop, and some money in her pocket (from the husband) was making life easier. Just as women had always been good wardens of flour and lentils and whatever their husbands brought from urban markets, now they were good at managing money. Divorce and polygyny continued to be rare. For couples, contentedness and discontent continued to hinge on how both partners discharged their respective responsibilities, whether the women in close proximity to the household liked or disliked one another, and whether inheritance and economic issues were handled equitably within kin groups.

---

[18] There are catches, though: a local woman said she had declined every suitor until, to her chagrin, a Seyyed family wanted her; she did not dare to refuse a descendant of the Prophet.

[19] Mothers with middle-class aspirations routinely absolved their sons of menial chores to prepare them for a better life, one depending on literacy and study.

Modernity in Health, Education, and Marriage

With the decline of the tribal chiefs' power and authority, governmental modernization programs flourished in Sisakht in the 1970s, especially in public health and education. At the same time, environmental degradation, loss of fields to the building boom, and the expansion of orchards made herding unprofitable, and women lost their most important economic tasks: processing milk and wool. They started to engage in elaborate homemaking and joked about becoming "lazy and fat" or "aching from sitting around so much." Public health programs accelerated population growth by increasing life expectancy and lowering the rates of infant/child mortality. The resulting population increase outpaced local economic resources. Already in 1965, parents expressed worries about their children's future and began to ask for contraceptives. Children no longer were an inevitable product of marriage, and their upkeep was becoming expensive. That "too many" children kept the family in poverty was a mantra that children heard in school and adults heard on the radio, from the doctor, and from each other. In many villages, this new ideology changed parental duties, adults' attitudes toward children, and the dynamics of intrafamily relations, including those of spouses, toward greater permissiveness and autonomy.[20] "Freedom" (*āzādi*) became a corollary of "progress" in the language of politics. For women, it included an easier workload, a permissive husband, a comfortable life. Men found it increasingly difficult to keep up with their wives' and children's expectations. Government-backed loans afforded amenities that soon were seen as necessities.

The other important feature of modernity was education. Truman's Point Four Program was introduced in 1950 in Iran. By 1960, the program made literacy locally available to tribal boys and girls by establishing tent-schools that moved with them. Now young local people, men and some women, trained in a tribal teacher-training school in Shiraz, began to teach students.[21] People regarded this as a watershed development: teaching was the first salaried job available not only to local young men but also to young women. Marriage and gender expectations became problematic in the bid for middle-class life, especially regarding money. In many (if not most) farm families, women had always been the managers of foodstuff in the house and now simply added the management of their husbands' wages or agricultural income to their chores, but salaried men did not accept this. For them, the management of their paychecks became a measure of their status and its validation, and for most this included managing the wife's salary, too, if she had one. "A paycheck is not like a sack of flour in the kitchen for my wife to make bread with," said a teacher.

---

[20] For the importance of the concept of "progress" in the area, see Reinhold Loeffler, "The Ethos of Progress." This permissiveness did not eliminate parental matchmaking, though. In 1994, when two young people from unrelated and socially unconnected families in town became engaged, the neighbors did not know what to make of it until a regular mosque-attendant pointed out that both fathers were famous singers in the mosque. By then mosque-circles had overlapped with other social spheres. Erika Friedl, "A Brief History of Childhood in Boir Ahmad, Iran," *Anthropology of the Middle East* 12/3 (2017): 6–19.

[21] President Harry S. Truman's "Point Four" development program included a tent-school program for nomads, led by M. Bahmanbegi, a Qashqa'i. It was a great success.

The first women teachers in Sisakht, three sisters from a former chief's family, provide good examples of these changes. Their literate father had no sons and taught the daughters to read and write. The eldest was "given" to a khan in a distant village in her early teens in a marriage arranged largely for political reasons. She had two children when her husband died. Rather than stay on in a levirate marriage, she decided to leave and become a teacher although she thereby lost custody of her children. Her in-laws' protest was loud, but she was backed by her own strong-willed, widowed mother and a maternal uncle and argued that her teacher's salary would facilitate a university education for her sons later. She was successful: her children have university degrees and have "made good progress"; she later married an amiable relative and opened a private school.

The next sister was accepted to the teacher-training school at the age of fifteen, before she married a cousin, who was also a teacher. It was generally agreed that the young people insisted on getting married over "everybody's" objections. The couple soon moved into separate quarters to avoid interference by relatives who called the young husband a rude spendthrift.[22] His salary was insufficient for their needs, but his wife insisted on managing her salary herself. There were harsh words. For the wife, teaching, managing household finances, and taking care of house and children while also being a servant (her term) to her husband proved exhausting, despite various helper arrangements. He complained about the lack of respect as the head of the family and about getting neither her salary nor the customary service of a wife who did not have an income, such as proper dinners. He had a "scrambled-egg wife," he said. Their disputes drew attention to the conflict between a working woman's time-constraints and a husband's customary expectations. When her husband died, she did not remarry but continued to teach, earned a college degree, and became the legendary principal of the local girls' high school, known for her wisdom, authority, teaching skills, and her temperament. Throughout the area, hers became a cautionary story: a wife with a job is incompatible with her husband unless she lets him manage her money.

The third sister also became a teacher. Betrothed early to the youngest son of a maternal aunt, she lived in his family's house after marriage and had full assistance with housekeeping and childcare from her aunt and cousins. Her husband managed both their salaries wisely: they had a car, a good house, and a peaceful life, in that order of importance.

For the next two generations, such cases highlighted the choices and their consequences for a young woman: either to aspire to a job with "money in your pocket" that elevated her status and made even divorce manageable but likely came at the price of a dissatisfied husband or else to be dependent on a husband who might or might not prove financially reliable and kind. For men, the choice was to either have a wife with a job and thereby endure curtailed wifely services, tensions in the house, neglected children, and perhaps no more money at his own disposal, or else to opt for a homemaker wife with no chance for progress in lifestyle in a one-salary family. For most men, and especially their mothers, a homemaker wife was still preferable.

---

[22] In androcentric societies, it is common for a husband to separate his wife from her own people to keep her subservient.

"Three years of elementary school is enough for a girl" became a glib expression in the 1980s.[23] Girls, however, disagreed. The main concern of many high school girls was to avoid becoming engaged before they had finished school.[24] To escape the "prying eyes" of young men and their scouts (men's sisters and mothers), the adolescent girls made themselves rare, went out firmly wrapped in long veils "looking at nobody," refused to talk to people on the telephone, and fought with their relatives (especially brothers and grandmothers) who wanted to see them "taken care of."

Despite the working women's conundrum, other women followed the three sisters' lead. As education students away from home, they studied hard and copied the tribal fashions of rich Qashqa'i women they met in school.[25] Back home, as teachers, they became powerful role models—glamorous, respected, and envied by their girl students.

The first local university graduates (starting in 1966) were men with good salaries in traditionally arranged marriages with homemaker wives. The first medical doctor, however, married a professional urban woman of his own choice, but his urban professional wife disdained village life. The couple moved away and had children, but the marriage developed problems, and the wife stopped working. This was the second example that local people recounted as a warning about letting young people choose their spouses: the young, no matter how well educated, have neither experience nor wisdom enough to choose wisely.

The marriage of a local female physician, in 1994, also served as an example. Repeatedly, she refused the marriage proposals of a well-off local man although they were approved by his and her people. However, his perseverance demonstrated that he was her "fate," she said, and all she could do was to insist on finishing her medical degree before the wedding. The couple moved away for well-paying jobs but experienced the usual problems: the husband's people said that he "had no wife" and the children had "no mother" because she worked "day and night"; the wife's people said that she had little support from her husband, no reliable help with housework and that her busy husband neglected his family. (The spouses did not complain, though.)

The desire for a "companionate marriage" was not an issue in any of these cases. (Even mild remarks by young women about their attraction to a suitor or husband appeared only in the last generation, in the late 1990s.) Rather, since the 1970s, the issues were overwork of women and disputes over authority, money, power, and services. For most working women, the pressure to perform the services expected from a mother/wife outweighed the benefits of the income from their jobs even if the salary stayed under their control.

This problematic condition increased after the Revolution of 1979. Throughout Iran, jobs were scarce, yet aspirations to a "modern," middle-class way of life continued.

---

[23] The Revolution of 1979 did not change this modernization evolution in Sisakht.
[24] The Iranian educational system has university admission quotas for women and for students from rural places, stoking girls' aspirations without fulfilling all of them, because competition for access to university education is intense, and it is a contentious political issue in Iran.
[25] Traditional tribal dress for women in the area is similar to that of Qashqa'i women in neighboring Fars Province. It consists of a cap, veil, and shawl covering the head, and several wide, long skirts, a long shirt, and a velvet jacket. Qashqa'i outfits were more elaborate, colorful, and expensive than Boir Ahmad women could afford.

These aspirations included having a nuclear family living in its own well-appointed residence, enjoying good food, chic clothes, and a car. Such demands could be satisfied only if a man had a good job. If his wife also worked, she likely asked her husband for help with domestic chores. This new division of labor was talked about "a lot," people said, and it caused discontent between spouses but brought little change in women's domestic responsibilities.[26]

Because of the 1979 Revolution, the 1980–88 Iran–Iraq war, the US-imposed sanctions, "the rule of the mullahs," and several other macro-socioeconomic conditions, even fewer jobs opened up for women in rural areas than in the cities. At the same time, a highly progressive and successful governmental family-planning program quickly curbed the population increase. As a result, fertility rates throughout the country, including in this part of the tribal area, dropped to astonishingly low levels.[27] However, lack of childcare in the new, smaller, independent families became the major stated reason why women did not look for jobs even though money was short. Yet, paradoxically, lack of jobs also was—and is—the reason given by couples for limiting the number of their children to "one or two," even if the mother stays at home: to bring up more than two successful children in a competitive world has become impossible on one salary, they say. Although Iranian women, including rural women, are among the best-educated in the Middle East, Iran has one of the lowest rates of women in the paid labor force.[28]

Obviously, there is more to this than a bad economy. Locally, one factor is the old, pervasive assumption that it is a man's (God-ordained) duty to care for the wife he has contracted and paid for and to provide for his children. In other words, the wife and children can demand of the husband/father full care and sustenance; a good provider is a successful, well-regarded man. Neglect is one of few legal reasons for a judge to grant a woman's petition for divorce. In traditional tribal law, ownership of a wife had included ownership of her products, be they children or valuable items such as woven rugs and butterfat or else her income from a job. By the same logic, a father's duty to take care of an unmarried daughter had included his claim on a part or all of her income, if needed. Upon marriage, these rights and duties were transferred to her husband.[29] Working

---

[26] This complaint remains widespread in Iran. In 2015, an urban university professor said that, no matter how tired she was, she had to cook a full dinner for her husband every night.
[27] On fertility management, see chapter 11 in Janet Afary, *Sexual Politics in Modern Iran* (Cambridge: Cambridge University Press, 2009); Agnes G. Loeffler and Erika Friedl, "The Birthrate Drop in Iran," *Homo: The Journal of Comparative Human Biology* 65/3 (2014): 240–55.
[28] The massification of undergraduate education in Iran resulted in more than half of all students being women, despite repeated attempts by the government to limit women's access to higher education. Yet, in 2017, women's participation in the labor force in Iran was less than 17 percent. See https://www.theglobaleconomy.com/Iran/Female_labor_force_participation/ (accessed January 9, 2019).
[29] In contrast, in urban conservative circles, fathers and husbands who permitted a daughter or wife to work forbade her to spend a penny of her salary on the household. In the 1940s, a school principal in Shiraz, Z. Qatrifi, reported that she could not even buy a pair of shoes for herself. Later, widowed young, the gold she had bought with her salary enabled her to bring up her children by herself (personal communication, 1994). In 2012, the urban parents of a teacher in Boir Ahmad who was living with her unemployed husband and his parents, insisted that she keep her salary: if her husband could not pay for her upkeep, it was his father's duty to pay, they said. In Sisakht, the few men with a salaried daughter or wife fit their financial behavior to the needs of the moment. An indebted man repeatedly asked his married working daughter for money, arguing that as her

both at home and in the workplace and handing the income to a demanding husband was an unattractive option for women. Rather, young women hoped for a well-off husband, a good provider who did not need her financial input. For the husband, it was beneficial to his comfort, status, and reputation to have a home-centered wife and well-groomed children, which showed that he was doing well and did not need the income from a working wife. There have been enough cases that "prove" the wisdom of such attitudes to make them appear valid even in a difficult economy.

The other pervasive assumption involves inheritance. As tribal custom makes men responsible for the upkeep of their children, a married son in the traditional economy expected enough animals and land from his father to make him independent soon after his marriage. This transfer of resources, which was counted as part of his inheritance, was jealously calculated and monitored by the other sons so as to prevent unequal distribution. (This also explains sons' disapproval of an elderly widowed father's remarriage: additional sons with his new wife would complicate the inheritance issue.) Nevertheless, younger sons felt disadvantaged because the elder brothers had first claim on "the best" of everything, and elder sons felt disadvantaged if the younger ones got an education and a salaried job, counting this as the young brothers' inheritance. Sisters did not inherit land and property at all, because their husbands were bound to take care of them. Brothers, however, had to have the wherewithal to support their own families. All this amounted to entitlement thinking by children and wives that changed marriage arrangements in the present generation since the turn of the twenty-first century.

Marriage in "the Times of the Children"

Local people aspire to what counts as comfortable, chic, new lifestyles in Iran, modeled on foreign television shows and the lives of expatriate cousins who send videos and occasionally even visit. Women desire education, clothes, beauty products, and travel from a father while unmarried; from a husband, they want a car, an apartment, furniture, jewelry, one child only, and travel.[30] Preferred jobs are "*lüx*," which means a desk job with good pay and good hours. For the past decade, the ubiquitous expression "there is no work" (*kār nist*) has meant lack of such good jobs throughout Iran.[31] Most jobs available in rural areas do not pay enough to let a man be the proud head of a household. Young people in Sisakht have to defer marriage: Thirty-year-old "girls" and "boys" are quite common. Young men feel stressed by being "nobody" at an age when their grandparents were called elderly. Young women suffer less, they say: they would rather stay with kind, poor parents than with a depressed, angry, poor husband. Besides, they may claim an allowance from the half-share of a father's inheritance

---

husband was taking care of her, she did not need her salary anyway. He never asked his sons for help.

[30] There is a general belief, supported by physicians, that depression in women is due to a lack of diversion such as travel can provide. A "good" husband takes his wife on trips.

[31] In 2015, I asked local high school students to rank the best fields of study. They placed pharmacy above medicine, and radiology above surgery on the basis of better pay and more flexible hours.

they are entitled to under sharia law. Most local older men have some income from agriculture or the sale of land that helps to make ends meet even if they support adult live-in children. Such support may even extend to an unemployed son's wife, because a father's responsibility includes the son's responsibilities as well. In 2004, a local, single female engineer declined a job in northern Iran, saying she would rather stay jobless at her father's house than live in a far away, small place with a small salary or be a servant for a mother-in-law. In social circles aspiring to a middle-class life, unemployment (*bikāri*) in effect has become a "luxury good."[32] A middle-class man with an income and a child has to justify why his wife is working, especially in a low-prestige, low-paying job like nursing, for example. Poorer rural women are less limited: many continue to work harvesting fruits, among other jobs, and manage their little income, invariably for the benefit of the household.

Arranged marriages do not make much sense under these circumstances and have become unpopular among the young, who count the right to choose a spouse as "freedom." Few parents still insist that their children marry relatives, but most want them to marry people within their social class and with good economic prospects, people who are known and can be trusted, and who "fit" their children's personality and habits. But the young find this rather difficult to do. Young men complain that young women have become "choosy" and their parents "greedy"; that the girl's family gathers intelligence about a potential suitor's economic standing before they even "look at him as a person." The contractual divorce-severance pay (*mahriyeh*) has risen so high in Iran that in 2015 the government tried to limit it to about $100,000 (in the form of gold coins), and young men and their families hesitate to commit themselves to what might be an economic disaster in the future. Stories are popular about predatory young women who marry to get a good divorce settlement. Young women complain that young men only want "beautiful girls" from well-to-do families to be cheap maids at home. Furthermore, weddings and wedding preparations have become so expensive that most grooms expect to be in debt for years. In 2015, the obligatory bridal makeup and rent for a white dress cost a teacher's monthly salary, and weddings had moved from courtyards with food cooked by women to costly fashionable parties in hotels with music and dancing. Among the tribal elite, expensive, neo-traditional, "tribal" fashions appeared at weddings, and gold jewelry, measured in weight, was de rigueur for the bride. People defended such financially painful extravaganzas by speaking of "the eyes of the people" or "keeping up with the Joneses": no groom wants to be called a cheapskate. Guests' wedding presents become important in local status rivalries when many families record and announce them publicly. In 2015, a local bank clerk joked that every year he had to spend the equivalent of one month's salary for gifts at relatives' weddings.

Aside from money in the marriage game, young men and women also wish for partners they can "talk to" and "like," who share their interests and have similar educational backgrounds; that is, they wish for a fledgling companionate relationship. But it is difficult to establish trust and ease if, in the words of a local woman, "he is gone all day and I am alone behind a closed door," or, in the words of a professional man

---

[32] This is a term used by A. J. Ghose, "The Luxury of Unemployment," *The Economist* 6/9 (2018): 65.

with a beautiful wife, "she visits her mother all the time and only talks about cosmetics." Inhabitants of small tribal towns know about urban, "modern" arrangements for cohabitation known as "white marriages" and intimate relations outside of marriage, but locally, it is unimaginable for a young man and woman to move in together in a "white marriage" or a temporary marriage (*sigheh*), surrounded by scandalized relatives.[33] One can do this only in a city, where there is more freedom, they say.

All this belongs to what young people in Iran generally call "freedom" (*āzādi*): freedom to participate in whatever their world has to offer, with little interference from authorities, be they the government, religious bodies, parents, or spouses. Rules of conduct have softened, and one learns early to bend them. Quiet illicit relationships are increasing, people say. Care of children is not included in this vision of a good life: children are expensive and demanding, and they limit one's movements, especially in the absence of relatives' help with childcare in the neolocal families. The same holds true for care of the elderly, which increasingly stresses couples.[34] Locally, several "old maids" with small salaries provide care for parents when this should be the responsibility of the youngest brother and his wife. Traditional, "cheap," more or less arranged, marriages still occur, but they are seen as a function of poverty and social stagnation now that wealth and chic living are most attractive.

Divorces initiated by women are increasing throughout Iran, including in the tribal areas. Reasons vary from traditional, wide-ranging "neglect" accusations to a husband's secret drug addiction, from "behaving like a khan or shah" to wanton ("unjustified") physical abuse, and from impotence to nondisclosure of a previous marriage. But divorced women's financial status suffers. A dissatisfied husband can easily divorce his wife without much justification, just as his ancestors did, but the new prenuptial monetary arrangements are a deterrent. By and large, young men and women and their parents have become distrustful of suitors (or potential brides) they do not know well, and they enlist far-flung relatives to scout their backgrounds. "Spies are everywhere," said a young woman. Brothers continue to be matchmakers: they see their sisters as theirs to barter with and their matchmaking as beneficial for the sisters because, alas, the brother's friend is a known person. Male teachers, too, use their position "to fish in the pool of young, bright pretties," as one told me, as a joke; he had married one of his students "fresh out of school" when she was sixteen, in 1998. For one local school principal, this custom was a reason for the education department to insist on female teachers for female students.

The changes in marriage customs create new problems for local people. For every wife a man imports from elsewhere, a local girl's chance to get married decreases. "Old maids" now are in every kin group, but there is no structure in place for them.[35] This

---

[33] Allowed in sharia law and recommended to limit illicit sexual relations among young people, a *sigheh* marriage is contracted for a specified time. It was never popular in respectable families.
[34] See also Mary Elaine Hegland, "The Need for a Center for the Elderly and for Widows Living Alone in the Shiraz Area." Paper presented at the First International Conference on Social Policy in the Islamic World, Tehran, May 12–13, 2018.
[35] A few local, single, professional women left Iran recently and married abroad. The reason given for the increase in marriage migration from Iran was that "Iranian husbands are too demanding." See Mary Elaine Hegland, "Social Mobility in the Shiraz Suburb of Aliabad: Living Standards, Marriage

causes misgivings and unhappiness. A young man, engaged to be married to a cousin before he left for a city job, "went crazy" about a secretary there. The resulting cancellation of the engagement with the cousin made enemies of their families. Another young man left his wife with his parents while studying in Tehran, where he married a student without telling her that he was already married. Eventually, it became known and caused a scandal, and both women divorced him on the legal ground that he had taken a second wife without the first wife's consent. And there is the sad story of a student who, unable to get the woman he fell for in the city where he studied, tried to kill himself.

Such stories were told at the beginning of the "Free Choice" movement, around 2000.[36] Meanwhile, "anything goes," as a young man said about business, politics, and marriage: "If you like your cousin, marry the cousin and make your mother happy; if you fancy a pretty fellow student, move in with her if you can afford it. But beware of the girls who are after you: most are bad women who take up with anybody for money." This includes married women whose husbands turn a blind eye to their liaisons because the additional income affords a better life. The "bad city girls" who like to be rich men's "*gerl frends*" create stories local people tell with glee.

Fear of polygyny has risen even in the countryside, where social controls and economic constraints have always made polygyny rare. In 2006, a local high school principal said that her female students' main concern was the fear that their fathers might try to "sell them" as second wives or would take a second wife. By 2015, local people talked about how acceptable it had become for wealthy urban men to take a second, young wife: it showed their economic prowess, and the new wife got a comfortable life in her own apartment. The romantic aspects of "love," however, are not much in evidence in any story.[37] A well-off, local business man with a young second wife assured me that he never would divorce his first wife because he "really loved" her, but his second wife said he meant that it was cheaper for him to pay the first wife's upkeep than to pay the divorce settlement.

Because modern marriages in Iran hinge on money, one may ask how people can aspire to a middle-class marriage and family, given the country's bad economy. One answer is government-sponsored loans and debts. Loans are "more important than salaries," said a bank clerk. Even more important, however, are smart people's economic opportunities in the robust, illegal "second economy." People see the same disconnect between behavior, morality, and law in their own behavior as "everywhere else": in government, with the mullahs, and in business. Everybody claims to have no other choice

---

and Desire for Diaspora." Paper read at the Fifteenth Conference of the European Association of Social Anthropologists, Stockholm, August 12–14, 2018.

[36] See, for example, Pardis Mahdavi, *Passionate Uprisings: Iran's Sexual Revolution* (Palo Alto, CA: Stanford University Press, 2009); Padideh Pakpour, *Identity Construction: The case of Young Women in Rasht* (Uppsala: Uppsala University Press, 2015).

[37] An example is the courtship story of a pious local professional woman who had been married for six years in 2015. "I thought that a freely chosen marriage was about passionate '*love.*' But the men around me, well: good-looking, plain, rich, dumb, shy boys—none made me look twice. There was this guy I talked with a couple of times in class, quiet and not much to look at, just kind and respectful. He was from a small village not far from my place, and once we took the same bus home and talked all the way. When he asked me to marry him I said yes, although I never had felt any *love*-passion. But we are happy!"

than to participate in it, if for no other reason than—again—the welfare and future of their children.³⁸ People call this difficult period "times of the children" (*doure baccyal*): rather than being viewed as an asset to the family, as they were in the past, many parents today see children as an economic drain, as behaving like "dictators" or "little shahs." The intrafamily power hierarchy is turned upside down: parents fulfill children's orders for goods and services and risk abuse when they fail. Working parents leave young children at home alone; university graduate "boys" and "girls" live with their parents, while old couples live alone because their children won't take care of them. A local sociology professor had a short explanation for the decrease in family commitments and for the low birth rate in Iran: "Why bother?" he said, meaning that these conditions further a kind of solipsistic hedonism, that is, in his opinion, morally unsound and alien to Iranian people's traditional ethos but endemic now "from top to bottom."

Marriage and Religion

The scarcity of references to Islam in this chapter is pointed: in the past, Islam in Boir Ahmad functioned as an ideology to justify (rather than create) social relations.³⁹ Local religion supported traditional sociopolitical structures or, vice versa, local people fitted their religion to their needs within politico-economic limits. Tribal law superseded Islamic law in many instances. Religion in the Islamic Republic may not make the economy better or people happier, but sharia-inspired laws regarding inheritance, marriage arrangements, divorce, custody, and fertility management have made local marital life easier. However, the laws did not topple the old hierarchies of authority and gender expectations. This created confusion. Most men (and women) use authoritarian aspects of religion to their advantage when they feel the need to emphasize traditional marriage and spousal relationships. In contrast, others, mostly women, are inspired by the same religion to encourage individuation and female authority in an Islamic feminism that opposes forced marriages and "frivolous" divorces, advocates "freedom," and motivates mistreated wives to speak up and claim their rights.⁴⁰ Rarely though, can anyone deny the effects of paternalistic, androcentric marriage-related customs that continue to prevail in the Islamic Republic's politico-religious milieu.

---

[38] Iran ranks 131 of 176 on the "Corruption-Perceptions Index 2016," *Transparency International* 2018. Available at www.transparency.org (accessed June 30, 2018). Locally, the term that normalizes most strategies in the black economy is *majbur*, compelled, forced: people claim they have no choice, just as they had none complying with a Khan's immoral requests.

[39] Local lived religion is not specific on marriage beyond supporting authoritarian, androcentric gender relations. See Reinhold Loeffler, *Islam in Practice: Religious Beliefs in a Persian Village* (Albany: SUNY Press, 1988); Erika Friedl and Reinhold Loeffler, "Eschatology in Boir Ahmad, Iran," *Anthropology of the Middle East* 13/1 (2018): 55–68; Hegland, "Wife Abuse and the Political System."

[40] A young woman much abused by her husband said that after participating in Qur'an classes, she was no longer afraid of her husband and was now holding her own in the house. Religiously motivated women's gatherings provide emotional support for women in the cities but are nearly absent in Boir Ahmad. See, for example, Sabine Kalinock, "Supernatural Intercession to Earthly Problems: *Sofreh* Rituals Among Shiite Muslim and Zoroastrian Women in Iran," in *Zoroastrian Rituals in Context*, ed. Michael Stausberg (Leiden and Boston: Brill, 2003), 531–46.

9

Changing Perceptions and Practices of Marriage among People of Aliabad from 1978 to 2018

New Problems and Challenges

Mary Elaine Hegland

When I arrived in Aliabad in September 2015, I went to stay with my friend from long ago, Esmat. She had recently bought a small house and was living next to the sister of another dear friend, Mina. One day, Mina's daughter Shahnaz was hosting several friends from her university classes. They were earning associate degrees in accounting at an institution located in a suburb on the Aliabad side of Shiraz. Not from Aliabad, at least two of the girls' families lived in apartments on the other side of Shiraz. I was invited to join them.

Shahnaz's two older sisters and her older brother were all married. Shahnaz was engaged and would be married in the summer of 2017. She was looking forward to marriage and liked to spend time with her husband-to-be and his family. She talked about the positive aspects of having children and looked forward to having babies. She expressed the hope that the marriage would turn out well.

The young women were talking about whether or not it is a good idea to get married. "Yes," Shukufeh said, "Marriage is okay if he has a pleasant personality and a good financial situation."

"No," Nazanin said, "I don't want to marry. I don't like marriage. You can always be afraid; maybe you will regret it."

Someone else added, "But a single life also has its regrets."

Then they asked me, "Do you think it is better to have a boyfriend or get married?"

Feeling rather shocked and put on the spot, wanting to avoid the possibility of answering in a way that would offend parents, I said, "I think it is good to study, work to get experience, and become more mature (*pokhteh misheh*) before getting married." (As an anthropologist, I should have turned the question around and used it to investigate their views, but I didn't think that fast.)

What they would do, the young women decided, is take it easy this coming term: take time off, think, and work on their health and figures. They'll go to the gym (*bashgah*). Shahnaz was trying to lose weight and went to a gym ten minutes away once a week.

Shahnaz's mother came in and commented, "My daughter-in-law (the couple lived in the apartment upstairs) goes to the *bashgah* (gym), the *daneshgah* (university), and the *arayeshgah* (beauty parlor). Now she should go to the *zaimangah* (labor and delivery hospital)."

The others said, "She is always telling her daughter-in-law to have a baby." The daughter-in-law had married three years earlier and was twenty-seven years old. Although her family was originally from Aliabad, they had lived in Shiraz and only moved back a few years ago. When the daughter-in-law came in a little later after driving back from the city, she presented a sophisticated image. Her hair was dyed different shades of blonde and in a chic short cut. She wore tight black pants and had beautifully done makeup. She spoke in a straightforward and open manner with her mother-in-law and father-in-law. She didn't show deference but behaved as one might with peers.

This encounter, early in my three-month fieldwork in fall 2015, introduces current dilemmas and concerns about marriage. Now marriage is perceived somewhat more as a choice than before; one has to make a decision, and any decision could prove to be the wrong one. For the majority of Aliabad women, the troubled economy and lack of good job opportunities, especially for women, along with constraints against women working means that there is not actually much of a choice. For lack of alternatives, usually, they must marry.

Later Shahnaz confided that she wasn't really interested in continuing her education. Her intent, it seemed, was to marry, have children, and live a life similar to that of her mother and two sisters—a life of domestic involvement and social engagement with relatives and in-laws in Aliabad.

Like Shahnaz, many Aliabad girls have access to post-diploma education in Shiraz, in other cities in Fars Province, or even at universities in other provinces. With iPhones, Twitter, and other social media,[1] in addition to class attendance, Aliabad university students' interactions and communication with their associates outside of Aliabad—their peer group—had become more frequent and significant for young women from Aliabad. Their worlds had expanded.

Also evident in this encounter was the common contrast between the older generation's views of marriage and the ideas and behaviors of some of the younger generation. Older women maintained the attitude that men should be providers and women should be homemakers. When a friend repeated my remark that Middle Eastern women have the lowest rate of employment outside of the home, and among them Iranian women have the lowest, older women exchanged pleased glances.

Shahnaz's mother wanted her daughter-in-law to have a baby, but many younger Aliabad women wanted to postpone having children and spend time pursuing their own interests and goals. Shahnaz's aspirations, however, were more like those of the older Aliabad women. One of her Shirazi cousins had said their Aliabad cousins were

---

[1] See Vahideh Golzard and Cristina Miguel, "Negotiating Intimacy through Social Media: Challenges and Opportunities for Muslim Women in Iran," *Middle East Journal of Culture and Communication* 9 (2016): 216–33.

not interested in reaching new goals or improving themselves. The city cousins saw a difference between rural and urban women's views insofar as personal development, marriage, family, and children were concerned. Sure, they would say, maybe Aliabad girls are getting more of an education than they did before, but they are still the same; they go on living like their mothers and grandmothers. In contrast, the city cousins say, they themselves want progress and better lives.[2] The world has changed, they say, and they want to change as well.

Many Iranians have been experiencing a dynamic period of questioning, change, and controversy about marriage. My participant observation for a total of three years among the people of Aliabad in 1978–79 and in the twenty-first century uncovered alterations in ideas and behavior regarding marriage over a period of forty years. Such transformations parallel those taking place elsewhere in Iran and figure among the dramatic cultural, social, political, religious, economic, and infrastructure changes that Iranians have experienced in the last four decades.[3] Whereas similar changes in Europe and America developed over centuries, the changes in Iranian society have been compressed into decades and, as a result, are all the more noticeable and in conflict with previous perceptions and practices. Along with new choices and modified relationships, new problems and dilemmas have emerged.

Marriage Perceptions and Practices in 1978–79

In the 1970s, marriage was still perceived as automatic at an early point in the life cycle. Parents saw the marriage of their children, along with becoming grandparents, as the apex of their lives. It was not too complicated, difficult, or expensive for parents to obtain a spouse for their children. For males and females to become complete human beings and adults, they were expected to marry and become parents. Marriage was seen as benefiting men and as necessary for the maintenance, guardianship, and protection of women. The perception of marriage as an intrinsic and necessary aspect of Muslim life was taken for granted. Even persons with disabilities generally married.

Marriage was seen as so valuable, positive, and religiously obligatory that better-off people might assist a young man who lacked the necessary means to marry. Such a donation was seen as bringing religious blessing and credit (*savab*) to the benefactor. In memory of sons who tragically died too young to marry, "wedding chambers" (*hejleh*),

---

[2] For discussion of another village where the emphasis on progress seems to have been much stronger, see Reinhold Loeffler, "The Ethos of Progress in a Village in Iran," *Anthropology of the Middle East* 6, no. 2 (2011): 2–14.

[3] For more discussion about such changes in Aliabad, see Mary Elaine Hegland (with Zahra Sarraf and Mohammad Shahbazi), "Modernization and Social Change: Impact on Iranian Elderly Social Networks and Care Systems," *Anthropology of the Middle East* 2, no. 2 (2008): 55–74; Mary Elaine Hegland, "Educating Young Women: Culture, Conflict, and New Identities in an Iranian Village," *Iranian Studies* 42, no. 1 (2009): 45–79; Mary Elaine Hegland, "Aliabad of Shiraz: Transformation from Village to Suburban Town," *Anthropology of the Middle East* 6, no. 2 (2011): 21–37; and Mary Elaine Hegland, *Days of Revolution: Political Unrest in an Iranian Village* (Stanford, CA: Stanford University Press, 2014).

decorated cubicles symbolizing bridal rooms, were built to stand in front of a bereaved family's home or at intersections, so that even the dead were symbolically "married."

Hoped-for attainments from marriage included adding a woman worker to the groom's family household and setting up a life-long partnership of gendered division of labor: women's labor benefited the men, and men provided material and financial support for women. Marriage enabled both men and women to achieve what society offered—membership in the community, children, sex, and a place in society. Generally, marriage did bring about these benefits, even if it did not necessarily bring companionship, emotional support, or intimacy. These benefits were not expected.

Most women did not expect marriage to bring them a significantly higher level of material advantage. Even in the 1950s and 1960s, Aliabad daily life was simple and minimal. Mud-brick homes of one or two small rooms lacked decorations. One could hope for a small, inexpensive Persian rug (*gelim*), a suit of clothing once a year, meat once a week or less, and rice not often either. People visited the public bathhouse every two weeks or once a month. Even radios had come to Aliabad relatively recently. Only two homes boasted a TV. Two automobiles were owned by village men, and a few shopkeepers owned an old pickup. Life was lived rather close to survival levels, but since the great majority of villagers lived at this level, people did not feel their deprivation as stigmatizing.

Problems did arise in marriages of forty and fifty years ago. Women wept, visited their mothers, went back to their fathers' homes for a stay, commiserated with women's circles of neighbors and relatives, and told stories of their miseries in the underground networks of women's communication. They visited shrines and made vows to wish for better relations in their marriage. Whether smoother or more difficult, marriages continued to occur, and divorce was virtually unheard of. When a woman faced marriage, the unknown was whether she would have an easy or a difficult time. Even if conditions proved to be difficult, she would persevere. As people said, *besuz o besaz* (burn and put up with it).

Influences Enabling Changes in Marriage

During the latter decades of the twentieth century, Aliabad evolved from an agricultural village of sharecroppers, traders, and some craftsmen that was owned by an absentee landlord and had about 3,000 inhabitants to a suburb of Shiraz with some 12,000–15,000 residents, including many in-migrants. Most men commuted outside of the community to work in factories, construction, services, businesses, or shops. Many people frequently went to the city for work, education, shopping, visiting relatives, pilgrimage, or errands. Many residents of Aliabad moved into Shiraz, and some returned to live in Aliabad. People, especially the young, felt as if they were a part of the city. Eventually, Aliabad was formally incorporated into Shiraz.

As a result, living styles changed. A room or two for a family around an extended family, dirt courtyard also housing farm animals gave way to urban-style, nuclear family, fired-brick homes with all the amenities. Aliabad families now own one or more cars. Virtually all homes have TVs, and satellite dishes bring programs from all over the world, many dubbed into Persian. Young people got desktop or laptop computers and the internet and then cell phones. Now almost all people carry their cell phones or smartphones wherever they go.

Along with closer contact with Shiraz, new opportunities, influences, and expectations for males and females have altered marriage dynamics.[4] These changes are the result of economic and living-style improvements; changes in means of subsistence; better transportation, travel, communication, social media, and access to global culture; more education, literacy, and access to a wider and more varied circle of social networks—especially for young people; more rural to urban migration and back-and-forth movement; increasing segregation between generations along with strengthening of youth culture and peer-group interaction; Islamic Republic government policies and actions and attitudes about them; economic improvements and then the economic decline of the last several years; and, finally, attitudes of hopelessness, bitterness, dissatisfaction, and a desire to escape as the only possible solution to problems on the part of many young people.

Twenty-First-Century Marriages: More Agency for Young People

Between 1978 and 2018, perceptions and expectations of the institution of marriage changed. Marriage is now seen as more for the sake of the young couple and freer from

---

[4] For more discussion about pre-Revolution and recent marriage and family attitudes and practices in Aliabad, see Mary Elaine Hegland, "Field Research in a Revolutionary Setting: Overlooking Sexuality in 1978–1979 Iran," Louise Lamphere and Maria-Luisa Achino-Loeb (eds.), *Journal of Anthropological Research, Special Issues on Omissions and Silences in Anthropological Fieldwork* 76, no. 1 (2020): 28–43; Mary Elaine Hegland, "Marriage Modifications in Aliabad from 1978–9 to 2018: Financial Improvements, Social and Cultural Changes Over-ride Shi'a Clerical Directives," in *The Global Dynamics of Contemporary Shi'a Muslim Marriage*, eds. Annalies Moors and Yafa Shanneik (New Brunswick, NJ: Rutgers University Press, forthcoming); and Mary Elaine Hegland and Maryam Karimi, "Child Marriages and Their Results: Insights from Women's Stories," in *Temporary and Child Marriages in Iraq, Iran, and Afghanistan,* eds. Seyeindehbehnaz Hosseini and Ourania Roditi (forthcoming). For elsewhere in Iran, see Roksana Bahramitash and Shahla Kazemipour, "Myth and Realities of the Impact of Islam on Women: Women's Changing Marital Status in Iran," *Critique: Critical Middle Eastern Studies* 15, no. 2 (2006): 111–28; Erika Friedl, "State Ideology and Village Women, " in *Women and Revolution in Iran,* ed. Guity Nashat (Boulder: Westview Press, 1983), 217–30; Erika Friedl, *Women of Deh Koh: Lives in an Iranian Village* (London, New York: Penguin, 1991); Erika Friedl, "Ideal Womanhood in Post-revolutionary Iran," in *Mixed Blessings: Gender and Religious Fundamentalism Cross Culturally,* ed. Judy Brink and Joan Mencher (New York: Routledge, 1997), 143–58; Erika Friedl, "Tribal Enterprises and Marriage Issues in Twentieth-Century Iran," in *Family history in the Middle East: Household, Property, and Gender,* ed. Beshara Doumani (Albany: State University of New York Press, 2003), 151–70; Erika Friedl, "New Friends: Gender Relations Within the Family," *Iranian Studies* 42, no. 1 (2009): 27–43; Erika Friedl, "A Thorny Side of Marriage in Iran," in *Everyday Life in the Muslim Middle East,* ed. Donna Lee Bowen, Evelyn A. Early and Becky Schulthies (Boomington: Indiana University Press, 2014), 122–32; Azadeh Kian-Thiébaut, "From Motherhood to Equal Rights Advocates: The Weakening of Patriarchal Order," *Iranian Studies* 38, no. 1 (2005): 45–66; Abbas Tashakkori and Vaida Thompson, "Cultural Change and Attitude Change: An Assessment of Post-revolutionary Marriage and Family Attitudes in Iran," *Population Research and Policy Review* 7, no. 1 (1988): 3–27; Soraya Tremayne, "Modernity and Marriage in Iran: A View from Within," *Journal of Middle East Women's Studies* 2, no. 1 (2006): 65–94; and Paul Vieille, "Iranian Women in Family Alliance and Sexual Politics," in *Women in the Muslim World,* eds. Lois Beck and Nikki Keddie (Cambridge, MA: Harvard University Press, 1978), 451–72.

the control and ownership of the groom's parents. This transformation did not take place without conflict, of course, as the following cases demonstrate.

About thirty years ago, Hushang became engaged with the approval of both sets of parents. Then a scandal developed; he became enamored with a sister-in-law's relative and wanted to break off the engagement with the first young woman. His parents were against it, but he stood fast and married the woman of his own choice. Hushang was able to do this because he had some higher education and a good job in a government department in Shiraz. For years, his parents did not interact with him. Then his father died, and the family went through intense conflicts over the inheritance. Only some years later, in 2003, did the extended family once again come together in the old village courtyard for a meal. The grandmother—Hushang's mother—came to the couple's home for a visit. I was present at both gatherings.

In contrast, the wife of an older brother, who had been chosen by his parents, was at the beck and call of her in-laws. This couple lived with his parents in their village home for some years and then moved into the city. This bride was well-behaved, devoted, and deferential to her mother-in-law as tradition dictated. Her mother-in-law might stay with her for extended periods, especially in the winter since her village rooms were not well heated.

The younger brother Hushang and his wife had become independent from the groom's parents immediately upon marriage; they lived separately from his parents. He had chosen his own wife, but the result was a disruption that lasted for years. His wife was not as giving, acquiescent, or accepting as the older brother's wife. The couple socialized much more with her relatives than with the husband's relatives.

Another family, well-off through land ownership and a real estate business, constructed a large, elegantly decorated and furnished home. They reserved the top floor for their eldest son. However, as his marriage arrangements proceeded, differences emerged. The bride and her family wanted a separate home for the young couple. The groom's father and mother were distraught, but eventually, they had to give in. The couple moved into a separate home in Shiraz. The two families were not on speaking terms. Even when the groom's parents lost their second son, the groom and his wife sat in a different area of the cemetery from the rest of the family. The groom's mother was bitter and angry. "They live their lives, and we live ours," she summed up. She does not care to interact with her son's family, she said, but she grieves for her granddaughter growing up without her. Choosing a different way may bring disturbances but may also suggest alternative possibilities to others.

Today there is less consensus about marriage—what marriage is, and what marriage should be. People hold diverse views, and these different perspectives regarding marriage can create conflict. Among those who have moved to Shiraz, who are more educated and more economically advantaged than allowed by the typical village cultivation and low-level commerce, change is more pronounced. Variation in the extent of change is apparent among families, individuals, socioeconomic classes, and ethnic groups.

One young woman friend explained the change in attitudes toward marriage among young people like herself as follows:

In the old days, no matter what happened, good or bad, people believed it was the Will of God. They lived like this; they were habituated to this way of thinking. In the past, women depended on their husbands or fathers. *Besuz o besaz.* (They burn, and they live with it.) They thought, "We're burning up, but we are forced to tolerate it."

Now people are not like this. Things have changed. They won't stay quiet. They think, "Why should we put up with this? We want a better life." This is why the divorce rate is higher now. Now they don't want to tolerate even half as much as before. They want to change their situation. My grandmother said something insightful. She said the reason why divorce has increased is that since women have gotten jobs; they think, "We have money so why should we go on tolerating things?"

Although her family was from Aliabad, this young woman had lived in Shiraz all her life. Her aunt (mother's sister) planned from early on that she would marry the aunt's son. The young woman gave in to her aunt's fond wish, although she insisted on earning her BS before the wedding. The young man had lived in Aliabad all of his life and, like so many Aliabad young men, had not earned his high school diploma. Financed by his father, he was running a cell phone shop in Aliabad. The young couple lived in Aliabad after the wedding. The young woman soon realized how incompatible they were, how unpleasant his behavior was, and how different their aims in life were, and in spite of terrific pressure, especially from her aunt, got a divorce.

Many things have changed about marriage in Iran, but one thing has not changed: a strong preference for cousin marriage among many people.[5] Sometimes parents very much want their daughter to marry a cousin, even if he is less educated and ambitious. However, if the woman has more education (which is common), lives in Shiraz, and enjoys wider worlds, the marriage may not go well. In yet another case, the parents persuaded a young woman who had grown up in Shiraz and received her BS degree to marry her village cousin who did not have a high school diploma. This marriage also ended in divorce. These two former husbands both found second wives who shared their own expectations and were satisfied with their domestic lives in Aliabad. The divorced young women who wanted wider worlds and more modern lives and relationships continued their pursuit of education and work. When sharp differences in education, culture, and ambition divide a couple, divorce often takes place in spite of the parents' wishes. Although many parents continue to favor cousin marriages, socioeconomic class and level of education are becoming more important for a successful marriage.

Young women often expect twenty-first-century marriages to be for the benefit of themselves as well as the husbands and to include more input from wives in decision-making. Even some women of the parental generation appreciate the greater voice of women in family discussions. For example, one grandmother said,

In those days, men conferred very little with their wives about what they wanted to do, maybe only 20 percent of the time. Thirty-five years ago, women were very

---

[5] The tradition of consanguineous (cousin and relative) marriage is frequently practiced in Aliabad, as well as in Iran in general, characterizing about a third of marriages, with some variation according to region.

little involved in household decisions. Women didn't have any say; they couldn't give their opinions. Now, men consult with them more like 80 percent of the time. The women give their opinions and have more influence in their own homes.

Now, since women have gone out into society more, they have more of a role in governing their households than in the past. I have seen this myself. In the old days, women were just at home. Women had less responsibility; they just prepared food, took care of the children, and did household work. Men's work was thought to be more important. Men thought that women were just in the house and didn't know much more than that; they didn't give much respect to women's opinions and didn't want to listen to their wishes. But now women are also out there working like men do. They are earning money like men, so men regard their views as more valuable and accept their opinions more. Now they listen more to women.

Although the woman quoted here was married young and had not worked outside of the home, all of her daughters were educated and worked; she was clearly basing what she said on their experiences. However, these young women were exceptions. Their family was well-off, and they had lived in Shiraz. The daughters had access to good education beyond high school and were able to attain high-status careers. The great majority of Aliabad women still do not work outside, although in recent years several young women have been finding ways to earn some money, such as opening small clothing or beauty shops or driving children to their schools.

Aliabad's young people are exposed to TV programs from other countries, smuggled-in films, and music videos from all over the world, the internet, websites, blogs, and social media. Watching other people's behavior and observing the results and learning about other countries and cultures have given many Aliabad women the desires and tools to go after their own interests to a greater degree. Several of the younger ones talked in admiring tones about anything "modern," (using the English term), and want to live a more "modern" way of life. Gaining more confidence through wider experiences and social interaction, young women—in Aliabad as well as elsewhere in Iran—have found more voice to express themselves.

Young people have gained more control over their own lives. Aliabad women enjoy greater and more independent mobility. Unmarried girls take taxis and buses into Shiraz by themselves. University students take trips in groups sponsored by their universities, even for several days, such as a flight to Mecca. They marry later, after developing more discernment and personal resources. Young Iranians have opportunities to meet members of the opposite sex through education, travel, and technology, such as cell phones and dating apps.

Twenty-first-century brides are usually free of control from their mothers-in-law. Brides do not follow the rules of staying home, which were especially strict in the early years of marriage forty years ago. Brides spent a great deal of time with their own families, especially the women.

While brides have gained more independence and power, mothers-in-law have lost power and influence. These days, the power struggle between brides and mothers-in-law is over almost before it begins. One of my close friends told me, "When I was a bride, it was the rule of the mother-in-law. Now that I am a mother-in-law, it is the rule of the bride." A twenty-first-century bride, she said, is willing to spend time with her mother-in-law only if she gets along with her and the mother-in-law does not try to control her.

Young people have developed autonomy and power in intergenerational relations. Aliabad young men's work and income are more often independent from their fathers, compared to earlier generations. Aliabad young people are often out of range of parental, kin, and community control. They possess resources that are not accessed as fully or at all by their parents, such as education and degrees, computer and internet capability, a wider circle of contacts, and knowledge about the larger world. They exhibit a greater sense of entitlement than their parents and grandparents did.

Examining a number of marriage cases suggests that young women now have many opportunities to get to know the groom before the wedding. They can often build emotional intimacy and make gradual transitions in sexual activity[6] before marriage. Brides make more material demands and expect a greater level of partnership in marriage—indeed, a companionate marriage.

These days, gender, generational, and marital relationships have been moving away from hierarchical relations and toward more discussion, negotiation, and openness.[7] The changes in marriage of recent years have given Aliabad women more status and power in the relationship with their own families, their husbands or husbands-to-be, and their husbands' parents.

Twenty-First-Century Aliabad Marriages: New Problems and Challenges

By 2018, for many people of Aliabad and nearby Shiraz, marriage had lost some of its sense of inevitability, permanence, and positive aura. Marriage, influenced by social and economic changes and by recent expectations of opulent weddings and marital homes, is now difficult for many to attain and fraught with potential pitfalls. New challenges are troubling Iranians. Struggles over gender and generational expectations, power-wielding, economic pressures, and the still-central place of marriage and family for women's social position, economic support, and identity often result in dilemmas and conflict.

The poor economy and lack of appropriate jobs for young men make marriage a highly problematic enterprise.[8] Many young men lack the current qualifications of

---

[6] See Hegland, "Marriage Modifications in Aliabad from 1978–9 to 2018," forthcoming.
[7] For more discussion about people questioning hierarchy, see Ibid.
[8] For more discussion about the difficulties young Iranians are facing, see Klara Debeljak, "Youth in Iran: A Story Half Told—Values, Priorities and Perspectives of Iranian Youth," *Young Publics Research Paper Series*, No. 1-Iran (May, 2013), http://www.intermedia.org/wp-content/uploads/Young-Publics-Research-Paper-Series-Iran.pdf; Saeed Kamali Dehghan, "'Desperate to Find a Way Out': Iran Edges Towards Precipice," *The Guardian* (July 20, 2018), https://www.theguardian.com/world/2018/jul/20/desperate-to-find-a-way-out-iran-edges-towards-precipice?CMP=Share_iOSApp_; Shahram Khosravi, *Young and Defiant in Tehran* (Philadelphia: University of Pennsylvania Press, 2009); Shahram Khosravi, *Precarious Lives: Waiting and Hope in Iran* (Philadelphia: University of Pennsylvania Press, 2017); Azadeh Kian, "Women and Politics in Post-Islamist Iran:

a good husband and provider. Aliabad young men continue their education at far lower levels than young women, and the lack of educated grooms for educated brides constitutes a significant challenge for marriage.⁹ Educated young women do not want to marry Aliabad young men who have less education and village backgrounds and culture. Often young men do not want a wife who is better educated either. Usually, women are faced with two choices: either marry a less-educated Aliabad man or remain single. As a result, marriages of young women with college degrees have sometimes resulted in unhappiness or divorce.

Young women may refuse a marriage offer arranged by others or a suitor they do not favor, or they may put off marriage to pursue higher education. However, refusing suitors may be dangerous; a young woman may end up single. In one case, in spite of quite a few proposals from Aliabad, a young woman who had grown up in Shiraz did not accept anyone. The parents did not force their daughter—usually this is not done these days. She continued her university education and received a degree in English translation. She was still without a husband after the age of thirty. Once when I was in the United States and talking with her by phone, she said in English—so her family would not understand, "I am looking for a husband."

Parents want their daughters to marry. Marriage and family are still central among Aliabad people and those who have moved into Shiraz. The great majority of girls and women do not work; even if they do, Aliabad females cannot earn enough money to be financially independent.

It has become more difficult for young people and their families to vet potential spouses. Many outsiders have moved into Aliabad, and the native population has also grown a great deal since the 1970s. Means of communication and mobility provide greater opportunities to meet others from outside of Aliabad. People who are not well known to the bride or groom's family may misrepresent credentials. A suitor may present himself as single when he is already married, as happened in one case. A young woman from Aliabad met someone at work who showed interest in her. Later, she found out he was married. Young people originally from Aliabad might find partners from elsewhere, and these outsiders may exhibit cultural differences or want to live elsewhere.

The Gender Conscious Drive to Change," *British Journal of Middle Eastern Studies* 24, no. 1 (2007): 75–96; Pardis Mahdavi, *Passionate Uprising: The Sexual Revolution in Iran* (Stanford: Stanford University Press, 2009); Azadeh Moaveni, *Lipstick Jihad: A Memoir of Growing up Iranian in America and American in Iran* (New York: PublicAffairs, 2006); Azadeh Moveni, *Honeymoon in Tehran: Two Years of Love and Danger in Iran* (New York: Random House, 2010); Norma Claire Moruzzi and Fatemeh Sadeghi, "Out of the Frying Pan, into the Fire: Young Iranian Women Today," *Middle East Report* 241 (2006): 22–8; Roxanne Varzi, *Warring Souls: Youth, Media and Martyrdom in Post-Revolution Iran* (Durham, NC: Duke University Press, 2006); Roxanne Varzi, *Last Scene Underground: An Ethnographic Novel of Iran* (Redwood City, CA: Stanford University Press, 2015); and Raz Zimmt, "Marrying Late: Young Adults and the Marriage Crisis in Iran," *The Forum for Regional Thinking* (July 10, 2016), http://www.regthink.org/en/articles/marrying-late-young-adults-and-the-marriage-crisis.

9   Also see Shashank Bengali and Ramin Mostaghim, "More Women in Iran Are Forgoing Marriage. One reason? The Men Aren't Good Enough," *Los Angeles Times* (November 11, 2016), http://www.latimes.com/world/la-fg-iran-unmarried-snap-story.html.

Men and their families may also feel suspicious about a potential spouse. They may feel they do not know her and her family as well as they should. When she is not a relative and not from Aliabad, her family can also misrepresent her qualifications.[10] Both men and women and their families might not suspect potential mates of deceit, secrecy, and lying until it is too late: "Marriage is like a watermelon. You don't know what is inside until you break it open" is an old Persian saying often invoked these days.

Insufficient funds for wedding expenses and setting up the young couple in their marital home, as well as high expectations for living standards, may force the postponement of marriage. Instead of wedding celebrations held in family homes and courtyards and serving home-cooked meals with one entrée accompanied by rice,[11] extravagant weddings are held at wedding gardens and halls rented at great expense by the groom's family. These weddings provide the main social events of the year. Preparation of the bride and groom and their families for the event means a huge cash outlay. Even guests must come with new, elegant clothes.

At the celebration, caterers serve a large variety of foods. A medley of fruits for each guest, plates of fancy cookies, and often bottled water are placed on the tables. Tea is served by a number of hired staff. The dinner features several types of kebabs, stews, various rice dishes, salads, and sodas. After the meal, the wedding cake will be cut and brought around. I have seen ice sculpture as part of the décor. Guests may be treated to colored strobe lights, a DJ—if not live music—for dancing, and large photos of the bridal couple in various poses on braced placards. Often a professionally made video of the young couple posing and cavorting in various chic settings is shown to the wedding guests—another output of money. Wedding parties are videotaped by professionals.[12]

Young women and their families make it clear there will be no wedding until the groom and his family have acquired a separate residence, which will be completely furnished by the bride's family. Forty years ago, a young man brought his young bride to his father's house where they were given a room of their own and shared the lives of

---

[10] For example, some years ago, an Aliabad man married a young woman from Shiraz, who supposedly had earned her high school diploma. Sometime after the marriage, the Aliabad family found out that she actually had not completed this degree.

[11] For a description of earlier Lar marriage customs, see Emily Wells Gianfortoni, "Marriage Customs in Lar: The Role of Women's Networks in Tradition and Change," *Iran and the Caucasus* 13 (2009): 285–98.

[12] For a description of a 2006 wedding in Rasht, see Soheila Shahshahani, "Wedding Ceremony in Turmoil," *Anthropology of the Middle East* 2, no. 1 (2007): 103–8. Based on a marriage celebration in Urmia, weddings, Shamsi Miri Ghaffarzadeh argues, are influenced by a number of factors and cannot be bifurcated into either traditional or modern. See Miri Ghaffarzadeh, "Traditional vs. Modern Wedding Ceremony in Urmia City of Iran," *The Social Sciences* 11 (2016): 3543–8.

For descriptions of some over-the-top Tehran weddings, see Moaveni, *Honeymoon in Tehran* and Tacita Vero, "Behind the Scenes of Iran's Growing Wedding Industry," *Slate Magazine* (January 9, 2017). http://www.slate.com/articles/news_and_politics/roads/2017/01/behind_the_scenes_of_iran_s_growing_wedding_industry.html. People complain about how extravagant weddings have become in other countries too. See Claire Heald, "Four Dresses and a Drone – Are Weddings Getting Out of Control?" *BBC News* (April 26, 2017), https://www.bbc.com/news/uk-39716582. (Thanks to Erika Friedl for pointing out the Heald article.) The trend toward extremely expensive, flashy weddings appears to be one more way in which Iranian weddings and marriages are replicating wedding and marriage trends elsewhere—in spite of attempts by clerical officials of the Islamic Republic to impose their own wedding and marriage culture on the Iranian population.

his parents. Now, a young man must have a job, an income, a car, and a separate home for the bride before he can get married.

Young women expect that their lives will be completely set up before marriage. The household items provided by the bride's parents are extravagant and comprehensive—large flat TV, living room and bedroom furniture, fully stocked refrigerator and freezer, and everything that should go into the house, even down to spices, toothpicks, and cleaning materials. When the bride's family brings all of the household furnishings, equipment, clothing, makeup, and male toiletries, relatives of both bride and groom are invited to come and see it shown off. The bride's mother must also buy all necessities for the first child (with funds provided by the bride's father), now including furniture, diapering needs, toys, store-bought chic clothing, strollers, and room decorations—everything needed for the child. The child is expected to have his/her own room in the couple's home. These greatly inflated expectations present a great challenge to the groom and his parents and the bride's parents to gather the necessary money.

Expectations of marriage are higher than in the past. Women may want more gold jewelry and higher living standards or yearn for romance and a companionate marriage, whereas young men might expect a more traditional marital relationship with a wife who caters to them and does not question them. Such expectations, if not realized, may lead to disappointment and dissatisfaction.

Sexual activity before marriage has become more common, especially for Aliabad men, and this concerns young women and their families. They worry that such behavior of young men might continue after marriage. In a very few cases, even women's extramarital sexual activities have come to light.

Forty years ago, young men were not addicted to opium or other drugs, and I did not know of a single man with a drinking problem. Now, addiction, drinking, and even death from overdose have become common in Aliabad, as elsewhere in Iran. These issues further add to marital problems. Women who are unhappy with their addicted husbands often just go on with them, but in some cases, they might separate from them, seek a divorce or even, very rarely, find other sexual partners. Men's deaths from overdose mean that more women are living as widows. Widowed and divorced women still find it difficult to find another marriage partner.

Although a divorced woman is still highly stigmatized, divorce now has become more common in Aliabad. Divorce rates in Iran are rising dramatically.[13] The possibility of divorce after marriage increases the feeling of uncertainty and trepidation about marriage among Aliabad girls and their parents. Women face almost insurmountable challenges in seeking economic and social self-sufficiency. A few young, divorced women in Aliabad, while living in their fathers' homes, have found partial employment, such as driving children to their schools in the city. One young divorced woman lives

---

[13] For information about divorce elsewhere in Iran, see Akba Aghajanian and Vaida Thompson, "Recent Divorce Trends in Iran," *Journal of Divorce & Remarriage* 54, no. 2 (2013): 112–5 and Correspondent in Tehran, "Why Are Young Iranians Losing Interest in Marriage?" *Al-Monitor, Iran Pulse* (June 2, 2015), http://www.al-monitor.com/pulse/oiginals/2015/06/iran-birth-rate-marriage-decline-divorce.html.

in her parents' home and commutes to work as a nurse in Shiraz. At least one divorced young woman of Aliabad, living at her father's home in Shiraz, has found work as a contractor for a city department. Exorbitant housing costs mean that Aliabad women generally could not find work that pays enough for them to afford a separate home. In any case, it would not be socially or culturally possible for a divorced younger woman of Aliabad to live apart from her family.

The great majority of women of Aliabad strategize, negotiate, and/or cooperate with men to attain their goals and desired living conditions in the absence of an independent income. Labor-market participation of Iranian women remains low, in spite of their advances in education, in part due to lack of jobs. Government jobs such as teaching, which remain gender-segregated, would be appropriate for women. However, many of these jobs as well as private sector employment do not pay well enough to support people which also discourages women from working outside of the home. People blame the current high rates of unemployment on US sanctions, governmental mismanagement, corruption, imports, lack of support for businesses, bureaucratic complications, and the fleeing of foreign companies after the revolution. The high birth rate after the 1979 Revolution, encouraged by the regime for nearly a decade, brought a dramatic increase in population, resulting in a high unemployment rate among the young.

In Aliabad, in the 1970s, if women worked outside the home, it meant the husbands or fathers were not capable of supporting them—a horrific commentary on their manhood. At the time, when I tried to get a girl to help me out with babysitting, her male relatives put an end to it. I was told that even occasionally bringing a gift back for her, after my travel and in lieu of pay, would not work. Today still, in Aliabad and elsewhere, it is problematic for women to work outside of the home. Women in Aliabad, and generally in Iran, are expected to have *appropriate* jobs if they work. Unless poverty absolutely forces otherwise, a job should have high status and not bring a female into contact with males. Nursing, although gender-segregated, deals with body fluids and brings little status. Even teaching in gender-segregated primary and secondary schools is no longer prestigious, nor does it pay well. Further, Aliabad schools are filled with the children of outsiders—Afghans, Lurs from more rural areas, and others—whom young women of Aliabad try to avoid. Girls and women of Aliabad generally do not have the resources and connections to compete for high-status work.

In Iran, a stay-at-home wife or other woman (the husband's sister, for example) indicates that the responsible male is capable of supporting her, bringing status to the man and the women in the family.[14] The law confirms this view. Women need their male guardians' permission to work; frequently, this permission is withheld. In Aliabad and elsewhere, most men do not want their wives, daughters, mothers, sisters, or other

---

[14] An article about women leaving work in India also suggests another reason for women's low labor-market participation in Aliabad and Iran. A World Bank study found that when Indian men's income stabilized, women dropped out of work and "engaged in status production at home." Soutik Biswas, "Why Are Millions of Indian Women Dropping Out of Work?" *BBC*, India (May 18, 2017), http://www.bbc.com/news/world-asia-india-39945473 (accessed May 20, 2017). Thanks to Erika Friedl for alerting me to this article and pointing out how this phenomenon in India could also apply to low female employment in Iran.

female relatives to work, as it would reflect badly on them and the family. Often women themselves are not interested in outside work. Although a minority of women in Iran work outside of the home in a great variety of jobs and careers, economic conditions, government policies, and cultural forces pressure women to stay at home, especially when they have children.

Custody laws continue to favor the father. A terrible result of divorce for a woman with children is loss of her children. Previously, Iranian law gave physical custody and guardianship of the children to their fathers—girls at the age of seven and boys at two. This has been changed, and now children can stay with their mothers for more years. Often fathers do not want the responsibility of caring for children and do not provide child support. Thankfully, most Aliabad divorces take place before children are born.

Given the poor labor market and legal, social, and cultural disincentives for women to work, especially in jobs considered inappropriate for women, women are rather at loose ends if they divorce. In Aliabad, they go back to their parents' homes. Without work or educational pursuits, they feel bored, uncomfortable, socially stigmatized, and isolated. As divorced women whose reputations are already questionable, social pressure, lack of appropriate transportation, and lack of funds may keep them from getting around much in the world outside of home. Given their age and non-virgin status and the negative attitude toward divorced women, it is difficult for them to find a second husband. These days, the likelihood of divorce after marriage has increased; therefore, the difficulty of finding another husband causes additional trepidation among unmarried girls and their families as they contemplate marriage. Even if they fail to attain the now-expected more companionate marriage, women feel they have little alternative to an unsatisfactory marriage.

Men also may feel forced to remain in an unsatisfactory marriage. If a wife wants to resist divorce, she has financial considerations in her favor. To divorce his wife, a husband is supposed to give her the *mahriyeh,* the marriage payment agreed upon in the original marriage contract. Because financial expectations are high, this amount is generally very large; most men cannot gather such a great sum. Husbands are further discouraged from divorce by the almost insurmountable financial requirements of a second marriage.

As marital and nuclear family relations have grown in significance, female companionship and circles have become less available. Although marriages among some younger people have become more intimate and sexually and socially satisfying than they were forty years ago,[15] changes in lifestyle mean that divorced women and women in less-than-satisfactory marriages find the former comforts of female companionship and circles and ties with extended kin and neighbors to be less available.[16] Women in unhappy marriages feel more isolated emotionally than their mothers and grandmothers did in similar situations.

---

[15] See Hegland, "Marriage Modifications in Aliabad from 1978–9 to 2018."
[16] For discussion about women's circles in earlier decades, see Mary Elaine Hegland, "Talking Politics: A Village Widow in Iran," in *Personal Encounters: A Reader in Cultural Anthropology,* ed. Linda S. Walbridge and April K. Sievert (Boston, MA: McGraw-Hill, 2003): 53–9; Nancy Tapper (Lindefarne), "The Women's Sub-society among the Shahsevan Nomads," in *Women in the Muslim World,* eds. Lois Beck and Nikki Keddie (Cambridge, MA: Harvard University Press, 1978): 374–98;

Pressures on Parents

In the mid-twentieth century, gifts to the bride before the wedding, wedding expenses, and setting up the home for the bridal couple required only a modest financial outlay; planning for a son or daughter's marriage did not cause parents consternation.

These days, the custom of the groom's father providing the home and the bride's family providing the household equipment has continued, but the financial expectations of both fathers have risen radically. Women and their families are no longer willing to accept a separate room in the groom's parental home. Many are not even satisfied with a separate apartment on a different floor in the in-law's house. If, as in some cases, the bride and groom and his parents initially live on different floors in one building, the in-laws are not expected to come upstairs without an invitation.

The exorbitant costs of their children's weddings and marital homes mean economic sacrifice for parents. Housing has become a huge expense.[17] These days, the father of the groom may buy a condominium for a young couple who live in Shiraz. For parents, these inflated expectations are a terrific source of stress. Sometimes even relatively well-off men have had to sell their land or take out large, high interest loans to pay for the son's house or the daughter's bridal home furnishings.

Parents find it much more difficult now to guide children or invoke their own greater experience and knowledge about life to make decisions about their children's lives. Their adult children may feel that their parents' experiences are not relevant to their own lives in a transformed world. Parents still feel obligated to find appropriate mates for their children, but they have much less control over their children, the process of finding mates for them, and setting up their adult children in their married lives. The challenges, potential pitfalls, and dangers in the course of selecting and acquiring marriage partners have become great. The path to a successful marriage is now fraught with uncertainty, fear, mistrust, anxiety, and tremendous financial burdens.

Parents feel responsible for the success of their children's marriages and go to great lengths to help the young couple live together in relative harmony. Mothers of girls commonly make efforts to mend problematic marriages; they do not want the humiliation of divorce for their daughters and the family. Mothers of sons also invest in saving the marriage. In one case more than ten years ago, a mother took responsibility for salvaging her son's marriage. Her son's wife had retreated to her parents' home and announced that she would not return to her husband until he provided them with a home separate from that of his mother and the other son and daughter-in-law.[18] The son considered divorcing his wife, but he would have had to pay her *mahriyeh*, and

---

and Sue Wright "Prattle and Politics: The Position of Women in Dushman-Ziari," *Anthropological Society of Oxford Journal* 9 (1978): 98–112.

[17] Hassan F. Golipour and Mohammad Reza Farzanegan, "Marriage Crisis and Housing Costs: Empirical Evidence from Provinces of Iran," *Journal of Policy Modeling* 37, no. 1 (2015): 107–23.

[18] The wife was using a time-honored tactic—often quite effective. A husband is embarrassed and extremely inconvenienced. He is left without a cook, cleaning lady, clothes washer, hostess, and, if she leaves the children with him, without needed childcare. Also see Mary Elaine Hegland, "Wife Abuse and the Political System: A Middle Eastern Case Study," in *To Have and to Hit: Cultural Perspective on Wife Beating*, eds. Dorothy Counts, Judith Brown, and Jacqueline Campbell (Urbana: University of Illinois Press, 1999), 234–51.

he did not have the funds. His mother then stepped in. She sold her hard-won home and courtyard and divided the money between her two sons to enable her older son to build a separate home for his wife.[19] The mother then put up a short wall around a small piece of land and gradually built herself a small home, in effect becoming a squatter.

Women who are experiencing marital difficulties frequently go home to their parents. In case of separation or divorce, the parents handle all expenses and arrangements. It would be economically, socially, and culturally impossible for a divorced younger woman of Aliabad to live apart from her family. In Aliabad, divorced women live with their parents. Parents, it seems, are eternally responsible for their children. Fathers provide financial support, and a divorced daughter's care is added to a mother's household tasks. One mother returned repeatedly to Shiraz courts trying to obtain her daughter's *mahriyeh*. These days, parents are not the authority figures they were fifty years ago; they mainly provide money and services for their children.

For the wedding celebrations and marriages of their children, the two sets of parents use up resources and then have much less for their own older age. Previously, adult children were responsible for the care of their elderly parents, and at least one usually lived with or near them. Today, young couples do not take much responsibility for their parents. Elderly family members, even an incapacitated, widowed mother, may be neglected by their children. The couple's own expenses are too great, and the bride wants resources to be used for her own nuclear family. The young people want to live their own lives, spend their time together, and go out together. The bride wants to run her own home.

An elderly man still retains high status in this patriarchal society. He may own property that the young hope to inherit, which motivates them to show him respect. A widowed mother, however, usually lacks resources. By the second decade of the twenty-first century, more than half of the elderly widowed women in Aliabad lived alone.[20] They may live in a home needing repair and cosmetic work. Although daughters would like to help, widows generally receive little help and sometimes even little attention from their children.[21]

The focus is now on the young couple who have more power. The bride is likely to be educated and her mother-in-law illiterate or semi-literate; the bride and her mother-in-law usually live in different worlds. Given different worldviews and ideas about who

---

[19] Thankfully, by my fall 2015 visit, this couple had arrived at a relatively more harmonious relationship. (The mother had become a widow as a young teenager and was forced to work to support herself and her two sons.)

[20] For more information about Aliabad elderly, see Mary Elaine Hegland, "Independent Grandmothers in an Iranian Village," *Middle-East Journal of Age & Aging* 4, no. 3 (June 2007): 28–31 and Mary Elaine Hegland (with Zahra Sarraf and Mohammad Shahbazi), "Modernization and Social Change: The Impact on Iranian Elderly Social Networks and Care Systems," *Anthropology of the Middle East* 2, no. 2 (September 2007): 55–73.

[21] In Iranian culture, the son, not the daughter, was expected to be responsible for elderly parents. (In actuality, this meant the care of his elderly parents fell upon his wife.) Much less expectation for assistance to parents weighed upon a daughter. Further, since the daughter was most often not working outside of the home, she herself had no income to use to help her parents. Although women are more emotionally attached and in closer relationships with their own parents than with their husbands' parents, wives were not to use their husband's resources to help their own parents.

has authority, it would be problematic for them to live in the same home or courtyard. Each may feel uncomfortable in the other's presence. Mothers-in-law have to tailor their expectations and wishes to the reality that their "interference" is not wanted.

Solitude is shunned in Aliabad; after a lifetime of living in close proximity and interaction with others, widows in Aliabad are faced with the difficult necessity of learning to live alone. Often, they say this is what they want, probably realizing that the young couple does not want them.

A bride in the first half of the twentieth century suffered under the harsh administration of her mother-in-law and husband and had to adjust to the expectations of others, but if she tolerated her situation with at least apparent acquiescence, she could hope for more respect and authority as time went on and she bore and raised children. Her daughters could become close companions and helpmates, and her sons could support and cater to her. She could look forward to eventually becoming a mother-in-law and administrator of a busy household herself.[22] The brides of the 1960s and 1970s, after many of them acquiesced and suffered under the demands of their mothers-in-law and husbands, now find themselves unable to reap their reward of becoming mothers-in-law in authority over the domestic arrangements of a large family.

Although I sympathize with the desire of younger people who are resisting authoritarian hierarchies for more self-determination and self-realization, as a senior myself with many friends of forty years among the parental generation whose company I enjoy when I go to Aliabad, I feel sympathy for them as well. They have devoted their lives to their children and want foremost to see their children close to them and well set up in life. The children expect a great deal of assistance, but then go off to their own homes. Their parents' responsibility for them does not seem to end, yet the children's responsibility for their parents often has low priority.

Marriage Strategies of Young People and Their Families

Iranians are trying to figure out how to cope with the opportunities, difficulties, and challenges around marriage that have emerged in the last fifty years. Young Aliabad/Shiraz women and men and their families have adopted several different strategies to deal with new influences, expectations, and dilemmas regarding marriage arrangements, weddings, setting up households for young couples, and managing relationships.

Some young women resist parental control and surveillance and have agitated for more self-definition, decision-making, and autonomy. Influenced by examples from elsewhere and a new sense of personal entitlement, young women may want to resist home-boundedness; subservience to in-laws; social control; traditional lifestyles of housekeeping, cooking, and childcare; and a social life centered on family, relatives, and neighbors. Many of them, especially those living in Shiraz or attending university there

---

[22] See Deniz Kandiyoti, "Bargaining with Patriarchy," *Gender and Society* 2, no. 3 (1988): 274–90.

or in other cities, desire a higher, more urban standard of living, more commodities, and romantic, companionate marriages. Many want access to a wider world. Some dream of the advantages they would have if they could go abroad, and a few want desperately to leave Iran.

Many young women of Aliabad have been able to postpone marriage by pursuing education although this may reduce their chances for marriage with an Aliabad man of similar status. Parents continue to prefer young men from Aliabad—ideally, relatives—as suitors, but usually only young men with a high school diploma—or even lacking one—are available for young women with a university degree.

A few women of Aliabad have remained unmarried even into their thirties and are working while living at home with their parents. One young woman became a nurse. She never married but cared for her elderly ill parents until they died. Then, as a woman in her fifties, she continued to work at a hospital and lived alone in an apartment in Shiraz—the only such case among Aliabad women that I know of. These examples are unusual among people in Aliabad and those now living in Shiraz. However, as new phenomena, they make other young women of Aliabad aware of alternative possibilities.

In the 1970s, women did not meet outsiders on their own. Now Aliabad girls can take taxis and buses on their own. A few girls travel with sisters or friends. Several educated women have been able to evade traditional married life in Aliabad and instead have married educated, professional men from outside of the settlement whom they met through education or travel. This is a recent innovation. Any such young woman would have to be extraordinarily lovely, educated, and intelligent; because of their village origin, most Aliabadi women would not be considered attractive partners by young, urban, middle-class men.

In Aliabad and elsewhere, young Iranian women and their mothers often perform pilgrimage, make vows, and perform rituals in hopes of finding a good husband. One mother devoted her *haj*, her pilgrimage to Mecca, to praying for a good wife for her son.

Many people in Aliabad, discouraged with their lives and chances in Iran, want to leave the country, feeling that such a move would solve their problems and provide them with wonderful lives. During my three months in Aliabad in the fall of 2015, most people with whom I spoke focused their conversations on hopes of leaving Iran and in 2018, people fixated even more on exiting. They compared economic and social conditions in various countries and discussed how to get out of Iran. Several decades ago, at least two men were able to leave Iran and married women in their new countries. Several young men have left more recently, and by 2020, at least four younger Aliabad women had emigrated for education. As far as I know, only one young woman from Aliabad has been able to marry a foreigner and, thereby, leave Iran.

Marriage with a man from elsewhere is not what parents prefer for their daughters, especially since it means the daughter will live elsewhere. They do want to see their daughters in successful marriages. Some marriages have taken place with men from other cities, and the brides have moved to new surroundings. Raised with very close relations with their parents and siblings, Aliabad women who live elsewhere can be lonely and depressed because of this separation. The personal resources one has developed for one kind of life may not be the right qualification for taking advantage of new opportunities when one lives in different circumstances. With access to media, such as cell phones and Skype, close and even frequent daily contact may be maintained, but it cannot take the place of physical proximity.

Several young women of Aliabad are exploring work possibilities created by increased conspicuous consumption and attention to women's appearance spreading throughout the country. A few young women have opened women's fashion boutiques in Aliabad. Several have taken classes and are operating beauty salons for hair styling, painting nails, makeup, and other forms of beautification, either in their homes or in a separate space. They thereby manage government and family-imposed rules of segregation and work restrictions on women and against interaction with non-related males. A few others, especially older widows with little other means, run small shops selling a variety of items to earn a meager livelihood and have some social interaction. As far as I know, though, none of the younger women are able to earn enough to maintain themselves. All are married or live with their families of origin.

One option for a young woman to have it all is to marry an "inappropriate" man. A young woman finished her education and then began working at the Aliabad health center. She grew older, and Aliabad people did not want an old bride. When she was in her thirties, a younger, less-educated man of tribal origin came to work in the health center. He liked her and wanted to marry her. By marrying him, she was able to have the family that she wanted, but at the cost of having to endure the stigma of marrying an outsider from a Lurish ethnic background, a group looked down upon by Aliabad people. Although the relationship seemed to work quite well, the marriage was perceived as a step down for the young woman.

During the latter years of the twentieth and early years of the twenty-first century, many Aliabad residents came into a great deal of extra money by going into the real estate business or by selling land obtained from land reform or that they had claimed after the revolution This enabled families to demonstrate their status by arranging luxurious wedding parties. However, by the second decade of the twenty-first century, most available land had been sold. Because of the shrinking real estate market and the downturn in the economy caused by sanctions and unsuccessful internal economic policies, most people no longer enjoy a financial surplus. Jobs for young men are difficult to come by. Fewer fathers have the capital to set up sons in shops, and by the fall of 2015, people complained that Aliabad shops and businesses no longer attracted customers. People were not buying because they had no extra money. By the spring of 2018, in particular when the United States announced that it was leaving the nuclear accord agreement, economic conditions worsened and have continued this downward trend. However, demands for extravagant weddings and households for bridal couples have continued.[23]

In the face of the tremendous financial challenges of marriage, young people and their families may take several courses of action. If fathers do not have land or have

---

[23] As I have not been in Iran since spring 2018, I cannot say for sure if such expectations have continued. By March 2020, people were facing increasingly challenging economic conditions because of the sanctions and internal inadequacies. Unfortunately, the coronavirus pandemic added even more severe liabilities to the economy and people's daily lives.

sold off what they had, they may be forced to look for opportunities to borrow money although non-government loans carry very high interest rates. The government has been making loans for marriages available although people complain that they are too small. Some parents accept the traditional practice of donations from guests (*shavash*) to help defray the tremendously high costs of a wedding. Young men and women often postpone marriage due to lack of funds.

Financial considerations may force a family to wait a long time between the *aqd*—the signing of the marriage contract—and the *arusi*—the wedding cerebration, which were previously held close together. By having a small, discreet marriage contract-signing ceremony, families may put off the costly wedding party and home setup, waiting and hoping to gather more funds. In the meantime, they may arrange lengthy marital visits for the young couple in the two parental homes.

Influenced by global media, young women hope for a companionate marriage with a romantic and intimate relationship rather than a utilitarian one. However, people must be mindful of the government laws that require gender segregation in public spaces and forbid social and intimate interaction between men and women who are not related. All sexual activity, physical contact, or even unsupervised social contact must take place within the context of marriage.[24]

The lived reality in Iran for many people, especially the young, diverges radically from the Shi'a Muslim culture promoted by the state's clerical rulers.[25] Even in Aliabad, many women no longer agree with the state's pronouncements about women, the demands for their seclusion and covering, or the limits on their mobility and behavior. Aliabad people do not support forced *ḥijāb*.[26] How does one spend time with one's

---

[24] Of course, extramarital sexual activity carries far less condemnation for men. Legally, they may have up to three permanent wives and an unlimited number of *sigheh* or temporary wives, a Shi'a Muslim type of marriage. Although in 1978–79, two Aliabad men had two wives, I do not know of any Aliabad men with two wives these days. I have heard of only one case of *sigheh* with a woman from a further-out village, which did not last long.

[25] See Anonymous, "Sexual Mores in Iran—Throwing Off the Covers: An Official Report Blows the Lid Off the Secret World of Sex," *The Economist* (August 9, 2014), https://www.economist.com/middle-east-and-africa/2014/08/09/throwing-off-the-covers.

[26] Also see Anonymous, "Official Report: Support for Compulsory Ḥijāb Plummets," *IranWire* (July 30, 2018), https://iranwire.com/en/features/5433.
    A recent survey found 82 percent of participating Iranian Facebook users between the ages of 18–33 supported "separation of religion and state," whereas in the MENA survey, for the general population of the Middle East and North Africa, the statistic was only 24 percent. See Janet Afary and Roger Friedland, "Critical Theory, Authoritarianism, and the Politics of Lipstick: From Weimar Republic to the Contemporary Middle East," *Critical Research on Religion* 6, no. 3 (December 2018): 243–68. For studies of questioning, negotiating, and resisting IRI laws and pronouncements about females and gender among women elsewhere in Iran, see Janet Afary, *Sexual Politics in Iran* (New York, NY: Cambridge University Press, 2009); Masserat Amir-Ebrahimi, "Transgression in Narration, The Lives of Iranian Women in Cyberspace," *Journal of Middle East Women's Studies* 4, no. 3 (2008): 89–118; Shahin Gerami, "DeTerritorialized Islamisms: Women's Agency of Resistance and Acquiescence," in *Routledge Handbook of Political Islam,* ed. Shahram Akbarzadeh (New York and London: Routledge, 2012), 191–204; Shahin Gerami and Melodye Lehnerer, "Women's Agency and Household Diplomacy: Negotiating Fundamentalism," *Gender & Society* 15, no. 4 (2001): 556–73; Elhum Haghighat, "Iran's Changing Gender Dynamics in Light of Demographic, Political and Technological Transformations," *Middle East Critique* 23, no. 3 (2014): 313–32; Azadeh Kian, "Islamic Feminism in Iran: A New Form of Subjugation or the Emergence of Agency?" *Critique Internationale* 46, no. 1 (2010): 45–66, http://www.cairn-int.info/abstract-E_CRI

fiancé, without flouting too outrageously the modesty laws and expectations? Terms and nuances are constantly negotiated. To interact with men—to act, in effect, against government directives—the couple may engage in *sigheh*.[27] This temporary marriage institution is allowed by Shi'a Muslim law but frowned upon by the public as it would bring shame to a woman and her family, result in loss of her virginity, and provide little protection for a woman and any offspring, both during the union and once it is terminated.

Only rarely have I heard of this institution used among people of Aliabad for the purpose of legally allowing an engaged couple to spend time together.[28] Generally a young woman and her family will not be in favor of a *sigheh*, which is not a guarantee of a formal marriage to come. They would be concerned that the bridegroom-to-be might renege on a formal marriage. Then the young woman, whose defloration was completed or suspected, would be in an unenviable position. For more legal and social protection, young women and their families much prefer to go through the *aqd*. Their families try to prevent others from knowing that the couple have had the *aqd*; they do not want to advertise the fact that the couple have likely begun sexual relations before the public wedding celebration.

In general, marriages are becoming more companionate; however, this is not the case with all unions. Some husbands are domineering, and some are physically, verbally, and emotionally abusive.[29] One husband in Aliabad refused to give his wife permission to see her own relatives. Because relations with female relatives are usually close, she felt lonely and depressed. While some women of Aliabad seek a divorce in

---

I_046_0045--islamic-feminism-in-iran-a-new-form-of-s.htm (accessed May 19, 2017); Azadeh Kian-Thiébaut, "From Motherhood to Equal Rights Advocates," 45–66; Mahdavi, *Passionate Uprising*; Ali Akbar Mahdi, "Iranian Women between Islamization and Globalization," in *Iran Encountering Globalization: Problems and Prospects*, ed. Ali Mohammadi (New York and London: RoutledgeCurzon, 2003), 427–48; Gousia Mir and G. N. Khaki "Globalization and Post-Islamic Revolution: A Changing Iranian Woman," *Journal of Globalization Studies* 6, no. 1 (May 2015): 74–90; Moaveni *Lipstick Jihad* and *Honeymoon in Tehran*; Arzoo Osanloo, *The Politics of Women's Rights in Iran* (Princeton, NJ: Princeton University Press, 2009); Fatemeh Sadeghi, "Negotiating with Modernity: Young Women and Sexuality in Iran," *Comparative Studies of South Asia, Africa and the Middle East* 28, no. 2 (2008): 250–9 and "Bypassing Islamism and Feminism: Women's Resistance and Rebellion in Post-revolutionary Iran," *Féminismes Islamiques* 128 (December 2010): 209–28, https://remmm.revues.org/6936?lang=en (accessed May 18, 2017); and Azam Torab, *Performing Islam: Gender and Ritual in Iran* (Leiden, Netherlands: Brill, 2006).

[27] For information about *sigheh*, see Shahla Haeri, *Law of Desire: Temporary Marriage in Shi'i Iran* (Syracuse, NY: Syracuse University Press, 1994).

[28] Temporary marriages (*sigheh*) apparently have been increasing in Iran although for most people such unions carried extreme stigma. In spite of regime propaganda, females—especially never-married young females—generally still want to avoid *sigheh* due to dishonor and lack of legal protection. See Parvaneh Masoumi, "Iran's Failure to Combat Prostitution," *IranWire* (February 27, 2018), https://iranwire.com/en/features/5196; Masud Moheb, "Really Brief Marriage with Benefits," *IranWire* (April 2, 2015), https://iranwire.com/en/features/453; and Robert Tait, "Iranian Minister Backs Temporary Marriage to Relieve Lust of Youth," *The Guardian* (June 4, 2007), https://www.theguardian.com/world/2007/jun/04/iran.roberttait.

[29] Domestic violence and abuse are even more common in Iran than in the United States. See Hamideh Hajnasiri, Reza Ghanei Gheshlagh, Kourosh Sayehmiri, Farnoosh Moafi, and Mohammad Farajzadeh, "Domestic Violence Among Iranian Women: A Systematic Review and Meta-Analysis," *Red Crescent Medical Journal* 18, no. 6 (May 17, 2016), https://www.ncbi.nlm.nih.gov/pmc/articles/PMC5006439/ and Zahra Tizro, *Domestic Violence in Iran: Women, Marriage and Islam* (New York: Routledge, 2013).

such cases, she felt unable to do so. Occasionally, she met secretly with her relatives. In contrast to her own dependent and abusive marital situation, her married daughter fared better. The young woman had received an education. She trained and worked as a beautician with another woman in a space near her mother's home.

Conclusion

For present-day Aliabadis, marriage is moving away from a taken-for-granted, permanent, highly significant step in the life cycle, followed by a more-or-less functional partnership to be endured even if difficult. Marriage has become altered and diversified as a result of changes in economic and educational conditions and greater exposure to the outside world. It has become a realm replete with higher hopes, complications, paradoxes, conflicts, and fears. A main focus of this study has been the internal critiques about marriage and how marriage is viewed by people in contemporary Iranian society with an emphasis on commentaries from Aliabad and Shiraz. Although some people saw positive changes in marriage (e.g., more acceptance of young people's partner choices and more wifely input in decision-making), frequent complaints about marriage changes arose. These included difficulties finding and vetting appropriate spouses, extravagant demands from potential brides and their families, and terrifically expensive engagement and wedding parties and homes for newlyweds. Marriage now involves competition for status in marriage choices, weddings, and post-wedding lifestyles as well as jousting over how couples should relate to each other and their relatives. All these issues have become part of the now crucial struggle for status, material goods, and other ways to show that one is better off than others—*cheshm ham cheshmi* (keeping up with the Joneses). Marriage, some people say, has become a business: just one more aspect of the materialism, extravagance, selfishness, individualism, and money-focused, entitled, and status-desiring aspects of the corrupted Iranian culture under the Islamic Republic.

Among Shirazis, some people say, marriage now involves competition over who holds power in the union. Older female informants have complained that wives give orders to their husbands, attempting to show them who is the boss. Wives may fail to show compassion for and gratitude to hardworking husbands; they may demand resources from their husbands to demonstrate their high status to outsiders.

According to some indigenous critics, young people want it all. They expect the traditional economic support from their parents for their now modern, urban-type homes and elaborate furnishings but also want their independence and nuclear family focus. Brides expect increased traditional economic support from their husbands but also want the personal freedoms and independence of European and American women they see portrayed in TV programs and films.

Marriage continues to be highly desired by a great majority of people of Aliabad even though the potential risks and the great financial costs cause anxiety and frustration and—for those who cannot manage it—hopelessness and discouragement. Parents still consider the marriage of their children to be a supreme duty, and they make every effort to achieve that end.

Women in Iran and the families who want the best for them are working within narrow parameters to improve their situations. Even when not directly stymied by law or policy, women face severe gender discrimination and pressure to fit into restrictive frameworks. Yet women are gaining influence within marriage and sometimes developing more intimate, egalitarian relationships, empowered by transformations in gender dynamics and their own modified gender and marriage ideas.[30] The private home space may offer better opportunities for transforming relationships than the outer world—visible and under the control of the Islamic Republic's clerical officials.

The diversity of marital strategies and examples of more companionate and less hierarchical marital relationships serve as models for other young women. Given exposure to more mutually caring marriages, a woman's expectations may be raised.[31] This sometimes results in disappointment but sometimes, if the spouse is sympathetic, enables them both to work toward a marriage that better reflects their wishes. Some of my most gratifying fieldwork moments have been spent in the presence of a few affectionate couples, clearly engaged in respectful, caring relationships.

---

[30] In spite of changes in marriage perceptions and practices in Aliabad, radical transformations (e.g., egalitarian relationships, both spouses working in and outside of the home, and sharing childcare) remain rare among Aliabad young women. While almost all couples live separately and out of the immediate control of mothers-in-law, most Aliabad women carry out domestic tasks during the day while their husbands work. Few Aliabad women, married or not, work outside of the home. They remain economically dependent on fathers, if they are unmarried or divorced, or husbands. Some husbands may depart somewhat from traditional norms by helping to set out and clear dishes and taking a more active role with children; the old gender division of labor remains in effect. Husbands retain formal authority, legally as well as through cultural beliefs. Still, some women, more or less subtly, negotiate the power dynamics of the relationship to their benefit.

[31] Also see Afary, *Sexual Politics in Iran*; Gerami, "DeTerritorialized Islamisms"; Gerami and Lehnerer, "Women's Agency and Household Diplomacy"; Kian-Thiébaut, "From Motherhood to Equal Rights Advocates"; Charles Kurzman, "A Feminist Generation in Iran?" *Iranian Studies* 41, no. 3 (2008): 297–321; and Jaleh Shaditalab, "Iranian Women: Rising Expectations," *Critique: Critical Middle Eastern Studies* 14, no. 1 (2005): 35–55.

10

Changing Established-Outsider Relations?

A Case Study of Bakhtiaris in Iran

Behrouz Alikhani

Introduction

According to the model of the "established and the outsiders" developed by Norbert Elias, a very close connection exists between "power" and "self-esteem." This means that members of established groups often ascribe their higher status and power to their assumed human superiority; accordingly, they perceive members of outsider groups as inferior. This principle is conceptualized as "the logic of emotions" and can be observed in various hierarchically structured group relationships. This chapter, which considers the practice of traditional marriages among members of different Bakhtiari nomadic tribes in Iran, examines such connections between power and self-esteem in human societies. It also addresses how changing the power balance to favor outsider groups over established groups affects the self-esteem of members of both established and outsider-interdependent groups.

The main point of departure of this study is memories of my childhood. I belong to a Bakhtiari nomadic tribe in southwestern Iran. Time and again, I observed how older men of my tribe, whose women had died or who wanted to marry a second wife, went to specific Bakhtiari nomadic tribes and married much younger women. During my studies as a sociologist, I started reflecting on this phenomenon, which until then had been just a "normal" and self-evident practice for me.[1] I have learned to question that practice and to look for deeper power structures that generate certain patterns of feeling, conduct, and action, and I started searching for theoretical models that could explain this specific form of social inequality in which some groups possessed higher power and status chances than the other groups.

Neither Marxist theories, which focus primarily on the material living conditions of conflicting groups, nor the individual psychological theories, with their emphasis

---

[1] Pierre Bourdieu, *Entwurf einer Theorie der Praxis – auf der ethnologischen Grundlage der kabylischen Gesellschaft* (Frankfurt am Main: Suhrkamp, 1979), 164–5. Pierre Bourdieu points out in "Outline of a Theory of Practice" how, as a result of innateness in a specific culture, certain "objective structures" become "internalized structures."

on single individuals, regardless of their group memberships, could provide a realistic description of the structure of such a relationship. Nor could theories that focus on differences, such as race, ethnicity, or religion, explain such hierarchical relations since the various Bakhtiari nomadic tribes all have the same language, social origin, and skin color, as well as the same religion. Also, studies on gender inequalities tend to reduce such a hierarchical relationship to only one of its aspects. In these cases, it was not primarily gender but a tribal background that played a crucial role in a person's stigmatization. However, being a woman and belonging to an "inferior" tribe meant double stigmatization. With the aid of "intersectional" models for the study of group inequalities, one could come closer to the core of such relationships.[2] The established-outsider model developed by Norbert Elias provides such an intersectional perspective.

The Established-Outsider Model

The established-outsider theoretical model, in my opinion, explains the structure of such relationships most realistically. It was first developed in the early 1960s, based on a "community study" in a suburb of London, anonymously called "Winston Parva." This model points to a relatively subtle and hidden kind of established-outsider relations in a working-class neighborhood. It concerns two groups whose members have the same socioeconomic origin, skin color, nationality, and religion, who nonetheless stand in an established-outsider relationship with each other. The members of the established group possess better cohesion and organization than the members of the outsider group merely because of the length of their residence at the place. Members of the long-established group have monopolized all of the important power and status positions in local administrative organizations, churches, and clubs and have closed their ranks against the newcomers. The outsiders, because of their relatively recent arrival, are at a disadvantage. They do not yet know one another well and lack close inter-group relations, which could eventually lead to group cohesion in competition with the established residents. The degree of stigmatization in Winston Parva is relatively low since the power differences between established and outsider groups are not very large. Hence, the way members of outsider groups are excluded is relatively hidden and subtle. One has to look very closely to see how members of the established group look down upon the members of the outsider group and exclude them from their own intimate circles.

Nearly thirty years later, Elias further developed this model in a study of the famous novel *To Kill a Mockingbird*, by the American writer Harper Lee, in which a black man in the small US town of Maycomb, Alabama, was murdered in the 1930s by members of the white community because of a mere suspicion that he had had a sexual relationship with a white woman. The suspicion that this black man had ignored the monopoly of white men was sufficient to hurt their self-esteem. To repair their injured individual and group self-esteem, members of the white group defied the laws. Their killing of

---

[2] Julia S. Jordan-Zachery, "Am I a Black Woman or a Woman Who Is Black? A Few Thoughts on the Meaning of Intersectionality," *Politics & Gender* 3, no. 2 (2007): 254–63, 255.

the black man was perceived as just and was intended to reaffirm their superiority, in accordance with the hierarchical relationship between white and black in the US society at that time.[3] This example allows a better understanding of the mechanisms of stigmatization since the power differentials between the established and outsider groups are considerably larger than in Winston Parva. In Maycomb, the reactions to the breaking of taboos are more open, violent, and brutal. The type and the degree of stigmatization, discrimination, and exclusion are quite different in these two studies. Although they differ in their *form* and *appearance* from each other, these examples share some *structural similarities*.[4] In his study of the novel, Elias attempts to shed light on such structural similarities among all established-outsider figurations. According to him, the study of differences based on appearances, such as race, religion, and nationality, might be misleading because they may distract from the real underlying structures.[5] Both studies are about two groups that are related as established and outsiders. One group more or less restrictively denies members of the other group access to key positions of power and status and defines them as being inferior.[6] The core of these hierarchical relationships is the unequal access to and distribution of power and status and the "self-esteem-relevant" experience of these differences in a given "scheme of self-esteem-relationships."[7] Members of the established groups equate their higher power and status with higher human quality and value, feeling that they justly deserve all their privileges.[8] This principle, captured by Elias as "the logic of emotions," can also be observed, he says, in other similarly structured group relations: "One can observe again and again that members of groups which are, in terms of power, stronger than other interdependent groups, think of themselves in human terms as better than the others."[9]

What all these established-outsider figurations have in common is that the members of powerful groups understand themselves as *better* human beings, equipped with a "group charisma," a *specific value*, which all its members share, and which remains unattainable by members of outsider groups. This "group charisma" is accompanied by a

---

[3] Norbert Elias and John L. Scotson, *The Established and the Outsiders* [Collected Works of Norbert Elias] (Dublin: University College Dublin Press, 2008), 226.
[4] Behrouz Alikhani, *Institutionelle Entdemokratisierungsprozesse, zum Nachhinkeffekt des sozialen Habitus in Frankreich, Iran und Deutschland* (Wiesbaden: VS Verlag, 2012), 86.
[5] Elias and Scotson, *The Established and the Outsiders*, 210.
[6] Similar to the concept used by Elias, the concept of power is a relational concept. "Power" is an attribute of relationships, and every human relationship is simultaneously a power relationship. Circumstances may alter these relationships to favor one side and disadvantage the other. Power relations can, therefore, constantly shift as the circumstances on which they depend undergo change (Norbert Elias, *What Is Sociology?* [Collected Works of Norbert Elias] (Dublin: University College Dublin Press, 2012), 111. It has extraordinary theoretical and practical consequences if the concept of power would not be used in a reified manner but in a connection with other words like power resources, power differentials, power chances, power balances, power potentials, power distributions, and power ratios. The sources of power can vary; they need not be economic. Sources of power are also sources of a person's self-esteem.
[7] Dawud Gholamasad, *Selbstbild und Weltsicht islamischer Selbstmord-Attentäter* (Berlin: Klaus Schwarz Verlag, 2006), 28.
[8] Elias and Scotson, *The Established and the Outsiders*, 224–5.
[9] Ibid., 1.

"group disgrace," which is attributed to all members of the outsider group.[10] Depending on the given power differences and the conscious experience of these differences, the reactions of members of the outsider group may vary widely. At the extremes, the members may accept the attribution of inferiority by the established group and absorb it in their self-image, or they may reject it completely. In the course of a potential shift in the balance of power alongside "functional democratization" in favor of members of an outsider group, especially in the case of the conscious experience of this shift, members of outsider groups could engage in counter-stigmatization.[11] However, this counter-stigmatization would only affect members of the established group if the available power differences become small enough. Otherwise, the attempt at counter-stigmatization by members of the outsider group could be deflected by the established group and have relatively little (if any) effect.

Elias defines such relationships as having a "universal regularity" that can be observed in all established-outsider figurations in the world. He cites examples from the Indian, Japanese, and Latin American societies to substantiate the universality of this model. The established groups in all these case studies ascribe *superior human characteristics* to their members and exclude all members of the other groups from closer contact with their own circles. Deviant behavior by any member of the established group would be classified as anomic and strongly sanctioned by the rest of the group. Thus, members of established groups more or less consciously try to maintain their own "self-esteem-enhancing" power and status monopolies by rejecting contact with outsiders:

> The closing [of] ranks among the established certainly has the social function of preserving the group's power superiority. At the same time, the avoidance of any closer social contact with members of the outsider group has all the emotional characteristics of what in another context has [come] to be called "the fear of pollution."[12]

Members of an outsider group pose a threat to the power and status privileges of members of an established group and also threaten the sources of their self-esteem. Any loss of power on the part of members of the established group would be automatically perceived as a loss of self-esteem and self-value. That is why established groups react so vehemently to a breach of taboos that are closely connected with their opportunities to

---

[10] Norbert Elias, *Gruppencharisma und Gruppenschande*. Hrsg. Jentges, Erik (Marbach: Deutsches Literaturarchiv Marbach, 2014), 7.

[11] The functional dimension of processes of democratization refers to the shifting of the power balance in favor of previously excluded outsider groups. Norbert Elias coined the term "functional democratization" to demonstrate the direction of social and political development from a hierarchically structured social and political order to a more even distribution of power resources in a society. Also, the process sociological concept of *function*, like the concept of *power*, is a concept of relationship. There are always functional interdependencies between individuals and groups in a society (Elias, *What Is Sociology?* 58–61). These functions are reciprocal and multipolar. What is symbolically called "society" is from a process sociological point of view nothing more than functional nexuses of interdependent people as individuals and groups. People or groups that have functions for each other exercise constraint over each other as well. Elias, *What is Sociology?* 71.

[12] Elias and Scotson, *The Established and the Outsiders*, 9.

exercise power. Channels of "praise and blame gossips" serve to effectively regulate the behavior of group members.[13] Depending on how loyal the members of an established group are and how well they adhere to the dominant norms and standards of their group, they might get rewarded or punished. In the course of their socialization, members learn the unwritten rules that must be respected and obeyed. They internalize these rules as constituent elements of their individual and group identity.[14]

According to Elias, this established-outsider model can be taken as an "empirical paradigm" for the investigation of similarly structured figurations in any human society.[15] In this way, the model can be tested repeatedly, complemented, and possibly revised. This method also reflects the general theoretical-empirical approach of Elias: first, set up a model based on an empirical example and then try to expand the scope of the model, using new empirical case studies from differently structured societies. "One can build up a small-scale explanatory model of the figuration one believes to be universal, a model ready to be tested, enlarged and if necessary revised by enquiries into related figurations on a larger scale."[16]

In this chapter, I seek to discover how far this model might serve as a "template" to explain the hierarchical relationships of different Bakhtiari nomadic tribes in southwestern Iran. I investigate why "downward marriage" (i.e., with members of lower-status tribes) has been vehemently proscribed and tabooed for members of higher-status tribes, especially when it involves procreation. Why are exceptions possible for considerably older men who could not easily marry a relatively young woman of their own tribe to manage their household, a responsibility that includes hard physical work for women? Are material living conditions the only reason that the members of some tribes feel superior to members of other tribes, whom they do not know personally? How have such hierarchical tribal relationships changed in the past decades? Have they undergone greater nationalization, urbanization, and individualization? And how have members of different formerly established and outsider tribes experienced themselves and their relationship to members of other tribes in the course of these transformations?

The Structure of Marriages in Bakhtiari Tribes

Bakhtiari nomadic tribes in Iran have a very complex web of relationships. Beyond concepts such as "ethnicity," "tribe," or "clan," there exist many other levels and layers of tribal subdivisions, which are hardly translatable into English. Each individual possesses a specific place in this web of relationships, which is difficult to change. The place and the position of every single individual can be easily traced back and identified in a very long chain of generations. The tribe affiliation is determined by the father. The

---

[13] Elias, *Gruppencharisma und Gruppenschande*, 28.
[14] Norbert Elias, *The Society of Individuals* [Collected Works of Norbert Elias] (Dublin: University College Dublin Press, 2010), 199–200.
[15] Elias and Scotson, *The Established and the Outsiders*, 3.
[16] Ibid.

relationship between different tribes used to be hierarchically structured. The history of tribal elimination struggles and the date of inception of such hierarchies is unknown. In a dominantly illiterate and prestate society, the tribal stories and narratives are passed on oral history from one generation to the next. The current recognizable manifestation of these differences is the very unequal distribution of pasture lands among different tribes. The best pasture lands, as the most decisive source of power in a society of stockbreeders and farmers, are possessed by the tribes with the highest places in the tribal hierarchy. For example, the tribe of Zarasfand possesses high-quality pasture lands because of its early close relationship with political commanders, called Khans." The Mowri tribe, which had a weak relationship with these Khans, received pasture lands of lower quality, despite the large number of its members. This historically developed power resource is enormously important in determining how members of different tribes perceive and evaluate themselves and others. The close link between "power" and "self-esteem" can be clearly demonstrated on the basis of this striking example. In other societies with established-outsider figurations, power differentials are lower, relatively hidden, and therefore more difficult to perceive.[17] However, the study of such overt examples can help in developing concepts and models that can capture even more subtle and hidden "distinctions" and their relation to self-esteem in more democratic societies:

> The need to make this distinction is self-evident in all cases in which individuals from the same class fraction or the same family, and therefore presumably subject to identical moral, religious or political inculcations, are inclined towards divergent stances in religion or politics by the different relations to the social world which they owe to divergent individual trajectories, having, for example, succeeded or failed in the reconversion strategies necessary to escape the collective decline of their class.[18]

This study is based on interviews that I randomly carried out between the summer of 2015 and the summer of 2017 with some members of three relatively established tribes, Galeh, Pebdeni, and Babadi, and one outsider tribe, Mowri. I asked eighteen members of the more established tribes, who were of different ages, genders, and educational backgrounds, about their personal opinions regarding marriages with members of two outsider tribes, Mowris and Arpenais. Due to some "tribal sensitivities," given the currently changed power balance that favors former outsider tribes, I managed to interview just four male members of the Mowri tribe about the same issues. Nowadays, as a result of the strong restructuring of Iranian society in the last four decades, talking about such hierarchical relationships is very unpleasant for members of the formerly outsider tribes. Such discussions may have negative, even violent, consequences for people who divulge them in public, as well as for all members of their tribe. Therefore, many members of my family and tribe warned me not to publicly discuss such "sensitive

---

[17] Ibid., 12.
[18] Pierre Bourdieu, *Distinction: A Social Critique of the Judgement of Taste* (London: Routledge, 1884), 111.

issues," which could also affect them. By publishing in a foreign language and not using actual names, I have tried to reduce the potential negative impact of debating such tabooed topics among members of different Bakhtiari tribes. I focused on marriage relationships because, in my opinion, I could come closer to the emotional reactions of members of different established and outsider groups regarding such an intimate and personal subject. Furthermore, marriage and types of marriage ceremonies in Bakhtiari tribes are considered a means of creating, broadening, and maintaining social relations among families and individuals and are, therefore, very important in the social lives of the tribes.[19]

None of the interviewees currently lives a nomadic lifestyle, though either they themselves were formerly nomads or came from nomadic families. They all live in small towns on the edge of the summer or winter pasture lands of their ancestors in Shahr-e Kord, Ahwaz, or in small cities around Isfahan. Most of the interviewees from the former established tribes expressed themselves in similar and clear ways. They argued almost entirely within the following framework: Behdarvands and Zarasfands, the two established tribes at the top of the tribal hierarchy, are "better." They have "better roots," "a better vein and blood," "a better nature," as well as "a better ancestry." In contrast, Arpenais and Mowris, the two outsider tribes, were regarded by them as "inferior," "without good origin and roots," "evil" and "less respectable." In almost all the interviews, the self-image of established tribes tended to be based on their perceptions of a minority of their "best" members. In contrast, the outsider tribes were defined by the "bad" characteristics of their group's "worst" members. For example, the Mowris were referred to as "criminals" and "thieves," and the Behdarvands were called "noble" and of "high value." This perspective is important for increasing the self-esteem of members of the established groups: "This pars pro toto distortion in opposite directions enables an established group to prove their point to themselves as well as to others; there is always some evidence to show that one's group is 'good' and the other is 'bad.'"[20]

In accordance with the structure of these nomadic tribes, the language that is used is very "concrete" rather than "abstract"; that is, the terms used are at a very "low level of synthesis."[21] Particularly, spatial terms such as "height" and "depth," or "up" and "down" symbolize not only the *position* of the tribes in the tribal hierarchy but also the *human quality* and *value* of their members. All these terms either enhance or diminish self-esteem, and as such they simultaneously include both the *power* and *value* aspects of human relationships. Next, I analyze nine selected statements from interviews with

---

[19] Mohammad Reza Shahbazi, "The Role of Marriage in Social Relations in Bakhtiari Tribe," *Journal Studies of Tribes and Tribals* 10, no. 1 (2012): 29–34, 29.
[20] Elias and Scotson, *The Established and the Outsiders*, 5.
[21] Norbert Elias, *The Symbol Theory* (London: SAGE Publication, 1995), 59. From the process sociological point of view, language represents the world as it is experienced by the members of a language community. According to Elias, everything that members of a language community may articulately experience and communicate to each other is located in their language and is passed down from one generation to others. Thus, language affects the perception of future generations about the world they experience. The close connection between "thinking," "knowledge," and "language" deserves more careful attention from the human sciences since the function of language extends beyond communication to orientation and control. Ibid., 69–70.

members of the established tribes. The selected statements are representative of the way that individuals perceive themselves and members of the former outsider tribes. The statements of the four members of the outsider tribe are analyzed at the end of this chapter. The translation of these statements from Lori to English has been a difficult task, because it has not always been easy to find concepts in the English language with the same meanings and connotations. Given these limitations, I have tried to convey the general content of the statements as accurately as possible.

The first statement is from Afshar, a 37-year-old man of second generation who lives in a small town near the summer pasture lands of his tribe. He is a lawyer and currently offers legal advice to different companies and individuals. He lives in the city of Farsan, near Shahr-e Kord, and he has maintained relatively close ties to the larger circle of his tribal kin, who still live as nomads, reside in the newly developed villages in former tribal areas, or live in smaller towns at the outskirts of the tribal areas. When asked whether he could imagine marrying a woman from one of the two abovementioned outsider tribes, he answered without delay:

> I will not marry a woman from the Mowri tribe. They are down (low). There are some redlines, which are not easily identifiable. These lines are deeply inside me. I am sure, I will have huge problems with myself if I marry a Mowri woman. I cannot do that. I will have children in my life later. I am convinced that if I marry a Mowri woman, I will lose both my social position and my face. I have my own tribal relationships. People would then surely think about me in a different way.

Afshar, as a member of a former established tribe, is aware of boundaries that must not be crossed, and he shares his respect for these external constraints with other tribal members, who believe as he does. He clearly fears the possible reaction of other group members if he were to breach the taboos. He wants to behave according to the tribal canon and standards to maintain his reputation (his "face") and his position. Afshar is afraid of being subjected to the "blame gossip" of other tribal members. He also uses prejudicial expressions when discussing the members of the two former outsider tribes, which show that he feels superior to them. He implicitly connects the higher position of his tribe in the existing hierarchy of tribes with his own higher human quality and value. The importance of this connection is evident in other interviews as well. The creation of a we-group with a specific group charisma is not only a conscious but also a less conscious praxis, and its importance persists, despite the fact that the former hierarchical tribal relationships no longer exist in contemporary Iranian society, and tribal membership no longer plays a significant role.

The next interviewee is Anush, a 61-year-old woman who, as a nomad, moved with her family when she was twenty-eight to a small town near the winter pasture lands of her tribe. Anush openly expresses the connection between the low status of outsider tribes and the low value and quality of their members in her eyes. This connection is again generalized when referring to members of the group as a whole. The fear of pollution in the case of a marriage with a member of a former outsider tribe is a very strong emotion for her:

Mowris do not have any roots. They have no correct descent. They are beggars. They are unable and low. The Mowri tribe was always a minor tribe. They have always followed commands. One would lose face if there would be a marriage. This is not possible at all. If somebody did that (marry somebody from the two outsider tribes) they would not be respectable anymore.

The statement of the 68-year-old Morvarid, who is among the second generation of her community to live in a city, is similar to that of Anush. For her, all members of outsider tribes have a "bad reputation," which is unlikely to change even if generations pass. For her, this negative reputation is something permanent, intrinsic, or even "biological." She believes that everyone born into these tribes automatically inherits and bequeaths that reputation. A person who marries into one of those tribes is subject to this bad fortune and would lose his or her purity: "Tribes like Arpenai, Mowri and Belivand have just a bad reputation. They are also bad. Some of them perhaps have gotten rich nowadays, but they do not have proper roots. They simply could not change this reality."

The terms "good family," a "good descent," and "good roots" are also crucial for Bibigol, a 75-year-old woman who has never lived a nomadic life and now lives in a village near the summer pasture lands of her tribe. In her view, one's origin and ancestry are permanent features of one's character:

Names of the father and grandfather are extremely important. You always have to ask whose son or daughter is someone. The son of a bad father will always remain the son of this bad father. In these tribes, you barely have people with good family, good origin, and ancestry. They have always been like that.

Amin, a 22-year-old man who studies and lives in Shahr-e Kord, and Mina, a 24-year-old woman who studies civil engineering at the university of Isfahan, are both of third-generation nomadic origin and hold similar views. Amin was asked why he thinks that he is better than Mowris and Arpenais and if that means that he would not marry a woman from either of those two tribes. He replied curtly, "No! You have veins and roots. I never would do it!" The answer to the "why" question was also very short: "Because it is a flaw."

Mina, who studies in one of the best universities in Iran, replied more or less the same:

"Veins and roots are very important. And the family is also important. Mowris do not have the right veins and roots. They are peasant and we are nobles. Even if individually the person is a good and economically successful person I would not marry him. I had such offers, but I rejected them. I do not like it. Acknowledgment [of other people] is very important."

The "redlines" thus seem extremely well-defined for many single people who are concerned about their community's view of them. Ignoring such views has consequences such as exclusion, blame gossip, and other kinds of social sanctions.

In the course of the interviews, I realized that, despite the continuity and similarities, there exist distinctive differences between members of different generations in these three established tribes. While the older members of the established tribes, such as

Anush, Morvarid, and Bibigol use terms such as "roots," "blood," "origin," "descent," or "family" to emphasize the inferiority of members of the outsider tribes, the younger members of these established tribes employ more modern terms from the Persian language, such as "race," "nature," and (increasingly) "genes." For example, 33-year-old Farnash is among the second generation to grow up in a small town on the outskirts of the summer pastures of his tribe in Shahr-e Kord. He expresses himself very directly:

> Like a watchdog which should have a good race, human beings also have different races. Some races embody biological superiority. "Bravery," "manhood" and "self-sacrifice" have always been important for Bakhtiaris. Some tribes possess such characteristics, some simply do not. Like different glasses which have different capacities, groups of human beings have different capacities as well. The Mowri tribe, for example, has a lower capacity. I would also never marry a woman from the Arpenai tribe. Although there are good Arpenais, these are a minority. Arpenai men do not have any masculine attributes. They are also physically weak. Their voice sounds like women's voices.

Karam, a 39-year-old, is an engineer and a member of the second generation of nomads living in the same city. He argues very similarly. He thinks that some tribes are "naturally" better than others. They create "brave men and real warriors." Their "nature" could not be changed through education or "cultural" changes. When asked why he thinks that "brave men and real warriors" belong to particular Bakhtiari tribes, he replied, "Some tribes could not create great men due to their weak genes and bad blood. Their men could not compete with the famous men from good tribes."

The next statement is from Masude, a 26-year-old woman who is in the second generation in her family to live in a city on the edge of the winter pasture lands of Bakhtiari nomadic tribes in Ahwaz. In her statements, one sees her internal contradiction. She lives in a large city with a relatively high degree of individualization, but she only maintains tribal relationships within and outside this city. When asked whether she would have problems if her daughter wanted to marry a man from the Mowri or Arpenai tribe in the future, she replied hesitantly:

> I personally have no problems if my daughter would marry a man from the Arpenai tribe. Only the fact that people would judge us would worry me a lot. Then, I would be ashamed. I, on my part, would not have any problems with such a marriage. The world has changed extremely, and we do not live as nomads anymore. But people say that the Arpenais are sexually promiscuous and easy going. People still are very sensitive towards this issue. One has to be very careful.

Her conflict is one that many Bakhtiaris from established tribes who now live in newly developed cities face. On the one hand, they live an urban life and are employed in modern professions and positions. On the other hand, in this highly transitional society—from a tribal to an urbanized state society—they rely on their own tribal relationships, which still have great regulatory effects and force them to keep to the old tribal canons and standards. The term "drag effects of social habitus"²² is a technical term coined by Nobert Elias. It refers to the continuity of the social habitus of a group of people which does not relate to the changed social reality any more. Such processes are closely connected to the fast-paced transition of the Bakhtiari nomadic society into a nationalized Iranian society.

Processes of Nationalization and the Change of Intertribal Power Relations in Favor of Former Outsider Tribes

Iranian society has been affected by a rapid process of modernization, urbanization, and individualization. The population increased from 18.9 million in 1957 to 33.7 million in 1977 and 75.1 million in 2011. During this process of transformation from a predominantly homogeneous and prestate tribal community to a mainly urbanized and individualized society, the number of people living in cities rose from 25 percent in the early twentieth century to 31.4 percent in 1957 and 71.4 percent in 2011.²³ According to Iran's Center for Statistics (p. 19), in 1977, there were only 210 cities in the whole country. By 2011, this number had increased sixfold to 1,331 cities, including eight cities with more than a million inhabitants. Similar to many other nomadic tribes in Iran, Bakhtiari nomads have been affected by such dramatic changes. At the beginning of the twentieth century, 90 percent of Bakhtiari nomads lived a nomadic life; in the year 2000, this number was less than 10 percent.²⁴

This process of urbanization had an enormous impact on the Bakhtiaris. This post-nomadic society has increasingly evolved into a nation-state society. The tribe as a "survival unit" has increasingly ceded its functions to newly created national institutions.²⁵ This trend has been accompanied by many loyalty struggles. There

---

²² Elias, *The Society of Individuals*, 188. The term "drag effect of the social habitus" in this sense refers to the consequences of transformation of self-experience of the people concerned "dragging" behind social transformation.
²³ Iran's Center for Statistics, census of 2011, Tehran, 17. To visualize the extremely rapid increase in population and its consequences for the people of Iran, it helps to compare this figure with the parallel increase in population of some more modern societies. In Germany, for instance, the population was 68.8 million in 1935, and it rose at a relatively slow pace to 71.4 million in 1957, 78.1 million in 1979, and 81.8 million in 2011 (Statistisches Bundesamt: Entwicklung der Gesamtbevölkerung Deutschlands von 1871 bis 2014: Wiesbaden).
²⁴ Javad Safinejad, *Irans Lurs* (written in Farsi) (Teheran: Atiyeh, 2002), 187.
²⁵ From a process sociological point of view, the "state" is the social organization that serves to protect and defend its members. States share these functions with other prestate survival units, such as extended families, clans, and tribes. These survival units highlight different forms of organization and social influence at different stages of integration and differentiation. The state level of integration differs from the other prestate levels in its degree of complexity and differentiation. States represent in this sense relatively stable institutions that monopolize physical violence and taxation. The creation of these monopolistic institutions is the result of long struggles of competition and elimination that were accompanied by processes of ascent and descent of human beings and their forms of integration. In the course of these processes, older units of organization and integration have been superseded. The disintegration of older units usually goes along with the formation of newer processes of integration at a higher level of social and political development. Under certain circumstances, however, these processes may be reversed. Norbert Elias, *The Germans* (Cambridge: Polity Press, 1996), 349–50.

already exist many conflicts between members of different generations and regions. Many members of the older generations have been habitually lagging behind the new reality.[26] The state-led processes of modernization have developed so rapidly in recent decades that many people have not been able to keep up with the pace. This "non-simultaneity of developments" among different functional, institutional, and habitual dimensions of transformation explains some of the major conflicts of the Bakhtiari society that have occurred in recent decades.

In particular, the Islamic Revolution dramatically changed the relationships among and within various tribes. This revolution, as Ayatollah Khomaini formulated it, was altogether a revolution of the "poor" and "marginalized" against the "rich" and the "oppressors."[27] Members of the outsider tribes, thus, were enabled to ascend in the postrevolutionary institutions. In contrast, members of the established tribes experienced downward social mobility. Many of them were accused by the Islamists of having a close relationship with the former regime. This upward mobility (for outsider tribes) and downward mobility (for established tribes) has led to power differentials, especially between people of Bakhtiari descent who live in the cities. If current trends continue in the next two or three generations, the hierarchy of the tribes might be forgotten by the people from the formerly established tribes. The replacement of tribal hierarchy by the new scheme of self-value relationships can be deduced from the statements made by some of the interviewees from formerly established and outsider tribes. Processes of individualization in the course of the increasing urbanization of nomadic areas have already changed the older and more familiar value systems among some members of the formerly established and outsider tribes. New functions and positions have by and large replaced older relationships, functions, and positions. Accordingly, the web of dependencies among different tribes has changed dramatically in favor of former outsider tribes in a nationalized society. According to the emerging scheme, a person's salary is the main criterion by which that person's position is evaluated. Therefore, some members of formerly established tribes, who have now been integrated into the new nationalized society, no longer decide and act according to the older, tribally oriented social codes and standards.

Generally, despite all the aforementioned "social prejudices" in larger cities, there is an increasing tendency to marry outside the strict borders of extended families and kinship relationships. The increasing participation of women in the growing public space and the emergence of new means of communication have created new opportunities for men and women to come in contact with each other beyond the old tribal channels of communication. The time when couples married without first seeing and talking to each other is over for many Bakhtiaris.

In what follows, I analyze the statements of two members of formerly established tribes and four members of a formerly outsider Mowri tribe to verify the impact of the changed power relationships on the members of different tribes and suggest possible directions of development in the future. These changes are due to processes

---

[26] Elias, *The Society of Individuals*, 188.
[27] Dawud Gholamasad, *Iran, die Entstehung der islamischen Revolution* (Hamburg: Junius Verlag, 1985), 461–3.

of functional democratization resulting from the rapid nationalization of Iranian state and society, as the accompanying disintegration of former "survival units" continues. For instance, Amirhossain, age fifty-four, a civil servant in Shahr-e Kord, is admittedly aware of the former tribal scheme of self-value relationships and their regulating power for members of formerly established tribes. However, he could imagine looking for a woman from an outsider tribe for each of his two adult sons:

> I would marry a Mowri girl for my son if she were a lecturer at the university or a doctor of medicine. Then I would not care about her father and mother. The personal character of humans is important.

For Amirhossain, having a doctoral degree in medicine and a high salary could replace the older tribal ascriptions. The "polluted" person from an "inferior" tribe would be a potential marriage candidate for his son if she were very successful according to the new, "capitalistic" scheme of self-value relationships. The merit of the person and not the collective background was Amirhossain's main concern. This kind of evaluation is a new and increasingly common phenomenon. In Pierre Bourdieu's view, before this period of individualization, "symbolic" rather than "economic" capital was crucial for measuring a person's value as a human being. But in a modern, functionally divided society, other sources are replacing the former sources of power and self-esteem.[28]

An interview with an illiterate 48-year-old man from a village near Kuhrang who lived a nomadic life until he was twenty-six was very revealing. In his case, the tension of the transition from a prestate nomadic society to a national society was clear. As a son of a former established tribe leader in Kuhrang, he talked in a contradictory way about differences between tribes and clans in terms of their roots and lineages, and he ranked himself higher than members of the former outsider tribes. He complained that everybody was now equal according to the new national laws. Until the time of his father, in his view, all the political, economic, military, and judiciary decisions were made by his ancestors. When asked whether he would let his son marry a woman from either of the two mentioned former outsider tribes, at first, he answered with a clear "no!" He said, "[. . .] because then I will lose him. He will go to her place." When I asked how it would be if he stayed at his own place, he replied,

> But this is a very awkward question! I do not know. Maybe they know it better. Nowadays, everybody marries everybody from every tribe he or she wants. But, some tribes have great leaders like Mohamad Gholi, Asgar or Esmail [some famous men from his tribe]. No matter how poor they are, they would stay great.

One senses the difficult situation in which the interviewee found himself. He seemed not to have thought about these unpleasant questions before. His body language demonstrated this tension. Finally, he contradicted himself again in responding to the

---

[28] Pierre Bourdieu, "The Forms of Capital," in *Handbook of Theory and Research for the Sociology of Education*, ed. J. Richardson (New York: Greenwood,1986), 241–58.

less emotional question of whether he thought tribal differences were being replaced by new ones, such as differences in wealth.

> Maybe it could replace. Yes, money is replacing these things. Nowadays, who is rich and has a couple of trucks or two or three billion is very important. One could see this in weddings and funeral ceremonies. One calls the name of newly rich people in loudspeakers, people whose fathers were nobodies.

The New Self-image of Members of Former Outsider Tribes

I was wondering how the dominance of the new "capitalistic" scheme of self-value relationships has impacted members of the Mowri outsider tribe. Mohsen, a 28-year-old, had a master's degree in political science and worked at a library in Shahr-e Kord. His answers show the rising importance of economic capital compared with the traditional "social and symbolic capital" of the people in the traditional tribal society:

> The old tribal hierarchy within and between tribes no longer exists. Just within families there are some older people who are respected. Nowadays money defines who has dignity. Money has replaced nobility. [. . .] Marriage is meanwhile seen as an opportunity to increase one's economic opportunities. The occupation of a person is very important. If the man or the woman is a doctor, a dentist or a pharmacist one would go for it, regardless of the family background of the person. Ninety percent of Bakhtiari families have changed and are moving away from traditional rules. For me the history of the person is more important that the history of her family. But still in the eyes of my family the history of the family is more important.

The next statement shows how, in the course of the nationalization of the Iranian state and society, the prestate structures have lost their function in favor of new state institutions. Ali, a 31-year-old illiterate peasant living in a village between Shahr-e Kord and Ahwaz, is from the Mowri tribe. In simple language, he explains how state institutions are replacing the hierarchical tribal institutions, which he clearly disliked. As a member of an outsider tribe that has gained more power in the last decades, he did not like my question about his tribe being lower in the tribal hierarchy in the past. He answered in an angry and annoyed way:

> You are asking awkward questions. I think these differences are nonsense. Nowadays, money is important. In different tribes there are different people. One has to decide by himself. We had recently a fight in our neighborhood. The young people did not listen to the opinion of the elders. Finally, the police came and solved the problem. The time of khans [a Bakhtiari political title] and nobility is gone. Everybody who has money is now a khan for himself. Now, people look for somebody in the government to get a job or position for their children.

In another statement, Zaher, a successful, 37-year-old businessman from the Mowri tribe who lives a prosperous life in Esfahan, refused to accept the narrative about the hierarchy of different tribes in the past. He vehemently denied that his tribe used to be placed at the bottom of the hierarchy:

> We had also our important persons as well as our courageous men and brave warriors. Mowri always had khans. Everybody knows that. You could read it in different books! Everybody knows Eskandar Zaheri Abdevand. He dared to loudly threaten people from Zarasfand tribe [a very established tribe] in one of their weddings.

The tale of how a leader of his tribe had once loudly opposed members of an established tribe at one of their most important gatherings was, for Zaher, a clear sign of the greatness of the whole Mowri tribe in a warrior society where bravery and militancy were the most desired features of a great man. At the same time, Zaher demonstrated that he did not live according to the former tribal standards. He stated that the status of a woman's tribe would not influence his decision to marry her. Similar to all the other three interviewed members of the former outsider Mowri tribe, and two of the eighteen members of the three former established tribes, Zaher emphasized the individualistic characteristics of his potential partner instead of her tribal affiliation. The emphasis on such personal characteristics by all the members of former outsider tribes indicates that they have adjusted to the new social life of a nationalized society where tribal affiliations no longer play an important role. Zaher stated,

> For me it is not important from which tribe I should choose my future wife. It depends on the person if I like her. My parents do not care from which tribe as long as we do not have any personal family or tribal fights with them. We actually marry different tribes. [. . .] Nowadays, nobody would say we are bad. Every tribe has good and bad people. I am claiming that our clan is the best clan within the Mowris.

Finally, a statement from Khedri, a 48-year-old man from the Mowri tribe who now owns a shop selling electronic devices, is also very revealing. Khedri embodied the new self-awareness of the members of outsider tribes. He completely rejected the old narratives about social hierarchies of different tribes. He tried to relativize the old stories by expressing his complete disregard of such tribal differences. In an indirect way, he criticized "some people" who thought they were better than other people, without trying to place them in a tribal landscape. This statement suggests that he was aware of the way members of former established tribes perceived members of his tribe:

> Some people think that they are better. But, if it comes to actions sometimes they are weaker than ordinary people. In this time and under this political regime everybody thinks he is a unique person. Mowris came earlier to cities and they learned the tricks of city life better than members of the other tribes. When they

visited the tribal regions, they could fool members of other tribes very easily. Mowris had many important persons. Maybe in the past they were weaker due to their poverty, but Mowris were neither peasant nor vassal [*raiyat*]. Poverty between different tribes was the problem.

We can also notice Khedri's emphasis on individualization. For him, life in modern times required skills other than nomadic skills of bravery and militancy. When I asked why some people still believed in such tribal hierarchies, he replied,

> Young people do not listen to the old people anymore. For me the family of the person is important and not her or his tribal background. All tribes are at the same level. Talking about tribal differences is nonsense. You should not believe in such myths. Even in a single family you have different persons. One of them could be stupid, the other one could be clever and so on. You cannot just take one person from one family and say the whole tribe is like that! Nowadays khans no longer exist. Everybody thinks that he is a khan. If you are literate and smart you should not make yourself small. You should believe in your individual abilities. In every tribe we could have such people. Such features are not hereditary. One should work on oneself.

Summary

Bakhtiari tribes in Iran have the same skin color, the same religion, and the same socioeconomic origin. However, most members of some tribes refuse to marry or have intimate relationships with members of other tribes who are perceived as inferior. In eighteen interviews that were carried out between the summer of 2015 and the summer of 2017 with members of three former established tribes and two former outsider tribes about intermarriage within tribes, sixteen interviewees rejected entering such a union. Older members of former established tribes mentioned "bad vein," "bad origin and ancestry," and "bad roots" of members of the two former outsider tribes as the main reasons for such rejection. The younger members additionally used more modern terms, such as "bad race," "nature," and "genes" to distinguish themselves. Such evaluations originate in the power differences among tribes in the hierarchical structured society of the past and their influence on self-evaluation. The high status of a tribe was used to define the superiority of its members. According to the principle of "the logic of emotions" in every established-outsider figuration, more power is often directly translated into superior human quality. All these distinctions still exist among many of the three former established tribes despite the great changes in power relations that have favored the former outsider tribes in the course of the rapid nationalization of Iranian society. This short study has shown that hierarchies still exist in the social habitus of many Bakhtiaris from former established tribes who now live in the cities.

In the new, more urbanized and individualized society, tribal background is no longer key for gaining social, political, and economic positions. Statements by four members of the former outsider tribes suggest that the symbolic capital of tribal background is much less important. Instead, the economic capital of individuals has increasingly become the main source of their power and self-esteem. The changing patterns of intertribal Bakhtiari marriages reveal the close connection between power and self-esteem in human societies. They also shed light on the importance of changing power balances among different established and outsider figurations for shifts in patterns of conduct and sentiment—the social habitus—among the people involved. The latter changes, however, may lag behind the changing power relationships for three to five generations, as we saw in the case of the former established Bakhtiari tribes.[29] The further restructuring of the social habitus of former established Bakhtiari tribes depends on the direction of development in the Iranian society and the strength of resistance of this social habitus.

---

[29] Elias, *The Germans*, 34.

Epilogue

The Rise in Non-standard Marriages in the Region

Janet Afary and Roger Friedland

Dramatic shifts in the Muslim Middle East in the institution of marriage have not been limited to Iran. In recent years, we have witnessed similar changes in the formation of unions in other countries of the Middle East (Turkey, Tunisia, and Egypt, among others), as well as in North Africa and South Asia. Marriage is delayed, and the age at first marriage for both men and women has gone up, while rates of marriage have been declining. These trends conflict with customary attitudes in the region, which regard marriage as a fundamental aspect of a man's or woman's transition to adulthood. Researchers in different parts of the region are also reporting significant increases in rates of nonstandard marriages in the Middle East, North Africa, and South Asia (SWANA) region. These unions—some religiously sanctioned and some not—are called *'urfi* (customary marriage), *misyar* (traveling marriage), and *mut'a* or *sigheh* (temporary marriage), making them different from formal marriage (*nekāh dā'em*). In addition, committed cohabitation among educated urbanites, similar to Iranian white marriages, are also appearing in other parts of the region, such as Tunisia. Because nonstandard unions are often not registered, it has been extremely difficult to document this trend.

In 2012–13 and again in 2017–18, we used Facebook banner ads in seven Muslim-majority countries to survey the young and computer-literate populations of Algeria, Egypt, Iran, Pakistan, Palestine, Tunisia, and Turkey, as well as those living in diaspora. We analyzed the responses of a cross section of those who took our survey and either expressed their attitudes about nonstandard marriages in the region or admitted that they were currently living in such a union, rather than in formal marriages. Our findings were quite diverse. Among others, we noticed a rise in the desire for love as a basis of mate selection in the countries we surveyed. Young people increasingly want love in their married lives, but they and the communities in which they live remain uncomfortable with the mating practices that have emphasized love in the West.

Our survey results showed that the future of romantic love in the Muslim world is tied up with the politics of gender and religion, and women's agency. The new courtship practices associated with love as a basis of marriage depend on that agency. Women's visibility issues—their ability to enter public spaces and to interact with men and their capacity to recognize and act upon their attraction to single men, which includes acting on their ability to say no—are significant issues in the SWANA world, issues that animate the conflict over religion's proper political role. Islamist organizations have taken an active role in addressing these challenges; indeed, some of the reasons for the popularity of Islamism among young people is that they are developing new organizations and new (Islamist) public spaces that would facilitate unions, whether through standard or nonstandard marriages.[1]

One key factor that has fueled this desire for love is the role of social media. In particular, Facebook has created new virtual public spaces where young women and men living in socially conservative societies can communicate to meet and engage in forbidden intimacies. But is cyberspace an alternate space for young people where the laws of social gravity do not apply, where they can pursue forbidden behaviors? Do young people in countries with more conservative social norms about young, unrelated women and men meeting in public space use the internet as an alternative space in which to interact and engage romantically? Our survey confirmed that this, in fact, is the case, as earlier studies on Brazil, India, and Morocco have shown. In general, Facebook and other online social platforms have created a new public sphere that allows for the recalibration and regendering of norms and interactions. In such places, the digital space becomes an alternative public arena where young people can interact, court, and love.[2]

The desire for love-based marriage in the internet age is coupled with the fact that throughout the SWANA region, many young people are postponing formal marriage until they are in their late twenties or thirties, while others are completely foregoing formal marriage. This delay is rooted in the many years it takes to receive a college education, find employment, and save enough to enter into a formal marriage, with all its expensive financial commitments, in a world where well-paid jobs are becoming scarce. It is also rooted in the fact that women are becoming more educated, often more so than the men in their cohort and, therefore, may not be able to find a partner in their community.

This environment has contributed to the rise of nonstandard marriages, specifically among college-age students. More than 10,000 self-identified Muslim respondents, who took our 2018 survey, provided us with data about their marital status. Of these, close to 3,500 were formally married and about 450 were in nonstandard unions. Our survey takers shared the following sentiments about nonstandard marriages.

- A vast majority of the men who engaged in nonstandard marriages (65 percent) had never been formally married compared to 47 percent of the women. A sizeable portion of the women (38 percent) were divorced, separated, or widowed.
- Nonstandard marriages were loving unions and not cold, transactional relations. A majority of men (60 percent) and women (53 percent) in nonstandard

---

[1] Roger Friedland, Janet Afary, Paolo Gardinali, and C. Naslund, "Love in the Middle East: The Contradictions of Romance in the Facebook World," *Critical Research on Religion* 4, no. 3 (Fall 2016): 229–58.

[2] For details, see Ramina Sotoudeh, Roger Friedland, and Janet Afary, "Digital Romance: The Sources of Online Love in the Muslim World," *Media, Culture, and Society* 39, no. 3 (February 2017): 429–39.

marriages loved their partners. These numbers were very close to those we have for couples in formal marriages.
- Our survey shattered the common assumption about nonstandard marriages that the wives entered such unions out of financial desperation. The overwhelming majority of the women in such unions—88 percent—were employed. So it is not surprising that only 5 percent of the women in our sample in such unions relied on their partners for financial support. In fact, 14 percent of the women were helping to support their male partners.
- But even wives in formal marriages were less reliant on their husbands than before. Only 29 percent of married women in our survey relied on their husbands for financial support. On the whole, 44 percent of the wives in our sample (in both types of marriage) were employed, suggesting that the traditional gendered division of labor in marriage is also breaking down.
- The key difference between formal and nonstandard marriage was the reciprocity of this love, a major factor contributing to the fragility of nonstandard marriages. When we asked our respondents in nonstandard unions if they thought their union would last a life time, the difference between men and women was dramatic. In our sample, 36 percent of women expected their union to last their whole life, but only 17 percent of the men had the same expectation."[3]

Women are now just as likely as their male counterparts to want love in their unions.[4] But for women, the risks associated with acting on this desire far outweigh those for men. The actionability of love depends on female agency, on the capacity of a woman to know and act upon her own desires. By expressing their approval of these transgressive behaviors and actually engaging in them, including entering into nonstandard marriages that are generally disapproved of by their relatives, women are making risky decisions about their own lives. While paying a heavy cost, these women, by their preferences and acts, are undermining the patriarchal norms of their societies; ultimately, they will change the meaning of love, marriage, and commitment in the region. Still, there does not seem to be any going back. With the greater availability of the internet and the expansion of social media among all classes of society, more young people will be able to move beyond traditional ways of finding a partner and will be able to exercise greater agency.

---

[3] See Afary and Friedland, "Temporary and Non-Standard Marriages in Contemporary Middle East, North Africa, and South Asia: A Facebook Survey," forthcoming.

[4] The yoking of romantic love and marriage is a globally modern and recent phenomenon. In the United States, in a poll of college students in the 1960s, two-thirds of the women said they would consider marrying a man they did not love if he met all their other criteria. It was late in the twentieth century, at a time when the rate of female participation in the labor force peaked at 60 percent, a majority of American women said that love was the most important factor in choosing a partner (S. Coontz, *Marriage, a History: From Obedience to Intimacy or How Love Conquered Marriage* [New York: Viking Press, 2005], 186). Until that time, men were more willing and able than women to make mate choices based on romance (E. Illouz, *Consuming the Romantic Utopia: Love and the Cultural Contradictions of Capitalism* [Berkeley: University of California Press, 1997], 209). See our earlier cited article, Friedland, Afary, et al. "Contradictions of Love."

All indications suggest that globalization and the need to survive in the digital age would further push women toward greater education. In such a world, the need for both husband and wife to have paid employment is more important than ever. These factors will further delay the age at which couples enter into a formal marriage, as has been the case in the West, making nonstandard unions more attractive and affordable. Ultimately, family law has to be changed throughout the region to address the increase in nonstandard unions and to provide greater protection for women, as well as for any children born in such unions, in case of divorce or the death of either partner.

Bibliography

Abbasi-Shavazi, M. J. and Askari-Nodoushan, A. "Family Life and Developmental Idealism in Yazd, Iran," *Demogr Res* 26 (2012): 207–38.

Abbasi-Shavazi, J., M. Inhorn, H. B. Razeghi-Nasrabad and G. Toloo. "The 'Iranian ART Revolution': Infertility, Assisted Reproductive Technology, and Third-Party Donation in the Islamic Republic of Iran," *Journal of Middle East Women's Studies* 4, no. 2 (2008): 1–28.

Abbasi-Shavazi, M. J., McDonald, P., and Hosseini-Chavoshi, M. *The Fertility Transition in Iran: Revolution and Reproduction.* Heidelberg: Springer Press, 2009.

Abbasi-Shavazi, J., H. B. Razeghi, Z. B. Ardekani and M. N. Akhondi. "The Socio-cultural Aspects of Gamete and Embryo Donation in Infertility Treatment," in *Essays in Gamete and Embryo Donation in Infertility Treatment: From Medical, Theological, Legal, Ethical, Psychological and Sociological Approaches*, ed. M. A. Akondi. Tehran: Centre for Research and Development in Human Sciences (Semat), 2006, 371–91.

Abdollahian, Hamid. "Generations and Gendered Perspectives," in *Pajouhesh Zanan*, saison 2, no. 3 (Autumn 2004).

Abrahamian, Ervand. *A History of Modern Iran.* Cambridge: Cambridge University Press, 2008.

Afary, Janet. *Sexual Politics in Iran.* New York, NY: Cambridge University Press, 2009.

Afary, Janet and Kevin B. Anderson. *Foucault and the Iranian Revolution. Gender and the Seductions of Islamism.* Chicago: The University of Chicago Press, 2005.

Afary, Janet and Roger Friedland. "Critical Theory, Authoritarianism, and the Politics of Lipstick: From Weimar Republic to the Contemporary Middle East," *Critical Research on Religion* 6, no. 3 (2018): 243–68.

Aghajanian, A., A. Tashakkori, V. Thompson, A. H. Mehryar, and S. Kazemipour. "Attitudes of Iranian Female Adolescents Toward Education and Nonfamilial Roles: A Study of a Postrevolutionary Cohort," *Marriage Fam Rev* 42, no. 1 (2007): 49–64.

Aghajanian, Akbar and V. Thompson. "Recent Divorce Trends in Iran," *Journal of Divorce & Remarriage* 54, no. 2 (2013): 112–25.

Aghajanian, A. and V. Thompson. "Female Headed Households in Iran," *Marriage & Family Review* 49, no. 2 (2013): 115–34.

Ahmad Khurasani, Nushin. "See Campaign for One Million Vote' Junbish Yek Melun Emza," *Rawayati as Dorun* (1386/2017).

Ahmadi, A. "Ethical Issues in Hymenoplasty: Views from Tehran's Physicians," *Journal of Medical Ethics* (2013). Published Online First.

Ahmadi, A. "Hymenoplasty in Contemporary Iran: Liminality and the Embodiment of Contested Discourses," in *Abortion Pills, Test Tube Babies, and Sex Toys: Emerging Sexual and Reproductive Technologies in the Middle East and North Africa*, eds. A. M. Foster and L. Wynn. Nashville: Vanderbilt University Press, 2016). Under contract.

Ahmadi, K., M. Barari, A. Ghaffari, and M. Purrezaian. "Temporary Marriage: Attitude and Tendency in Iran," *Journal Divorce & Remarriage* 53, no. 7 (2012): 533–42.

Ahmadinia, S. 2017. Available from: www.Mehrkhaneh.IR

Akhavan, N. *The Iranian Internet: Interventions in New Media and Old Politics*. Ph.D. thesis, University of California, Santa Cruz, 2007.

Akondi, M. A. (ed.). *Modern Human Reproductive Techniques from the View of Jurisprudence and Law* (in Persian). The Avicenna Research Institute in association with the Academic Publishing House for the Social Sciences, 2001.

Akondi, M. A. (ed.). *Essays on Gamete and Embryo Donation in Infertility Treatment: From Medical, Theological, Legal, Ethical, Psychological and Sociological Approaches*. The Avicenna Research Institute in association with the Academic Publishing House for the Social Sciences, 2006.

Alhojailan, M. I. "Thematic Analysis: A Critical Review of Its Process and Evaluation," *Proceedings of the WEI International European Academic Conference*, 2012, pp. 39–47. Accessed February 17, 2016. http://www.westeastinstitute.com/journals/wpcontent/uploads/2013/02/4-Mohammed-Ibrahim-Alhojailan-Full-Paper-Thematic-Analysis-A-Critical-Review-Of-Its-Process-And-Evaluation.pdf. December 2012.

Alikhani, Behrouz. "Institutionelle Entdemokratisierungsprozesse, zum Nachhinkeffekt des sozialen Habitus in Frankreich," *Iran und Deutschland*. Wiesbaden: VS Verlag, 2012.

Althusser, Louis. *On the Reproduction of Capitalism*. New York: Verso, 2014.

Amir-Ebrahimi, Masserat. "Conquering Enclosed Public Spaces," in *Cities: The International Journal of Urban Policy and Planning* 23, no. 6 (2006): 455–61.

Amir-Ebrahimi, Masserat. "Blogging from Qom, Behind Walls and Veils," *Comparative Studies of South Asia, Africa and the Middle East* 28, no. 2 (2008): 235–49.

Amir-Ebrahimi, Masserat. "Transgression in Narration, The Lives of Iranian Women in Cyberspace," *Journal of Middle East Women's Studies* 4, no. 3 (2008): 89–118.

Amir-Ebrahimi, Masserat. "Weblogs and the Emergence of a New Public Sphere in Iran," in *Publics, Politics and Participation: Locating the Public Sphere in the Middle East and North Africa*, ed. Seteny Shami. New York: SSRC Books, 2009, 326–56.

Amirmazaheri, Amirmasoud, Leila Shiri Gheydari, and Mahshid Shahidi. "Spreading Modern Rationality and Forming the New Patterns of Family; A Study of Cohabitation Style in Tehran," *IAU International Journal of Social Sciences*, 6, no. 4 (2016): 45–54.

Anonymous. "Iran: Human Rights Abuses Against the Kurdish Minority," *Amnesty International*, July 2008, pp. 1–58. Available at www.amnesty.org/download/Documents/MDE130882008ENGLISH.pdf. Accessed June 27, 2018.

Anonymous. "Sexual Mores in Iran—Throwing Off the Covers: An Official Report Blows the Lid Off the Secret World of Sex," *The Economist*, August 9, 2014. http://www.economist.com/.

Anonymous. "Official Report: Support for Compulsory Ḥijāb Plummets," *IranWire*, July 30, 2018. https://iranwire.com/en/features/5433.

Anonymous. "Corruption-Perceptions Index 2016," Transparency International 2018. Available at www.transparency.org. Accessed June 30, 2018.

Ansary, Nina. *Jewels of Allah: The Untold Story of Women in Iran*. Plano, TX: Revela Press, 2015.

Arafi, Ali Reza. "Preface," in *The Theoretical Foundations for Fundamental Transformation of the Education System in the Islamic Republic of Iran*, Ministry of Education, Islamic Republic of Iran N.p.: n.p., n.d.

Asgharzadeh, Alireza. *Iran and the Challenge of Diversity: Islamic Fundamentalism, Aryanist Racism, and Democratic Struggles*. Gordonsville, VA: Palgrave Macmillan, 2007.

Ayatollah Muhammadi Golpayeghani. "ezdevaj sefeid sharm avar ast," *Ruznameyeh Sharq*, 10 Azar (1393/2014).
Azad Armaki, Taqi. "Khanevade-yeh sefeid, chaleshi buniyadi barayeh khanevadeh Irani," *Zanan Amruz* 1, no. 5 Mehr (1393/2014).
Azad-Armaki, T., Sharifi-Sai, M. H., Isari, M., Talebi, S. "Cohabitation: Emerging New Family Form in Tehran," *Cultural Resources* 3, no. 1 (2012): 43–77.
Bahramitash, Roksana and Shahla Kazemipour. "Myth and Realities of the Impact of Islam on Women: Women's Changing Marital Status in Iran," *Critique: Critical Middle Eastern Studies* 15, no. 2 (2006): 111–28.
Bartky, S. L. *Femininity and Domination: Studies in the Phenomenology of Oppression*. New York: Routledge, 1990.
Baym, N. K. *Personal Connections in the Digital Age*. Cambridge: Polity Press, 2010.
Baym, N. K. "Social Networks 2.0," in *The Handbook of Internet Studies*, eds. M. Consalvo and C. Ess. Oxford: Wiley-Blackwell, 2011.
Bazeley, P. "Analysing Qualitative Data: More than 'Identifying Themes'," *Malaysian Journal of Qualitative Research* 2, no. 2 (2009): 6–22. Accessed February 17, 2016. http://www.researchsupport.com.au/bazeley_mjqr_2009.pdf.
Beck-Gernsheim, Elisabeth. "Transnational Lives, Transnational Marriages: A Review of Evidence from Migrant Communities in Europe," *Global Networks* 7 (2007): 271–88.
Bekker, M. H. J., J. Rademakers, I. Mouthaan, M. de Neef, W. M. Huisman, H. van Zandvoort, and A. Emans. "Reconstructing Hymens or Constructing Sexual Inequality? Service Provision to Islamic Young Women Coping with the Demand to Be a Virgin," *Journal of Community & Applied Social Psychology* 6 (1996): 329–34.
Bell, D. and B. Kennedy. *The Cybercultures Reader*. London and New York: Routledge, 2000.
Bengali, Shashank and Ramin Mostaghim. "More Women in Iran Are Forgoing Marriage. One Reason? The Men Aren't Good Enough," *Los Angeles Times*, November 11, 2016.
Biswas, Soutik. "Why Are Millions of Indian Women Dropping out of Work?" BBC, India, May 18, 2017. http://www.bbc.com/news/world-asia-india-39945473. Accessed May 20, 2017.
Boe, Marianne. *Family Law in Contemporary Iran. Women's Rights Activism and Shari'a*. London: I.B. Tauris, 2015.
Bologne, Jean Claude. *Histoire du célibat et des célibataires*. Paris: Fayard, 2004.
Bordo, S. *Unbearable Weight: Feminism, Western Culture, and the Body*. Berkeley: University of California Press, 2003.
Bourdieu, P. *Outline of a Theory of Practice*. New York: Cambridge University Press, 1977.
Bourdieu, P. *Entwurf einer Theorie der Praxis – auf der ethnologischen Grundlage der kabylischen Gesellschaft*. Frankfurt am Main: Suhrkamp, 1979.
Bourdieu, P. *Distinction: A Social Critique of the Judgement of Taste*. London: Routledge, 1984.
Bourdieu, P. "The Forms of Capital," in *Handbook of Theory and Research for the Sociology of Education*, ed. J. Richardson. New York: Greenwood, 1986, 241–58.
Boyd, D. *It's Complicated: The Social Lives of Networked Teens*. New Haven: Yale University Press, 2014.
Brown, I. "Internet Censorship: Be Careful What You Ask For," *Social Science Research Network* 4, no. 4 (2008): 1–12. Accessed June 7, 2015. http://papers.ssrn.com/sol3/papers.
Butler, J. *Gender Trouble: Feminism and the Subversion of Identity*. New York: Routledge, 1990.

Butler, J. *Bodies That Matter: On the Discursive Limits of "Sex,"* New York: Routledge, 1993.

Carline, A. "Resignifications and Subversive Transformations: Judith Butler's Queer Theory and Women Who Kill," *Liverpool Law Review* 27 (2006): 303–35.

Carsten, J. (ed.). *Cultures of Relatedness: New Approaches to the Study of Kinship*. Cambridge: Cambridge University Press, 2000.

Charsley, Katharine and Alison Shaw. "South Asian Transnational Marriages in Comparative Perspective," *Global Networks* 6 (2006): 331–44.

Charsley, Kathrine. "Unhappy Husbands: Masculinity and Migration in Transnational Pakistani Marriages," *Journal of Royal Anthropological Institute* 11 (2005): 85–115.

Cindoglu, D. "Virginity Tests and Artificial Virginity in Modern Turkish Medicine," *Women's Studies International Forum* 20 (1997): 253–61.

Clarke, M. "Islam, Kinship and New Reproductive Technology," *Anthropology Today* 22 (2006): 17–22.

Clarke, M. "Children of the Revolution: Ayatollah Khamenei's "Liberal" Views on In Vitro Fertilisation, " *British Journal of Middle Eastern Studies* 34, no. 3 (2007): 287–303.

Clarke, M. *Islam and New Kinship: Reproductive Technologies and the Shariah in Lebanon*. New York and Oxford: Berghahn Books, 2009.

Clarke, M. "Neo-Calligraphy: Religious Authority and Media Technology in Contemporary Shiite Islam," *Comparative Studies in Society and History* 52, no. 2 (2010): 351–83.

Clarke, M. "Islamic Bioethics and Religious Politics in Lebanon," in *Islam and Assisted Reproductive Technologies: Sunni and Shia Perspectives*, eds. M. Inhorn and S. Tremayne. New York: Berghahn Books, 2012, 261–84.

Clarke, M. "The Judge as Tragic Hero: Judicial Ethics in Lebanon's Sharia Courts," *American Ethnologist* 39, no. 1 (2012): 101–16.

Conrad, P. *The Medicalization of Society: On the Transformation of Human Conditions into Treatable Disorders*. Baltimore: The Johns Hopkins University Press, 2007.

Constable, Nicole. "A Transnational Perspective on Divorce and Marriage: Filipina Wives and Workers," *Identities: Global Studies in Culture and Power*, 10 (2003): 163–80.

Constable, Nicole. *Romance on a Global Stage*. Berkeley: University of California Press, 2003.

Constable, Nicole. "A Tale of Two Marriages: International Matchmaking and Gendered Mobility," in *Cross-Border Marriages: Gender and Mobility in Transnational Asia*, ed. Nicole Constable. Philadelphia: University of Pennsylvania Press, 2005, 167–86.

Correspondent in Tehran. "Why Are Young Iranians Losing Interest in Marriage?" *Al-Monitor, Iran Pulse*, June 2, 2015. http://www.al-monitor.com/pulse/originals/201 5/06/iran-birth-rate-marriage-decline-divorce.html

Debeljak, Klara. "Youth in Iran: A Story Half Told—Values, Priorities and Perspectives of Iranian Youth," *Young Publics Research Paper Series*, No. 1, Iran, May, 2013, InterMedia Research and Consulting Europe and InterMedia Groups in Washington, DC and Nairobi, Kenya and Small Media, London. http://www.intermedia.org/wp-c ontent/uploads/Young-Publics-Research-Paper-Series-Iran.pdf

Dehghanpisheh, Babak. "Rise in Divorce in Iran Linked to Shift in Status of Women," *Reuters World News*, 22 October (1393/ 2014).

Del Rosario, Teresita C. "Bridal Diaspora: Migration and Marriage Among Filipino Women," *Indian Journal of Gender Studies* 12, nos. 2 and 3 (2005): 258–60.

Deliovsky, Katerina. *White Femininity*: Race, Gender, & Power. Halifax, Nova Scotia: Fernwood Publishing, 2010.

Donaldson, D. M. "Temporary Marriage in Iran," *Muslim World* 26, no. 4 (1936): 358-64.
Edgardh, K., and K. Ormstad. "The Adolescent Hymen," *Journal of Reproductive Medicine* 47 (2002): 710-14.
Edmunds, June and B. S. Turner. *Generations, Culture and Society*. Philadelphia: Open University Press, 2002.
Edwards, J. "Explicit Connections: Ethnographic Enquiry in North-West England," in *Technologies of Procreation: Kinship in the Age of Assisted Conception*, eds. J. Edwards, S. Franklin, E. Hirsch, F. Price and M. Strathern. London: Routledge, 1993, 60-85.
Egel, D. and D. Salehi-Isfahani. "Youth Transitions to Employment and Marriage in Iran: Evidence from the School to Work Transition Survey," *MEDJ* 2, no. 1 (2010): 89-120.
Eich, T. "A Tiny Membrane Defending "Us" against "Them": Arabic Internet Debate about Hymenorrhaphy in Sunni Islamic Law," *Culture, Health & Sexuality* 12 (2010): 755-69.
Eich, T. "Constructing Kinship in Sunni Islamic Legal Texts," in *Islam and Assisted Reproductive Technologies: Sunni and Shia Perspectives*, eds. M. Inhorn and S. Tremayne. New York and Oxford: Berghahn Books, 2010, 27-52.
Elias, Norbert. *The Symbol Theory*. London: SAGE Publication, 1995.
Elias, Norbert. *The Germans*. Cambridge: Polity Press, 1996.
Elias, Norbert. *The Society of Individuals* [Collected Works, vol. 10]]. Dublin: UCD Press, 2010.
Elias, Norbert. *What Is Sociology?* Enlarged edition, [Collected Works, vol. 5]. Dublin: UCD Press, 2012.
Elias, Norbert. *Gruppencharisma und Gruppenschande*. Hrsg. Erik Jentges. Marbach: Deutsches Literaturarchiv Marbach, 2014.
Elias, Norbert, and John L. Scotson. *The Established and the Outsiders* [Collected Works of Norbert Elias]. Dublin: University College Dublin Press, 2008.
Emmans, S. J., E. R. Woods, E. N. Allred, and E. Grace. "Hymenal Findings in Adolescent Women: Impact of Tampon Use and Consensual Sexual Activity," *Journal of Pediatrics* 125 (1994): 153-60.
Esfandiari, Golnaz. "Rise in Cohabitation Has Iran Officials Railing Against 'White Marriage," *Radio Free Europe. Radio Liberty*, 6 December (2014). Available at http://www.rferl.org/articleprintview/26728820.html.
Esfandiari, Hale. "The Role of Women Members of Parliament, 1963-88," in *Women in Iran: From 1800 to the Islamic Republic*, eds. Louis Beck and Guity Nashat. Urbana, IL: University of Illinois Press, 2004, 136-62.
Espiritu, Yen Le. *Home Bound: Filipino American Lives Across Cultures, Communities, and Countries*. Berkeley: University of California Press, 2003.
Essen, B., A. Blomkvist, L. Helstrom, and S. Johnsdotter. "The Experience and Responses of Swedish Health Professionals to Patients Requesting Virginity Restoration (Hymen Repair)," *Reproductive Health Matters* 18 (2010): 38-46.
European Commission. *Migration and Social Integration of Migrants* (2003): 11.
Farahani, F. *Diasporic Narratives of Sexuality: Identity Formation Among Iranian-Swedish Women*. Stockholm: Stockholm University Press, 2007.
Farshidi, N. *Virginity Still a Commodity in Iran*, 2011. http://iwpr.net/report-news/virginity-still-commodity-iran. Accessed February 10, 2011.
Ferdows, Adele K. "Gender Roles in Iranian Public School Textbooks," in *Childhood in the Muslim Middle East*, ed. Elizabeth Warnock Fernen. Austin: University of Texas Press, 1995, 325-36.
Fereidooni Somayeh. *Girls' Narrative of University Experience*. Jameeshenasan, Tehran, 2015.

Financial Tribune. Iran Ranked World's 7th Instagram User, 2018. Accessed February 15, 2019. https://financialtribune.com.
Floor, W. *A Social History of Sexual Relations in Iran*. Washington, DC: Mage Publishers, 2008.
Foucault, M. *The Birth of the Clinic: An Archaeology of Medial Perception*. Paris: Presses Universitaires de France, 1963.
Foucault, M. *Discipline and Punish: The Birth of the Prison*. Paris: Editions Gallimard, 1975.
Foucault, M. *The Will to Knowledge: The History of Sexuality*, Vol. 1. Paris: Editions Gallimard, 1976.
Franklin, Sarah, and Helena Ragoné, eds. *Reproducing Reproduction: Kinship, Power, and Technological Innovation*. Philadelphia: University of Pennsylvania Press, 1998.
Friedl, Erika. "State Ideology and Village Women," in *Women and Revolution in Iran*, ed. Guity Nashat. Boulder: Westview Press, 1983, 217–30.
Friedl, Erika. *Women of Deh Koh: Lives in an Iranian Village*. London and New York: Penguin, 1991.
Friedl, Erika. "Women's Spheres of Action in Rural Iran," in *Shifting Boundaries: Women and Gender in Middle East History*, eds. N. Keddie and B. Baron. New Haven, CT: Yale University Press, 1992.
Friedl, Erika. "Ideal Womanhood in Postrevolutionary Iran," in *Mixed Blessings: Gender and Religious Fundamentalism Cross Culturally*, eds. Judy Brink and Joan Mencher. New York and London: Routledge, 1997, 143–58.
Friedl, Erika. "New Friends: Gender Relations within the Family," *Iranian Studies* 42, no. 1 (2009): 27–43.
Friedl, Erika. "Tribal Enterprises and Marriage Issues in Twentieth-Century Iran," in *Family History in the Middle East: Household, Property, and Gender*, ed. Beshara Doumani. Albany: State University of New York Press, 2012, 51–170.
Friedl, Erika. "A Thorny Side of Marriage in Iran," in *Everyday Life in the Muslim Middle East*, eds. Donna Lee Bowen, Evelyn A. Early and Becky Schulthies. Boomington: Indiana University Press, 2014, 122–32.
Friedl, Erika. "A Brief History of Childhood in Boir Ahmad, Iran, *Anthropology of the Middle East* 12/3 (2017): 6–19.
Friedl, Erika. *Folksongs from the Mountains of Iran. Culture, Poetics and Everyday Life*. London: I. B. Tauris, 2018.
Friedl, Erika and Reinhold Loeffler. "Archaeology and Cultural Memory in Boir Ahmad, Southern Zagros, Iran," *Archiv für Völkerkunde* 61–62 (2013): 138–231.
Friedl, Erika and Reinhold Loeffler. "Eschatology in Boir Ahmad, Iran," *Anthropology of the Middle East* 13/1 (2018): 55–68.
Garmaroudi, S. "Gestational Surrogacy in Iran: Uterine Kinship in Shia Thought and Practice," in M. *Islam and Assisted Reproductive Technologies: Sunni and Shia Perspectives*, eds. Inhorn and S. Tremayne. New York: Berghahn Books, 2012, 157–93.
Gerami, Shahin. "DeTerritorialized Islamisms: Women's Agency of Resistance and Acquiescence," in *Routledge Handbook of Political Islam*, ed. Shahram Akbarzadeh. New York and London: Routledge, 2012, 191–204.
Gerami, Shahin and Melodye Lehnerer. "Women's Agency and Household Diplomacy: Negotiating Fundamentalism," *Gender & Society* 15, no. 4 (2001): 556–73.
Ghaffari, M., S. Rakhshanderou, and Y. Mehrabi Afsoon Tizvir. "Using Social Network of TELEGRAM for Education on Continued Breastfeeding and Complementary Feeding of Children Among Mothers: A Successful Experience from Iran," *International Journal*

of Paediatric 5, no. 7 (2017): 5275–86. Accessed March 12, 2019. HYPERLINK "http://ijp.mums.ac.ir/article_8570.html" http://ijp.mums.ac.ir/article_8570.html

Ghaffarzadeh, Shamsi Miri, "Traditional vs. Modern Wedding Ceremony in Urmia City of Iran," *Social Sciences* (Pakistan) 11, no. 18 (2016): 4338–43.

Ghaffarzadeh, Shamsi Miri, "Traditional vs. Modern Wedding Ceremony in Urmia City of Iran," *Social Sciences* (Pakistan) 11, no. 14 (2016): 3543–8.

Ghasemi, A. "Women's Experiences of Work in the Iranian Broadcast Media (IRIB): Motivations, Challenges, and Achievements," *Feminist Media Studies* 13, no. 5 (2013): 840–9. Accessed February 17, 2016. http://www.tandfonline.com/doi/abs/10.1080/14680777.2013.838367.

Ghodsi, T. F. "Tying a Slipknot: Temporary Marriages in Iran," *Michigan Journal of International Law* 15, no. 2 (1994): 645. Accessed June 7, 2015. https://litigation-essentialslexisnexis.com/webcd/app.

Gholamasad, Dawud. *Iran, die Entstehung der islamischen Revolution*. Hamburg: Junius Verlag, 1985.

Gholamasad, Dawud. "Zum Umbruch im nachrevolutionären Iran," *Orient* 42 (2001): 617–38.

Gholamasad, Dawud. *Selbstbild und Weltsicht islamischer Selbstmord-Attentäter*. Berlin: Klaus Schwarz Verlag, 2006.

Ghorashi, H. *Ways to Survive, Battles to Win: Iranian Women Exiles in the Netherlands and United States*. New York: Nova Science Publishers, Inc., 2003.

Gianfortoni, Emily Wells. "Marriage Customs in Lar: The Role of Women's Networks in Tradition and Change," *Iran and the Caucasus* 13 (2009): 285–98.

Ginsburg, Faye, and Rayna Rapp. "The Politics of Reproduction," *Annual Review of Anthropology* 20, no. 1 (1991): 311–43.

Ginsburg, Faye, and Rayna Rapp. "Introduction: Conceiving the New World Order," *Conceiving the New World Order: The Global Politics of Reproduction*. Berkeley: University of California Press, 1995.

Giroux, Henry. *Neoliberalism's War on Higher Education*. Chicago, IL: Haymarket Books, 2014.

Glaser, Gabrielle. *Stranger to the Tribe: Portraits of Interfaith Marriage*. Boston: Houghton Mifflin, 1997.

Golchin, Masoud, and Saed Safari. "Kalan shahr Tehran va zuhur neshaneha-yeh ulgu-yeh tazeh as ravabet zan va mard muttalleh zamineh, farayand va payamadha-yeh ham-khanegi," *Faslnameh Tahgigat-e Farhangi-e Iran* 10, no. 1 (Spring 1396/2017): 29–57.

Goldstein, E., H. Megally, D. PoKempner, and M. McClintock. *The Internet in the Mideast and North Africa: Free Expression and Censorship*. Washington, DC: Human Rights Watch, 1999. Accessed June 9, 2015. https://www.hrw.org/report/1999/07/01/internet-middle-east-and-north-africa-free-expression-and-censorship.

Golipour, Hassan F. and Mohammad Reza Farzanegan. "Marriage Crisis and Housing Costs: Empirical Evidence from Provinces of Iran," *Journal of Policy Modeling* 37, no. 1 (2015): 107–23.

Golzard, Vahideh and Cristina Miguel. "Negotiating Intimacy through Social Media: Challenges and Opportunities for Muslim Women in Iran," *Middle East Journal of Culture and Communication* 9 (2016): 216–33.

Goodyear-Smith, F. A., and T. M. Laidlaw. "What Is an "Intact Hymen"? A Critique of the Literature," *Medicine, Science and the Law* 38 (1998): 289–300.

Gordon Tuula. *Single Women: On the Margins?* Hampshire: Macmillan Press LTD, 1994.

Graham, M. and S. Khosravi. "Reordering Public and Private in Iranian Cyberspace: Identity, Politics, and Mobilization," *Journal of Identities: Global Studies in Culture and Power* 9, no. 2 (2010): 219–46. Accessed June 9, 2015. http://www.tandfonline.com/doi/abs/10.1080/10702890212204.

Gramsci, Antonio, *Selections from the Prison Notebooks*. London: Lawrence & Wishart, 1971.

Gramsci, Antonio. *Selections from Political Writings, 1910–1920*. London: Lawrence & Wishart, 1977.

Griswold, Eliza. "The 22 Syllables That Can Get You Killed," *BBC*, November 16, 2016. Available at www.bbc.com/culture/story/20161116. Accessed November 20, 2017.

Haeri, Shahla. "Power of Ambiguity: Cultural Improvisations on the Theme of Temporary Marriage," *Iranian Studies* 19, no. 2 (1986): 123–54.

Haeri, Shahla. *Law of Desire: Temporary Marriage in Shi'i Iran*. New York: Syracuse University Press, 1989.

Haeri, Shahla. "No End in Sight: Politics, Paradox, and Gender Policies in Iran," *Boston University Law Review* 93 (1992): 1049–62.

Haeri, Shahla. "Temporary Marriage and the State in Iran: An Islamic Discourse on Female Sexuality," *Social Research* (1992): 201–23.

Haeri, Shahla. "Temporary Marriage and the State in Iran: An Islamic Discourse on Female Sexuality," Reprinted in *Women and Sexuality in Muslim Societies*, ed. Pinar Ilkkaracan. Istanbul: A Publication of Women for Women's Human Rights – New Ways, 2000, 343–61.

Haeri, Shahla. "The Institution of Mut'a Marriage in Iran: A Formal and Historical Perspective," *Islam. Critical Concepts in Sociology* 3 (2003): 154–72.

Haeri, Shahla. "Women, Religion and Political Agency in Iran," in *Contemporary Iran: Economy, Society, Politics*, ed. Ali Gheissari, Oxford University Press, 2009, 125–49.

Hafezun. *Dating Site for Temporary Marriage*, 2015. Accessed June 9, 2015. http://haroo.ir/.

Haghighat, Elhum. "Iran's Changing Gender Dynamics in Light of Demographic, Political and Technological Transformations," *Middle East Critique* 23, no. 3 (2014): 313–32.

Hajnasiri, Hamideh, et al. "Domestic Violence among Iranian Women: A Systematic Review and Meta-Analysis," *Red Crescent Medical Journal* 18, no. 6 (2018), Published online May 17, 2016. https://www.ncbi.nlm.nih.gov/pmc/articles/PMC5006439/

Halder, D., and K. Jaishankar. "Cybersocializing and Victimization of Women," *Temida* 12, no. 3 (2009): 5–26. Online. http://www.doiserbia.nb.rs/img/doi/1450-6637/2009/1450-66370903005H.pdf.

Hanassab, S. "Sexuality, Dating, and Double Standards: Young Iranian Immigrants in Los An-geles," *Iranian Studies* 31 (1998): 65–75.

Hartsock, N. "Foucault on Power: A Theory for Women?" in *Feminism/Postmodernism*, ed. L. J. Nicholson. New York: Routledge, 1990, 157–75.

Haskell, Rebecca, and Brian Burtch. *Get That Freak: Homophobia and Transphobia in High Schools*. Halifax, Nova Scotia: Fernwood Publishing, 2010.

Hatam, N. *Iran: Internet Dating Website Launched by State*, 2015. Accessed June 1, 2015. http://www.bbc.co.uk/news/world-middle-east-32833363.

Hawwa, Sithi. "From Cross to Crescent: Religious Conversion of Filipina Domestic Helpers in Hong Kong," *Islam and Christian and Muslim Relations* 11 (2000): 347–67.

Heald, Claire. "Four Dresses and a Drone - Are Weddings Getting Out of Control?" *BBC News*, April 26, 2017. https://www.bbc.com/news/uk-39716582

Heckman, S. "The Question of Materiality," in *Body and Flesh: A Philosophical Reader*, ed. Donn Welton. Malden, MA: Blackwell Publishers, 1998, 61–70.

Hegland, Mary Elaine. "Wife Abuse and the Political System: A Middle Eastern Case Study," in *To Have and to Hit: Cultural Perspective on Wife Beating*, eds. Dorothy Counts, Judith Brown, and Jacqueline Campbell. Urbana: University of Illinois Press, 1999, 234–51.

Hegland, Mary Elaine. "Talking Politics: A Village Widow in Iran," in *Personal Encounters: A Reader in Cultural Anthropology*, eds. Linda S. Walbridge and April K. Sievert. Boston, MA: McGraw-Hill, 2003, 53–9.

Hegland, Mary Elaine. "Independent Grandmothers in an Iranian Village," *Middle-East Journal of Age & Aging* 4, no. 1 (June 2007). http://www.me-jaa.com/me-jaa11June07/independentgrandmothers.htm.

Hegland, Mary Elaine. Hegland, Mary Elaine, with Zahra Sarraf and Mohammad Shahbazi. "Modernization and Social Change: Impact on Iranian Elderly Social Networks and Care Systems," *Anthropology of the Middle East* 2, no. 2 (2008): 55–74.

Hegland, Mary Elaine. "Educating Young Women: Culture, Conflict, and New Identities in an Iranian Village," *Iranian Studies* 42, no. 1 (2009): 45–79.

Hegland, Mary Elaine. "Aliabad of Shiraz: Transformation from Village to Suburban Town," *Berghahn Journals* 6, no. 2 (2011): 21–37. *Anthropology of the Middle East*. Oxford and New York.

Hegland, Mary Elaine. *Days of Revolution: Political Unrest in an Iranian Village*. Stanford, CA: Stanford University Press, 2014.

Hegland, Mary Elaine. "Marriage and Sexuality in Revolutionary Context: Iranian Perceptions and Practices, Contents and Meanings," *Journal of Anthropological Research*, forthcoming.

Hegland, Mary Elaine. "Marriage Modifications in Aliabad from 1978–9 to 2018: Financial Improvements, Social and Cultural Changes Over-ride Shi'a Clerical Directives," in *The Global Dynamics of Contemporary Shi'a Muslim Marriage*, eds. Annalies Moors and Yafa Shanneik, Rutgers University Press Series on The Politics of Marriage and Gender: Global Issues in Local Contexts, forthcoming.

Hegland, Mary Elaine. "The Need for a Center for the Elderly and for Widows Living Alone in the Shiraz Area," Paper presented at the First International Conference on Social Policy in the Islamic World, Tehran, May 12–13, 2018.

Hegland, Mary Elaine. "Social Mobility in the Shiraz Suburb of Aliabad: Living Standards, Marriage and Desire for Diaspora," Paper read at the 15th Conference of the European Association of Social Anthropologists, Stockholm University, August 12–14, 2018.

Hegland, Mary Elaine. "XXXXX in Janet Afary and XXX (eds.)," *The Changing Nature of Family and Marriage in Contemporary Iran*. London: I.B. Tauris, 2020.

Henry-Waring, M., and J. Barraket. "Dating and Intimacy in the 21st Century: The Use of Online Dating Sites in Australia," *International Journal of Emerging Technologies and Society* 6, no. 1 (2008): 14–33. Accessed May 8, 2015. http://eprints.qut.edu.au/32317/.

Higgins, Patricia J., and Pirouz Shoar-Ghaffari. "Women's Education in the Islamic Republic of Iran," in *The Eyes of the Storm: Women in Post-revolutionary Iran*, eds. Mahnaz Afkhami and Erika Friedl, 19–43. Syracuse: Syracuse University Press, 1994.

Higgins, Patricia J., and Pirouz Shoar-Ghaffari. "Changing Perception of Iranian Identity in Elementary School Textbooks," in *Childhood in the Muslim Middle East*, ed. Elizabeth Warnock Fernen, 337–63. Austin: University of Texas Press, 1995.

Hobbs, M., Owen, S. and Gerber. L. "Liquid Love? Dating Apps, Sex, Relationships and the Digital Transformation of Intimacy," *Journal of Sociology* 53, no. 2 (2017): 271–84.

Accessed March 4, 2019. https://journals.sagepub.com/doi/pdf/10.1177/1440783316 662718.
Hojat M., R. Shapurian, H. Nayerahmadi, M. Farzaneh, D. Foroughi, M. Parsi, and M. Azizi. "Premarital Sexual, Child Rearing, and Family Attitudes of Iranian Men and Women in the United States and in Iran," *Journal of Psychology* 133 (1999): 19–31.
Horst, H., and D. Miller. *The Cell Phone: An Anthropology of Communication*. Oxford: Berg, 2006.
Hugill, David. *Missing Women, Missing News: Covering Crises in Vancouver's Downtown Eastside*. Halifax: Fernwood Publishing, 2010.
Hunt, Chester and Richard Coller. "Intermarriage and Cultural Change: A Study of Philippine-American Marriages," *Social Forces* 35 (1957): 223–30.
Hussaini, Seyyid Hassan, and Mina Azizi. "Barresi ghavanin va siyasathayeh hemayati as khanevadehh dar duvran-e pas as engilab-e Islami-e Iran," *Mutalle'at-e Zan va Khanevadeh* 4, no. 1 (Spring and Summer 1395/2016): 34–7.
ICEF Monitor. *Using Social Media to Reach Students in the Middle East and North Africa*, 2015. Accessed July 28, 2015. http://monitor.icef.com.
Imtoual, A., and S. Hussein. "Challenging the Myth of the Happy Celibate: Muslim Women Negotiating Contemporary Relationships," *Contemporary Islam* 3 (2009): 25–39.
Inhorn, M. C. *Quest for Conception: Gender, Infertility and Egyptian Medical Traditions*. Philadelphia: University of Pennsylvania Press, 1994.
Inhorn, M. C. "Interpreting Infertility: Medical Anthropology Perspectives," *Social Science & Medicine* 39, no. 4 (1994): 459–61.
Inhorn, M. C. *Infertility and Patriarchy: The Cultural Politics of Gender and Family Life in Egypt*. Philadelphia: University of Pennsylvania Press, 1996.
Inhorn, M. C. "The 'Local' Confronts the 'Global': Infertile Bodies and New Reproductive Technologies in Egypt," in *Infertility Around the Globe: New Thinking on Childlessness, Gender, and Reproductive Technologies*, eds. M. C. Inhorn and F. Van Balen. Berkeley: University of California Press, 2002, 263–82.
Inhorn, M. C. "The Worms Are Weak – Male Infertility and Patriarchal Paradoxes in Egypt," *Men and Masculinities* 5, no. 3 (2003): 236–56.
Inhorn, M. C. *Local Babies, Global Science: Gender, Religion, and In Vitro Fertilization in Egypt*. New York: Routledge, 2003.
Inhorn, M. C. "Global Infertility and the Globalization of New Reproductive Technologies: Illustrations from Egypt," *Social Science & Medicine* 56, no. 9 (2003): 1837–51.
Inhorn, M. C. 'Middle Eastern Masculinities in the Age of New Reproductive Technologies: Male Infertility and Stigma in Egypt and Lebanon," *Medical Anthropology Quarterly* 18, no. 2 (2004): 34–54.
Inhorn, M. C. "Fatwas and ARTS: IVF and Gamete Donation in Sunni v. Shi'a Islam, " *Journal of Gender, Race and Justice* 9, no. 2 (2005): 291–318.
Inhorn, M. C. "'He Won't Be My Son': Middle Eastern Muslim Men's Discourses of Adoption and Gamete Donation," *Medical Anthropology Quarterly* 20, no. 1 (2006): 94–120.
Inhorn, M. C. "Making Muslim Babies: IVF and Gamete Donation in Sunni versus Shi'a Islam, " *Culture, Medicine and Psychiatry* 30 (2006): 427–50.
Inhorn, M. C. "Masturbation, Semen Collection and Men's IVF Experiences: Anxieties in the Muslim World," *Body and Society* 13, no. 3 (2007): 37–53.
Inhorn, M. C (ed.). *Reproductive Disruptions: Gender, Technology and Biopolitics in the New Millennium*. New York: Berghahn Books, 2007.

Inhorn, M. C. "Right to Assisted Reproductive Technology: Overcoming Infertility in Low-Resource Countries," *International Journal of Gynecology and Obstetrics* 106 (2009.): 172–74.

Inhorn, M. C. "Globalization and Gametes: Reproductive 'Tourism,' Islamic Bioethics, and Middle Eastern Modernity," *Anthropology and Medicine* 18, no. 1 (2011): 87–103.

Inhorn, M. C. *The New Arab Man: Emergent Masculinities, Technologies, and Islam in the Middle East*. Princeton, NJ: Princeton University Press, 2012.

Inhorn, M. C., and S. Tremayne (eds.). *Islam and Assisted Reproductive Technologies: Sunni and Shia Perspectives*. New York and Oxford: Berghahn Books, 2012.

Iran's Center for Statistics, Census of 2011, Tehran. Statistical Centre of Iran, Tehran, The Islamic Republic of Iran.

Iranian Government, Office of Statistics and Demographic Information and Immigration. Available at https://www.amar.org.ir/Portals/0/Files/yearbook1394/yearboo94_3-8.pdf.

Iranian Parliament's Legal Research Group. "Provisory Marriage and Its Impact on the Adjustment of Illegitimate Sexual Relation," May 2014.

Islam and Christian-Muslim Relations, 12 (2001): 39–60.

Jafari, Elahe. "Taghir-e mafhum khanevadeh as ejdevajeh sefeid ta hamjensgaraei, neghahi be sabak zendeghi," *aseibha va chalesh-ha, Faslameyeh Mutalle'at-te Siyanat as Huqugeh Zanan*, no. 8 (Summer 1396/2017): 138–65.

Jamieson, L. *Intimacy: Personal Relationships in Modern Societies*. Cambridge: Polity Press, 1998.

Janks, Hillary. *Literacy and Power*. New York: Routledge, 2010.

Jordan-Zachery, Julia S. "Am I a Black Woman or a Woman Who Is Black? A Few Thoughts on the Meaning of Intersectionality," *Politics & Gender* 3, no. 2 (2007): 254–63.

Kahn, S. M. *Reproducing Jews: A Cultural Account of Assisted Conception in Israel*. Durham, NC: Duke University Press, 2000.

Kalinock, Sabine. "Supernatural Intercession to Earthly Problems: *Sofreh* Rituals Among Shiite Muslim and Zoroastrian Women in Iran," in *Zoroastrian Rituals in Context*, eds. M. Stausberg. Leiden and Boston: Brill, 2003.

Kamali Dehghan, Saeed. "'Desperate to Find a Way Out': Iran Edges Towards Precipice," *The Guardian*, July 20, 2018. https://www.theguardian.com/world/2018/jul/20/desperate-to-find-a-way-out-iran-edges-towards-precipice?CMP=Share_iOSApp_

Kandiyoti, Deniz. "Bargaining with Patriarchy," *Gender and Society* 2, no. 3 (1988): 274–90.

Kar Mehrangiz. *Shuresh, ravâyati zananeh az enghelâb* (Rebellion, a feminine narration of the Iranian Revolution) 2006, Baran, Sweden.

Karimain, Nader, and Samaneh Salari. "Rabeteyeh hamkhanegi dar Iran, barresi keifi va 'alal-e angezehayeh gerayesh be on," *Mutalle'at Ravanshenasi Baleini*, no. 21 (Winter 1394/2015): 177–200.

Karimi Majd, Roya. "Ezdevaj safeid, utaqi ba dar-e baz," Radio Farda. Accessed June 13, 1395/2016. http://www.radiofarda.com/articleprintview/27776567/html.

Karimi, Pamela. *Domesticity and Consumer Culture in Iran, Interior Revolutions of the Modern Era*. London: Routledge, 2013.

Karimi, R. The Hymen Restoration Operation: The Fashion in Iran. 2011. http://www.radiofarda.com/content/f4_curtain_surgery_iran_fashion/2281901.html. Accessed January 21, 2011.

Karimian N, and E. Zarei.. A Qualitative Study of Women Participating in Cohabitation in Three Iranian Cities 2016.

Katz, J. E. and R. Rice. *Social Consequences of Internet Use: Access, Involvement, and Interaction*. Boston: MIT Press, 2002.
Kaye, Evelyn. *Crosscurrents: Children, Families, and Religion*. New York: C.N. Potter, 1980.
Keddie, Nikki. *Modern Iran, Roots and Results of Revolution*. New Haven and London: Yale University Press, 2003.
Kember, S. and J. Zylinska. *Life after New Media: Mediation as a Vital Process*. Cambridge: MIT Press, 2012.
Keren, M. *Blogosphere: The New Political Arena*. Plymouth: Lexington Books, 2006.
Khatam, A. "The Islamic Republic's Failed Quest for the Spotless City," Middle East Report. [Online] (2009): 44–9. Accessed July 28, 2015. http://www.merip.org/mer/mer250/Islamic-republics-failed-quest-spotless-city.
Khiabany, G. *Iranian Media: The Paradox of Modernity*. New York: Routledge, 2009.
Khorasani, Noushin Ahmadi. *Iranian Women's One Milllion Signatures Campaign for Equality: The Inside Story*. Bethesda: Women's Learning Partnership for Rights Development and Peace, 2010.
Khosravi, Shahram. *Young and Defiant in Tehran*. Philadelphia: University of Pennsylvania Press, 2009.
Khosravi, Shahram. *Precarious Lives: Waiting and Hope in Iran*. Philadelphia: University of Pennsylvania Press, 2017.
Kiamanesh, Ali Reza. *UNICEF: Global Education in Iranian Guidance Schools: Achievements and Prospects*. Tehran: UNICEF Iran, 2004.
Kiamanesh, Ali Reza. *UNICEF: Global Education in Iranian Primary Schools: Achievements and Prospects*. Tehran: UNICEF Iran, 2004.
Kian, Azadeh. "Women and Politics in Post-Islamist Iran: The Gender Conscious Drive to Change," *British Journal of Middle Eastern Studies* 24, no. 1 (1997): 75–96. Accessed July 25, 2009. http://www.tandfonline.com/doi/abs/10.1080/13530199708705639.
Kian, Azadeh. "From Motherhood to Equal Rights Advocates: The weakening of Patriarchal Order," *Iranian Studies* 38, no. 1 (March 2005): 45–66.
Kian, Azadeh. "Women and Politics in Post-Islamist Iran: The Gender Conscious Drive to Change," *British Journal of Middle Eastern Studies* 24, no. 1 (2007): 75–96.
Kian, Azadeh. "Islamic Feminism in Iran: A New Form of Subjugation or the Emergence of Agency?" *Critique Internationale*, no.46/1 (2010): 45–66. http://www.cairn-int.info/abstract-E_CRII_046_0045--islamic-feminism-in-iran-a-new-form-of-s.htm. Accessed May 19, 2017.
Kian, Azadeh. "Gendered Citizenship and the Women's Movement in Iran," in *Iran: A Revolutionary Republic in Transition*, eds. Rouzbeh Parsi. Chaillot Papers (1390/ 2012): 61–79.
Kousha, Mahnaz. *Voices from Iran*. Syracuse: Syracuse University Press, 2002.
Kurzman, C. "A Feminist Generation in Iran?" *Iranian Studies* 41, no. 3 (2008): 297–321.
Lacar, Luis. "Balik-Islam: Christian Converts to Islam in the Philippines, 1970–1998," *Islam and Christian-Muslim Relations* 12, no. 1 (2001): 39–60.
Lacar, Luis. *Muslim-Christian Marriages in the Philippines*. Quezon City, Philippines: New Day Publishers., 1980.
Lambert, A. *Intimacy and Friendship on Facebook*. Houndmills: Palgrave Macmillan, 2013.
Landinfo (The Country of Origin Information Centre) Report: Honour Killings in Iran. 2009. http://www.unhcr.org/refworld/docid/4a704f352.html. Accessed May 15, 2011.

Lauth Bacas, Jutta. "Cross-Border Marriages and the Formation of Transnational Families: A Case Study of Greek-German Couples in Athens," 2002. http://www.transcomm.ox.ac.uk/working%20papers/WPTC-02-10%Bacas.pdf. Accessed on December 15, 2018.

Lee, Michelle and Nicola Piper. "Reflection on Transnational Life-Course and Migratory Patterns of Middle-Class Women - Preliminary Observation from Malaysia," in *Wife or Workers*, eds. Nicola Piper and Mina Roces. Oxford: Rowman & Littlefield Publishers, Inc., 2003, 121–36.

Leung, L. and P. S. Lee. "The Influences of Information Literacy, Internet Addiction and Parenting Styles on Internet Risks," *New Media & Society* 14, no. 1 (2012): 117–36. Accessed July 28, 2015. http://nms.sagepub.com/content/14/1/117.short.

Lindegaard, M. R., and A.-K. Henriksen. "Sexually Active Virgins: Negotiating Adolescent Femininity, Colour and Safety in Cape Town," in *Transgressive Sex: Subversion and Control in Erotic Encounters*, eds. H. Donnan and F. Magowan. New York: Berghahn Books, 2009, 25–46.

Livingstone, S. "Taking Risky Opportunities in Youthful Content Creation: Teenagers' Use of Social Networking Sites for Intimacy, Privacy and Self-Expression," *New Media & Society* 10, no. 3 (2008): 393–411. Accessed May 20, 2015. http://nms.sagepub.com/content/10/3/393.short.

Loeffler, Agnes G., and Erika Friedl. "The Birthrate Drop in Iran," *Homo. The Journal of Comparative Human Biology* 65/3 (2014): 240–55.

Loeffler, Reinhold. "Boir Ahmadī I: The Tribe," in E. Yarshater (ed.), *Encyclopaedia Iranica* IV/3 (1989): 320–4.

Loeffler, Reinhold. "The World of the People of Deh Koh," in *The Nomadic Peoples of Iran*, eds. R. Tapper and J. Thompson. London: Azimuth Editions, 2002.

Loeffler, Reinhold. "The Ethos of Progress in a Village in Iran," *Anthropology of the Middle East* 6/2 (2011): 1–13.

Lyn, Parker (ed.). *The Agency of Women in Asia*. Singapore: Cavendish, Marshall International, 2005.

Mahboobi, E. "White Marriage Contemporary Iran Imperial," *Journal of Interdisciplinary Research* 2, no. 12 (2016).

Mahdavi, Pardis. *Passionate Uprising: The Sexual Revolution in Iran*. Stanford: Stanford University Press, 2009.

Mahdi, Ali Akbar. "Iranian Women between Islamization and Globalization," in *Iran Encountering Globalization: Problems and Prospects*, eds. Ali Mohammadi. New York and London: RoutledgeCurzon, 2003.

Makvand, Raziyeh. "Negaresh zanan va mardan-e mujarad shahr-e Tehran be ham-bashi va barresi-yeh 'avamel-e moasser bar an," *Payan-nameh Karshenashi Arshad*. Tehran: Al-Zahra University, 1396/2017.

Mardomsalari (2013). *Average Age of Marriage in Iran*. Accessed June 9, 2015. http://mardomsalari.com/template1/News.aspx?NID=174830.

Marranci, Gabriele. "Muslim Marriages in Northern Ireland," in *Migration and Marriage: Heterogamy and Homogamy in a Changing World*, eds. Barbara Waldis and Reginald Byron. Berlin: LIT Verlag Berlin-Hamburg Munster, 2006, 40–84.

Masoumi, Parvaneh. "Iran's Failure to Combat Prostitution," *IranWire*, February 27, 2018. https://iranwire.com/en/features/5196

Mayer, Egon' *Love and Tradition: Marriages Between Jews and Christians*. New York: Plenum Press, 1985.

Mehran, Golnar. "The Socialization of School Children in the Islamic Republic of Iran," *Iranian Studies* 22 (1989): 35–50.

Mehran, Golnar. "Ideology and Education in the Islamic Republic of Iran," *Compare* 20 (1990): 53–65.
Mehran, Golnar. "The Creation of the New Muslim Woman: Female Education in the Islamic Republic of Iran," *Convergence* XXIV, No. 4 (1991): 42–52.
Mehran, Golnar. "Social Implications of Literacy in Iran," *Comparative Education Review* 36, no. 2 (1992): 194–211.
Mehran, Golnar. "A Study of Girls' Lack of Access to Primary Education in the Islamic Republic of Iran," *Compare: A Journal of Comparative Education* 27, no. 3 (1997): 263–77.
Mehran, Golnar. "Lifelong Learning: New Opportunities for Women in a Muslim Country (Iran)," *Comparative Education* 35, no. 2 (1999): 201–15.
Mehran, Golnar. "The Paradox of Tradition and Modernity in Female Education in the Islamic Republic of Iran," *Comparative Education Review* 47, no. 3 (2003): 269–86.
Mernissi, F. "Virginity and Patriarchy. Women's Studies International Forum 5," *Control and Sexuality: The Revival of Zina Laws in Muslim Contexts*, eds. Mir-Hosseini, Z., and V. Hamzic. London: Women Living under Muslim Laws, 1982, 183–91.
Miles, M. B. and A. M. Huberman. *Qualitative Data Analysis: An Expanded Sourcebook*. London: Sage Publications, 1994.
Milligan, Jeffrey Ayala. "Religious Identity, Political Autonomy and National Integrity: Implications for Educational Policy from Muslim-Christian Conflict in Southern Philippines," *Islam and Christian Muslim Relations* 12 (2001): 435–48.
Ministry of Education, Islamic Republic of Iran. *Fundamental Reform Document of Education (FRDE) in the Islamic Republic of* Iran. N.p.; n.p., 2011. Accessed June 4, 2017. http://www.dres.ir/safeschool/Downloads/FRDE.pdf.
Ministry of Foreign Affairs, Islamic Republic of Iran. *The Country Report of the Islamic Republic of Iran on the Ten Year Evaluation of Implementing the Commitments Undertaken in the World Summit for Children (WSC)*. N.p.: n.p., 2000.
Minuei, Zahra. "Barresi-yeh abad-e huquqi-yeh ezdevajeh sefeid," *Zanan* 1, no. 5 (1393/2014).
Mir, Gousia and G. N. Khaki. "Globalization and Post-Islamic Revolution: A Changing Iranian Woman," *Journal of Globalization Studies* 6, no. 1 (May 2015). http://www.socionauki.ru/journal/articles/281744/. Accessed May 19, 2017.
Mirfakhraie, Amir. "*Curriculum Reform and Identity Politics in Iranian School Textbooks: National and Global Representations of "Race," Ethnicity, Social Class, and Gender*," PhD diss., The University of British Columbia, 1998. https://open.library.ubc.ca/cIRcle/collections/ubctheses/24/items/1.0055443 1998.
Mirfakhraie, Amir. "Racialization of Asia, Africa and the Americas, and the Construction of the Ideal Iranian Citizen: Local and Global Representations of Colonialism, Geography, Culture and Religious Diversity in Iranian School Textbooks," in *Africa's Many Divides and Africa's Future: Pursuing Nkrumah's Vision of Pan-Africanism in an Era of Globalization*, eds. Charles Quist-Adade and Vincent Dodoo. Newcastle upon Tyne, UK: Cambridge Scholars Publishing, 2015, 217–53.
Mirfakhraie, Amir. "Constructions of Phobias, Fractured and Stigmatized Selves, and the Ideal Citizen in Iranian School Textbooks," in *Manufacturing Phobias: The Political Production of Fear in Theory and Practice*, eds. Hisham Ramadan and Jeff Shantz. Toronto, ON: University of Toronto Press, Scholarly Publishing Division, 2016, 69–115.
Mirfakhraie, Amir. "A Social Justice Approach to Iranian School Textbooks as Racist Frameworks of Othering and a Critique of the Imperialism of Anti-Imperialism," in

Iran's Struggles for Social Justice: Economics, Agency, Justice, Activism, eds. Peyman Vahabzadeh. New York: Palgrave Macmillan, 2017, 99–125.

Mirfakhraie, Amir. "Discursive Formations of Indigenous Peoples in Iranian School Textbooks: Racist Constructions of the Other," *Journal of Curriculum Studies* 50, no. 6 (2018): 754–71. Accessed October 4, 2018. https://doi.org/10.1080/00220272.2018.15 28302.

Mirza, M. "Internet Difficulty in Iran," DW, 2016. Accessed March 12, 2019. https://www.dw.com/fa-ir/ایران-در-اینترنتی-زوجیابی-دشواری/a-19061799

Moallem, Minoo. *Between Warrior Brother and Veiled Sister. Islamic Fundamentalism and the Politics of Patriarchy in Iran*. Berkeley: University of California Press, 2005.

Moaveni, Azadeh. *Lipstick Jihad: A Memoir of Growing up Iranian in America and American in Iran*. PublicAffairs, 2006.

Moaveni, Azadeh. *Honeymoon in Tehran: Two Years of Love and Danger in Iran*. New York: Random House, 2010.

Moghadam, F. E. "Commoditization of Sexuality and Female Labor Participation in Islam: Implications for Iran, 1960–90," in *In the Eye of the Storm: Women in Post-revolutionary Iran*, eds. M. Afkhami and E. Friedl. Syracuse: Syracuse University Press, 1994, 80–97.

Moghissi, H. "Away from Home: Iranian Women, Displacement, Cultural Resistance and Change," *Journal of Comparative Family Studies* 30 (1999): 207–17.

Mohammadi, A. *Iran Encountering Globalization: Problems and Prospects*. London: Routledge, 2003.

Mohammadpur, Ahmad. "Disembedding the Traditional Family: Grounded Theory and the Study of Family Change among Mangor and Gaverk Tribes of Iranian Kurdistan," *Journal of Comparative Family Studies*, 44, no. 1 (2013): 117–XI. Accessed June 8, 2018. https://ezproxy.kpu.ca:2443/login?url=https://search.proquest.com/docview/1431 071305?accountid=35875.

Moheb, Masud. "Really Brief Marriage with Benefits," *IranWire*, April 2, 2015. https://iranwire.com/en/features/453

Mooney, Nicola. "Aspiration, Reunification and Gender Transformation in Jat Sikh Marriages from India to Canada," *Global Networks* 6 (2006): 389–403.

Moore, H. L. *A Passion for Difference: Essays in Anthropology and Gender*. Bloomington: Indiana University Press, 1994.

Moruzzi, Norma Claire, and Fatemeh Sadeghi. "Out of the Frying Pan, into the Fire: Young Iranian Women Today," *Middle East Report* 241 (2006): 22–8.

Mostaghim Ramin, Sarah Parvini. "White Marriage' a Growing Trend for Young Couples in Iran," May 29, 1394/2015. Available at, http://www.latimes.com/world/middleeast/la-fg-iran-white-marriage-20150529-story.html.

Musavizadeh, Meysam, Muhsen Bagheri Tavani, and Adel Nahvi. "Deidghah-e huquqi nasbat be ezdevaj sefei'd dar Iran", *Avalien Hamayesh Aseib va Aseib Zudaei Shekaf bein Nasli (Azmunha, Chalesh ha, va rahkarha)*. Bushehr: Moasseseh Farhangi va Honari-yeh Bam. Pajuhesh-e Parvaz Junub (1396/2017).

Najmabadi, Afsaneh. "Hazards of Modernity and Morality: Women, State, and Ideology in Contemporary Iran," in *Women, Islam and the State*, ed. Denize Kandiyoti. Philadelphia: Temple University Press, 1991, 48–76.

Najmabadi, Afsaneh. "Veiled Discourse–Unveiled Bodies," *Feminist Studies* 9 (1993): 487–518.

Najmabadi, Afsaneh. "(Un)veiling Feminism," in *Women and Islam: Critical Concepts in Sociology*, eds. Haideh Moghissi. Vol. III (London: Taylor and Francis, 2005).

Nakamatsu, Tomoko. "Complex Power and Diverse Responses: Transnational Marriage Migration and Women's Agency," in *The Agency of Women in Asia*, ed. Lyn Parke. Singapore: Cavendish, Marshall International, 2005, 158–81.

Niazi, Mohsen and Leyla Parniyan. "Classification of Friendships Between Two Opposite Sexes Among Young Girls in the City of Kerman," *Zan dar Towseh va Siyasat*, no. 47 (Winter 1393/2014): 576–59.

Nicola Piper and Mina Roces. "Sisterhood is Local: Filipino Women in Mount Isa," in *Wife or Worker? Asian Women and Migration*, eds. Nicola Piper and Mina Roces. Oxford: Rowman & Littlefield Publishers, Inc., 2003, 73–100.

Nobles, Allison. "A Potential Dark Side to Iran's White Marriages," *Clippings*, p. 2/5. Accessed June 9, 1395/2016. https://thesocietypages.org/clippings/.

Oberling, Pierre. *The Qashqa'i Nomads of Fars*. Berlin: De Gruyter Mouton, 2017.

One Million Signatures Demanding Changes to Discriminatory Laws. BBC Persian, Wednesday, January 24, 2007.

Osanloo, Arzoo. *The Politics of Women's Rights in Iran*. Princeton, NJ: Princeton University Press, 2009.

Paidar, Parvin, *Women and the Political Process in Twentieth-Century Iran*. Cambridge: Cambridge University Press, 1995.

Pakpour, Padideh, *Identity Construction: The Case of Young Women in Rasht*. Uppsala: Uppsala University Press, 2015.

Parkin, R., and L. Stone (eds.). *Kinship and Family: An Anthropological Reader*. Oxford: Blackwell Publishing, 2004.

Parla, A. "The 'Honor' of the State: Virginity Examinations in Turkey," *Feminist Studies, Inc.* 27 (2001): 65–88.

Parrenas, Rachel. "The Care Crisis in the Philippines: Children and Transnational Families in the New Global Economy," in *Global Women: Nannies, Maids, and Sex Workers in the New Economy*, eds. Barbara Ehrenreich and Arlie Hochschild. New York: Metropolitan Books, 2002, 39–54.

Piper, Nicola and Mina Roces, eds. *Wife or Workers*. Oxford: Rowman & Littlefield Publishers, Inc, 2003.

Poortman A, and B Hewitt. "Editorial for Special Collection on New Relationships from a Comparative Perspective," *Demographic Research* 37 (2017): 13–24.

Purhonen Semi. "Zeitgeist, Identity and Politics in the Modern Meaning of the Concept of Generation," in *The Routledge International Handbook on Narrative and Life History*, General Editor: Ivor Goodson, (and Part editors). London and New York, Routledge, 2017, 167–78.

Qasemi, Somayeh. Hassan Muhadesi Gilavaei. "Mutalle-yeh jam'eh shenakhti durughgui dar ravabet beyna jensi zuvjhayeh Tehran," *Pajuheshnam-yeh Zanan Pajusheshga-yeh Ulum-e Ensani va Mutalle'at-e Farhangi* 8, no. 3 (Fall 1393/2014): 87–116.

Qur'an. Translated by Muhammad Habib Shakir. New York: Tahrike Tarsile Qur'an, Inc. 1987.

Ragoné, Helena. *Surrogate Motherhood: Conception in the Heart*, Boulder, CO: Westview Press, 1994.

Rahimi, B. "Censorship and the Islamic Republic: Two Modes of Regulatory Measures for Media in Iran," *Middle East Journal* 69, no. 3 (2015): 358–78. Accessed July 28, 2015. http://muse.jhu.edu/journals/the_middle_east_journal/v069/69.3.rahimi.pdf.

React. "Iran's Youth Find Their Unconventional Way to Romance amid Strict Dating Laws," January 28, 2019. *Cornell Student Articles on Topical Affairs*. Accessed February

5, 2019. https://blogs.cornell.edu/react/2019/01/28/irans-youth-find-their-unconvent ional-way-to-romance-amid-strict-dating-laws/
Reyes, Victoria. *Filipina Military Brides: Negotiating Assimilation and Cultural Maintenance with a Bi-Cultural Setting.* A Senior Thesis, The Ohio State University. 2006.
Richie, Beth E. *Arrested Justice: Black Women, Violence, and America's Prison Nation.* New York: New York University Press, 2012.
Roces, Mina. "Sisterhood Is Local: Filipino Women in Mount Isa," in *Wife or Worker,* eds. Piper, Nicola and Mina Roces. Oxford: Rowman & Littlefield Publishers, Inc, 2003.
Romano. Dugan, *Intercultural Marriage: Promises and Pitfalls.* Nicholas Brealey Publishing Intercultural Press, 2001.
Sadeghi, Fatemeh. "Negotiating with Modernity: Young Women and Sexuality in Iran," *Comparative Studies of South Asia, Africa and the Middle East* 28, no. 2 (2008): 250-9.
Sadeghi, Fatemeh. "Bypassing Islamism and Feminism: Women's Resistance and Rebellion in Post-revolutionary Iran," *Féminismes Islamiques* 128 (2010): 209-28.
Safi, Sana. "Why Female Suicide in Afghanistan Is so Prevalent," *BBC News,* July 1, 2018. Available at www.bbc.co.uk/news/world-Asia-44370711. Accessed August 18, 2018.
Safinejad, Javad. Irans Lurs. (written in Farsi). Teheran: Atiyeh, 2002.
Salehi-Isfahani, D. "Growing Up in Iran: Tough Times for the Revolution's Children," *BJWA* 15, no. 1 (2008): 63-74.
Sanasarian, E. "Politics of Gender and Development in the Islamic Republic of Iran," *Journal of Developing Societies* 13 (1992): 56-68.
Sawicki, J. *Disciplining Foucault: Feminism, Power, and the Body.* New York: Routledge, 1991.
Schneider, Susan. *Intermarriages: The Challenge of Living with Differences Between Christians and Jews.* New York: Free Press, 1989.
Serendip, G. "Exploring the Real Iran, with Social Media as Your Guide," *The Guardian,* 2016. Accessed January 31, 2019. https://www.theguardian.com/travel/2016/apr/19/ exploring-iran-travels-facebook-instagram-couchsurfing
Shaditalab, Jaleh. "Iranian Women: Rising Expectations," *Critique: Critical Middle Eastern Studies* 14, no. 1 (2005): 35-55.
Shahbazi, Mohammad Reza. "The Role of Marriage in Social Relations in Bakhtiari Tribe," *Journal Studies of Tribes and Tribals* 10, no. 1 (2012): 29-34.
Shahghasemi, E., H. Masoumi, A. Manijeh, and T. Bijan. "Liquid Love in Iran: A Mixed Method Approach," *Mediterranean Journal of Social Sciences* 6, no. 1 (2015): 138-44. Accessed July 28, 2015. http://www.mcser.org/journal/index.php/mjss/article/view/ 5520.
Shahidian, H. "To Be Recorded in History. Researching Iranian Underground Activities in Exile," *Qualitative Sociology* 24 (2001): 55-81.
Shahshahani, Soheila. "Wedding Ceremony in Turmoil," *Anthropology of the Middle East* 2, no. 1 (2007): 103-8.
Shirazi, F. "The Contribution of ICT to Freedom and Democracy: An Empirical Analysis of Archival Data on the Middle East," *Electronic Journal of Information Systems in Developing Countries* 35, no. 6 (2008): 1-24. Online: http://www.ejisdc.org/ojs2/index php/ejisdc/article/view/499.
Shirazi, F. "Free and Open Source Software versus Internet Content Filtering and Censorship: A Case Study," *Journal of Systems and Software* 85, no. 4 (2012): 920-31. Accessed May 20, 2015. http://www.sciencedirect.com/science/article.

Skalli, L. "Communicating Gender in the Public Sphere: Women and Information Technologies in the MENA," *Journal of Middle East Women's Studies* 2, no. 2 (2006): 35–59. Accessed February 1, 2019. http://www.ikhtyar.org/wp-ontent/uploads/2014/06/

Sloane, E. *Biology of Women*. Albany: Delmar, 2002.

Smith, Dorothy E. "The Standard North American Family: SNAF as an Ideological Code," *Journal of Family Issues* 14, no. 1 (1993): 50–65. Accessed March 4, 2016. https://doi.org/10.1177%2F0192513X93014001005.

Statistisches Bundesamt: Entwicklung der Gesamtbevölkerung Deutschlands von 1871 bis 2014: Wiesbaden.

Strasbburger, Gaby. "Transnational or Interethnic Marriages of Turkish Migrants: The (In) Significance of Religious or Ethnic Affiliations," in *Muslim Networks and Transnational Communities in and Across Europe*, eds., Stefano Allievi and Jorgen Nielson. Boston: Brill, 2003, 194–242.

Strathern, Marilyn. *After Nature: English Kinship in the Late Twentieth Century*. Vol. 1989. Cambridge: Cambridge University Press, 1992.

Strathern, Marilyn. *Reproducing the Future: Essays on Anthropology, Kinship and the New Reproductive Technologies*. Manchester: Manchester University Press.

Suzuki, Nobue. "Tripartite Desires: Filipina-Japanese Marriages and Fantasies of Transnational Traversal," in *Cross-Border Marriages: Gender and Mobility in Transnational Asia*, eds. Nicola Piper and Mina Roces. Philadelphia: University of Pennsylvania Press, 2005, 124–44.

Tait, Robert. "Iranian Minister Backs Temporary Marriage to Relieve Lust of Youth," *The Guardian*, June 4, 2007. https://www.theguardian.com/world/2007/jun/04/iran.robertttait

Tapper (Lindisfarne), Nancy. "The Women's Sub-society among the Shahsevan Nomads," in *Women in the Muslim World*, eds. Lois Beck and Nikki Keddie. Cambridge, MA: Harvard University Press, 1978, 374–98.

Tashakkori, A. and Thompson, V. "Social Change and Change in Intentions of Iranian Youth Regarding Education, Marriage, and Careers," *International Journal of Psychology* 26, no. 2 (1991): 203–17.

Tashakkori, A. and Thompson, V. D. "Cultural Change and Attitude Change: An Assessment of Post-revolutionary Marriage and Family Attitudes in Iran," *Population Research and Policy Review* 7 (1988): 3–27.

Tohidi, N. "Iranian Women and Gender Relations in Los Angeles," in *Irangeles: Iranians in Los Angeles*, eds. R. Kelley, J. Friedlander, and A. Colby. Berkeley: University of California Press, 1993, 175–217.

Tolentino, Roland B. "Bodies, Letters, Catalogs: Filipinas in Transnational Space," *Social Text* 48, 14, no. 3 (Fall 1996): 49–76.

Torab, Azam. *Performing Islam: Gender and Ritual in Iran*. Leiden: Brill.

Torabi, F., A. Baschieri, L. Clarke, and M. J. Abbasi-Shavazi. "Marriage Postponement in Iran: Accounting for Socio-economic and Cultural Change in Time and Space," *Popul Space Place* 19, no. 3 (2013): 58–274.

Tremayne, Soraya. "Modernity and Marriage in Iran: A View from Within," *Journal of Middle East Women's Studies* 2, no. 1 (2006): 65–94.

Tremayne, Soraya. "Law, Ethics and Donor Technologies in Shia Iran," *Assisting Reproduction, Testing Genes: Global Encounters with New Biotechnologies*. New York and Oxford: Berghahn Books, 2009, 144–63.

Tremayne, Soraya. "The 'Down Side' of Third Party Donation: Challenging the 'Happy Family Rhetoric' in Iran," in *Islam and Assisted Reproductive Technologies: Sunni and Shia Perspectives*, eds. M. Inhorn and S. Tremayne. New York and Oxford: Berghahn Books, 2012, 130–56.

United Nations World population prospects: The 2012 revision. New York: United Nations, 2013. https://population.un.org/wpp/Publications/Files/WPP2012_HIGHLIGHTS.pdf

Unnithan-Kumar, M. "Female Selective Abortion – Beyond Culture: Family Making and Gender Inequality in a Globalising India," *Journal of Culture, Health and Sexuality* 12, no. 2 (2009): 153–66.

Usta, I. "Hymenorrhaphy: What Happens Behind the Gynaecologist's Closed Door?" *Jour-nal of Medical Ethics* 26 (2000): 217–18.

Varzi, Roxanne. *Warring Souls: Youth, Media and Martyrdom in Post-Revolution Iran*. Durham, NC: Duke University Press, 2006.

Varzi, Roxanne. *Last Scene Underground: An Ethnographic Novel of Iran*. Stanford: Stanford University Press, 2015.

Vatandoust, Gholam Reza. "The Status of Iranian Women During the Pahlavi Regime," in *Women and the Family in Iran*, eds. Asghar Fathi. Brill, 1985, 114.

Vaziri, Mustafa. *Iran as Imagined Nation: The Construction of National Identity*. New York: Paragon House, 1993.

Vero, Tacita. "Behind the Scenes of Iran's Growing Wedding Industry," *Slate Magazine*, January 9, 2017. http://www.slate.com/articles/news_and_politics/roads/2017/01/behind_the_scenes_of_iran_s_growing_wedding_industry.html

Vieille, Paul. "Iranian Women in Family Alliance and Sexual Politics," in *Women in the Muslim World*, eds. Lois Beck and Nikki Keddie. Cambridge, MA: Harvard University Press, 1978, 451–72.

Vigh, H. "Motion Squared: A Second Look at the Concept of Social Navigation," *Anthropo-logical Theory* 9 (2009): 419–38.

Wiles, Janine. "Sense of Home in Transnational Space: New Zealanders in London," *Global Networks*, **7**, no. 2008): 116–37.

Wilkerson, J., and R. Parkin (eds.). 2012. *Modalities of Change: The Interface of Tradition and Modernity in East Asia*. New York and Oxford: Berghahn Books.

Williams, J. A. "Unholy Matrimony? Feminism, Orientalism, and the Possibility of Double Critique," *Signs (Chic Ill)* 34, no. 3 (2009): 611–32.

Wright, Sue. "Prattle and Politics: The Position of Women in Dushman-Ziari," *Anthropological Society of Oxford Journal* 9 (1978): 98–112.

Yaghmaian, B. *Social Change in Iran: An Eyewitness Account of Dissent, Defiance, and New Movements for Rights*. New York: SUNY Press, 2008.

Zahedi, Ashraf. "Negotiating between Shi'a and Catholic Rituals in Iran: A Case Study of Filipina Converts and Their Adult Children, " Anthropology of the Middle East 13 (2018): 82–96.

Zahedi, Ashraf. "State Ideology and the Status of Iranian War Widows," *International Feminist Journal of Politics* 8 (2006): 267–86.

Zahedi, Ashraf. "Transnational Marriages, Gendered Citizenship, and the Dilemma of Iranian Women Married to Afghan Men," *Iranian Studies* 40 (2007): 225–39.

Zimmt, Raz. "Marrying Late: Young Adults and the Marriage Crisis in Iran," *The Forum for Regional Thinking*, July 10, 2016. http://www.regthink.org/en/articles/marrying-late-young-adults-and-the-marriage-crisis

Zontini, Elisabeth. "Immigrant Women in Barcelona: Coping with the Consequences of Transnational Lives," *Journal of Ethnic and Migration Studies* 30 (2004): 1113–44.

Zulfaghari, Abolfazl and Akram Ramazani. "Aseib shenasi ravabet kharrej as urf dukhtaran," *Pajuheshnameyeh Madadkari Ejtema'i* no. 4, (Summer 1394/2015): 197–236.

Notes on the Contributors

Janet Afary is the Mellichamp Professor of Religious Studies at the University of California, Santa Barbara. She is the author of *Sexual Politics in Modern Iran* (2009), winner of the British-Kuwait Friendship Society Book Prize given by the British Society for Middle East Studies.

Azal Ahmadi received her BA in Philosophy from Wellesley College and her MA in Medical Anthropology from the University of Oxford. Her dissertation research focused on migrant female sex workers living with HIV in Senegal. At the time of her sudden death, she was a doctoral student in Social and Behavioral Interventions Program at Johns Hopkins School of Public Health.

Behrouz Alikhani received his MA in Political Science from Teheran University and his PhD in Sociology and Social Psychology from the Leibniz University of Hanover. Currently, he is a lecturer and researcher at the Institute of Sociology at the Westphalian Wilhelms-University Muenster in Germany. His main research focus is on democratization and de-democratization processes and social inequalities.

Masserat Amir-Ebrahimi is an independent researcher. She holds an MA in Urban Sociology and a PhD in Human, Economic, and Regional Geography from the University of Paris X Nanterre. She has worked on several urban and sociocultural projects in Iran and has taught in the Department of Environment at Tehran University and in the Department of Cultural Studies at the University of Science and Culture (Elm va Farhang) in Tehran. In 2002, she was awarded an International Collaborative Research Grant by the Social Science Research Council (SSRC) Program on MENA for her project "Authority and Public Space in Iran." She was the executive and scientific coordinator of "Atlas of Tehran Metropolis" (2005). In 2006–7 and 2011, she was twice Professor Nikki Keddie—Balzan Fellow at the University of California, Los Angeles (UCLA), where she taught in the departments of Sociology and Geography. In 2014, she was a fellow in the Department of Near and Middle Eastern Studies at Trinity College Dublin. Currently, she is working on a project entitled, "Ethnicity, Gender and Public Space in Iran." Her research and publications focus on women, youth, Tehran, public space, and cyberspace.

Jesilyn Faust received her BA in Political Science from California State University, Long Beach, where she was a nationally ranked debater, and an MA in Spanish Language and Literature from the same institution. She is currently a PhD candidate in the Department of Global Studies at the University of California Santa Barbara and is completing a transregional analysis that includes Northern Africa, Latin America, and the Caribbean societies. Jesi's current projects include translating Bartolome de las Casas's *Brevisima relacion de la destruccion de Africa*.

Erika Friedl is E. E. Meader Professor Emerita of Anthropology at Western Michigan University, where she taught between 1971 and 2000. Her years of ethnographic research in the tribal areas of Iran have resulted in many articles and seven books, from *Women of Deh Koh* (1991) to *Religion and Daily Life in the Mountains of Iran* (2021), and in several dozen academic articles. In 2020 she was honored with the Lifetime Achievement Award of the Society for Iranian Studies for her past and ongoing scholarly work on Iran.

Roger Friedland is an Emeritus Professor of Religious Studies and Sociology at the University of California, Santa Barbara. He seeks a religious sociology of institutional order equally applicable to market value, love, and salvation. His essay "The Logic of Practice: Ontologies, Teleologies and the Problem of Institution" was published in 2019 in M@n@gement. He is also working with Janet Afary and Maria Charles on the relationship between gender, love, and intimate life among tens of thousands of respondents in seven Muslim-majority countries.

Vahideh Golzard holds a BA degree in Media and Communication from the University of Tehran. She studied International Studies at the University of Leeds and received her PhD in 2013. Her dissertation was on *Women and Cyberspace in Iran*. It focused on women's use of the internet in Iran and their perceptions of empowerment. Her main research interests are related to social media and the empowerment of Muslim women. She teaches Arab media, politics and society, audiovisual culture, and Persian language at the University of Leeds and has been a guest lecturer at other institutions in the UK.

Mary Elaine Hegland is Professor Emerita in Anthropology at Santa Clara University and the author of *Days of Revolution: Political Unrest in an Iranian Village* (2014). Mary has lived and worked in Iran for periods from 1966, including three years of field research in "Aliabad" and nearby Shiraz between 1978 and 2018. Her publications have focused on women, gender, and family; revolution, politics, and religion; women and Shi'a Muslim rituals in Iran and Pakistan; and Iranian elderly and gender relations in Iran and among Iranian Americans in the Bay Area of California. Her current research focuses on gender, sexuality, and early and child marriage among Iranians in the twentieth and twenty-first centuries.

Cristina Miguel is a senior lecturer in Digital Communication at Leeds Beckett University, UK. She holds a PhD in Media and Communications from the University of Leeds, UK. Her doctoral thesis investigated intimacy in the age of social media, with a special focus on gender issues. Her research interests include digital culture (network intimacy, online dating, and online privacy) and digital economy (sharing economy, the political economy of social media, and influencer marketing). Her most recent book is titled *Personal Relationships and Intimacy in the Age of Social Media*. She has also published numerous academic articles in *Convergence*, *Social Media + Society*, *Middle East Journal of Culture and Communication*, and *MedieKultur*, among others.

Amir Mirfakhraie received his PhD from the Faculty of Education at the University of British Columbia. He teaches sociology at Kwantlen Polytechnic University. His research interests focus on anti-colonial pedagogy, anti-racism, textbook and curriculum studies, decolonization of knowledge, and Iranian transmigration to Canada.

Maryam Sheipari is Assistant Professor of History at Zahedan University, Iran. She received her PhD from Shiraz University in 2012, ranking first in her graduating class. She is a modern historian by training, foremost engaged in contemporary Iran and the modern world. Dr. Sheipari's more than twenty-five peer-reviewed articles concentrate on women, economic history, journalism, and foreign policy. Her coauthored manuscript in Persian entitled *Persian Women and Newspapers of the Constitutional Period: A Portrayal (1906-1911)* was published twice (2007, 2009) and won the Sediqeh Dowlatabadi Award for Women's Studies. Another volume, now under publication, is a study of the Iranian press during the nationalization of Iranian oil under Dr. Muhammad Mosaddeq.

Soraya Tremayne is a social anthropologist and founding director of the Fertility and Reproduction Studies Group (FRSG), as well as a research associate at the Institute of Social and Cultural Anthropology, University of Oxford. She was formerly the director of the International Gender Studies at the Department for International Development Studies, University of Oxford; the founding chair of Social Analysis and Anthropology Associates—SA3 Limited—a consultancy firm specializing in the development and aid projects; Lecturer in Social Anthropology at Tehran University; and Director of the Ethnographic Museum of Tehran. She is also the founding co-series editor of the Fertility, Reproduction, and Sexuality series, with Berghahn books. She served on the Council of the Royal Anthropological Institute between 1993 and 2014, as a council member, a vice president, and a member of the Finance Committee.

Gholam Reza Vatandoust is a professor of Near Eastern Studies and History in the Department of International Relations at the American University of Kuwait. Until 2007, he served at Shiraz University (formerly Pahlavi University) in Iran. He is an affiliate of the Middle East Center, the Jackson School of International Studies, and the History Department of the University of Washington, where he taught as the Giovanni Costigan visiting professor. He was the recipient of the Getty Institute Fellowship, won the outstanding Research Fellow at Shiraz University and was recognized for his contributions to the Province of Fars. His book *The CIA Documents on the 1953 Coup and the Overthrow of Dr. Mosaddeq of Iran* (2001) was named winner of the Best Book Award in the Fars Province. His coauthored manuscript in Persian entitled *Persian Women and Newspapers of the Constitutional Period: A Portrayal (1906-1911)* was published twice (2007, 2009) and won the Sediqeh Dowlatabadi Award in Women's Studies. His *Selected Texts: A Reference Guide to the History of Iran* is now in its ninth edition. He has served as editor and contributor to scholarly journals and has published in both English and Persian.

Ashraf Zahedi is a sociologist and research scholar. She has conducted research at the Centre for Middle Eastern Studies, University of California, Santa Barbara; the Beatrice Bain Research Group, University of California, Berkeley; the Institute for Research on

Women and Gender, Stanford University (the Clayman Institute for Gender Research); and the Centre for Middle Eastern Studies, University of California, Berkeley. She has taught at Boston University, Suffolk University, and Santa Clara University. Zahedi has published many academic articles and is, with Jennifer Heath, the coeditor of *Land of the Unconquerable: The Lives of Contemporary Afghan Women* (2011) and *Children of Afghanistan: The Path to Peace* (2014). Zahedi and Heath's forthcoming edited volume, *Book of the Disappeared: The Transnational Quest for Justice*, will be published by the University of Michigan Press.

Index

abortions   2, 74, 152
Afary, Janet   21
ahl-e ketab   39
Ahmadi, Azal   5–6, 125 n.1
Ahmadinejad, Mahmoud   17, 26
Aliabad marriages   7, 174–96
  changes, influences enabling   177–8
  parents, pressures on   188–90
  perceptions/practices (1978–79)   176–7
  problems/challenges   182–7
  radical transformations   196 n.30
  twenty-first-century   178–87
  young people and their families, strategies of   190–5
Alikhani, Behrouz   7–8
alimony; *see* marriage
Althusser, Louis   77
Amir-Ebrahimi, Masserat   3, 112, 116
andaruni   116
aqd   193
Armenians
Arpenais tribe   202–3
arranged marriages   2–3
ARTs; *see* assisted reproductive technologies (ARTs)
arusi   193; *see also* marriage; wedding
Aryan identity   85
'*ashayir* (nomadic tribes)   80, 84, 105; *see also* tribes
assisted reproductive technologies (ARTs)   6, 141–51
Avesta   129

Babadi tribe   202
bā-ḥejāb/bā-ḥījāb (veiled)   80, 94
bā-īmān (believer)   80, 87–8, 91
Bakhtiari tribes (case study)   197–213
  established-outsider theoretical model   198–201
  former outsider tribes, new self-image of members of   210–12
  intertribal power relations, change of   207–10
  marriages structure in   201–7
  nationalization   207–10
  urbanization   207–8
Baluch   104
bekarat; *see* virginity
bī-ḥījāb (unveiled)   80
bī-īmān (nonbeliever)   80
biopower   126
birth control   1–2; *see also* family, Iranian, planning
biruni (outer compartment of a house)   116
blogs   116, 118–21; *see also* social media
Boir Ahmad   155–73
  global lifestyle, aspirations to   156
  marriage
    in distant past   158–63
    modernity in   165–9
    Pahlavi modernity   163–4
    and religion   173
    in times of children   169–73
  modernity in   156
    health, education, and marriage   165–9
    Pahlavi   163–4
  traditional life, local people's recollections of   155–7
Bologne, Jean Claude   12–13, 31
breastfeeding   151
Burned Generation (*Nasl-e Soukhteh*)   16
Butler, Judith   126–8

child custody   2, 18, 24, 72, 166, 187
childless families   92
child-marriage   158, 159 n.10
"Children of the Revolution"   15
Christians   4, 34, 38–40
clerics   56, 145–6
companionate marriage   2–3, 167, 182, 185–7, 191, 193; *see also* marriage

consanguineous connectivity 148
contraceptives 1–2
Convention on the Rights of the Child 81
cousin marriages 148, 160, 180 n.5; *see also* kinship, marriages
cultural hegemony 77
Cultural Revolution of 1980 4, 24, 32
custody of children 2, 18, 24, 72, 166, 187
cyberspace 215; *see also* social media

dating 3, 121–3
dating apps 123; *see also* social media
Deh Koh 6–7
democratization 200, 200 n.11, 209
digital *andaruni* 113, 119–21; *see also* social media
divorce (talāq) 2, 11, 18, 91, 56, 72
downward marriage 201; *see also* marriage
dress code 36; *see also* ḥijāb

education 3–5, 7–8, 13, 20–1, 27, 32, 37, 45, 68, 81–2
Elias, Norbert 197, 207
emigration 157
employment 27
endogamous marriages 3; *see also* marriage
eshgh 136; *see also* love
established-outsider theoretical model 198–201
Ettela'at-e Banovan 20
extended family 88

Facebook 112, 116, 118–21, 214–15; *see also* social media
family, Iranian 4–6, 11–12, 79–108
 curricula 81–3
 dāyemi (formal) 86
 education system 81–3
 ethnicization of 99–107
 extended 88
 ideal 88, 92
 ideological codes 80
 and kinship 6, 141–52
 law 18, 21, 24, 55–6
 male-centrism 88–9
 marriages 84–8
 martyrdom, discourse of 90–1
 motherhood 90
 nuclear 84–8
 patriarchal discourse 89–90
 pedagogy 81
 planning 1–2, 168
 racialization of 99–107
 rights, roles, and obligations 92–9
 Shiʿi-centric image of 99–107
 sigheh 86, 171 n.33 (*see also* marriage, temporary marriage; *mutʿa*)
 single-parent 88–9
 structures 85
 textbooks 81–3, 99–107
 (trans)national ideological codes 81–3
family-planning programs 1–2
Family Protection Law 24, 55–6, 55 n.2
father-in-law 175
fatwa (religious ruling) 139
femininity 137–9
feminism 127, 173
Ferdows, Adele 83
fertility rates 1, 11, 17, 85, 168
Filipinas 4, 32–54
 cultural reproduction and maintenance 48–50
 emotional and cultural adjustments 43–5
 family relations, dynamics of 41–3
 Filipino-Iranian children, social experiences of 50–3
 as foreign maids 32
 migration 34–7
 Muslim men, image of 40–1
 research methods 37–8
 romancing and marrying Iranian men 38–40
 social integration 45–8
 transnational communities 34
 transnational marriages of 34–7, 53–4
 in transnational spaces 33–4
 women, image of 40–1
 working overseas 33
Filipino-Iranian children, social experiences of 50–3

fiqh   70, 94, 98; *see also* Islamic laws
folk songs   157 n.5
Foucault, Michel   126–8
freedom (*āzādi*)   23, 135–6, 165
Friedl, Erica   6–7

Galeh tribe   202
gender   127–8
gender segregation   13 n.5, 164
generations, Iran   14–18
   First (*nasl-e avval*)   15–16
   Fourth (*nasl-e chaharom*)   17–18
   Second (*nasl-e dovvom*)   16
   Third (*nasl-e sevvom*)   16–17
gheyrat (honor/zeal)   136
globalization   111
Golpayegani, Ayatollah   70 n.42
Golzard, Vahideh   5
Gramsci, Antonio   76–7
Green Movement in 2009   17, 76

ḥalāl/permitted   80, 91; *see also*
   ḥarām/forbidden
ḥarām/forbidden   80
health   86, 108, 157
Hegland, Mary   7
heterosexual marriages   1, 55, 85, 87–8;
   see also marriage
Higgins, Patricia   82–3
ĥijāb   15, 24, 93
homosssexuality   69, 87–8, 94, 127, 137
honor killings   125
Huberman, A. Michael   114
hymenoplasty (hymen repair), in
   Iran   5–6, 125–40
   cases   133–5
   femininity   137–9
   hymen (pardeh bekārat)   130
   medicalization   126–8, 137
   narratives/discourses
      surrounding   132–6
   power   126–7
   resignification   137–9
   as resistance   127–8, 136–7
   setting/methods   131–2
   social control   126–7

ideal family   88, 92
ideological hegemony   77

ijtihād   145–6
īmān (faith)   93–4
immigrants   74
individualism   11–12
infant mortality rates   158, 163, 165
infertility   141–52; *see also* kinship
inheritance rights, of women   98,
   169–70, 173, 179
Inhorn, Marcia C.   144–5
Instagram   123; *see also* social media
intermarriages   2
internet   5, 111; *see also* social media
in vitro fertilization (IVF)   144–5;
   see also assisted reproductive
   technologies (ARTs)
   third-party gamete donation   141–4,
      148, 152
Iran   2
   ARTs in   6
   Bakhtiaris in (case study)   197–213
   educational system   165–9
   family   4–6, 11–12, 78–108
   generation, concept of   15–18
   hymenoplasty in   5–6, 125–40
   kinship in   6, 141–52
   medicalization of virginity in   128
   social media in   5, 111–24
   surrogacy in   149–50
   technology in   5
   third-party gamete donation in
      141–4, 148, 152
   and virginity   128–30
   white marriage in   55–78
   women, emergence of   11–31
Iranian Revolution of 1979   1, 3, 15–16,
   22–3, 32, 167–8; *see also* Islamic
   Revolution
Iranians marriage   2–8, 11, 84–8; *see also*
   marriage
   in Aliabad   174–96
      influences enabling changes
         177–8
      parents, pressures on   188–90
      perceptions/practices (1978–79)
         176–7
      problems/challenges   182–7
      twenty-first-century   178–87
      young people and their families,
         strategies of   190–5

in Boir Ahmad (1900-2015) 155-73
    distant past 158-63
    modernity 165-9
    Pahlavi modernity 163-4
    and religion 173
  cousin marriage 148, 160 (*see also*
    kinship, marriages)
  patriarchal/heteronormative
    construction of 87
  rate of 11
  in rural and tribal sectors of
    society 6-8
  social media and 5, 115-18, 121-3
  transnational 4
  white 3-4, 8, 11-12, 55-78
Islamic laws 6, 24, 91, 97, 115-17, 139, 142, 173
Islamic Republic of Iran
  Islamist laws 6, 24, 91, 97, 115-17, 139, 142, 173
  Islamist organizations 2, 6, 21-2, 49, 141-2
  Islamist politics 7-8, 21-2, 163, 165, 202, 214
  Islamist women 1-3, 5-8, 11-31
  hokm-e Islami 70
  race 4-5, 34-6, 52-4
  white identities 82
  white marriage 3-4
Islamic Revolution 2, 111-12, 208; *see also* Iranian Revolution
IVF; *see* in vitro fertilization (IVF)

jahiziyeh (trousseau) 75
Jews 129

kadkhodā (village elder) 156
Karbaschi, GH 25-6
Kayhan 70
khans 156-7, 157 n.7, 202
khastegar (suitor) 132; *see also* marriage
khastegari (marriage proposal) 133; *see also* marriage
Khatami, Mohammad 17, 26
Khomeini, Ayatollah 25, 82, 93, 102-3, 111-12, 208
Kian, Azadeh 25
kinship 6, 141-52
  ARTs 143-51

and family 6, 141-2
in Islamic societies 143-51
marriages 3, 146-8
methodology 142-3
milk 151
Kousha, Mahnaz 72
Kurdish
  marriage 85
  women 84-5

leftist movements 16, 21-2
love 1-2, 21-2, 36, 42-3; *see also eshgh*; headings beginning sex...; romance

Mahdavi, Pardis 26
mahram, 80, 87, 146, 146 n.17, 148
male infertility 141, 148-9
Mannheim, Karl 14-15
marriage; *see also* Iranians marriage
  age at first 1, 214
  Aliabad 7, 174-96
  companionate 2-3, 21, 167, 182, 185, 187, 191, 193, 196
  cousin 148, 160
  downward 201
  for girls 3
  formal 8, 56, 58, 61-2, 67-77, 115, 194, 214
  institution of 2-3
  Iranians 2-8, 84-8
  and love 1-2, 21-2, 36, 42-3
  in Muslim Middle East 214-17
  in North Africa 214-17
  and sex 1
  shirbahā 159
  social media and 5, 115-18, 121-3
  in South Asia 214-17
  technology and 5
  temporary marriage 1, 4, 8, 56, 86-7, 115, 146, 148, 171, 194 (*see also mut'a*; *sigheh* (temporary marriage))
  transnational 4, 32, 34-7, 53-4
  in United States 183
  virginity 5-6 (*see also* virginity)
  white 3, 55-78
marriage contract (*aqd nāmeh*) 159
martyrdom, discourse of 90-1

medicalization   126–8, 137
Mehran, Golnar   83
mehriyeh   61, 98, 129–30
menarche   161 n.14
middle classes   2, 7, 18, 21–4, 37, 112
Miguel, Cristina   5
milk kinship   151
Mirfakhraie, Amir   4–5
misyar (traveling marriage)   214
modernity
   and family   19–21, 37–8, 84–5
   and gender   13–20, 31, 85
   of Islamist organizations   94
modernization
   in Iran   116, 165–9, 207–8
   Islamic Republic era   165–9
   Pahlavi era   7, 156, 163–4
mojtahid (religious leader)   96
motherhood   90, 96–7
mother-in-law   42–4, 150, 159–62, 170, 175, 179–82, 189–90
Mowri tribe   202–3
Muslim Middle East, marriages in   214–17
mutʿa   56, 214; see also marriage, temporary marriage; *sigheh* (temporary marriage)

nafaqeh (maintenance)   98
na-mahram   80, 87–8, 146–7; see also *mahram*
nejabat (purity)   128–9
nekāh (formal marriage)   56, 115, 214
North Africa, marriages in   214–17
nuclear family   84–8

online dating   121–3; see also social media
online intimacy   5, 112–13, 118–21; see also social media
   digital *andaruni*   119–21
   risks/barriers in   118–19

Pahlavi, Muhammad Reza Shah (r. 1941–79)   3, 12, 15, 18
Pahlavi era (1925–79)   2, 15–17, 156
   abortion   2, 74, 152
   divorce   2, 11, 18, 56, 72, 91
   dress code   36

education of girls   27
employment of women   27, 31
Family Protection Law   18, 24, 56
feminism   127, 173
marriage in   18–21, 26
polygamy   2, 24, 74, 76, 87
sexual relationships   26
Pasdaran (Islamic Revolutionary Guard Corps)   25
patriarchal discourse   89–90
patrilineal (*pedar tabāri*)   84
Persian language   101
Philippines   4, 32–54
polygamy   1–2, 24, 74, 76, 87
polygyny   162, 164, 172
post-Khomeinism   25–7
power   127, 197, 199 n.6, 202, 212–13
pregnancy   73–4, 160–1
progress (*pishraft*)   165–9, 165 n.20
prostitution   56; see also sex workers

Qalibaf, Mohammad   17–18
Qashqaʾi tribes   167 n.25
Qom   132
Qurʾan   39, 45, 95, 99, 145, 159

racism   5, 36, 50, 105–6
rape   129–30
resistance   127–8, 136–7
revolution, Islamic   22–3
Revolutionary Guards   24–5; see also Pasdaran (Islamic Revolutionary Guard Corps)
romance   32–54, 185

Sadeghi, Fatemeh   114
Sawicki, Jana   127
segregation (gender)   13 n.5, 112, 123
self-censorship   118
self-esteem   197–9, 202, 212–13
sex education   26, 129
sexual awakening   129
sexual inegalitarianism   6
sexuality   86–8, 126–30
sexual relationships   160–1, 160 n.12
sexual revolution   26
sexual violence   134–5
sex workers   34–5
Shāhnāmah   82, 100–1

sharia 24, 56, 147
Sheipari, Maryam 4
Sherkat, Zahra 69
Shi'i Islam 82, 99–107
Shirazi, Farid 116
sigheh (temporary marriage) 56, 89, 115, 171 n.33, 214; *see also mut'a*
single households 12–14, 31
single-parent family 88–9
single women 11–15, 28, 31, 78, 90
Smith, Dorothy 80
social media 5, 214–15
   Asymmetric Digital Subscriber Line (ADSL) service 118
   blogs 116, 118–21
   digital *andaruni* 113, 119–21
   elements 113
   Facebook 112, 214–15
   heterosexual relationships and 112
   internet 5, 13, 17, 26, 43, 55, 111–23, 178, 181–2
   Internet service providers (ISPs) 117
   Instagram 123
   in Iran 5, 111–24
   for Muslim Iranian women 111–12, 114–18
   online dating 121–3
   online intimacy 5, 112–13, 118–21
   proxy servers 117
   self-disclosure in 5
   services 114
   social networking sites (SNSs) 117
   Telegram 123
   Tinder 123
   Twitter 114
   Weblogestan 116
   weblogs 112
   YouTube 114
sources of emulation (*marja' al-taqlid*) 145
South Asia, marriages in 214–17
Standard Iranian Family (SIF) 80, 88, 107–8
Standard North American Family 56
state-administered hegemony system 76–7
suicide, female 162
surrogacy 149–50

Tagalog 49–50
talāq (divorce) 2, 11, 18, 56, 91
technology 5, 26
teen pregnancies 158
Tehran 11–12, 18–19, 86
   Filipina brides in 39–40
   hymenoplasty in 131–2
   migrant women *vs.* Tehrani women 28–30
   single woman in 27–8
Telegram 123; *see also* social media
textbooks 81–3, 85, 99–107
Tinder 123; *see also* social media
transnational communities 34, 49, 53
transnational marriages 4, 32, 34–7, 53–4; *see also* marriage
Tremayne, Soraya 6, 125 n.1, 145
tribes
   'ashayir 80, 84, 105
   Bakhtiari 197–213
   Qashqa'i 167 n.25
   tribal groups 156–7
      tribal dances 159 n.11
      tribal dress 167 n.25
Truman's Point Four Program 19, 165
Twitter 114; *see also* social media

Ummah 82
Ummat-e Islamī 80, 84, 98, 108
unveiling 20, 80, 94
urban middle-class women 18–19
'urfi (customary marriage) 214

Vatandoust, Azadeh 85 n.1
Vatandoust, Gholam Reza 4
veiling 1, 112; *see also* unveiling
Velāyat-e Faqih 80, 82, 87, 94–5, 98
virginity 6, 125–40; *see also* hymenoplasty (hymen repair), in Iran
   curtain of 130
   examinations 130
   govahiye bekarat (virginity certificate) 129
   Iran and 128–30
   medicalization of 128
   narratives/discourses surrounding 132–6
   recreating 132

themes in narratives of   135–6
women's manipulation of
        medicalization of   137
voting   97

Weblogestan   116; *see also* social media
Weblogs   112; *see also* social media
wedding   8, 39, 44, 67, 73–5, 129, 132–5;
        see also Iranians marriage;
        marriage
    shirbahā   159
white identities   82
white marriage   3–4, 8, 11–12, 55–78
    consequences   72–5
    definition   56
    freedom from parental
        intervention   73
    government attitude on   69–71
    overview   55–7
    professional women   59–61
    Shiraz, carpet weavers of   61–2
    social enigma   71–5
    survey of   62–8
widowed women   90, 189
women, emergence of   11–31
    First Generation   15–16
    Fourth Generation   17–18
    freedom   22–3

    gaining independence within
        family   19–21
    generational theory to   14–15
    Islamic Republic, building of   24–5
    lifestyle   12–13
    living alone   11–14
    migrant *vs*. Tehrani   28–30
    post-Khomeinism   25–7
    private life   21–2
    public spaces   22–3
    religious rights over   24
    revolution   22–3
    Second Generation   16
    single   11–14, 27–8
    Third Generation   16–17
    trajectory of   30–1
    urban, middle-class women before
        revolution, lives of   18–19
Women's Organization of Iran (WOI)   2

youth   12–13, 15–16, 21–8, 31, 88, 70
YouTube   114; *see also* social media

Zahedi, Ashraf   4
Zanan   69 n.34, 112
Zanan-e Emruz   69, 69 n.35
Zan-e Rouz (Today's woman)   20
Zoroastrians   129

www.ingramcontent.com/pod-product-compliance
Lightning Source LLC
Chambersburg PA
CBHW072140290426
44111CB00012B/1926